MARTIN KYRLE'S

LITTLE BLUE NIGHTBOOK

© Martin Kyrle 2013

By the same author:

Martin Kyrle's Little Green Nightbook

The Liberals in Hampshire – a Part(l)y History
Part 1 Southampton 1958-65: object lessons
At the international Winchester Writers' Conference in 2013 a shortened version entered anonymously (as per house rules) for the Local History competition was awarded a 'Highly commended'.

In preparation:

Martin Kyrle's Little Orange Nightbook

The Liberals in Hampshire: Part 2: Chandler's Ford 1965-72

Jottings from the Trans-Siberian Railway
Sample pages of this journal of a month spent traversing Siberia and then Mongolia in 2012 was entered anonymously (as per house rules) in another competition at the above-mentioned international Winchester Writers' Conference in June 2013. Described by the adjudicator as 'a brilliantly written account of a very long journey', it was awarded third prize. The full version will be lavishly illustrated with photographs.

Front cover and illustrations by Derek Snowdon
Europe and Asia maps sourced from <u>d-maps.com</u>

All rights reserved. No part of this publication may be reproduced, stored in a retrieval system or transmitted in any form or by any means without prior permission of the publishers.

ISBN 978-0-9575220-1-5

Printed by Sarsen Press

CONTENTS

		page
	Introduction	1
A	In at the beginning	5
B	A Window on the East (with acknowledgements to Peter the Great)	15
C	'...to Caunterbury they wende' (Chaucer)	25
D	... and Plan A	39
E	'Tis an ill clutch that blows nobody any good...	45
F	Returning to normal	53
G	Stone me!	59
H	'The Good Old Days' – or were they?	67
I	An island life that is no longer	73
J	That's pretty steep!	79
K	Twinning makes the strain	89
L	'I'm from Brum!'	99
M	Sardines!	105
N	Phew!	113
O	Corks!	121
P	A tour de force?	129
Q	Belle Île or bust!	139
R	Althing's for all men?	147
S	Schier delight!	157
T	...the farther you go, the farther you still have to go!	167
U	Bator late than never?	173
V	Plan B to the end of the world	181
W	As one life reaches its climax, two others begin	189
Y	Faith in the future	197
Z	If the opposite of 'uncouth' is 'couth', so the opposite of 'out of kilter' must be 'in'.	203
	Epilogue	213
	Acknowledgments	214

INTRODUCTION

The *Little Green Nightbook,* first published in May 2010, was intended to introduce readers to the first of what might well become a trilogy of collections of personal anecdotes, of which this volume is the second to appear. Whatever may be said of the variety, interest or whimsy of the stories in the first volume, those in this one will be equal *(you have been warned!).* Great care was taken not to put all the 'best' stories in the more outlandish locations in the first – 'Green' – 'nightbook', thereby condemning the subsequent colours to carry all the dross. If you enjoyed the *Little Green Nightbook*, you will equally enjoy this one, its first successor.

The idea of writing up these reminiscences in the hope that they might be entertaining to other people occurred to me in 2003 when, having lost my seat on the local borough council for a second time and having by then notched up twenty years' service, I decided that it was an appropriate moment to call it a day. The village I represented was five miles from my home, and if I went to visit someone at the far end it was a round trip of twenty miles (and sometimes when I got there they'd be out, so it would be a wasted journey to boot). I reckoned I'd done my stint, and henceforth I'd do my politics where I lived – meaning that if I was out delivering leaflets and it started to rain I could nip back home and have a coffee and read the paper or make a phone call while interfering with the cat, instead of having to sit in the car in a lay-by twiddling my thumbs waiting for the weather to clear.

The first story I wrote was about how, driving in rural Brittany with my wife, Margaret, (now, sadly, my *late* wife, as she died in the summer of 2011) we were merely passing through an unremarkable village we'd never heard of when we noticed that it had two churches. One, though built in Gothic style, looked fairly modern and we knew from experience that in such buildings there's rarely anything of interest to a tourist; but the other church, apparently derelict, had a bent spire. This aroused our curiosity. We parked the car and went to look more closely, and the story about what befell us there appeared in the *Little Green Nightbook* under the little village's name *(and no, I'm not going to give the game away by saying what it was! You'll have to read the book and come across it)*. When I finished writing that story, methought 'I have a lot more stories like that in my memory bank. Some are comparatively recent, often driving around France with Margaret, but some date from my student days in the 1950s when the world was a very different place and my adventures (if one can glamorise them enough to call them that) took place at a time when Europe was still recovering from the ravages of the Second World War. My experiences, escapades, balls-ups even, took place in conditions which no longer pertain and can't be replicated. A modern reader might find them entertaining simply because they are being told against a backdrop which is totally alien to what a contemporary traveller in those places would experience now.' The other thought was, 'When I die, these stories will die with me. So better get them down on paper!'

In the Introduction to the *Little Green Nightbook* I explained in jocular detail who I was, my family and social background, experience of life and so on, to give the reader some sort of mind's-eye picture of where – as the cliché goes – I was 'coming from' and to emphasise to him or her that the book had no serious purpose or 'message' and was intended solely to entertain. This volume is a companion to its predecessor, so rather than repeat my biography I would respectfully advise anyone anxious to know something about *me* to 'read all about it!' as set out in the previous book. This may sound suspiciously like a ruse to sell more copies – but I assure you I speak in good faith. Someone who's read the *Little Green Nightbook* and is now moving on to the *Blue* one won't want to read again all that guff about my family, education, national service etc. etc. et bloody cetera.

The *Little Green Nightbook* carried a firm request – let's face it: strict instructions! – not to read it straight through but one story at a time prior to turning off the bedside light and going to sleep. Same again here: to get the most pleasure from the *Little Blue Nightbook* you should as before exercise iron self-control and not read it straight through like a novel, but take it one letter at a time each night. No story bears any connection either in time or place with the previous or following one – they are all free-standing, and designed to take the reader – with his or her connivance – to who-knows-where, who-knows-when. As there is no continuity, nothing is gained from reading one story and then proceeding straight to the next in the hope of maintaining the story line – there simply isn't one! The only common factor linking two consecutive stories is that they happened to me in the place and at the time indicated, either alone or with a companion.

Enjoy!

Goodnight.

The first story begins, unsurprisingly, with the letter A.
But that's for tomorrow.
Like I said – *goodnight!*

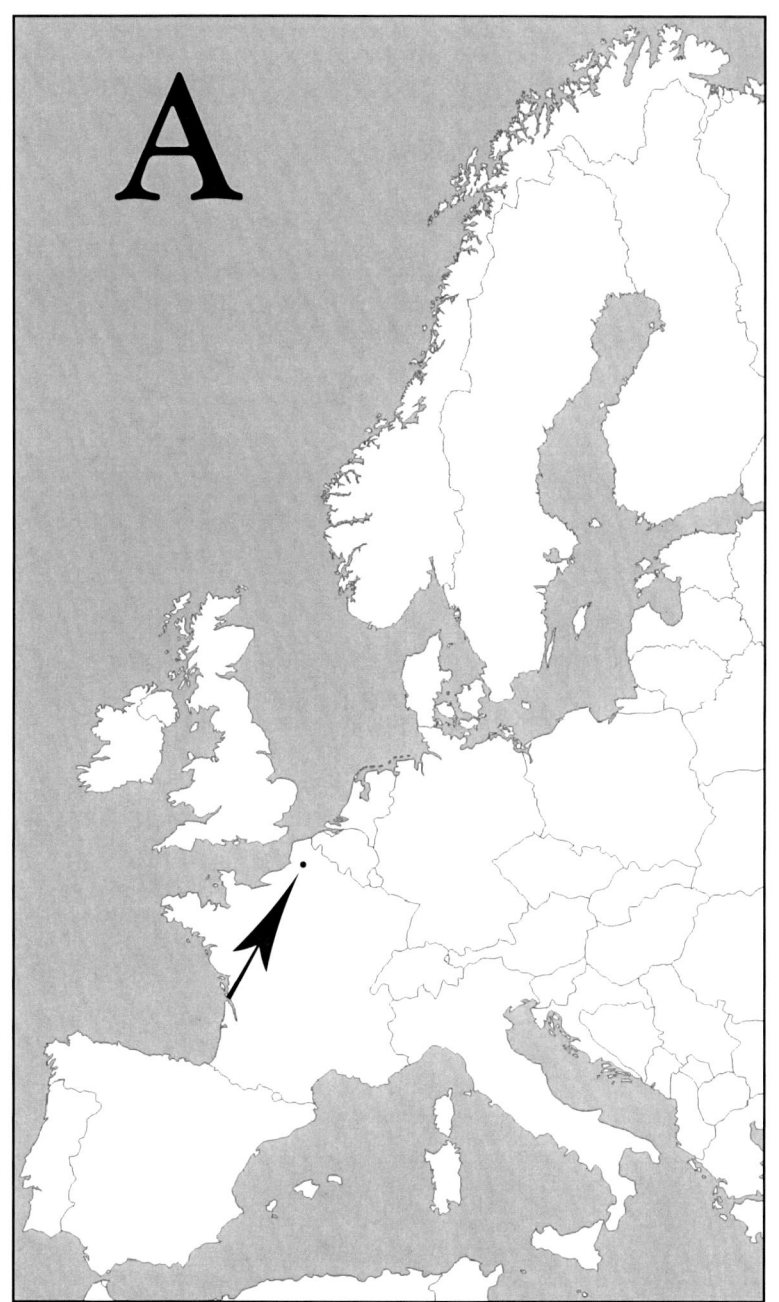

AGINCOURT

In at the beginning

'Who are the couple at the end of the table?' I asked my host, the Mayor of Harfleur. The *Fête de la Scie* was over for another year. We were finishing a busy day in typical French fashion, around the table in a local restaurant. The other guests, apart from ourselves, were all Harfleur councillors or their spouses whom I knew from previous visits. Except for one couple.

'She's a member of the council from Azincourt', said Michel, interrupting.

Our host, Gérard, the mayor, nodded.

'Why are they here?' I asked.

'We're working on an idea for mutual co-operation in promoting our tourism, something along the lines of English visitors interested in the Hundred Years' War coming here to see where Henry V started his campaign in 1415 when he laid siege to our town and then set off for Calais to take his army home and ended up facing our King on the battlefield at what you English call Agincourt. You know the rest.'

'Will you introduce us?'

The result was that I got into conversation with the village councillor from Azincourt who, accompanied by her husband, was also a civic guest at Harfleur's fête. Azincourt is only a tiny village, with a population of some 300 people. They get as many as 15,000 English tourists in a year, far more than they can cope with, all wanting to see the site where on 25 October 1415 one of the decisive battles of the Hundred Years' War took place, a battle which everyone in England has heard of if not through school history lessons then through Shakespeare's play – which they probably know through the famous film starring Laurence Olivier or its more recent re-make by Kenneth Branagh.

'Harfleur's Act I of Henry's journey', she told me. 'We're the finale. Perhaps our two councils together could work up a tourist trail designed for English visitors to start here in Harfleur, follow

Henry's route and end up with us, stopping *en route* at other villages or small towns where he threatened the local people, took the surrender of their castle, attempted to cross the Somme and so on.'

It sounded like an idea worth examining. Henry V is one of England's most famous medieval kings, and tourists would be interested in visiting places where important events during his reign took place; in particular, they would all know about the siege of Harfleur and the Battle of Agincourt and, given a bit of help and encouragement, would like to visit both of them. An increase in tourist numbers would boost the local economy, so both places would benefit if they got together and offered some sort of package along the lines of 'With Henry V to Agincourt!'.

The councillor from Azincourt was equally puzzled by our presence.

'What brings you two to Harfleur? I thought English tourists all went to Honfleur. Did you make a mistake and mix them up?'

'No. We've been to Honfleur on several occasions, but today we're here in Harfleur as the mayor's guests. We come from Eastleigh, which is as close to Southampton as Harfleur is to Le Havre and he thought we might face similar problems marketing ourselves as he does, both of us being, so to speak, overshadowed by a larger neighbour and he might learn something by talking to us. Basically, what he wanted to do was pick our brains. So he wrote to our tourist office and they invited him to come over with some of his colleagues – councillors and officials. We entertained them during their visit as we're both councillors and Margaret's portfolio includes responsibility for promoting Eastleigh's tourism. They invited us back during their annual *Fête de la Scie*, and we've been coming most years ever since – at our own expense, mind – and that's why we're here now.'

But this is supposed to be about Agincourt. Enough of Harfleur But you would enjoy their spring *Fête*, so go if you can. It's usually the first week-end in April.

You may have noticed two different spellings; Agincourt is the English version of the name of a village which on French maps is spelled not with a *g* but a *z*. The story goes that in the aftermath of the battle Henry asked someone where they were, and when told the name of the château visible on the horizon told his secretary to use it. Unfortunately the man wrote it down with a "g" instead, and it's stayed that way in English ever since. But if you're planning to go there, don't go looking for "Agincourt" with a *g* on a French map!

The lady councillor from Azincourt then explained why she and her husband were here in Harfleur.

'When visitors arrive they are disappointed because there's really nothing to see – just a field – so we decided that what we needed is a proper museum. But not your ordinary local museum with a few rusty halberds laid out in display cases and pictures of knights in armour. Azincourt's a bit special, and the site of one of the major battles between us and the English during The Hundred Years' War. We need a proper visitor centre explaining to visitors what medieval life was like, how people lived, how they fought, what their weapons were like and what skills and techniques were required to use them effectively.

Equally important, a proper visitor centre could explain to people of today why kings in medieval times apparently spent so much of their time fighting and then invited their erstwhile enemies to banquets and displays and married off female members of their immediate family to each other. Exhibits could show the political map of Europe at the beginning of the fifteenth century and how different it is from today's. What court life was like. Explain, showing historical documents, what relations were like between nobles and kings and nobles and each other, including when fighting each other and when not.

No way could we in tiny Azincourt afford to build such a centre, so the money has had to come from the *département* and the French government. In fact, several million euros have been spent on creating a showcase 'medieval experience', and we're having the official opening in three months time. Would you like to come?'

You bet!

So three months later, at the end of June and bearing presents as well as our official invitation from the mayor of Azincourt, we booked ourselves into *Les 3 Luppars* in Arras and drove to the village for the grand opening ceremony. The new centre, I'm bound to say, is truly amazing, and very well thought through. The entrance is designed to look like a row of bows pointing skywards with arrows notched, the view that the French knights at the start of the battle would have had of the front row of Henry's archers, bows 'loaded' just waiting for the order to loose. This architectural bull's-eye underlines the importance at that time of the longbow, the contemporary weapon of mass destruction. In the battle it was the English archers' mastery of this new powerful weapon coupled with Henry's mastery of tactics which enabled them to cut down the flower of the French nobility and gave the English a most unexpected victory in a contest where they were outnumbered three or four to one and the French were over-confident.

Azincourt Visitor Centre

Michel had been invited to represent Harfleur at the opening ceremony and we succeeded in finding him in the crowd before the formal ceremony started. This consisted of lengthy speeches, but I managed to sneak out of the marquee and go round the exhibits. One of Margaret's persistent complaints about visiting museums with me was that I want to read every word of every label, which

is all the more irritating for her when they're in French and I have difficulty in translating specialist historical terms. No one seems to have thought of publishing a specialised dictionary for foreigners who visit French museums, as the usual pocket variety doesn't have room for words for the individual bits of a knight's armour. When I was at school we had a joke about what comprised essential French phrases, and we all tried to think up the most unlikely, e.g. 'Lo! The postillion has been struck by lightning' and 'I've left my theodolite in the belfry'. But a glossary of technical and historical terms on a bi-lingual hand-out from museum reception would help.

I'm bound to say that in this exhibition the curatorial staff have got it absolutely right: both languages are used, but the French versions are much longer than the English. This is because the French are trying to explain to their own, French, tourists all about the contemporary situation in France at the time and the politics of the wars, whereas English visitors, with perhaps less time available, only really want to know what something is, who somebody is or what's happening in the picture. They reckon, I suppose, that English tourists with a serious interest in the history of that period can probably read French anyway, so there's no need to put all the details in English.

I judged from the distant sound of applause when the ceremonial speeches were over and it was safe to return to the crowd in the marquee and avail myself of a drink. We sought out the mayor and presented him with a print of the Westgate in Southampton, through which Henry V passed when he embarked on the campaign. Thus he had a picture of where Henry started, to hang in his office at the place where it ended. On our return to England later that week we submitted a story and picture to our local paper the *Hampshire Chronicle*, and sent him a copy. He did not acknowledge receipt and we never heard another word, but that's the French for you.

The battlefield itself is just farmland, but there are some interesting attempts by means of life-size two-dimensional men-at-arms positioned at the crossroads or peering at you from roadside hedgerows to tell the tale of what happened on this spot six hundred years ago. One can hardly expect the French to 'celebrate' a battle which they so comprehensively lost when they had overwhelming numerical superiority and should have won, but facts are facts. Azincourt is the site of a famous battle which had profound repercussions at the time and the only thing which prevented Henry succeeding in his ambition of uniting France and England under one king – himself – was that he contracted dysentery and died at the early age of 35, contrary to all expectations pre-deceasing

Charles VI of France by six weeks. But because he died when he did and the English campaign faltered, the 1420s belong not to England inspired by Henry but to France inspired by Joan of Arc. France was rescued from the invader and the French for their part had something to celebrate: the raising of the siege of Orléans by the Maid and the crowning of their own king, Charles VII, in the cathedral at Reims in defiance of the English who had crowned Henry V's infant son Henry VI as King of France at Rouen.

Odd that a chance meeting in a restaurant in Harfleur should result in us being present at an important cultural and historic event: the opening of the Azincourt visitor centre!

Goodnight.

The author presents the Mayor of Azincourt with a picture of the Westgate in Southampton, through which Henry V led his army when embarking to invade France in 1415.

June 2001

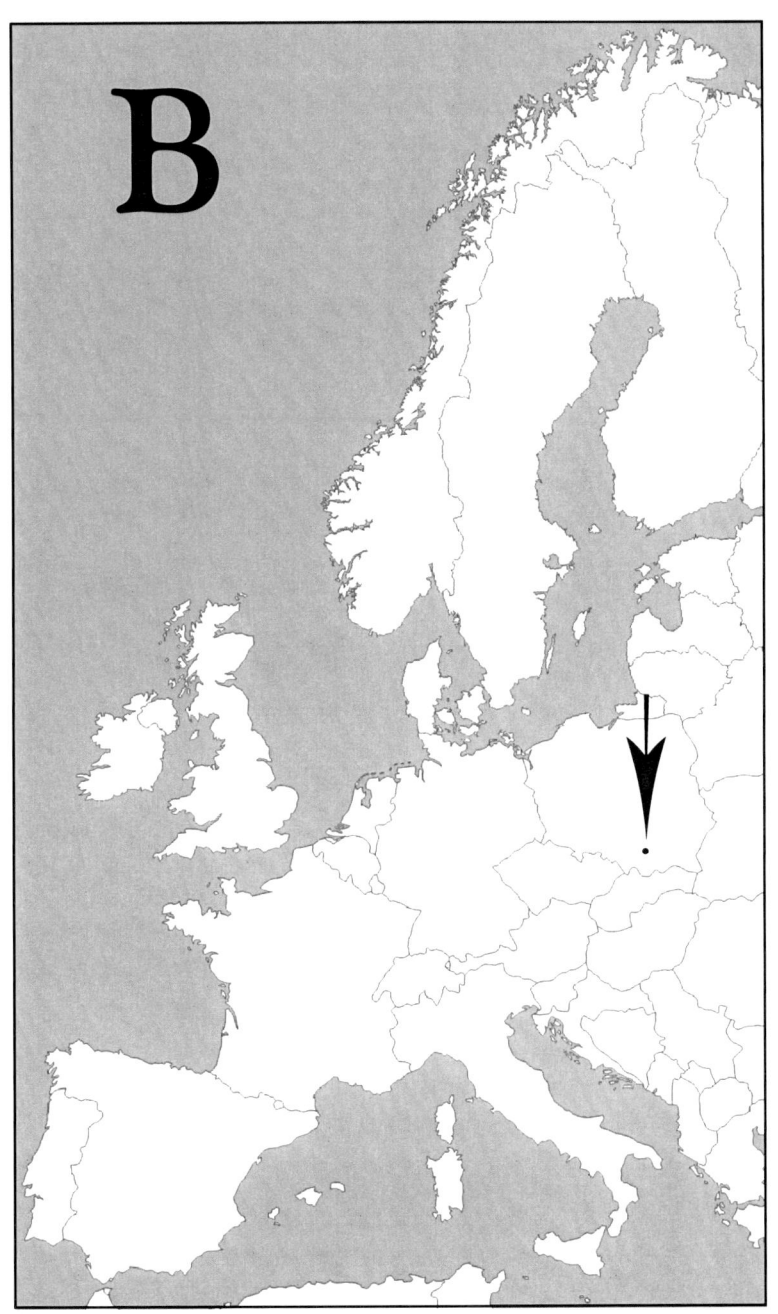

BIEŻANÓW

A Window on the East
(with acknowledgements to Peter the Great)

In my student days I belonged to an organisation called International Voluntary Service for Peace (IVSP. Later they dropped the "P"). Volunteers were often students during vacations, but some were older and there were even full-timers, who devoted their whole lives to the organisation and were paid a small salary. Before being allowed to join a camp overseas a prospective volunteer had to take part in at least one camp in his or her home country, just to make sure that they had the essential 'volunteer' frame of mind, were prepared to work conscientiously unsupervised and could fit in with an international group where the working language of the camp might not be their own. The bargain was simple: food and accommodation were provided free by the host organisation you were doing the work for, but you received no pay. How you made the journey from your home to the camp was your business – IVSP didn't pay anyone's fare. Most of us hitch-hiked. Having served my probationary stint in England (as recounted in the *Little Green Nightbook, q.v.*), I volunteered for a camp on the continent. As luck would have it, IVSP had just successfully concluded lengthy and difficult negotiations to set up a joint East-West camp with volunteers from both sides of the Iron Curtain working together. It was to be in Poland. I jumped at the chance as I had just graduated and was seeking funding for a PhD in Polish history.

The pioneer East-West camp was just outside Kraków at a small place called Bieżanów, so my route would take me by train to Strasbourg and then on the Paris-Warsaw express across Czechoslovakia. I recall quite clearly my first crossing of the Czech border because it was so utterly different compared to 46 years later on a coach going to Prague for the Christmas market. My first time was by train across the border at Cheb through a deep cutting and when I looked up I saw the muzzle of a sentry's sub-machine gun sticking out from the top of the watchtower and glinting in the sun. The border between East and West was heavily delineated, with two high barbed wire parallel fences stretching to the horizon in both directions and the land between them mined, we were assured, and armed patrols all the way along under orders to shoot anyone trying to cross. By contrast, the border between Czechoslovakia and Poland appeared to be nothing but a line of ploughed furrows in a field and there was minimal delay with frontier formalities. Who, after all, was likely to be stowing away to get out of Communist Czechoslovakia into Communist Poland? On the other hand, there was a popular joke at the time about a dog running across from Czechoslovakia into Poland who meets another dog coming the other way.

'Why are you leaving Poland?' asks the Czech dog.

'I'm going to Czechoslovakia to have a good feed', says the Polish dog, 'Why are you leaving Czechoslovakia?'

'I'm going to Poland to have a good bark.'

To get the joke, bitter as it is, if you consider the implied differences in how the Communist dictatorships in the two countries functioned you can work it out for yourself, even though it's no longer appropriate. The Iron Curtain is long gone, and now both Czechs and Poles live in democracies.

Leaving the train at Kraków I immediately faced a problem experienced in those days by every independent traveller: because it was not permitted to have Polish currency, zlotys, outside Poland I had absolutely no Polish money. OK perhaps if you were a businessman and took a taxi from the airport to your hotel and the driver waited outside while you changed a traveller's cheque at reception. I was travelling alone by public transport with nothing but a rucksack, and what I needed when I left the station was the equivalent of about fourpence for the bus fare to the hostel I was booked into. I explained this as best I could to the ticket collector, who I realised afterwards must have heard it many times before from odd bods arriving from the West penniless because of his own country's strict currency regulations. But he smiled, explained where the hostel was and which bus to catch and then put his hand in his pocket and gave me the fare. I don't suppose he ever realised just what a fillip his spontaneous action gave to Anglo-Polish relations, and that I would be recalling his kindness to a total stranger over fifty years after the event.

In case you're wondering how I managed to communicate at all, let me explain. I was aware that despite communist propaganda about all the peoples in Eastern Europe loving the Russians for freeing them from Nazi tyranny in fact most Poles loathed them, but as I was immediately recognisable from my appearance as being from the West (to start with, I had a beard), and as no Pole would expect a Westerner to speak Polish it was actually quite acceptable for me to speak Russian as the next best thing. But this created an interesting dilemma: no one ever *answered* me in Russian! Older people in southern Poland who had been to school in the days when it was part of the Austro-Hungarian Empire would reply in German, hoping I would know that language as well; others in default of knowing any English would use bits of whatever Western language they'd picked up. I remember a positively surreal conversation in a bookshop in Warsaw a few weeks later, when I asked in Russian for a particular book displayed in the window, the shop assistant replied slowly in Polish and refused to be deflected. She obviously understood every word I said (after all, Russian was compulsory in Polish schools at that time), but absolutely no way would she speak Russian to me even though it would have made everything so much easier. It was extremely illuminating about how ordinary Poles really felt towards their saviours. But I got the book.

Visitors from the West were not common in Poland in the mid-fifties, so at the hostel I was soon the centre of attention for local students eager to have their first-ever conversation in English with a native speaker. They were very keen to grill me about life in the West, and were fully aware that it wasn't anything like the picture painted by official propaganda. Ida, a student at the Jagiellonian University but originally from Szczecin, gave me her address, and we exchanged letters for a couple of years. Jacek and Leszek volunteered to take me to my final destination next day, Bieżanów being about twenty minutes by bus from Kraków. Getting this far had not been uneventful, and there was more to come.

The camp had not been organised by IVSP's HQ in London but by our Belgian branch, which meant that the working language of the camp was French. This widened my language experience, in particular when they got the cards out one evening after work and, discovering I could play bridge, proceeded to teach me how to bid in French. Our work consisted of levelling ground for a railway manoeuvring depot, which was not the sort of work IVSP would normally agree to do. The camp leader explained that they were keen to make contacts across the Iron Curtain and it was this or nothing. In the West IVSP volunteers did manual work of a socially useful nature, helping disadvantaged groups. In the communist paradise in the East, of course, there *were* no disadvantaged groups. In the face of obstinate official refusal to admit that there was any requirement for the sort of work organisations such as ours normally did, what they had offered us was all we were going to get. The leaders of IVSP swallowed hard, I suppose, and accepted the deal as the only way of getting a foothold in Eastern Europe. It was a departure from normal practice, but then running the first-ever camp in a communist country with young people from both sides of the Iron Curtain living and working together was not normal practice, either. The pay-off was getting a foot in the door, so to speak, and the hope that we could help improve mutual understanding and in due course organise a parallel East-West camp in the West, with East Europeans being allowed to travel to take part.

In the Tatra Mountains with Jim Riordan from England (l) and Palle Rossen (r) from Denmark

Our working day began at seven, and there was a rota each morning to rise at five for a half-hour tramp across the fields to a farm to collect milk for breakfast. We went in pairs, one who'd made the trip the day before to show the newcomer the way, and then the newcomer did the old hand bit the next day and so on until we'd all taken our turn. We worked, pick and shovel, until two, and went back to our hut for dinner. When there was a sudden downpour which flooded our work area we were put instead to moving an enormous pile of bricks hand-to-hand in a human chain. The rest of the day was our own, and the Polish members of our camp organised group visits to Kraków to see the sights in one of the most beautiful medieval cities you could wish for and to meet other young people for more East-West contact. They also arranged visits to the salt mines at Wieliczka, to Zakopane in the Tatra Mountains near the Czech border and to another place of interest in the vicinity which under its Polish name of Oświęcim doesn't strike a chord but is infamous when said in the German version: Auschwitz.

The Black Wall, Auschwitz, where inmates were lined up and shot. An urn of flowers is placed in front as a memorial

The duration of the camp was two weeks, and having made no plans for my return home I set off for Warsaw where I had heard that it was possible to hitch a lift to Gdynia on the British Embassy lorry which made the journey every week to collect supplies for the staff, many foodstuffs and what to us were ordinary household items being unobtainable in Poland at that time. I was joined on this leg of my journey by Kirsten, a Danish girl I had palled up with at the camp, who assured me that there were Danish cargo boats at Gdynia scraping a living from what little trade there was between Denmark and Poland. We struck a bargain: I would do the talking at the embassy and get us both a lift on the official lorry, and when we got to Gdynia she would find us a Danish ship and fix a passage to Copenhagen.

Sitting in the cab of the lorry I had a grandstand view of the Polish countryside, and was struck by the large number of horse-drawn farm wagons on the road whenever we approached a town.

They were farmers taking produce to market, too poor to have cars, lorries or even tractors. We arrived in Gdynia, but in the meantime Kirsten had decided that she wasn't yet ready to leave Poland and her new-found Polish boyfriend and so would not be crossing the Baltic with me after all. But she kept her side of the bargain and found me a ship.

'You come with us to Denmark?' asked the captain. 'That'll be £5.'

For his return voyage the only cargo the skipper had been able to find was birch strips for binding barrels of butter. They weighed almost nothing, so with inadequate ballast we were high in the water. In consequence, we rolled and pitched in the Baltic swell and I retired to my bunk to avoid letting the side down by publicly succumbing to seasickness, and stayed there until we docked the next day.

'You haven't eaten anything!' said the skipper, as I prepared to disembark – and gave me £3 back.

It was Sunday morning, a wonderfully bright, sunny August day. I was the only traveller going through customs, and the duty officer who stamped my passport seemed rather surprised at this rather scruffy Englishman with his rucksack coming into his country from sort of the wrong direction, i.e. from Poland. But no questions were asked, he just stamped me as entering the country and I set off to find a bed for the night before exploring the city the next day.

Goodnight.

July 1958

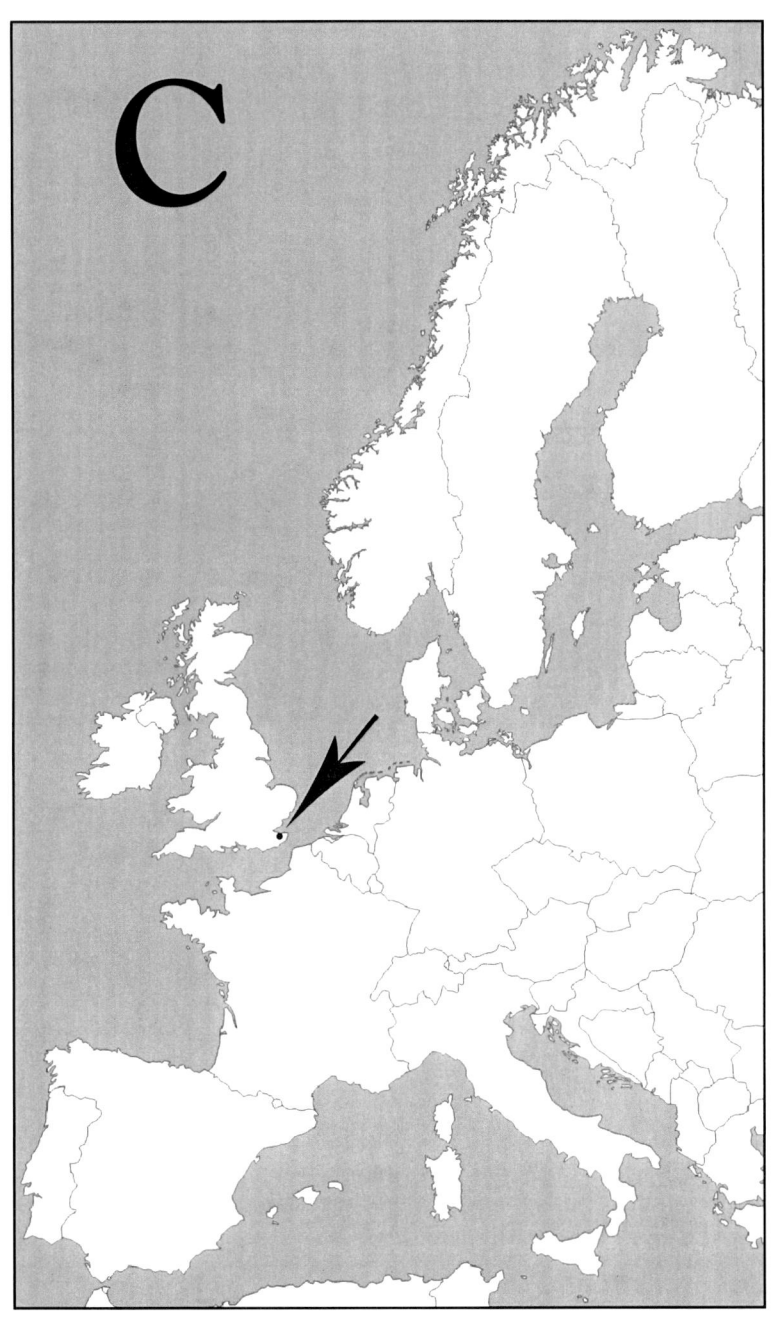

CANTERBURY

'...to Caunterbury they wende' (Chaucer)

Margaret didn't feel up to taking me abroad as my birthday treat – her doctor had forbidden her to fly and in February we had foregone our customary week at our time-share in Lanzarote. My natal day is in mid-March, and whereas one year she'd taken up a special offer in our local paper to take me to Dinan for the weekend this time she suggested a jaunt to Canterbury as a less stressful alternative – especially as it would be me doing the driving and there wouldn't be the physical demands associated with the ferry crossing. She'd always wanted to see the cathedral but had never managed it. My only visit was a whistle-stop half a century ago.

What probably decided her was an advert in our daily paper by a new hotel actually situated in the cathedral precincts, offering weekend stays at knock-down prices and including free parking and free admission to the cathedral itself. A booking there would enable us to solve an anticipated problem with parking, which even out of season is not likely to be easily resolvable in a city which attracts foreign tourists in their thousands to see the site where Roman Christianity first established itself in England in 597 when Pope Gregory the Great sent St Augustine on a mission to convert the pagan Saxons. He chose his opportunity well, for although King Ethelbert of Kent was a heathen his wife Queen Bertha was a Christian and had her own chaplain and the use of a church in which to pray daily.

Canterbury may boast England's oldest and most important cathedral, but finding it presented unexpected problems. Unlike many other cathedrals it doesn't have a spire – compare, in particular, Salisbury, whose spire rises 123m / 404ft and in its day was the tallest building in England. Canterbury's cathedral is almost completely quarantined from the town by an unbroken defensive wall of tall buildings which in former times protected it against attack while providing living and working space for the clerks when the Church provided the royal civil service and the archbishop was a principal advisor to the King and from time to time his Chancellor. The Church's power is much diminished in our day, but even if the buildings which surround the cathedral to keep out the mob are no longer required for administrative functions – lay or ecclesiastical – they are still there, effectively hiding it from public view. Our hotel advertised that it was located in the cathedral grounds – but we couldn't find the cathedral!

Entering from the west by the medieval gateway and following signs and the old walls, we eventually got into the city itself and spotted an access road into the cathedral precincts, but a sign clearly told us 'Authorised traffic only'. We interpreted this to mean people on church business, so we continued on our way and found ourselves right in the middle of the town's fully pedestrianised centre driving on a road reserved solely for delivery or emergency vehicles – and just as the local secondary school was disgorging its pupils! 'What now?' 'MIND THAT CHILD!' 'How the hell do we get out?' 'What happens when a traffic warden spots us and we get booked?' Surprising how you sweat in a crisis – especially when you're in a crowded place where you know you shouldn't be and are the unwanted focus of attention.

As luck would have it, there were a couple of traffic wardens patrolling, so I drove over to them and wound down the window. 'We're strangers, and we're lost! How do we get out? We're booked into a hotel in the cathedral precincts, but we can't find a road in, so how do we get to it?' She explained. 'But it's marked 'Authorised traffic only'. 'You're staying at the hotel?' 'Yes.' 'Then you're authorised.' 'Oh.' Makes sense when you think about it, but it would be a great improvement if they added another sign saying 'Hotel **** access for guests' or some such to avoid misunderstandings. Driving in the pedestrianised zone was embarrassing, to say the least – and I'm sure we weren't the first visitors who made the same mistake.

We were surprised at how comparatively small the centre of Canterbury is, and the limited number of top class places for a proper lunch or dinner. A couple were housed in old buildings and there were some pleasant continental restaurants where we ate well enough, but for such a major tourist hub we just expected to be tripping over them. Maybe the damage done by World War II bombs was more decisive, and cafés and restaurants can make more money catering for the lower end of the market – students and back-packers. But then medieval pilgrims didn't always have very much money, so the present-day pattern in supplying comestibles is probably the outcome of centuries of experience.

The first historic building we visited after doing a full tour of the cathedral was the Eastridge museum, which soon after the murder of St Thomas à Becket in the cathedral in 1170 was built as a place to stay for poor pilgrims visiting his shrine.

The underground Roman museum fascinated us, the result of one of the aforesaid bombs leaving a crater and revealing to public view for the first time in almost two millennia the existence of a Roman house. Its mosaic floors are still in their original positions, and overall the exhibits are very well laid out, with clear explanations – a model for us all – and lots of question papers and games for children. The Chaucer Experience – if I can call it that – was totally different. To be visited with tongue well stuffed into cheek, but enjoyable in its light-hearted take on medieval life –

Members of
Southampton University Operatic Society

present

COX AND BOX
(Triumviretta in One Act)

by

F. C. Burnand and Sir Arthur Sullivan
(By Permission of Bridget D'Oyly Carte)

and

The TELEPHONE
(Opera Buffa)

by

Gian-Carlo Menotti

at

8.0 p.m.

in the

UNIVERSITY THEATRE

26th - 27th - 28th - JUNE, 1958

The Entertainment will commence with the arrival of the Queen of Sheba.

'COX and BOX'

Directed by :
IAN THOMAS

Dramatis personae :

JAMES JOHN COX	A Journeyman Hatter	MARTIN KYRLE
JOHN JAMES BOX	A Journeyman Printer	BRIAN KEITH-SMITH
SERGEANT BOUNCER	A Lodging House Keeper— with military reminiscences	ARTHUR BARKER

SCENE: A room in Sergeant Bouncer's Establishment.

TIME: Late nineteenth century.

The action takes place in the lodging house kept by Sergeant Bouncer, and concerns his efforts to conceal from his two lodgers the fact that, unbeknown to them, they share the same room! His ruse is discovered when Mr. Cox unexpectedly receives a day's holiday, and returns home to find a stranger (Mr. Box) in his room. After initial misunderstandings, including a concertina solo, a challenge to a duel and a " dulcet dirge," the two lodgers discover that among their many things in common is their parentage, and decide to continue sharing the room.

There will then be an INTERVAL of five minutes, followed by a CONCERT (devised and directed by Martin Kyrle), which will begin with

L'Arlésienne—Farandole   (*Bizet*)   The Accompanists

Based on a play by Daudet and first produced in 1872, " L'Arlésienne " tells of the love of a Provençal farmer for an unworthy dancer from Arles. The farandole consists of the alternation and ultimate combination of two themes—a march and a Provençal dance.

Marriage of Figaro---Voi Che Sapete   (*Mozart*)   Hilary Taylor

Cherubino sings this in Act II complaining to Susanna that ladies take no notice of him as he is so young.

On 26-28 June 1958 —

Cavalleria Rusticana—Romance and Scene (*Mascagni*) Rosemary Storkey
The scene is the square of a Sicilian village, where Santuzza sings of how she has been betrayed by Turiddu. Before he went away to the wars Turiddu had been in love with Lola who, having tired of waiting for him to return, has now married Alfio, the village carrier. Discovering this on his return, Turiddu turns to Santuzza, but discards her to return to Lola, taking advantage of Alfio's frequent absences on business.

The Barber of Seville—Largo al factotum (*Rossini*) Ian Thomas
Dating from 1816, this well-known comic opera revolves around the machinations of that loveable rogue, Figaro. In this famous aria he laments the hardships of the life of a barber and general jack-of-all-trades, who never has a moment's peace!

Tales of Hoffman—Doll Song (*Offenbach*) Hilary Taylor
Olympia, described as Spalanzani the doll-maker's daughter, is presented to her "father's" guests, and in singing to them reveals the automaton-like delivery one might expect from a mechanical toy which has to be continually wound up.

Carmen—Toreador's Song (*Bizet*) Brian Keith-Smith
It is the beginning of Act II; the scene—a tavern. There are shouts from without: "Long live Escamillo!" Enter the toreador—a debonair figure in his fine costume, and the idol of the crowd.

Samson and Delila—Delila's Song (*Saint-Saens*) Marian Palmer
In this song, Delila calls to the Philistines to enter Samson's house and trap him.

Die Zauberflöte—Duet, Act II (*Mozart*) Marian Palmer
Ivor Levinson
After almost despairing of ever finding his lover, Papageno, the bird-catcher, is told by the Genii to set his magic bells ringing. When he does so his love Papagena appears, and the two sing of their happiness at being reunited.

Rigoletto—La Donna è mobile (*Verdi*) Martin Kyrle
Gilda who has been jilted by the Duke, sees him go into a tavern and sing this buoyant song over his wine—so much in keeping with the Duke's character.

Merrie England—The Waltz Song (*German*) Hilary Taylor
This is Bessie's song from Act II in praise of the delights of love.

The Desert Song (*Romberg*) Brian Keith-Smith
This is the theme song from the well-known operetta.

Die Zauberflöte—In diesen Leiligen Hallen (*Mozart*) Ivor Levinson
The High-Priest Zoroaster here tells of the glory and riches of the halls of wisdom over which he rules, protected by the shield of light.

INTERVAL of 10 minutes

---

all three of us were on stage —

'THE TELEPHONE'

Produced by:
BRIAN KEITH-SMITH

Dramatis personae:

LUCY	ROSEMARY STORKEY
BEN	IAN THOMAS

SCENE: Lucy's apartment in New York.
TIME: The present.

First produced in 1947 in New York, "The Telephone" is usually seen as a curtain-raiser to Menotti's longer work "The Medium." The action takes place in Lucy's apartment while Ben is trying to propose to her. He is continually thwarted by calls on the telephone, and in despair has to rush off to catch a train. Taking a last chance, he telephones Lucy from the station and proposes. This time the telephone is his friend.

Stage Manager	JOHN TAYLOR
Paintings by	KIRSTEN THOMPSON
Wardrobe Mistress	CELIA PHILLIPS
Make-Up by	BRIAN LEWIS
Lighting by	MIKE RUSSELL, JOHN LANE, PAT WOOSTER, PETER LANIGAN
Prompter	VARIOUS
Front-of-House Manager	IAN PURVIS
Front-of-House Manager	MARGARET ROUND
Treasurer	IVOR FASTCAR
Publicity Manager	IAN THOMAS
Programme compiled by	MARTIN KYRLE
Accompanists	KENNETH BROOKS, PETER LAMBERT

Musical Director:
RAYMOND TURLEY

Modern Furniture lent by	TYRRELL & GREEN LTD.
No Smoking by	REQUEST

Printed by	G. F. WILSON & CO. LTD.

while Margaret (under her maiden name) was Front of House Manager bedbugs and all – and the tribulations of the then prevailing *modus vivendi*. But unless you are familiar with the text of *The Canterbury Tales* you won't get all the jokes.

Eastridge Museum

Wandering idly, we attracted the unexpected attentions of a punter touting for business – a real one, selling tickets for a trip on his punt. We'd not expected such an essentially summertime activity to be on offer so early in the season. Maybe it was a fine day and he thought he might get lucky and attract some bonus punters? (*Sorry!*). Replete with straw boater and virtually non-stop explanation of flora and fauna, he did an excellent job, all the time either standing to punt us along the canal or sitting to row us when he reached the river – and warning us well in time to lie back flat on our cushions when approaching a low bridge. What was particularly disarming was that as a combination of boatman and natural history guide he knew his stuff and appeared to be enthusiastically enjoying himself as well as serving his customers.

Leaving Canterbury to make our way home we'd arranged to stop off near Ashford to visit two old friends from our university days, Arthur and Marian. The singular fact about Marian is that she is the only person I am still in contact with who was actually at school with me – we go back that far. When I went up to university after completing my national service who should be at the top of the steps up to the West Building – the student part of the university – on my first day but Marian – who at school I'd known by her first name, which she would prefer not to be made public so we'll stick to her second name. 'It's Martin Kyrle! What are you doing here?' 'It's ***** Palmer! What are you doing here?' 'Same as you, and I'm not called ***** any more, I'm called Marian'. 'Right'.

We were thrown together mainly through our membership of the university's Operatic Society. In the spring of my first year we put on HMS *Pinafore*, with me in the chorus and Marian in the role of Little Buttercup. Later Arthur came on the scene and we staged *Cox and Box* with me as Cox and Arthur playing Sergeant Bouncer, the landlord. Marian is bigger-built than Arthur and a couple of inches taller, and when I learned of them pairing up I asked her confidentially, 'Who carries the stool?', as for her the description 'little' in 'Little Buttercup' was – and is – entirely inappropriate. But they were soon clearly getting serious, and one day during a rehearsal Marian took me to one side and whispered in my ear, 'I wish they made Arthurs in larger sizes'. It didn't stop them going the whole hog and getting married and having two daughters, and at the present time they've been married for fifty-four years.

Another memory of our student G *&* S productions was what happened in *Patience*. I was the producer and Marian had the part of Lady Jane, one of Gilbert's standard contralto roles of an older woman losing her looks and desperate for a husband, and set up to be the butt of some heavy-handed sarcasm on stage. There's a well-known comic duet with one of the male leads, Bunthorne, which when it ends and the two singers have left the stage it's by custom encored and they perform it again but instead of just walking off at the end make their exit in some absurd way just for laughs. In our production, for the first encore Marian went into the wings and came back with a wheelbarrow, shoved Bunthorne into it and pushed him off with his legs kicking wildly (uproar!). Follow that! She did. They came on for the second encore and at the end she grabbed Bunthorne, threw him over her shoulder and marched off stage carrying him in a fireman's lift, arms and legs waving frantically. Brought the house down.

Marian comes from Fareham and is a life-long Labour supporter, following her father who was an unsuccessful council candidate until right at the end of his life when he finally got elected but died soon after. Our conversations, therefore, have always veered into politics, and in former times converged around the pointlessness of her being Labour in a place like Fareham and me being a Liberal practically anywhere. Things changed when I won a seat on the council to join Margaret, who then progressed to become Mayor for the first time – even though my parliamentary ambitions came to nothing (four elections, four second places). The sad thing now is that both Marian and Arthur are suffering the ravages of old age, her with crippling osteoarthritis leaving her walking with two sticks and Arthur fighting vascular dementia. What makes the situation particularly poignant so far as I'm concerned is that they're both younger than me – though this is partly counterbalanced by the fact that at least they're both still alive, and older than Margaret was when she died. It's a funny old world, *innit*, and there just ain't no justice. But good to see them again, and reminisce over old times and audience reactions to our long-past and long-forgotten performances when we trod the boards.

To round off a lovely birthday weekend we made another diversion before heading for home: take the opportunity to visit Ightham Mote, a remarkable survival of a 14th century moated manor house which belongs to the National Trust and is so evocative and 'chocolate box perfect' that it frequently does precisely what you'd expect: it appears in pictures on boxes of chocolates. Off the beaten track in a secluded and heavily-wooded valley, it lay half-forgotten for centuries and thus escaped modernisation and remains as it has always been, intact and entirely authentic.

Goodnight.

Ightham Mote courtyard

D

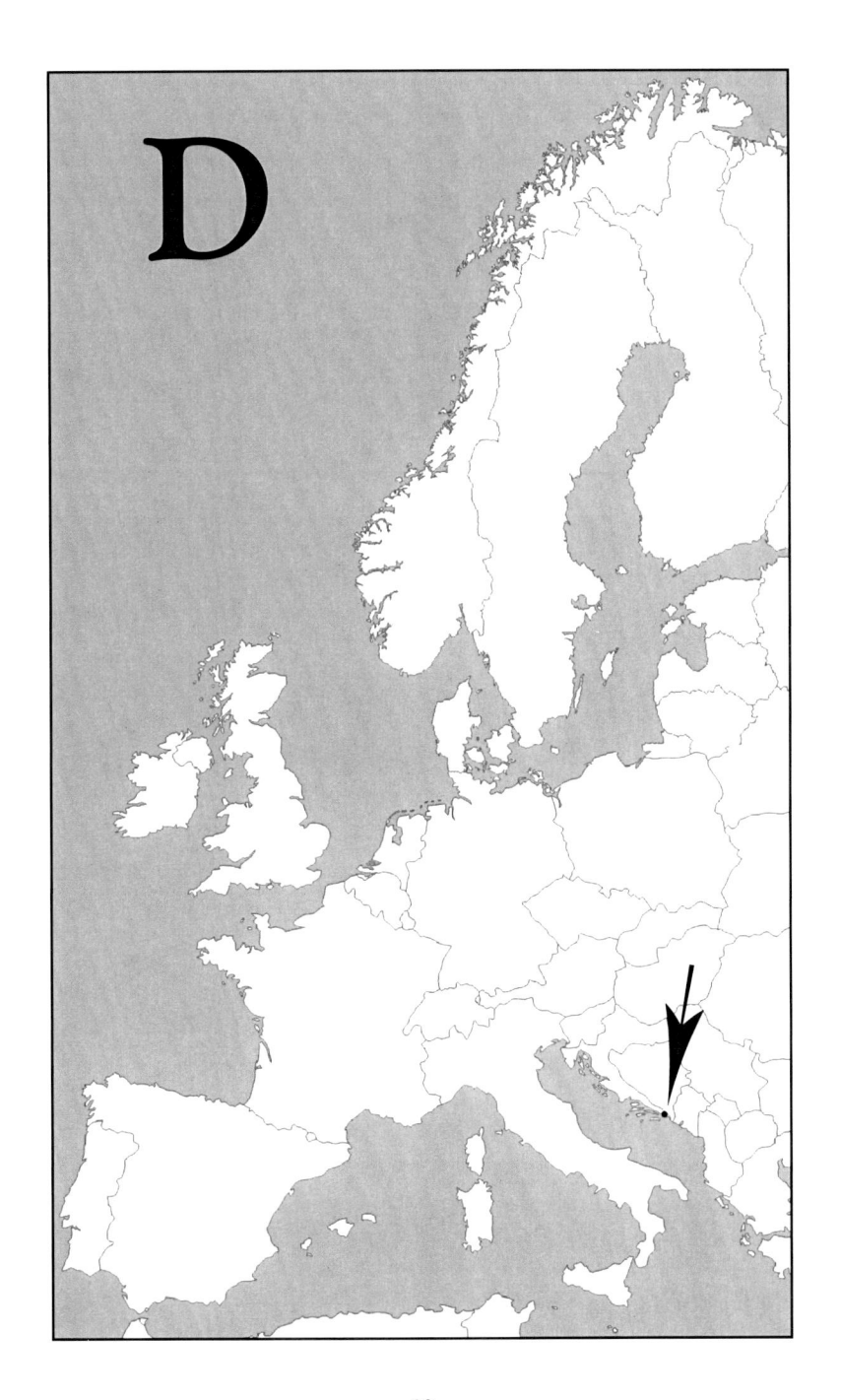

DUBROVNIK

... and Plan A

It had taken us thirteen hours overnight on the train from Sarajevo when by dawn's early light we crested the hills outside Dubrovnik and saw a hillside covered with cypresses all standing like a medieval army with spears at the ready waiting for the order to attack, and beyond them the Adriatic. You can read about that under S *(though not in <u>this</u> book)*.

Dubrovnik was all it's cracked up to be, and you can get a brochure from your friendly neighbourhood travel agent if you want a guided tour. All I need say is that we enjoyed walking the walls and reading up a brand new subject: the history of the Republic of Ragusa. We then set about finding out how to make our way up the coast to Rijeka and on into Austria to reach the refugee camp at Linz where we were scheduled to start work in time to meet our deadline.

Before taking the ferry, we determined to have a swim. A mistake, as Bob almost immediately trod on a sea urchin, which was not amused and retaliated by leaving a load of its spines embedded in his foot. For the entire duration of the ferry ride up the coast, at any moment we were sitting down anywhere Bob would take off his sandal and commence picking at his foot with his penknife, trying to tease out yet another urchin spine. Not a pretty sight, but at least it kept other passengers away. Especially with me looking them straight in the eye while furtively pointing sideways at my clearly deranged companion, gazing upwards into the sky and shaking my head slowly. Bob claimed to have once got to the front of a queue in a chemist's shop by declaiming in a loud voice of his companion at the time, 'They must have *something* for the black palsy', whereupon everyone else in the shop turned pale and sidled out through the door, leaving Bob at the counter where he was able to ask for the bottle of aspirins he'd come for. But what else could you expect from someone who was the only boy in his class at school whose parents had no children?

Boarding the ferry was a free-for-all, but we'd worked out Plan A in advance – a version of which I still employ when travelling minus car but with wife. I would carry both our rucksacks, 'doing a donkey out of a job', as my grandfather used to say. Bob would go ahead unencumbered, get a ticket and weave his way through other passengers who were technically ahead of us in the queue and make for the point of the bow *(translation for landlubbers: up at the sharp end)*. He would there mark out our territory by taking off his coat, sandals or whatever to show that this bit was taken, with the implication that he was awaiting his friend who, let me warn you, is 18 stone, of unpredictable disposition when crossed and chews hammers as a hobby (*i.e. not a professional, but a hammer-chewer*). Baring his teeth and coughing convulsively or doing a bit more urchin spine-picking with an open penknife also helped keep other passengers at a safe distance. In due course I would arrive, nonchalantly sauntering at the back of the crowd of embarkees, and simply deposit the two rucksacks and sit down. Being as far for'ard as it was possible to get had the advantage that you had the gunwales to lean against and only had other passengers next to you on one side and no one trying to go past you as there was nowhere past you to go.

Our first stop was the island of Hvar, but not enough time to disembark and explore. Another time, perhaps. Then into harbour at Split, and an afternoon to kill. The Roman emperor Diocletian built a palace at Split, and why I remember it so well is that inside the walls there were various kiosks and one of them sold the finest ice cream I've ever tasted. It was also so hot that when we found the road was lined with palm trees we took to walking along each tree's shadow from root to canopy and then darting as quickly as possible in a straight line to the base of the next one and then repeating the zigzag manoeuvre. Must have looked a bit like a film take for 'The Invasion of the Crab-men', but when you're wearing clothing for all seasons, not stripped off in shirt-sleeves for a heat wave, you are pretty desperate to get out of the direct heat of the sun.

The Dalmatian Islands are very picturesque, and I made a mental note to come back one day and explore them at leisure. Again, I'm still waiting – nearly sixty years later.

Rijeka was an interesting place, and we had time to go shopping. In restaurants in Sarajevo and Dubrovnik I had drunk coffee made in the Turkish fashion in individual brass pots with long handles, and I was determined to buy a set to take home as a souvenir. Prices in tourist shops were beyond my pocket. We found ourselves in the local market, where the prices being charged by the craftsmen were even higher. Then a thought struck me: where do the locals buy theirs? Answer: in the ironmongery section of a general store. Indeed, the prices there were a small fraction of the others, and I duly acquired my souvenirs. For the remainder of my student years I was able to impress colleagues and numerous girlfriends with my genoo-ine bedou-ine Turkish coffee made in the authentic way and in the proper utensils – 'Oh', I'd reply laconically when asked where they came from. 'I picked these up during my travels in the Balkans'.

Travel snobs aren't new . . .

But I hope I've grown out of it.

Reminds me of an incident in the wardroom when I was stationed in the naval barracks in Chatham. Most of us midshipmen were training to become cypher officers, but there were two who weren't. They were *the* most frightful poseurs you could ever wish to meet – or rather, wish *not* to meet. They were always bragging to each other in loud voices about where they'd been or who they'd met – never about anything they'd actually *done*, which was what riled the rest of us. If they'd ever accomplished anything worth boasting about, we wouldn't have minded. Eventually one of them, propping up the bar with his friend, was heard to remark, 'Is that the fifteenth or sixteenth country we've visited?' in the sort of stage whisper people adopt when they're saying something for the benefit of everyone else within earshot, expecting to create an impression. It was one brag too often. One of our number rose from his chair with his glass of beer in his hand, walked up to the bar and emptied the contents over the bombastic little shyster's head and without saying a word returned to his chair.

There was absolute silence. Made the point for all of us, we thought.

But if that's what you do to the next saloon bar bore you run into swanking to the assembled company about how Barbados is *so* last year, don't try to blame me for putting the idea into your head if you end up getting a fourpenny one.

Goodnight.

August 1956

E

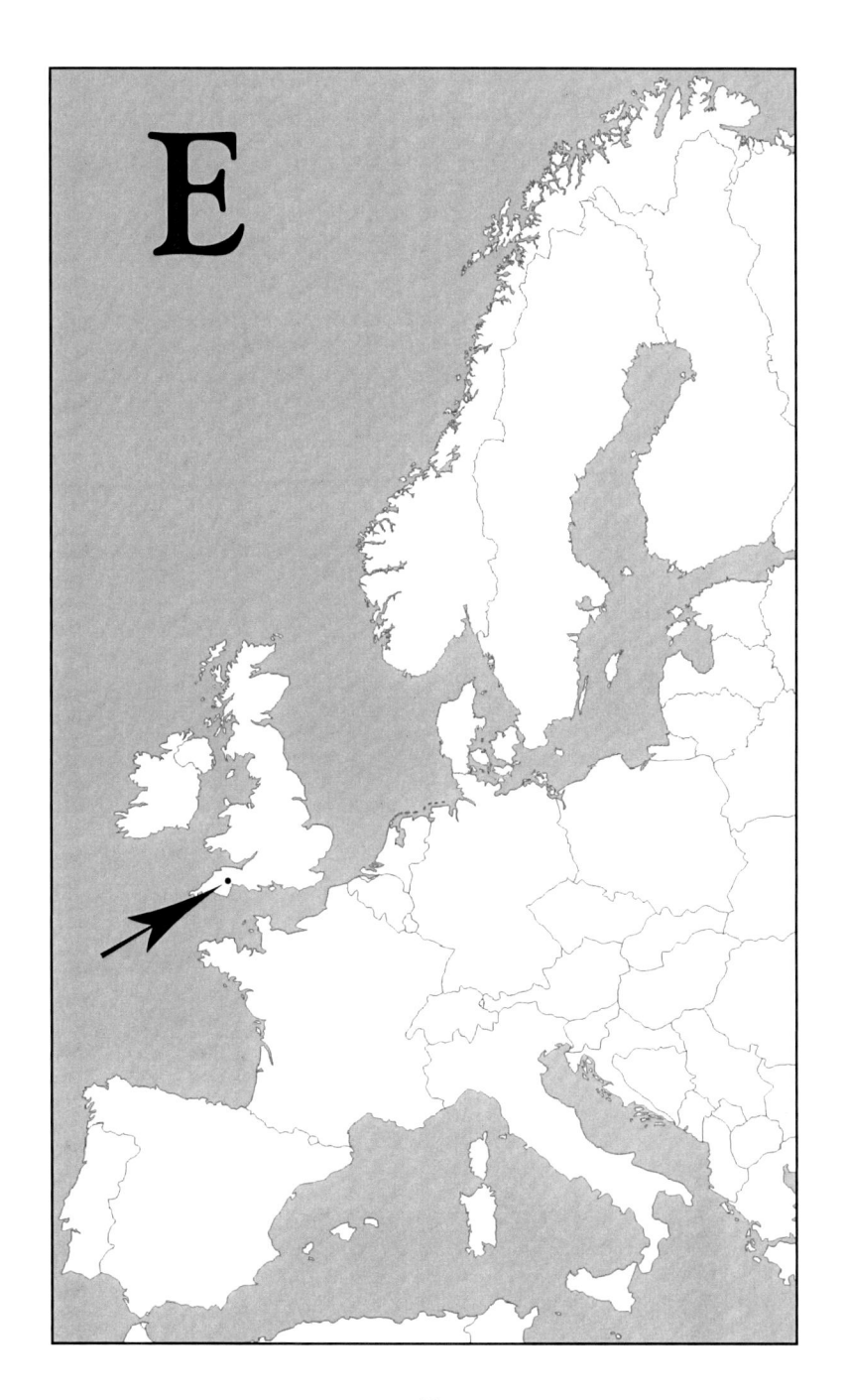

EXETER

'Tis an ill clutch that blows nobody any good...

On Wednesday the men were coming to our flat in Dartmouth to install the rest of the double glazing, so on Tuesday we drove down.
At least, that was the plan. The Almighty had other ideas.
When we changed over drivers Margaret found the clutch beginning to slip. Yes, I'd noticed it, and was intending to take it in to my local garage next week and get it fixed. Unfortunately, I hadn't told the clutch that salvation was in the offing, and ten miles short of Honiton going up a hill just after some roadworks it burned out, choking the driver behind in black smoke. That's it. Call the AA.
Luckily we had lunch with us – sandwiches with the remains of last Sunday's joint – and had planned to stop as usual in a lay-by as the weather was decent for the time of year (mid-December). The AA promised to be with us within the hour, but in fact the patrolman turned up after forty minutes. No emergency repairs were possible – the smell was proof enough that the only 'repair' was a new clutch. So he hooked us up on a towbar and headed off to the AA's nominated garage in Exeter, twenty miles away. Requires enormous concentration being towed at speed along a motorway when all you can do is steer and try to keep directly behind the towing vehicle but with no control over anything else. Also has a tendency to render the trousers a bit damp.
Part of my deal with the AA is a free hire car in case of such an emergency, but the problem was that the garage was on one side of the city and the firm hiring the car on the other. Being on our way down for a stay of several days we had a bootful of luggage, all of which had to be unloaded and stacked however we could in the patrolman's vehicle, which wasn't designed for such a contingency. But we managed it, and jammed ourselves into the front seats of his van and took it in turns to breathe in. If Margaret and I hadn't been married, one of us would have been done for assault.

We'd been coming down to the West Country for many years, ever since, in fact, I first brought my then fiancée to visit her prospective mother-in-law in Dartmouth in 1958. We came to the river bank at the Higher Ferry on the opposite side of the town, saw it laid out before us in the sunshine and fell in love with it on sight. When our boys were small and money was tight we used to come down for long weekends B&B, and at a time when Humphrey liked to get up at some godforsaken hour in the morning we'd give him 50p the night before and instruct him to go to the newsagent just down the road and buy us our morning paper and bring it back at eight o'clock and not a moment earlier. We felt quite confident that an 8-year old wouldn't come to any harm alone on the streets of Dartmouth in the early morning, and he never did – even though when he'd bought the paper instead of coming straight back to our guest house he used to go down to the South Embankment and walk along the river and come back from the opposite direction. The 1970s were more innocent times. Not so sure I'd take the same view nowadays.

Another reason bringing us to the West Country over the years was that my mother remarried for a second time in Flavel Church in Dartmouth, moved from there to Totnes, then to near Newton Abbot, then to Foxholes near St Austell, then to Newlyn, then to Penzance and finally to Long Rock on the road to Marazion. We visited in school holidays, and often stopped off at Dartmouth on the way home to extend the break. In all those years, we always drove straight past Exeter on the A38 or by-passed it on the road across Dartmoor via Moretonhampstead and only once went into the city – to visit the cathedral.

Exeter Quay *photo: Exeter City Council*

So being now by happenstance in the city again, once we'd been deposited by the AA patrolman at the hire car firm and had picked up our temporary vehicle we thought it only made sense as we had time to spare to make the most of our chance visit and explore the city before heading on to Dartmouth. We found Exeter to be a quite delightful place, especially when we left the cathedral precinct and found our way down to the river where in the days when ships were a lot smaller they delivered goods to merchants and loaded cargo for shipment. We managed a short walk through the main shopping area, but by then it was time to go – we had to get to Dartmouth (not very far), but when we got there we had to unpack our stuff for the rest of our stay and do a bit of shopping for fresh supplies like, for example, tomorrow's breakfast.

There are pros and cons to having a second home, when you come to think about it. Before buying bricks and mortar we came to Dartmouth for a few days in a year, but then perhaps not again for several years afterwards. So walking around the picturesque old part of the town was always a delight, unsullied by over-familiarity. Once you buy, you feel under pressure to come down not just every year but every month to make sure you're getting your money's worth and at a more mundane level just to keep an eye on things and cut the grass, re-paint a wall, pick the post up off the doormat and so on. After a few years, going down to your holiday home is no longer a holiday but a chore – you go because you have to, not because you particularly want to. Learning this lesson by experience, I always stood firm when Margaret wanted us to buy a place in France, where she very much enjoyed the lifestyle (as do I) and the cuisine. My objection was this: as things are, we can go to France four or five times a year (which we did right up to the time of her death), but always to different places to see new things, and as for those places we liked from previous visits we can always make a detour or just pop in for an overnight stay and have dinner in that nice restaurant or walk up that medieval cobbled street again or whatever. If we buy somewhere, then we'll have to go back to that same place every time and we'll lose our present freedom to explore all over – and added to that over time we'll get bored with the place because we'll have seen everything within range and there's nothing new left to do or see 'cos we've done it all and seen it all. Is that what you want? Answer: No. So we never did buy ourselves a *pied-à-terre*, and now that she's no longer here I'm glad I don't have the responsibility of managing a property on the other side of the Channel and having to make regular visits alone just to see that everything's alright. Keeping tabs on our flat in Dartmouth is difficult enough (a round trip of

300 miles), without having the added encumbrance of needing to book a ferry.

That's not to imply, let alone say, that I have any regrets about buying where we did. Anyone who knows Dartmouth knows that parking is difficult at any time, and impossible in the town in the summer. When we went house-hunting, we laid down three essential criteria: there had to be two bedrooms, so that we could go down with a friend if needs be, or lend the flat to friends with a child or friends who were not married to each other; it had to have a parking space of its own, not on the public highway, so that we could be sure that no matter at what time of the day or night we arrived we'd always have somewhere to park the car; and thirdly, it had to be walking distance from the town centre, so that once we'd arrived we could leave the car on site and not need it in order to get to the town itself.

Our choice fell on a basement flat which met our three demands, and we enjoyed many a short break over twenty years until finally deciding that we preferred exploring France and getting lost in the French countryside to retracing our steps month in and year out across Dartmoor – beautiful though that can be, especially in winter. When the suggestion across the breakfast table that 'it's time we went down to the flat' was met with a curl of the lip rather than a smile, I knew the time had come to re-think: sell up, or at least let it to a permanent resident. And so the situation remains. Between tenants we enjoyed some more short breaks, which were just like old times because we hadn't been for a couple of years and we thoroughly enjoyed reacquainting ourselves with restaurants, cafés and local shopkeepers we'd got to know over the years. The rental income paid for many a trip to France, so we had our holidays 'free' just as was the case – in pure economic terms – when we used to spend our holidays in our own (second) home.

So there you have it. A story which starts off about a chance mechanical breakdown leading to a revelatory visit to an ancient cathedral city, moves on to a few nuggets of folksy family history in historic Dartmouth and finally ends with some gentle philosophising on the subject of second homes.

And no doubt the local Tourist Boards will have no reason not to be pleased, either.

As a postscript, you may not have heard the following limerick, which was current during my student days and was regularly included in rugby club sing-songs:

> *There was a young lady of Exeter,*
> *All the boys used to crane their neckseter.*
> *But one silly sod*
> *Got six months in quad*
> *For waving his organ of sexeter.*

Goodnight.

December 2005

F

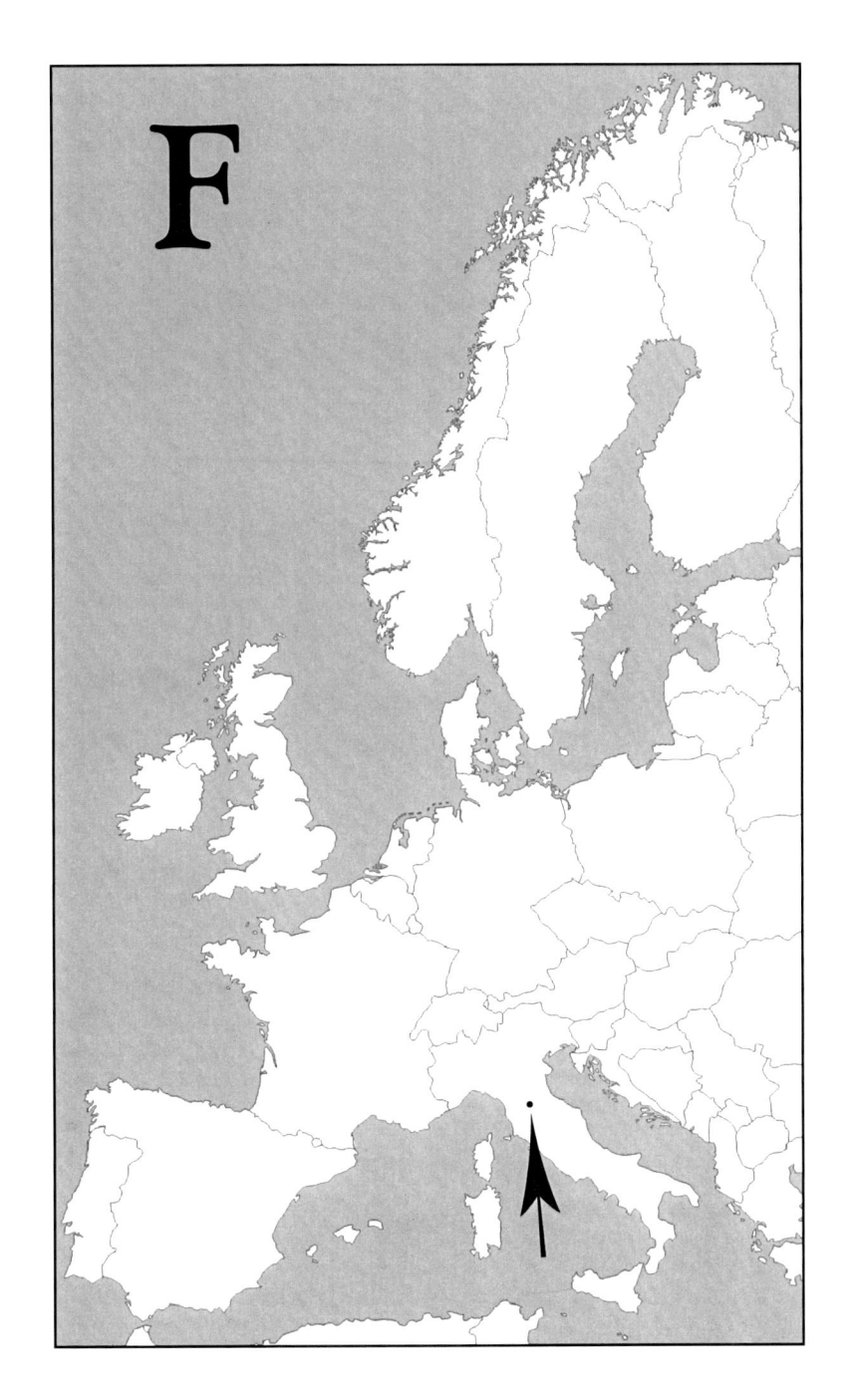

FIRENZE

Returning to normal

When you're mayor of the borough, for one whole year someone always opens the door for you, you enter every room first, everyone stands up, you get first pick of the buffet and your coffee's hot when they serve it. Well, there's a lot more to it than that, but you get the idea.

But it means that for that year you are *Numero Uno*, until your year is up and you pass the chain of office over to your successor. From being 'Madame Mayor' one day – I'm talking about Margaret, not me – the next morning you're back to 'Who?' and 'How do you spell your name?'. It can be quite a shock to the system. Moral: enjoy it while it lasts, but remember the bowing and scraping is to you as the office-holder, not to you as a person.

We decided that the way to smooth the transition from First Citizen back to normal life was to get right away for a week as soon as possible after the end of Margaret's mayoral year, and take a holiday somewhere a bit exotic. We'd both long wanted to visit Florence, so that's what we did.

And who should be on the plane but our MP, Sir David Price, and his wife – on last because of her need for wheelchair space. The significance of his appearance on this flight becomes apparent when I explain that at the general election two years before I'd been one of his opponents, so we'd been acquainted for a long time. Contrary to most people's presumptions about politicians in opposing parties, we had a high degree of mutual respect and got on quite well when we met at functions. But I did remark to Margaret that perhaps he was just making sure that he wouldn't have to face me at an election again as I was leaving the country and, this being Italy, just to make sure he'd been in touch with his local friends in *Cosa Nostra* and was coming in person to make sure his instructions were carried out. . .

It struck us as strange that a major city such as Florence didn't have its own airport – you flew to Pisa and took the train. But we settled into our hotel in the suburbs (couldn't afford city centre accommodation) and travelled in by bus every day to visit the historic sites. The mayoral year had been very strenuous, and what we really wanted was a good rest and some gentle sight-seeing without having either to rush around to some tour guide's schedule or worry about which side of the road to drive on. That's why we travelled by public transport, and independently instead of taking a package tour.

Being myself well versed in European history I was able to really enjoy seeing so many buildings which I had read about or seen in pictures. Having lunch in a beautiful square, I shuddered slightly to recall that Savonarola had been burned alive for heresy outside the building opposite – the same building, it was still there – and imagined what the crowd scene would have been like back in 1498, in contrast to the ambience we were enjoying sitting in the sunshine over a meal and a bottle of wine without a care in the world. In Rouen one of our favourite restaurants for lunch is *Les Maraîchers*, just across the road from the site where Joan of Arc was burned at the stake – in this case only memorials and plaques mark the spot, as Second World War bombs destroyed the originals. Two doors away is *La Couronne*, which claims to have records going back to 1345 and so to be the oldest restaurant in France. This means that if you have a sufficiently sick sense of humour you can imagine yourself (or maybe one of your ancestors – who knows, one of them might have been there at the time) sitting in that very tavern on 29 May 1431 watching the sweating English soldiery arranging the faggots around *La Pucelle* and the executioner lighting his torch in readiness while you stick your knife into a meat pie and shout at the pot boy to bring you another tankard – 'Hurry up! Those flames are going to be really, really hot when they barbecue the witch and the thought's making me thirsty!'. As I said, you have to have a sufficiently sick sense of humour . . .By way of an expiative palliative, let me offer you this one: in a medieval recipe for thick broth there appears the instruction: '*When the cauldron is boiling fiercely, pop in a scullion*'.

But it's not unusual for tourists who visit sites of historical interest to find themselves at some location where centuries ago scenes of unspeakable horror took place, yet here you are as a tourist relaxing and drinking coffee as though nothing had ever happened and the locals are just getting on with their everyday lives – serving the said coffee, selling papers, having lunch, going to the hairdresser's, meeting a date, pushing a pram or buying new shoes for the kids. If you've ever, for example, walked amongst the ruins of Pompeii, you'll know what I mean. However tranquil it looks now, it was a bit different on 24 August 79AD.

We had one nasty moment during our stay. I was strap-hanging in the bus into town when I happened to catch sight of the headline in the paper over another passenger's shoulder. The only Italian I knew was through singing Verdi and Puccini in my student days in the Operatic Society, but I could just make out that there'd been some disaster in Belgium, with pictures of a sports stadium and numbers of dead and injured and comments about English football hooligans. I suddenly twigged: it was the match between Liverpool and Juventus at the Heysel Stadium in Brussels, and something terrible had happened and the Brits were to blame. My immediate thought was: 'What's happened, and will we be at risk here in Italy because the moment we open our mouths it's obvious that we're English?'

As I couldn't be sure I'd read the story properly we decided to minimise our risks and head back to the safety of our hotel and ask the receptionist to explain. He told us that English football supporters had attacked Italian fans and numerous deaths had resulted. I asked him straight:

'Is it safe for us on the streets of Florence?'.

He was reassuring.

'Of course you are. It wasn't you!'

'Maybe so, but we're English and if someone here's lost his cousin because of English hooligans and he wants revenge or just to vent his anger, any English person will do.'

'No worries. We Florentines aren't like that.'

As it turned out, he was right. We encountered no hostility whatever.

I recalled this episode some years later, when staying in a pub in the far south-west of Ireland. One day while we were there news came through of an IRA bomb attack in the North, where a bus carrying British soldiers had been blown up and eight of them killed. Our landlord and all his customers went out of their way to assure us that it had nothing to do with them and they didn't support the IRA, let alone condone atrocities. As one of them put it: 'We don't want the North anyway. It's as much as our government can manage to look after the eighteen counties we've already got, without adding another six!'

At the end of our lovely week, steeped in history, art and Italian wine, we took the train back to Pisa and got on the plane home. And who was on it too? Believe it or not – Sir David and his wife.

Goodnight.

May 1985

G

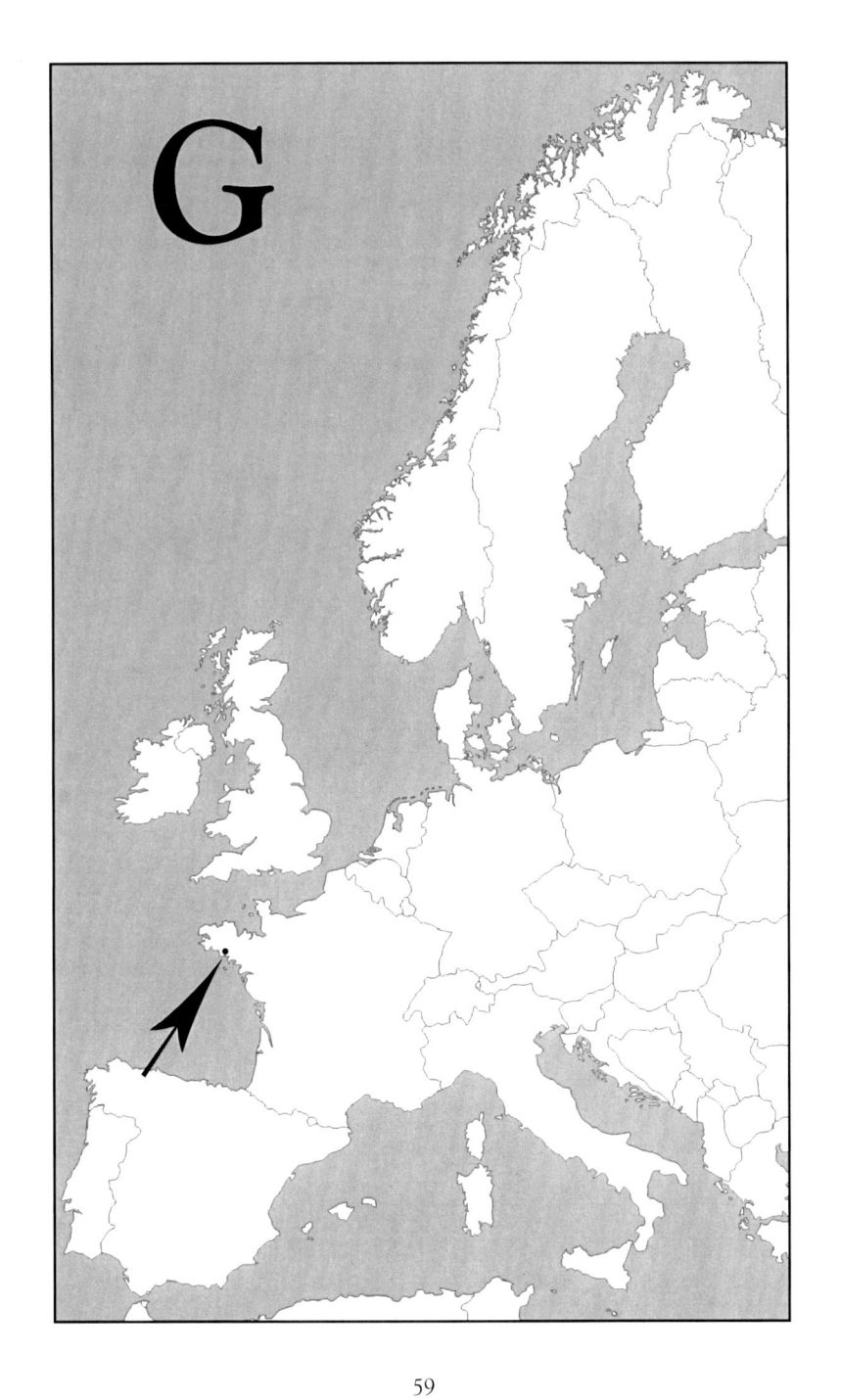

GAVRINIS

Stone me!

Margaret had always wanted to take a proper look at Carnac, one of the largest neolithic sites in the world with dead straight lines of standing stones stretching over a kilometre. The town is divided into two distinct areas, a couple of kilometres apart: Carnac proper and the seaside resort of Carnac-Plage, which is full of cafés, restaurants, hotels and holidaymakers and their children (the beaches are excellent, so no wonder!). But in our opinion 'old' Carnac boasted some rather more interesting restaurants, and whenever possible we opted to make the short drive up the hill to eat there. It also has an interesting church, with a statue on an outside wall of St Cornelius, Pope 251-3, who according to legend fled persecution under Emperor Trebonianus Gallus *(no – I'd never heard of him either)* and was pursued to Brittany, where the Roman soldiers chasing him were turned into stones and that accounts for the lines of standing stones to be found outside Carnac... Legend is a wonderful thing!

We'd rented a *gîte* in Carnac-Plage for convenience, as a central point to explore the area, but had considerable trouble finding it when we arrived because the street nameplate was not on the side of the road facing us as we approached but on the opposite side – which meant we only found it when, having got lost, we turned round and came back. Added to which, our little road was a cul-de-sac, so no way in from the other end so therefore no nameplates. The *gîte* was comfortably furnished and we thought we were in for a relaxing stay, until we tried to use the shower and the tap wouldn't budge, leaving us with the dilemma: do you increase the amount of force and risk breaking the tap and flooding the bathroom, or do you forego showers and just wash down using the washbasin? Not what you expect when you've paid top dollar for a house for a week in high summer. Things reached their nadir when the night before we were due to leave the lock in the front door jammed and we could only get out of the house by climbing through a window.

As is our wont, we sought out the local 'little train' and took a tour of the area. The Carnac-Plage version takes passengers for a joy-ride along the coast through the town and on to other nearby resorts, and then veers off into the countryside along the road which runs parallel to the neolithic site, giving passengers an excellent view of its entire length. Next day we went back in the car so that we could wander amongst the stones and read the guidebook and the helpful information panels erected by the local authorities.

Margaret's wishes now having been satisfied, it was my turn. My light-hearted goal of visiting every island off the French coast accessible by a public ferry turns up some difficult destinations. Gavrinis is one such.

Off the French coast it may be, but it's not in the sea but in the virtually land-locked Gulf of Morbihan. So small you wouldn't notice it on an ordinary map, the fact that it's the location of the highest neolithic tumulus in the whole of Brittany means it's highlighted on all the appropriate tourist brochures.

The problem is: how to get there.

It's only about twenty kilometres west of Vannes as the crow flies, but with such an indented coastline it's double that in road mileage (or should that be "kilometrage"?). You'd expect the principal ferry to the island to start out from Vannes, as the main centre for visitors, tourists, archaeology groupies and, as it's also the capital of that part of Brittany, where there is the greatest concentration of hotels.

Vannes is the starting point for many ferries, in particular for the "real" ones serving the ordinary residents on the two islands in the Gulf which are not in private hands, namely the Ile d'Arz and the Ile aux Moines, which need a regular commercial ferry to get to the mainland for shopping, private business (seeing their dentist, perhaps?) in the same way that the rest of us might need a bus to the local supermarket or a train service to go to a theatre in the next town. But not for Gavrinis, oh no!

There are two possibilities. One is from Port Navalo, on the tip of the Presqu'île de Rhuys and an hour's circuitous drive from Vannes, and when you get there you'd be doubling back on yourself. The other is from Locmariaquer, on the opposite side of the Gulf. But that's a small place well off the main road north-west of Vannes, and also at the end of yet another peninsula so on the way to nowhere. In other words, you wouldn't be going there by car *en route* for anywhere else. If you went there, it would be for a purpose.

Well, of course, we *had* a purpose: to catch the ferry to Gavrinis – what else?

Ferry? Well, I suppose so. Room for a couple of dozen passengers in comfort – but possibly that reflects the number of passengers who normally want to cross the mouth of the Gulf to get to Port Navalo. It took fifteen minutes or so, then fresh passengers embarked for the journey up to the top of the Gulf to deposit us all on Gavrinis.

We were blessed with a calm day, bright sunshine and perfect visibility. The Gulf is dotted with islands, most very small and often tree-covered or if privately owned featuring a single house and a rudimentary landing stage. But with no commercial traffic it was very relaxing. On our approach to Gavrinis we passed near another archaeological curiosity: an adjacent islet with a set of stones running from dry land into the water which are partly submerged at high tide. Students and enthusiasts occasionally visit it, but we had a perfect view and could take pictures from various angles – enough to satisfy any non-specialist tourist.

Being a monument of major importance, Gavrinis itself boasts a proper jetty and a stout iron fence surrounds the tumulus to prevent unauthorised or unaccompanied visitors. Public access is through a locked gate – open only during visiting hours. Guided tours only, to protect such a unique and valuable site. But the detailed illustrative panels carry explanations only in French. Well, this is France – but how many tourists have a working knowledge of archaeological terms in a language other than their own? Many of the specialist words are not found even in a standard dictionary, let alone in the pocket variety a tourist might be carrying. A site of international importance should, surely, also allow for the probability that some visitors – even experts or specialists – have only a limited command of French. I've encountered similar obstacles elsewhere and at other times – as, probably, have you. Not that we in England are any better in facilitating understanding of historic sites for foreign visitors by helping out with a glossary of terms for those whose English may be good enough for ordinary business – travelling around, booking hotels, enquiring about bus tickets, shopping or eating out – but who may not know the words 'keep', 'moat' or 'drawbridge'. If they're francophone they may think that the English word 'dungeon' means the same as French 'donjon' (which actually *is* a keep), whereas in reality our similar-sounding word is totally misleading because it refers to something which could be fifty (vertical) metres wide of the mark, if you follow.

The tumulus on Gavrinis has been dated by experts to c3700BC and was abandoned, they tell us, around 3000BC. It consists of a dolmen covered by a cairn of stones, the entrance to which was not discovered until the first serious excavation was undertaken in 1835. The mound of stones has a diameter of about 50m and in modern times a padlocked door has been added which helps protect the interior from the weather and also prevents unauthorised entry. A passage 14m long, a metre or so wide and between 1½m and 2m high leads to a chamber 2½m square. By the light of the guide's torch the side walls, which consist of a continuous line of enormous granite boulders, can be seen to be entirely incised with typical neolithic patterns of concentric circles, axes and what experts say may be representations of animals and gods. No one knows for sure. One's ability to see the carvings is not helped by the corridor being packed, as the guide takes in about two dozen people at a time.

A question every visitor has in his mind is that the granite blocks weight many tonnes so how on earth did our neolithic ancestors transport them to an island? The truth is, Gavrinis wasn't an island when the dolmen was built because the water level in the Gulf was some 15m lower. Even then, the questions remain: how did they manage to dig up such enormous blocks and transport them, and the other unanswered question: why? Comparisons with Stonehenge come to mind: how and why? And what sort of society was it that thought such tremendous effort was worth it and persisted over centuries?

Goodnight.

May 2010

H

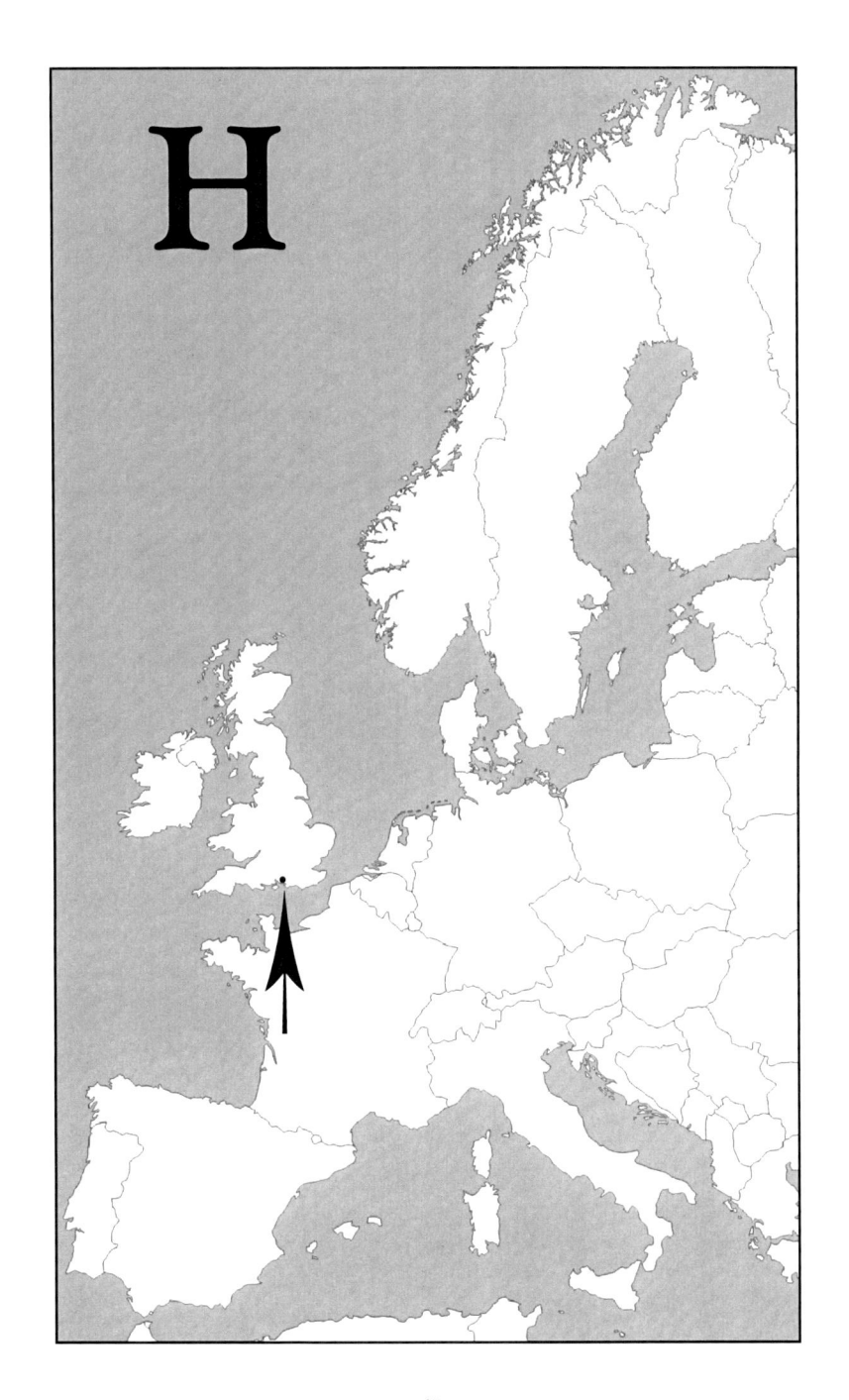

HORNDEAN

'The Good Old Days' – or were they?

When I was a schoolboy one of the ways us lads could make a bit of cash to supplement our pocket-money (assuming we got any) was to work for the local farmers in early autumn 'stooking', i.e. going out into the fields and walking behind the harvester and picking up a sheaf of corn in each hand and banging the tops together and then two more and so on to make a 'stook' consisting of six sheaves. Then move on and build another stook. All day long. Damned hard work, in the broiling sun and your forearms covered in pin-pricks from the cut ends of the corn. I think our pay was 1s 3d an hour (yes – 6p in our money, but the cost of living was entirely different in those days).

The other way to get hold of some extra funds was to work on the Post Office at Christmas.

Horndean Post Office was also a general store, with the proprietor's name over the doorway: 'B.J. BISH'. As postmaster, Mr Bish took me on as a 'temp' at 15, without seeming to bother about regulations which I think stipulated a minimum age of 16. He signed me on again the following year and in fact every year until I left school. I think he was glad to be able to take on a grammar school boy who could read and who, living in Clanfield on the outer reaches of his area, knew all the by-ways and lanes leading to outlying cottages and farms and who could therefore be relied upon to deliver their post.

I had to sign on by 6 a.m., which meant cycling from my home, a distance of a couple of miles. We started in the sorting office at the back of the premises, where I helped the regular postmen sort the incoming mail and put it into rounds. When this was complete I went out on a post office bike carrying the additional mail with one of the 'regulars', delivering to my own village and the surrounding farms. We did everything by bike – wind, rain or snow notwithstanding – and as this was in the middle of the South Downs we had some pretty demanding hills. They may not be very high, but they are often very steep.

I remember Horndean from a much earlier age than 15, from five in fact. When I reached that age and had to go to school, for some reason my grandparents who were bringing me up sent me to school in Blendworth, half a mile up the hill from Horndean, instead of to the village school in Clanfield. This meant that between the ages of five and eight I walked half a mile from my home up to the main A3 to catch the bus, went three stops to Horndean, got off and walked up the hill to the school in Blendworth and then repeated the journey at the end of the school day. Starting as an unaccompanied five-year old, remember, carrying my satchel with books, pens etc. and in all weathers.

Blendworth School was a single-storey building with a two-storey house attached, where Mrs Byrne, the head teacher, lived. There were two classrooms. Miss Miller, on the upper edge of middle age, took the five- to seven-year olds in one room, Mrs Byrne took the rest in the other. We sat two to a double desk, which had a bench seat attached on a black iron frame and holes for two inkwells and a groove for pens and pencils when not in use. The sloping top was hinged and when lifted revealed a space to store books and one's sandwiches for lunch (there was no school kitchen, nor any provision for hot food or drink). The desks stood in rows going back five deep to the rear wall, with two rows making up a 'standard', i.e. an age group. So Standard 4 was the two rows on the teacher's left, who'd be eight-year olds. Next to them and directly in front of Mrs Byrne were two rows of nine-year olds, and then on her right the top Standard, those in their final year before going on to secondary school. The three classes would all be doing different subjects, so Mrs Byrne might be teaching Standard 4 English, i.e. how to write and spell, Standard 6 might be having a history lesson, and sitting between the two would be Standard 5 doing nature study – all at the same time and in the same room and with just one teacher.

Our playground was a tarmac area bounded by a low fence of rounded iron railings facing the road and painted black, then at right angles a flint wall on the other side of which was the churchyard.

At the far end was the boys' urinal, consisting of a three-sided brick construction with the back wall and trough sealed with bitumen and open to the sky. Why Nan – my grandmother – chose to send me here – two half-mile walks and a bus fare – instead of to the much nearer village school in Clanfield – a mile-and-a-half across the fields, and no bus fare – I never found out, but as it turned out she withdrew me when I was eight and sent me to Clanfield School instead.

Back to Horndean. After we'd completed our morning round – usually not before two o'clock – we returned to sort mail for the afternoon shift. As well as two deliveries a day we even did a complete round on Christmas morning (for double time, so well worth it) and I got home for my Xmas Dinner at about two o'clock, having been up since five. We had a van for parcels, and my particular pleasure was to be assigned to this duty as that meant I had to knock on people's doors to deliver their parcel and if it had some interesting stamps on it I could ask if I could have them for my collection. Usually people were quite happy to give me the stamps, which otherwise they'd have thrown away, especially if it was a bitterly cold day and they took pity on the snow-covered post boy standing at their door in a howling gale. Some would tear them off there and then and give them to me, others would tell me to collect them next time I called. I built up quite a tidy collection that year! A lot of the stamps I got were, of course, from neighbours or other people living in the village whom I knew. Some of them, knowing that I was interested, kept their stamps for me long after I'd stopped being a 'temp' postie and would call me over when I was riding my bike along the lane or if they met me in the shop buying the weekly groceries for Nan and tell me they'd got some more stamps for me and to pop in and collect them. I sometimes got a cup of tea as well, or in hot weather a glass of lemonade. And sometimes an errand to run – e.g. post the reply to the letter from the country from which the stamps had come that I'd just been given. Seemed the least I could do – especially as the outcome would probably be another batch of stamps.

Harry, one of the regular postmen, had a specially adapted bike.

One pedal was fixed at full stretch for his foot to rest on and didn't go round, leaving his other leg to do all the pedalling. He'd been injured in the War (the First one, of course), and had an artificial leg but no control over the knee movement so could power the wheels on his bike only with his good leg. Despite all the hills, he seemed to manage them on his one-legged bike. At least he could always be absolutely sure that no one else would take it!

A last word about Horndean. During the two months of low temperatures and high snowfall we had no buses for six weeks and if I wanted to get to school at Purbrook, seven miles away, the buses which normally ran from Portsmouth to Petersfield could only get that far, and I had to walk to Horndean in the morning – hoping there'd be a bus to Purbrook – and then in the afternoon the reverse walk – about two miles – home. I had to try to get to school regardless of the weather conditions, as I was due to sit for my school certificate in the summer and one's entire future depended on success in that examination.

Goodnight.

December 1948

Afterthought: Anyone wanting to make stamp collecting illegal could write to the papers calling for philately to be stamped out.

I

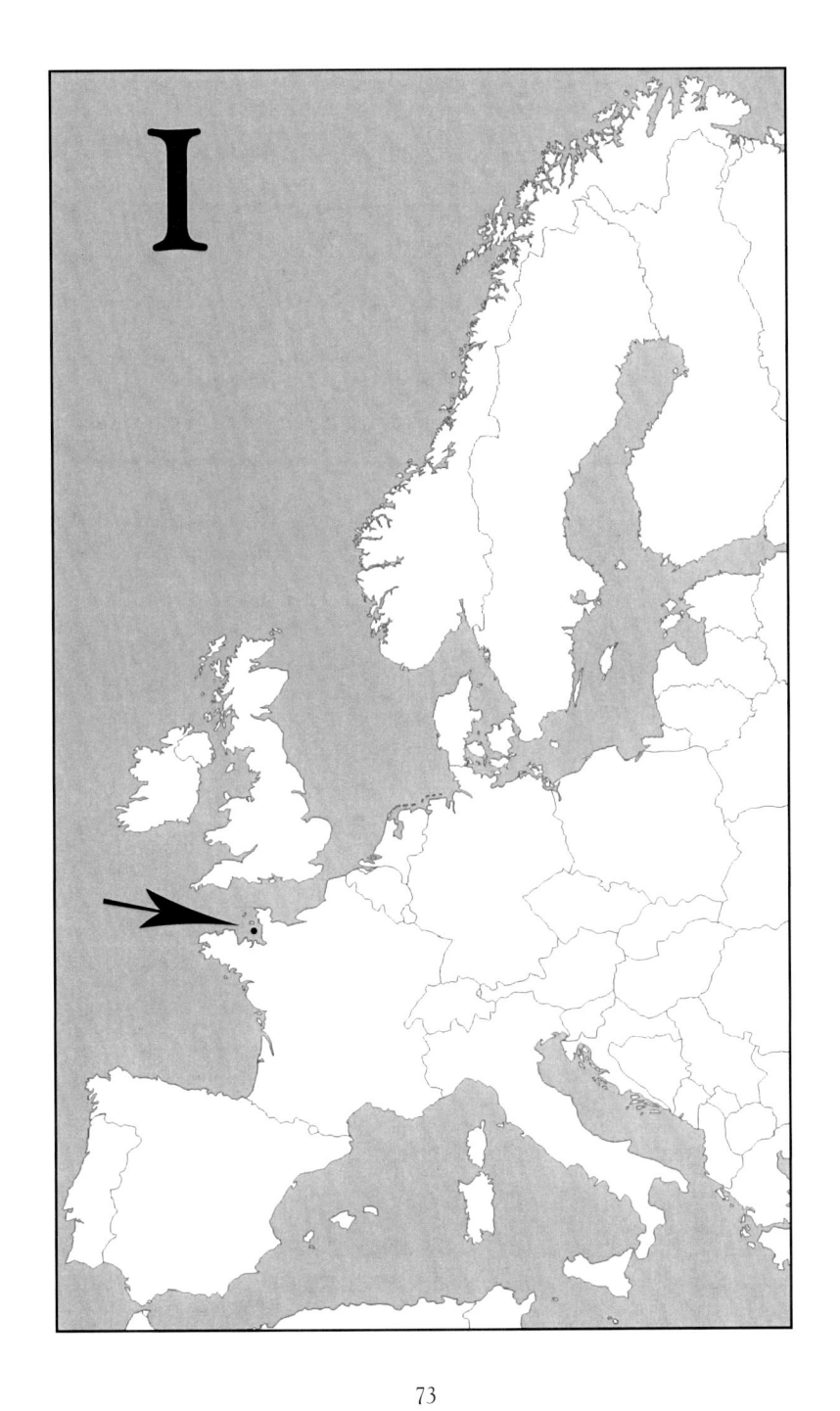

ÎLES CHAUSEY

An island life that is no longer

Most people think of the Channel Islands as being 'ours', i.e. part of the United Kingdom. Say that to a Channel Islander and s/he'll jump on you straight away and point out that as the last surviving relic of the Duchy of Normandy whose Duke, William, conquered England in 1066 it's actually the other way round. They're not part of us, we're part of them. They are subject to the English crown as the Queen is the lawful successor to the dukes of Normandy, but absolutely *not* subject to the English Parliament. Jersey and Guernsey have their own parliaments, stamps and coins to prove it.

But to the south there's another cluster of islands in the Channel which are part of France: Chausey and the surrounding rocky islets. Not many people know that, as they say. Officially there are 52 of them, but with a difference between high and low tide of 14m (about 45 feet in old money) many are submerged at high water, so it depends when you count them; allegedly there are 365 at low tide – one for each day of the year. From Granville the main island is visible some 17km distant on the horizon, and has a lighthouse (now automated – the last lighthousemen left in 2008) and a hotel, a restaurant and a café all open to visitors in the summer months. In the old days the islanders scraped a living by keeping a few sheep, harvesting seaweed and fishing – especially for lobsters. But the island priest locked the chapel for the last time and moved to the mainland in the 1970s and practically everyone else followed him a decade later, as these activities no longer provided a decent living. The little island school was abandoned and the workers' cottages sold off as holiday homes. Out of season the island retains only about thirty inhabitants, most of them maintenance staff. Elsewhere away from the landing stage there are a couple of private residences visible to passers-by through ornate gates at the end of long drives. However, these gates don't appear to be attached to completed walls, so more for appearance than security.

At low tide there are innumerable sandy beaches, rocky coves and delightful views over jagged rocks, but when the tide comes in you need to grab your clothes and picnic gear and leg it to above high water mark otherwise you will be caught out by the precipitate and unexpected speed at which the water comes up the beach.

It was the last weekend before the season ended, so as soon as we'd settled into our hotel in Granville I headed down to the ticket office in the harbour to make sure we were safely booked on the boat the following morning. I didn't want us to turn up and find it was full. As it happened, several hundred French holidaymakers seemed to have had the same idea because the weather forecast was bright sunshine, and altogether three boats laden with day-trippers made the crossing that day. But we were the only foreigners, and in fact I've never met any other English person who's been there. The voyage takes fifty minutes. The boats dropped everyone off and then tied up in the bay until five o'clock, when everyone clambered back for the return run. Being a crew member sounded like a real doddle.

Like a lot of others, our first thought on landing was refreshment. At the top of the slipway was the café and behind it the restaurant, so we headed for the one farther away as possibly likely to be less crowded. While ordering coffee I noticed the word *homard* scrawled in chalk on a little blackboard hanging beside the door to the kitchen. And at a knock-down price – about a quarter of what you'd expect to pay normally.

Now there's a thought . . .

'Is that available today?' I asked the chap behind the counter.

'Yes. Caught this morning. They're in the tank in the kitchen. Choose the one you want.'

I'm not inordinately fond of lobster, but this seemed too good an opportunity to miss. I'll see what Margaret thinks.

'Do you fancy a fresh lobster for lunch? It's only thirteen quid for the two of us.'

'OK. Why not? It'll make a change.'

I beckoned.

'Come and choose.' I didn't mention that they were still . . .

'Oh! no! It's alive!'
'Yes. I said they were fresh. Now which one do you want?'

It feels a bit mean to point at a poor old lobster in a tank, claws tied together with red string, and condemn him to death just to grace your plate. But if we didn't eat him someone else would, as there weren't very many *homards* in the tank and there were a lot of customers behind me in the queue.

Grillé mayonnaise, he was very tasty!

We set off along the path leading to the far end of the island, but it twisted and meandered and the time required turned out to be a lot longer than we'd expected. However, we'd out-walked every other tripper off the boats, so as we were likely to be able to have the beach to ourselves wherever we stopped there seemed little point in walking farther just for the sake of it. We chose a lovely little bay with fine sand, piled our clothes and baggage above the high water mark and made our way down for a bathe. The water was hardly deep enough to swim in, as the slope of the beach was so gentle. But then I'm not much of a swimmer, and this dip at the end of September was the only time all that year that I went in the water.

When the tide turned we moved back without hanging about; like the wise virgins we were, being on the lookout for this phenomenon and aware that getting caught might be mildly funny if all that happened was that you got your belongings wet but could be rather more serious if you got cut off. There were no lifeguards, and although there was a lifebelt on a stand at the top of the beach that's not going to be a lot of use if there's no one there to throw it to you. Visitors were warned by notices at the landing stage that the incoming tide could be dangerous, and to take note and not put themselves at risk.

We were disappointed to find the disused chapel locked, as we'd expected it to be opened on days when there would be visitors. The same with the schoolroom. A small terrace of workers' cottages, now private holiday homes, also seemed to be unoccupied and locked, which was a shame because we'd have liked to see the domestic arrangements of the former inhabitants and try to imagine what life must have been like for them. *[Memo to the Tourist Board: why not open one cottage and furnish it 'as was' so that visitors can enjoy a look at a time capsule?]*. We resisted the temptation to venture onto private property and peer through the windows, just in case they *were* occupied and it was just a case of the owners not leaving the front door open because they were enjoying an afternoon snooze. Or they were – well, you can imagine what else they might be doing on a balmy afternoon on holiday, without me spelling it out in words of one syllable.

It's quite hard to conjure up a picture of life in centuries past for people struggling against the odds living and working, marrying and dying on such a tiny island within sight of the mainland. But the story of Chausey was explained on boards put up near the slipway, which is how we learned that it was still inhabited for a generation after the war and not finally abandoned until the 1980s. Life must have been harsh in winter; little of the land seemed to be much above sea level, and one could imagine during mid-winter gales the spray blowing across from one side of the island to the other. On a beautiful sunny day in late summer, though, it was ideal for a family day out with the kids. Many of our fellow trippers had not gone exploring but had passed their time sitting around near the café and looking at the private boats moored all around the slipway.

Lazy days in the sun.
Goodnight.

September 1999

J

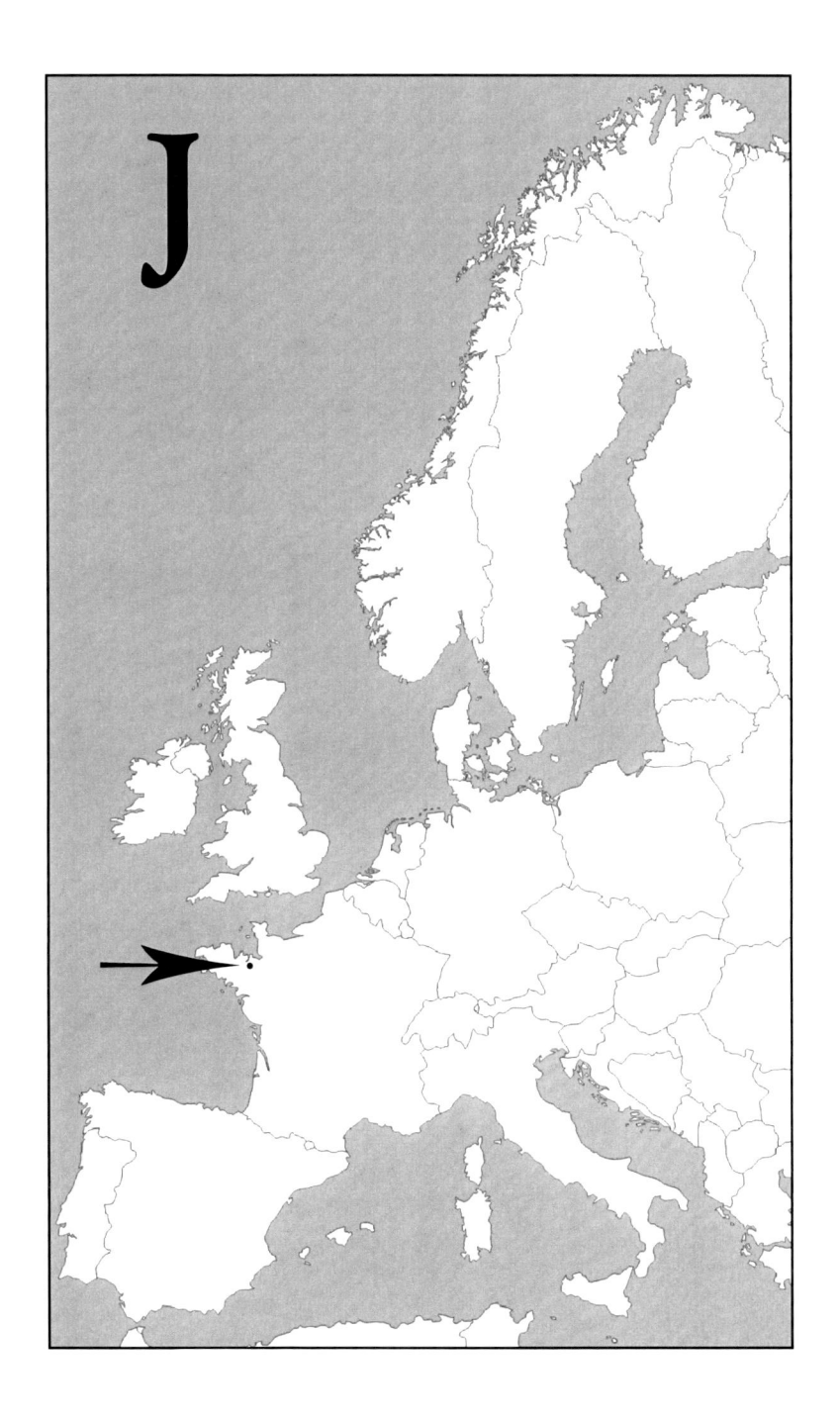

THE JERZUAL

That's pretty steep!

The Jerzual is the cobbled road in Dinan up which goods were transported in the Middle Ages half a kilometre from the river to the town, and which has been preserved much as it was – retaining as well its challenging gradient at certain points of between 1:3 and 1:4. It's a real physical struggle to walk up from the port to the Old Town when it's dry underfoot, highly problematic when the cobbles are wet. On one occasion returning to our hotel after dinner in a restaurant down by the river my umbrella blew inside out! Thankfully, there are stone benches randomly situated on which to catch your breath, or wait for your partner to catch up.

One of my favourite holiday destinations, Dinan was from the 13th century onwards heavily fortified by the dukes of Brittany and still retains many of its original medieval buildings as well as the bulk of its defensive walls, with their associated towers and gateways. It claims to have the highest number of *'maisons à porche'* in France – houses whose upper storeys overhang the ground floor and are supported on massive wooden pillars. It fell into economic decline in the 18th and 19th centuries. Modernisation and redevelopment didn't take place simply because in the absence of much commercial activity no one could see any profit.

This wonderfully preserved historic gem is usually awash with tourists, especially from Britain. But how we first discovered it was most odd.

If you've read the first book in this series, my *Little Green Nightbook*, you may remember me telling you that I had a friend, Claude, whose way of thanking me for helping him win a seat on the county council (I was his election agent) was to offer us the use of his flat at Ouistreham on the coast of Normandy for a free holiday. We started by exploring the countryside round about, then the nearby metropolis of Caen, then ventured farther afield to Bayeux and Arromanches and the various beaches where the D-day landings took place in June 1944. Eventually, after a couple of years of holidays based on Claude's flat, we ran out of nearby places to visit which we hadn't been to before and needed to be a bit more adventurous and spread our net.

One day we set out with the intention of going as far west as we could while still leaving ourselves time to get back in daylight (I don't like driving at night on the 'wrong' side of the road). We ended up crossing the border into Brittany, and came to a fork in the road. (You mean a family staying at a campsite had dropped some cutlery? No. The other sort of fork – silly!). To the right, Dinard. To the left, Dinan. They sound much the same to an unattuned foreign ear. 'One of these is a seaside resort full of yachties', I said to Margaret. 'The other one is a medieval town which I've read about in tourist brochures'. But I can't remember which is which!' We plumped to go left.

As we drove up the main road into the vast market square in the heart of the town – the *Place du Guesclin* – I exclaimed to Margaret with an air of triumph 'This is it! This is the one we want.' We parked, had a quick look round and headed back to Ouistreham while the light held. But having seen Dinan, we were hooked and knew we'd be back. And we were – we came back time and again for twenty years!

The original town sits on a bluff above the River Rance, and was encircled by a massive defensive wall with towers and gates. These are still much in evidence, and permit the city to stage – in alternate years ending with even numbers – a medieval festival, the *Fête des Remparts*, over a weekend in July. Costumed townsfolk saunter through the streets, many shopkeepers don fifteenth century attire and itinerant tradesmen, jugglers, beggars and lepers lurk in alleyways and men-at-arms camped out below the walls engage in hand-to-hand combat or re-enact a medieval siege. Behind the basilica of Saint Sauveur lies a small park – le Jardin des Anglais – where there's enough space to set up a camp and dedicate it to demonstrating some chosen aspect of medieval life. At the fête one year, for example, the chosen theme was 'Construction in the Middle Ages', i.e. how a cathedral was built, what instruments an architect would have employed and demonstrations of cutting stone and timber with medieval tools. At the next fête the theme was how justice worked; on another occasion it was 'Medicine in the Middle Ages'. I know, because we visited each time and saw what was going on.

The *pièce de résistance* of the *Fête des Remparts* is the jousting, which takes place in a sanded arena between the two largest round towers, some 40m high and in one of which the museum is housed. Tiers of seats are erected facing the curtain wall (€10 each) and right in the middle is a 10m high double doorway which following announcements by the Master of Ceremonies and a fanfare of trumpets is opened for the knights – usually six in number, with their squires and ostlers on foot carrying additional gear – to emerge mounted on their destriers, fully accoutred in plate armour and chain mail and armed with fifteenth century weapons, to be greeted by roars of welcome from loyal supporters in the crowd. My own initial reaction the first time I witnessed this carefully stage-managed spectacle was to wonder how the men facing them for real in a battle must have felt, seeing the enemy at full gallop coming to get them with swords, lances and mace-and-chain – all designed to rip you in half or smash your skull in. They must have been absolutely terrified! The origin, I suppose, of the modern phrase describing such a situation: 'shit scared'.

About two-thirds of the way up to the town the Jerzual passes through the original fortified gateway, Le Petit Port, and one year in order to attend the *Fête* we rented a *gîte* located upstairs in a building only 20m away, looking out onto the street in front and from our bedroom at the back affording a view over a vacant meadow under the walls about the size of three football pitches. Here we were delighted to discover that a band of visiting Viking traders had laid out a longboat and were explaining to onlookers how they built it, and from their camp fire offering a taste of Viking food to those willing to risk it. A band of troubadours performed just under our window, their playing of medieval instruments

Up the Jerzual. View through Le Petit Port, Margaret in the background

...and down. View from Le Petit Port. (Yes, that's me!)

occasionally accompanied by a troupe of dancers performing a round and inviting spectators to join in and learn the very simple movements – usually nothing much more complicated than a sideways step-and-a-hop and then in reverse while keeping time with the music.

Dinan-Port

At the bottom of the Jerzual is Dinan-Port, where in the past goods transported by river from the coast were unloaded and lugged up to the town on pack animals or by sweating porters. Nowadays it's a picturesque quarter with a medieval bridge still used (carefully!) by motor vehicles, and with a row of roadside restaurants and cafés along the river bank. There are also several restaurants actually on the Jerzual itself, in one of which on one occasion I received an unexpected bonus. I'd been placing our order in French – despite, or perhaps because, the place was full of loud English tourists barking at the waiting staff in English and I wanted to reassure the proprietor that we aren't all like that. When we'd finished our main course he came over, leaned conspiratorially over my shoulder and whispered, '*Do you know what a 'trou normand' is?*'. '*Yes*', I replied, '*it's a small glass of Calvados to clear the palate between courses.*' Whereupon he reached into his top pocket and produced two glasses and placed them on the table in front of us and filled them with the said spirit. I took this to be a mark of appreciation for being clients who were polite to him and his staff, and who didn't assume that the louder we shouted at them in English the more likely it would be that they'd understand. Since that memorable occasion ownership of the restaurant has changed – twice – but it's still an atmospheric place to eat and in colder weather there is the added pleasure of watching meat being roasted on its open hearth.

I'm sure other towns in France would challenge this eulogy with counter-claims, and they may well be right – it's just that I haven't found them yet. As you read in the first letter in this book, we have several times been to Harfleur for their *fête*, but it can't begin to compare as it's only a tiny fraction of the size of Dinan, lacks a medieval centre full of half-timbered buildings and its walls have long since disappeared (a few stubby remnants stand a metre or so high down by the river). I actually prefer to be in Dinan when it's not the *Fête*, simply because not being packed with actors and re-enactors and an influx of tourists who've come to watch them it's more likely I'll be able to get a table at a favourite restaurant or crêperie without having to book or wait a long time if I haven't.

But had it not been for Claude's generosity all those years ago we would never have found it in the first place, so wouldn't have enjoyed for a couple of decades the recurrent pleasure of a short stay or stopover to renew our familiarity with the Old Town and savour Breton cuisine down beside the river or on the Jerzual.

Goodnight.

August 1990

K

KIMRY

Twinning makes the strain

Most commonly 'town twinning' is an English town twinned with one in France of similar size and with possibly some economic similarity – Eastleigh, where I live, was twinned back in 1963 with Villeneuve-St-Georges on the outskirts of Paris because both were 'railway towns'. As our French twin was also twinned with a town in Württemberg we ended up with a three-way twinning to include Germany. Each year our mayors exchange visits or send a representative to lay wreaths at the commemoration of the Armistice in 1918, which so far as I know is unique.

Kornwestheim, in what was then West Germany, was also twinned with a town in East Germany and through them with a town in the Soviet Union – Kimry, astride the Volga some 70kms or so north-west of Moscow. Being in the 'rich' West, the good burghers of Kornwestheim offered economic help to their twin towns, such as when they refurbished a factory they gave the old equipment to their poorer twin to replace equipment there which was even older and even less efficient.

One of the purposes of twinning is to increase mutual understanding. So when your guests arrive you meet them, take them for a meal, both sides make speeches and present formal gifts and then over the next day or so – twinning visits seldom last more than three days – show them the highlights of your town: a visit to a factory or school, a site of historic interest if you have one, a nice restaurant in a bucolic setting – you get the idea. And a tour of your Town Hall or similar building, where the Mayor or his substitute tries to explain how local government works and you try to work out how it compares with the way you do it in your own country.

The inevitable problem is: what to put in, what to leave out. You can't get it all in in three days. The problem is, we all try. The inevitable result is that the visitors are walked off their feet, get overtired with the strain of listening to protracted explanations in a language they don't understand and which then has to be translated – requiring even more concentration, especially if you're out of doors, trying to hear against a background of traffic or wind. On the assumption that your visitors will only visit your town the once, you are determined to show them *everything*. The truth is, many of those visitors will come again on a subsequent 'twinning' visit. In my own case, for example, I went for the first time when Margaret was Mayor, then nine years later I was Mayor myself so another round of visits – leaving aside other occasions in between as part of a delegation jointly celebrating an anniversary of some kind and finally accompanying Margaret again when she was Mayor for a second time.

The Russians would like us in Eastleigh to make it a four-way twinning, but that isn't likely because of the distance and the consequent travel costs. However, our Twinning Association is a different matter, because we have no public funding and our members are enthusiasts who believe in the cultural value of twinning and we pay our own way out of our own pockets. That was the situation when the mayor of Kimry invited us – the Twinning Association – to send a delegation. We'd pay for our visas and our fares to Moscow, he would host us once we got to Russia.

Corridor in the Sovietsky Historical Hotel

Our first problem was Moscow's traffic, and its customary gridlock meant that we took two hours just to get from the airport to our hotel. Because of our delayed arrival our hosts decided that it was too late to proceed home so put us up instead in the Sovietsky Historical Hotel, built in 1952 on Stalin's orders but in the grandiose style of the mid-nineteenth century. Very sumptuous! Even had a harpist to provide a soothing background during breakfast, who was very appreciative when I sought her out to thank her.

Our hosts thought that we shouldn't come to Moscow and leave straightaway without being given a tour of Red Square and seeing the Kremlin. A splendid idea – but when we duly arrive in Kimry itself what are you going to omit from the programme to allow sufficient time? You see where this is going?

Then yet another delay before departing for our ultimate destination: we were taken to an evening performance of a new rock opera in a wonderful auditorium. This gave me an opportunity to see for myself just how the Russians – young and old and of both sexes – dress up for an occasion. They could certainly teach us in England – especially our young people – a thing or two! One would expect the young and sexy to dress fashionably, but I'd never seen so many high heels on shoes and boots. All ages seemed to have dress sense and natural flair.

Our hosts managed something of a gastronomic *tour de force* by introducing us to the cuisine of Ukraine and Azerbaijan in restaurants in Moscow and then in Kimry laying on a folk group to sing and play for us at a dinner of typical Russian dishes.

On the last night we were taken 20kms out to a yacht club on the Volga, where in summer rich Muscovites come to enjoy the river, though at this time of year – April – ice fishing (making a hole in the ice and sitting over it hoping to catch a fish) was still possible in the shallows (the main river was by now free-flowing). As the dinner progressed so did the jokes (more and more risqué!) and then our principal guide (who didn't speak any English, she just looked after us and made sure no one got left behind when the bus moved on) sang a folk song and invited us to respond. No one volunteered, because she had a very nice voice and we knew none of us was that good. However, in such a situation national pride comes into play. I leaned across and observed to the mayor that we'd been in Russia for four days criss-crossing the Volga and through the window at this very moment there it was shining in the dim moonlight, and so far no one had sung us the Volga Boat Song. He murmured that he wasn't much of a singer, so I said, in Russian, '*Well, if you won't sing it, I shall have to*', not letting on that I only knew one verse. I went over to our hostess and said, '*Come on, Tatiana, you and me – a duet!*'. I don't think our Russian hosts will forget the role reversal of having an Englishman singing the Volga Boat song to *them*, and it will always be one of my most hilarious memories – and at the same time serendipitous for being sung while actually able to see the eponymous river.

Historically, Kimry was renowned for its shoemaking industry – they were the official suppliers of boots for the Russian army which fought Napoleon, and a boot is featured on the town's coat of arms. The visits to factories, schools, clinics and young people's activity centres left me with a strong impression that despite economic difficulties Kimry seemed to offer far more to its young people than would be the case in an English town of comparable size (50,000 inhabitants). The civic authorities provide the venue and the staff and expect the parents to pay for their children's personal equipment, e.g. their costumes if their hobby is, say, dance. At a time when here in England the government is cutting funding for youth clubs, the contrast is stark. I remember half a century ago sitting in the youth hostel in Bremen and asking the warden who built it, and being told 'Hitler'. Stalin had the same vision when he built his 'Pioneers Palaces': provide young people with somewhere where they all want to go because there's so much to do there, and you keep them off the streets, out of trouble and in many cases allow them to acquire a skill in, say, music, theatre or sport. If young people grow up loving their country because of what it gives them then when the time comes they will defend it – which may have been his intention all along (in a military sense). Our wish might be more peaceful though no less imperative: that our children grow up wanting to defend our country's values of freedom of speech, toleration of differences between people, racial harmony, sexual equality and so on. A sound investment?

I mentioned economic problems. The roads were in general in a poor state in the town, with wide holes which led our driver to weave all over the road to avoid them. Outside my second floor hotel room was a fire escape. At least, there was a door leading to an iron platform, with a stair leading – well, it didn't lead anywhere because the metal staircase was lying on the ground below where it had fallen after rusting through. 'In case of fire, go through the emergency door and, *er* – jump!'

Then there were the wooden houses dotted around the town which we'd assumed were derelict but which were in a poor state of repair simply because the owners couldn't afford to modernise them. We were taken to a home for children rescued from abusive parents where some had run away from their own homes to escape violence and find sanctuary; that other endemic Russian phenomenon, excessive drinking amongst the male population, remains a problem.

In the restaurant

I've always enjoyed twinning visits and the opportunity to see more of another country, talk to its inhabitants and learn more about its culture, its current problems and how it's tackling them – whether visiting in my official capacity (when I had one) at public expense, or privately, paying my own way. In my experience the Russians and Germans are more internationally-minded than the English, with the French somewhere in between. People who've gone through the standard English education system seldom have reasonable command of any foreign language, unlike their contemporaries on the continent. Is this cause or effect? I'm not sure.

Because the programme constantly overran we never had time to go shopping and spend some of our roubles until on the final

The fire escape outside my hotel room. On the left of the platform the ladder to the ground has rusted away!

morning on the way to the airport we stopped off at the Sunday market. An unusual feature were stalls selling brightly coloured paper flowers – something to brighten up the long Russian winter when fresh ones would be too expensive for most ordinary people. Inside the covered market hall the stalls were packed tightly together, and I bought some very tasty biscuits and admired the profusion of fresh fish and meat which we for obvious reasons couldn't buy. I also bought a short-handled brush, exactly what I wanted to sweep the floor of my garden shed. As our luggage was all packed ready to go on the plane I had to just push it under the strap round my case and hope they wouldn't make a fuss at the baggage check-in. When questioned, I explained that it was a last-minute present for my wife – which elicited approving smiles. When I said we didn't have brushes like this in England one of them laughed out loud and remarked to me – in English – that he was glad that Russia was more advanced than England. English-speaking Russian border officials with a sense of humour? What a contrast with the Soviet era when I made my first visit!

Goodnight.

April 2011

L

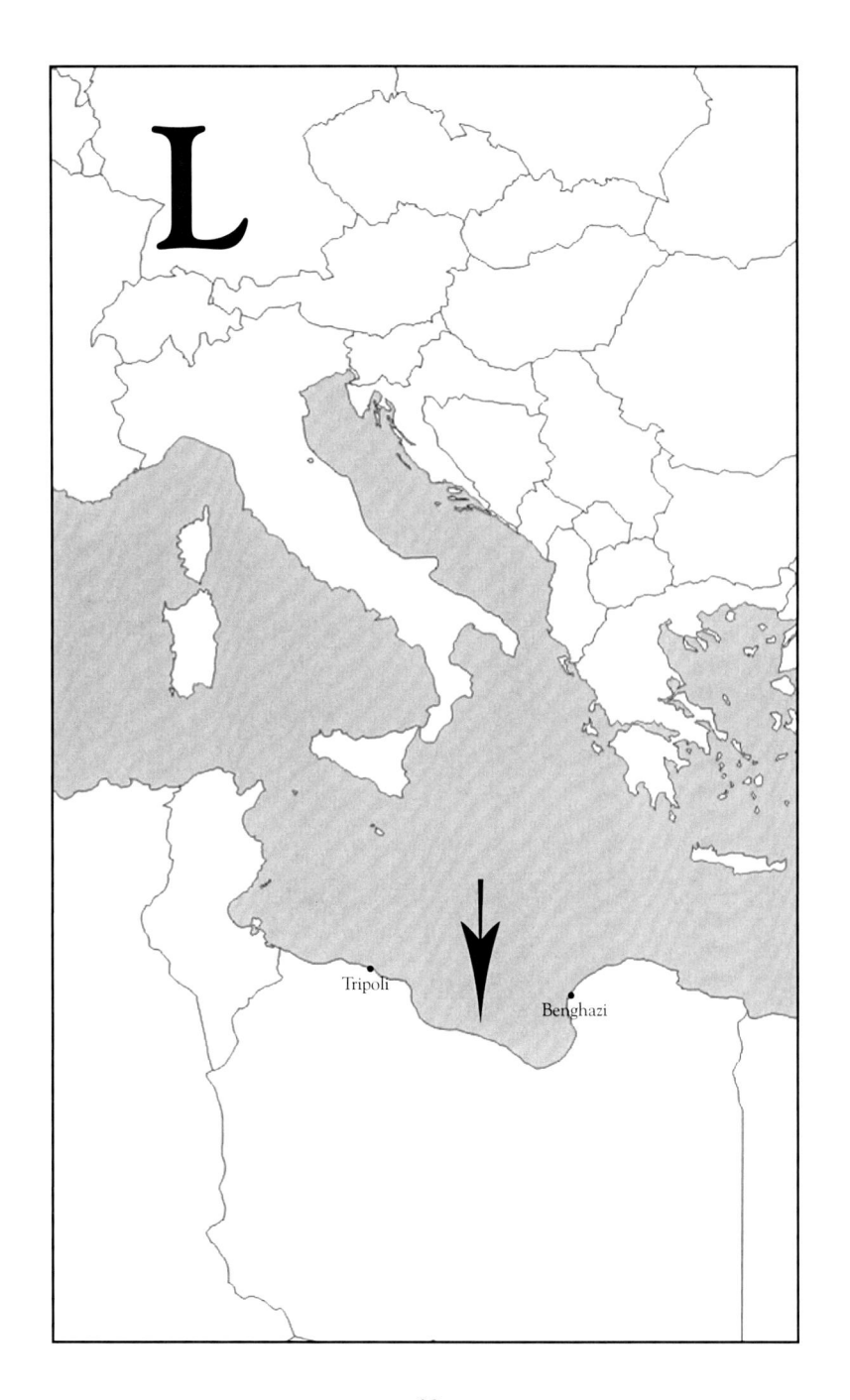

Tripoli

Benghazi

LIBYA

'I'm from Brum!'

These words spoken to me over half a century ago are still fresh in my mind, and I have never ceased to wonder at the quirks of memory – how one can forget important things, but something of absolutely no apparent consequence can stay firmly fixed in one's mind.

Perhaps it wasn't what was said, but by whom and where. By an Arab teenager, of all people, just outside Tripoli, of all places. This is how it happened.

Having been in Malta for some nine months and nearing the end of my time as a national serviceman, I was due some leave. I couldn't afford to go where most other naval personnel went when they had long leave, namely to Sicily – midshipmen weren't paid much and even though I had just shipped my first ring and was now a Sub-Lieutenant I hadn't held the rank long enough to have accumulated any savings. It looked as though I'd be confined to days out, which wasn't a very attractive prospect as I'd already visited nearly all Malta's historic and pre-historic sites during weekends and odd days off, using the local bus service. There was, of course, the companion island of Gozo. But you can have enough of pre-history and vast churches. Some other time, perhaps. What I want is a change.

As luck would have it, the Commander-in-Chief, Lord Mountbatten, was a friend of King Idris of Libya and decided to pay him a visit. Not on his own or by air; he'd take a cruiser and give the ship's company a bit of sea training to justify the expense. I enquired if they had any spare berths, and was told that there was space in the midshipmen's quarters. As I was officially on leave I wouldn't have to do anything, I could just be a passenger. The thought of a free trip, sitting in the gunroom swigging gin and all the mids calling me 'Sir', appealed. As a bonus, I'd leave Europe for the first time and get in a few days in North Africa in a country I wouldn't otherwise have much chance of getting to.

Anchored off Tripoli, the C-in-C hosted a party for local dignitaries. Attendance by officers was compulsory, including passengers – I might be excused duties, but that didn't extend to exemption from the duty of assisting with hospitality. So I had my first experience of trying to entertain and engage with people with whom I had no common language, our guests being Libyan army and navy officers who spoke only Arabic. Also, of course, being Muslims they didn't drink alcohol, so we couldn't resort to the armed forces' age-old method of breaking the ice with incomprehensible foreigners: ply your guests with copious booze, get 'em plastered and then even if your verbal communication doesn't extend beyond the equivalent of 'Cheers!' at least when they wake up next day in their own beds having been carried ashore paralytic they'll remember that they had a really good time with you last night and will regard you ever after as a friend. What other justification is there for diplomatic receptions, if not that? What better justification does one *need*?

Being, as I said, officially on leave, I was free to spend as much time ashore as I wanted. I managed one serious visit, to the ruins of the famous Roman amphitheatre at Sabratha. Four of us hired a jeep, and while doing so were accosted by some likely lads from the locality who attempted to worm their way into our company for reasons best known to themselves but which you can probably guess at as well as we could at the time. They were after our money, whether by over-charging us for some service or other or, if that didn't work, then straightforward pocket-picking would do. They spoke English with good accents, but it rapidly became evident that they had not learned it at school – they'd probably never been to school – but from the radio. So when one of them asked me where I came from and I said 'Portsmouth', he replied with the phrase at the top of this story: 'I'm from Brum'. I'm sure he didn't know what it meant, it was just something he'd heard someone say on the wireless, and he'd mimicked it. He had no idea that 'Brum' was a very particular place in England, in fact Birmingham, England's second city, and that anyone who came from it would have for starters a distinctive Brummie accent. We needed no further evidence that these were young lads on the make, and we got into our jeep and headed out into the desert as fast as we could before they had a chance to make their next move.

The Roman Theatre of Sabratha

I was surprised to see just how narrow the cultivated coastal strip was, just a couple of miles inland and agriculture appeared to stop dead and the land dissolved into desert. Nowadays I suppose everyone knows this, everyone's seen the films, documentaries and TV travelogues and read the colour supplements. But back in the early '50s we were not so aware of the outside world. TV was in black-and-white, and so expensive that most households didn't have it anyway. The full-colour travel programmes we are nowadays all familiar with were yet to be made, so all I knew about the Libyan Desert was what I'd read about in books, not seen in pictures. So seeing it at first hand was, in the true sense of the phrase, an 'eye-opener'.

We stayed only a few days in Tripoli before raising anchor and heading for the country's second city, Benghazi, where in the market I bought as a small souvenir a Tripolitanian camel pipe, which to this day hangs on my conservatory wall. I explain to visitors that it is entirely authentic, and is exactly as played by Tripolitanian camels. I recall seeing a banana tree for the first time – again, commonplace nowadays when virtually everyone goes to Spain on holiday and has seen such things from toddlerhood. But this tale is set in the '50s, before foreign holidays in the sun were the norm. For as long as most of us can remember Libya was ruled by Colonel Gadaffi, yet who was it I said the C-in-C was going to see? Yes, the *King*. Few nowadays will remember him, or even know Libya ever even *had* kings.

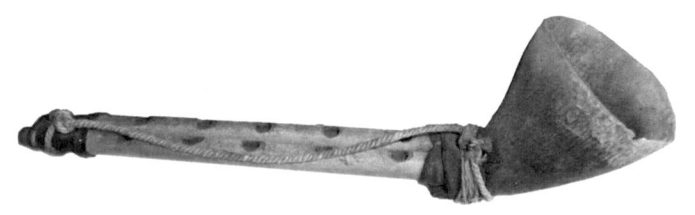

But I still remember those pushy Arab teenagers who might have fooled us into thinking they were genuinely friendly had one of them not lobbed in those fatally inappropriate and unlikely words in just too perfect English, to whom I would nowadays probably reply, 'My other leg plays '*The Bluebells of Scotland*' '.

Goodnight.

July 1954

M

MACAU
Sardines!

I'd always wanted to go to Hong Kong, as when I was a small boy Pa – my grandfather – had told me many stories of his time on the Far East Station in the 1890s and I'd seen photos of himself dressed in Chinese costume when he'd gone ashore somewhere up the Yangtze – something apparently lots of sailors did for a souvenir; and two, a pile of heads, all with pigtails, after a spate of executions.

But the place which fascinated me even more was Macau.

Adrian had moved to Hong Kong in 1985 with his wife, Myrtle (my sister-in-law) and their two sons, Paul and Matthew, and spent his time flying around the Pacific capitals on business. But he took time off at Christmas, and had invited Margaret and I to join them for the festive season. He agreed to take us on a day-trip to Macau, mainly because he wanted to take us to Hernando's Hideaway, a noted restaurant which served Portuguese cuisine out on one of the islands away from the town itself. He hired a vehicle something like a glorified golf buggy the moment we landed, and we piled in and headed off over the new bridge which now connected all the islands and had replaced the ferries which for centuries had been the only connection. It seemed strange ordering from a menu in Portuguese proffered by a Chinese waiter, when being about as far from Portugal as it was possible to get. After the meal we drove to the far end of the second island, Coloane, where we were able to visit the chapel dedicated to St Francis Xavier, a Jesuit missionary who in the mid-sixteenth century brought the gospel to the Far East as far as Japan and died on an island near Macau in 1552. There are also relics of priests martyred for their faith.

A Portuguese frigate was anchored offshore, flying the ensign aft. Nothing very spectacular about that, you might say. Macau was a Portuguese possession, so why shouldn't they have a warship there and of course it would be flying the national flag. But it was by the time of our visit the *last remaining* Portuguese possession, the last surviving remnant of the Portuguese overseas empire which had collapsed in the 1970s and it only remained in Portuguese hands because the Chinese refused to accept it back so long as Hong Kong remained British. The other thought which came into my mind was how small an area Macau occupied, and I tried to picture a wartime map of the Far East when everywhere for a thousand miles or more in any direction was under Japanese occupation and coloured black and right in the middle was this tiny, *tiny* pinprick of white – neutral, because neither Japan nor Portugal had declared war on the other. It must have been a strange experience for the inhabitants at that time, completely surrounded as they were by the armies of a country which was massacring Chinese everywhere else but which stopped its troops at their border out of diplomatic niceties because the Chinese there were Portuguese subjects and even though the colony was theirs for the taking had they been so minded.

The second time we visited, five years later, we were on our own. Well, on our own insofar as we were the only Europeans; the boat was absolutely packed with Hong Kong Chinese all set for a day out, mostly to the casinos. Gambling was banned in China, and even in Hong Kong the only betting permitted was at the races. If you wanted to chance your luck at the tables, you had to take the ferry to Macau. Which many did at weekends.

But we were in for a rough crossing. A storm was brewing, and as the boat hit the first large wave and bounced all the Chinese passengers shrieked with glee. Another wave, a bit stronger. More whoops.

'This is going to end in tears.'

'But *we're British*. Mustn't let the old country down, stiff upper lip and all that. Think of the Empah, what? Show the natives what it was that made the British Empah great.'

So we sat tight, clenched our stomachs and swallowed hard. For an hour, at least. Being sea-sick when we were the only Europeans on board would have been just too hideously embarrassing. We managed to hold out, but it was not an experience I would want to repeat. I am, after all, decidedly *not* a good sailor even though I got in a fair bit of sea time when I was in the Navy, and I don't like it when it's rough.

By the time we reached Macau all the other passengers were decidedly the worse for wear, a lot had been visibly ill and the rush to get on to dry land would have finished off anyone with a weak heart. Every man for himself, and as for the women – they used their elbows. Once on shore we were hit by driving rain, and the wind was so strong it blew my umbrella inside out. What were we supposed to do? We'd come to potter round the town, but we'd get soaked if we did.

When in a strange town and it's pissing down there is one reliable stratagem. Lunch. At least we'd be in the dry.

Sardines seemed a strange dish to order, as a staple of Portugal but on the wrong side of the world, washed down with *Mateus Rosé* in that distinctive-shaped bottle. But when in Rome, etc. Despite being entirely surrounded by oriental faces we were not in China, but in a part of metropolitan Portugal. Macau was quintessentially, aggressively, perhaps even desperately, Portuguese, had been for four centuries even if only on a microscopic scale and it was going to stay that way until the day it was handed back to the government in Beijing regardless of the fact that the date for this occurrence had actually been set and everyone knew there were barely a couple of years left before the Macanese took their orders

The Cathedral of St Paul was destroyed by fire in 1835 and only the south façade survived.

The Senate building

from there instead of from Lisbon. At the end of 1997 the sun would finally set on the Portuguese Empire of overseas possessions, other than Madeira and the Azores where the inhabitants really are Portuguese and predominantly European. All-ee same-ee Goa, and after the War the French didn't quibble or stand on ceremony in handing over Pondicherry when India became independent.

We'd set out intending to spend a day wandering about the main and back streets of this time-capsule mini-state, but in such weather it was best to accept an unkind fate and abort – there was just no point in hanging about. Best see if we can get an earlier boat back. Such a good idea that almost everyone else who'd been on the boat with us that morning had had it too – the terminus was absolutely jam-packed and it was almost impossible to move, let alone get to the ticket kiosk and enquire. Margaret was given the brush-off twice by a ticket clerk, when fortunately a Chinese in a tweed jacket, smoking a pipe and looking every inch the country gent reminded us in perfect English that this was the Orient and not the West and manners were different. Turned out he'd been a diplomat in Vienna, and was aware of the contrast between how officials treat the public in the West and in the East. He helped us get our bookings changed. So we did strike lucky and get an earlier boat back, repeating our earlier demeanour of stiff British upper lip and air of 'You call this rough weather? Why, back home we get worse than this on village duck ponds.'

Goodnight.

December 1995

N

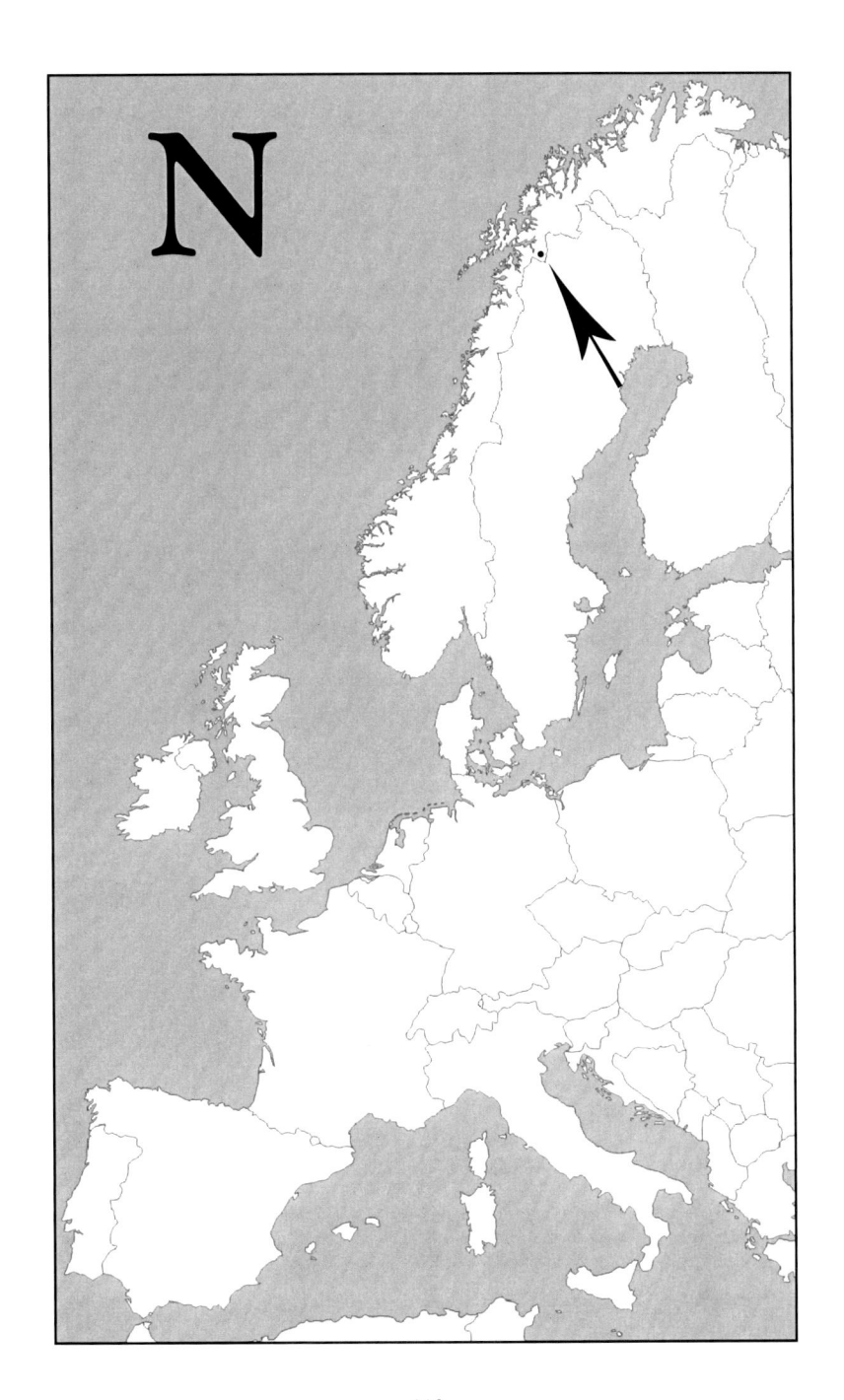

NARVIK

Phew!

It had taken us a whole day to get from Brekkvasselv to Majavatn, and we still needed – somehow – to get to Narvik and a lift was the only direct way. 'If we can't get a lift, what's Plan B?'
'Get the train.'
'There's no railway from here to Narvik.'
'No. The train goes across the border into Sweden, where we can change and get a train north to Kiruna. The Swedes have to have a railway up there because it's an iron mining area. Swedish ports on the Gulf of Bothnia are frozen up in the winter, so they export it via Narvik because it's an ice-free port.'

We set off for the station – well, halt – and found that there was a train at one o'clock – and that was the only one. They had just one a day. So – we've got till one o'clock to get a lift, and if no luck then after a day and a half of standing here we give up and proceed on public transport. Hope we can find the money.

Ten o'clock came, no luck. Eleven. Nossink. Twelve. Nowt. Give up, better get down to the station – sorry, halt – in case it's early. Hang on – there's a car coming – one last try. Bugger me – it stopped!

The driver and his friend had just been down to Trondheim to buy a car, had found what they wanted and were off to sign on in the Norwegian Air Force for their national service. And where would this be? Bugger me again – Tromsø, some way beyond Narvik. That's over five hundred kilometres north of here! Now that's what I *call* a lift!

We put our gear in the boot, and settled into the back seats. Having no common language, conversation was virtually impossible. Signs. We'll stop here for lunch, you pay for yours, we'll pay for ours. Stop for coffee, we insisted on paying. Here we are at the spot where the road crosses the Arctic Circle, so let's stop and look at the monument and do what all tourists do: pose standing astride the line across the road with one foot in the Arctic and

one not. Keep going, but there's no continuous road to Narvik. It stops at the shore of the fjord and you take the car ferry across to the shore opposite, likely as not just a small uninhabited islet, drive across it to get the next ferry and then continue in this disjointed manner and we have to make it to the first of the ferries at Fauske before they shut down the service for the night. We didn't make it. As we drove down to the shingle, there was the little ferry heading out into the sound.

What now?

We'll just have to stop here for the night, and catch the first ferry when they start again in the morning. We couldn't all sleep inside the vehicle, so by signs we indicated that we'd leave it to them and we'd sleep outside. Seemed only fair, and anyway we had groundsheets and sleeping bags, which they hadn't.

I got out first and did a quick reccy. There were no buildings, not even a ticket office or whatever, to provide any shelter – though luckily it was fine, dry and midsummer – midnight sun, and all that; the road ran through a totally empty landscape and stopped at the water's edge where the ferry came up to the shingle; passengers just got on the ferry if it was there, or hung around if it wasn't until it came back. The land was strewn with boulders and I searched out one by the roadside with a flat surface as my resting place for the night and went back to the car to retrieve my rucksack and sleeping bag.

As I approached the car I became aware of a strange smell – something like a combination of industrial-strength garlic and the inside of a Japanese wrestler's jockstrap. Getting nearer, it became overpowering. Then I saw that Mike was still in the back of the car, but his face contorted in what looked like the final stages of asphyxiation as he scrabbled dementedly at the door handle in his frantic efforts to get out. He did. He gasped fresh air and his face colour subsided from boiled beetroot to its normal pallor.

'What's up?'

'Can't you smell it?'

'Yes. What is it?'

'The driver took his shoes off!'

When you consider that I could smell it twenty feet away, what must it have been like inside the car? To this day I can't conceive how those two fellers managed to sleep together all night inside the car in such a stench.

The ferry at Fauske was the longest of the several crossings on the road north. At each stop, Mike would leap out of the car and yank off his socks and sandals and plunge his feet into the nearest stream – regardless of the temperature of the water and notwithstanding our experiences at Trondheim with immersion in seawater at such latitudes – to try to get some relief from the mozzies' attentions of the previous night when we'd camped by the lake at Majavatn *(as related in another book in this series – but which one would be telling!).* We could only guess what the locals thought: 'The English are renowned for their strange customs' – *shrug*. Fortunately, in this part of Norway there was always a stream handy – or the seashore by the ferry landing stage.

Next morning we ate a little chocolate for breakfast, got back in the car, caught the first ferry and arrived without further mishap in Narvik. Hand-shakes all round, thanks very much, good luck. It was midday. We were 200kms north of the Arctic Circle, yet the sun was so fierce we had to stand in the shade to get out of it to look at our town map to locate the youth hostel where we planned to spend the night. As usual, bugger's luck – it was right at the far end of town and up a hill, presumably because it was purpose-built and they'd had to find a suitable piece of land, and beyond the confines of the existing town at the top of a long incline was the only place where they could find a site big enough and cheap enough for their purposes. The view was dominated by a large mound of iron ore brought in by rail from the mines at Kiruna, across the border in

Narvik in the 1950s

Sweden, so no wonder the site was cheap!

I spent a summer in Malta as part of my national service, yet that day in Narvik has stayed in my memory as the hottest day I ever experienced. It sounds unbelievable that North Norway could be hotter than the middle of the Mediterranean – but that's how it felt at the time and how I remember it. So hot that for the first and only time in my hitch-hiking days I stopped dead, sat myself down in some shade and refused to go any further. 'I'm not moving from here until it gets cooler. The hostel won't be open at this time of day anyway.' When at last the hostel opened and I got a bed I more or less collapsed and slept the clock round, so probably I was suffering from mild heatstroke, brought on by the combination of heat and wearing clothing which was too heavy.

Final proof that the temperature wasn't a figment of my imagination came when we saw a cat sitting on a doorstep. You know what? It was so hot he'd got his top button undone.

Goodnight.

August 1959

O

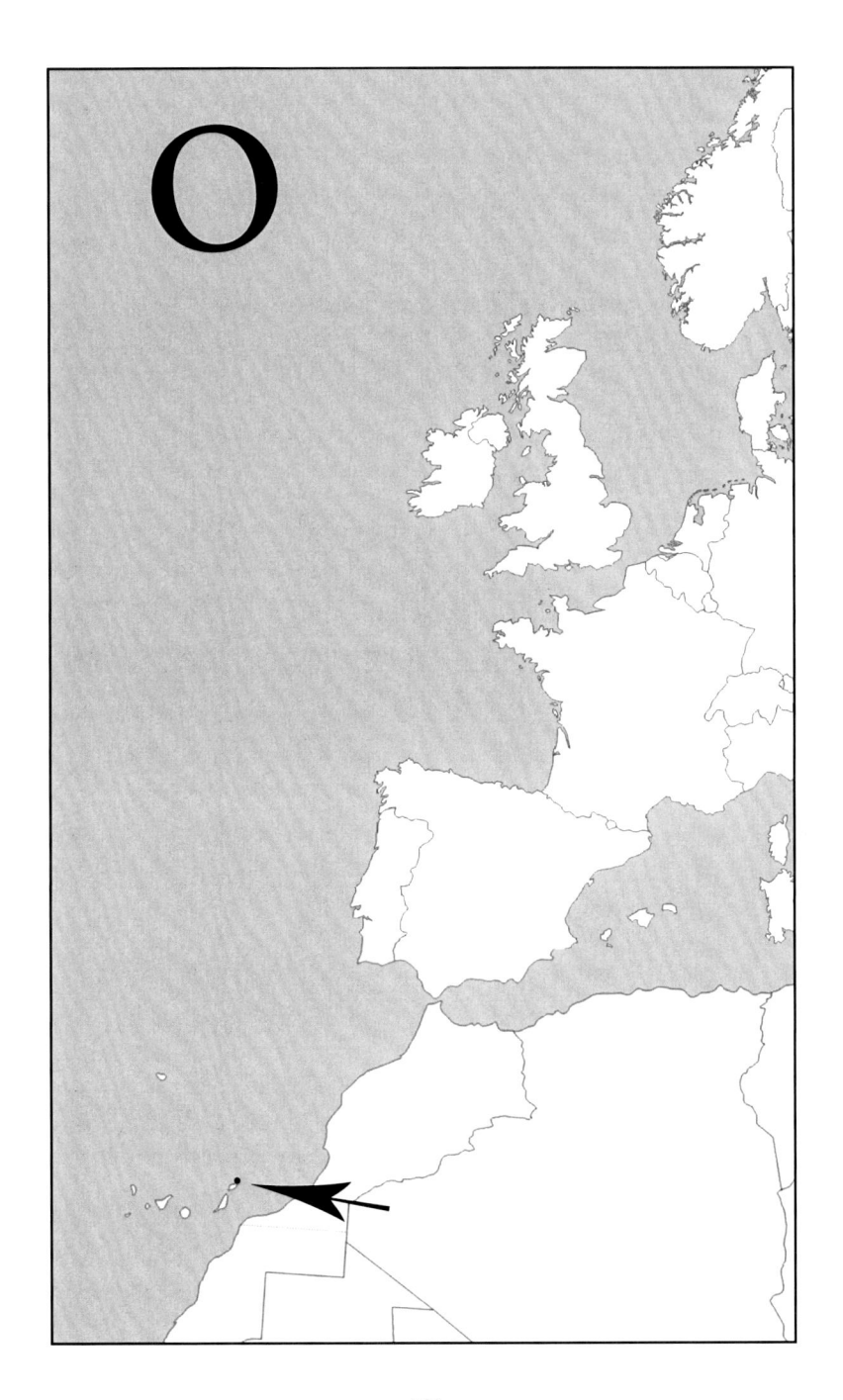

ÓRZOLA

Corks!

It took me ten years, but I finally made it to La Graciosa, the smallest of the Canary Islands with a resident population (of 700). There are buses to the ferry terminal at Órzola, a small fishing village at the northern tip of Lanzarote noted for its seafood restaurants, but from my time-share in Puerto del Carmen I could never work out a way to get there, catch the ferry and then get back the same day. The situation resolved itself when Mike joined me for a week and said he'd be quite happy to hire a car, as he drives an automatic at home.

Foreign tourists seldom make the crossing to set foot on La Graciosa, but many thousands see it from the Mirador del Rio, a vantage point directly opposite the main settlement, Caleta del Sebo, where the passenger ferry docks. From near the top of the cliffs which dominate the north shore of Lanzarote the viewer enjoys a panoramic view of the whole island from a height of 1,630 feet (nearly 500m). End-to-end it's about eight kilometres by four and, except where a hill gets in the way, you can see it all laid out in front of you. Not that there's much to see. It's rocky, barren and flat, with a few conical hills which rise steeply from the bare terrain as if plonked down from above by some giant chess player, and the dominant colour is brown: rock and sand. There are no trees, nor in fact any signs of anything green, and as there is no natural water source fresh water has to be piped in from Lanzarote. A network of tracks can be seen leading out of Caleta and disappearing into the distance on their way to remote beaches or to the only other cluster of houses, a shoreline hamlet away to the east. A number of pleasure boats can be seen tied up in Caleta's tiny harbour. As one would expect, there are several waterfront cafés ready to greet visitors alighting from the ferry, but all the buildings are one or two storey and from this lofty viewpoint there doesn't appear to be a main square, a church or any large administrative building to act as a focal point.

The previous day we'd picked up the car and I'd taken Mike, nowadays a keen photographer who works with a tripod, to the former capital of Lanzarote, Teguise, because it has a number of eighteenth century houses and some typical Canarian wooden balconies which I thought he would find worth pointing a lens at. There isn't much of historical interest anywhere on the island because in the past it never had a very large population nor many nobles or important officials living in style in grand houses. The reason for this was that until Napoleonic times it was constantly exposed to random raids by Barbary pirates from Morocco, Algiers, Tunis and Tripoli. At that time North Africa was still nominally part of the Ottoman Empire, and the Sultan of Turkey authorised locally-based corsairs to roam the Mediterranean and the Atlantic as privateers and prey on the merchant shipping of Christian countries or raid their coastal villages in return for a share of the profits. In addition to robbery and general pillage these pirates carried captives off to be sold in their slave markets. This ever-present danger inhibited the settlement and development of the Canary Islands, especially of the two closest to Africa, Lanzarote and Fuerteventura.

At the end of the eighteenth century the newly-independent United States faced demands for tribute from the rulers of the Barbary States amounting to almost one-sixth of the entire national budget, and Congress was forced to make a choice: either keep American merchant vessels safe from attack by corsairs by paying regular tribute to the Dey of Algiers, the Pasha of Tripoli *et al,* or build a navy and deal with them once and for all. The Americans' success in the Second Barbary War in 1815 forced the Dey to agree to give up attacking U.S. merchant ships and holding captives for ransom and to return all captives currently held in slavery. The U.S. benefited from knowing that henceforth its merchant vessels would be able to go about their business in safety, but the suppression of piracy was equally beneficial to the inhabitants of all coastal villages and islands in the Atlantic such as the Canaries who hitherto had had to live in constant fear of pirate attacks.

As well as La Graciosa I also wanted to visit the Castillo de Santa Barbara at Teguise, which from the crest of a 450m bluff commands views over much of the centre of the island and out to sea on three sides and houses a museum of piracy. The problem for the tourist is access: it's up a steep, winding dedicated road and there is no bus. Now we have a car, so at last I'll be able to get there. But my stomach tells me it's time for lunch, and on the advice of the charming lady in the tourist office in Teguise we head for her recommended restaurant. Everything nicely timed, and then we'll be off to the castle. Only we hadn't realised that at four o'clock they close the road by lowering a barrier, and when we turned up at twenty past three it was already in place. Aaaaargh! Come back tomorrow.

Tomorrow is planned the trip to La Graciosa, but as we missed out on the *castillo* due to the road being closed we'd better do that on the way, because there won't be another chance – it's Wednesday, Mike's last day before flying home, so now or never. No barrier across the road this time, so on up the switchback access road, wonderful panoramic views over the centre of the island and then park outside the castle. This is impressively inaccessible – a flight of stone steps leads up to a small platform onto which, in former times, a drawbridge would have been lowered at right-angles, and then in through the narrow castle gateway. The guardrooms

The only way into the Castillo de Santa Barbara (and no, you don't have to get past the watchman!)

are now laid out with the story of Spain's attempts to settle the Canary Islands and the problems with pirates, especially during the seventeenth and eighteenth centuries, and enemy attack during wars with England or France. Everyone knows that Lord Nelson lost his right arm; it's not so well known where he suffered the injury. Answer: during a British attack on Tenerife in 1797.

The ferry across El Rio, the strait separating Lanzarote from La Graciosa, leaves every hour or so from Órzola and takes a little over half an hour. It's quite a small boat, and we progress gracefully out of the harbour into the strait and the moment we pass the end of the breakwater – BOOM! We're hit by an absolutely enormous swell and bounce about all over the place like a cork in a tumble drier, and first-time passengers could be forgiven for thinking that at any moment we're going to turn turtle and sink with all hands! I'm on the upper deck and hanging on for dear life, but thoroughly enjoying the exhilarating experience because I can see the captain in the wheelhouse and from the expression on his face he is obviously totally unperturbed, so this rolling and pitching must be normal. The harbour of Órzola is protected on the west by the Punta Fariones, a rocky peninsula jutting out into the sea, with a navigation beacon on its point. Once we pass this the open strait is flat calm and the excessive motion stops as suddenly as it started, and we proceed close inshore under the shadow of the cliffs, trying to pick out the Mirador del Rio where we'd been the previous day. We make landfall in the harbour of Caleta without further excitement.

I can quite see why holidaymakers enthuse about going to La Graciosa with their children for a day out on the beach – there's sand everywhere, including the streets (instead of tarmac). After a restorative coffee at a café overlooking the harbour and time spent gazing in awe at the lowering cliffs of Lanzarote on the other side of El Rio we set off to explore. It doesn't take long. There are only a few dozen houses, several bars, a couple of small shops and supermarkets but, as I'd previously observed from the Mirador, there isn't any sort of built-up town centre with a town hall and also – which surprises me – no signs of a church. A hundred metres or so inland from the harbour the houses come to a dead stop and to our amazement the unmade, sandy track running along behind the last houses is furnished with a row of new lamp posts! What on earth *for* when there isn't any traffic? Where did the money come from, and was the expense justified? A rough track leads away into the distance across a barren landscape, giving access by taxi (visitors can't bring cars) to various remote and deserted beaches.

A question I often ask myself when visiting out-of-the-way places: what do the people who live here permanently do with themselves in their leisure time? Tourists don't mind the lack of things to do – they've come to relax or perhaps, as is certainly the case here, admire the view or enjoy the quiet beach and watch the children splashing about in the shallow water. But if you *live* here – what then? You can't spend every leisure hour paddling. No matter how impressive the cliffs of Lanzarote are, you can get fed up with just looking at them and surely you must get frustrated with living in a tiny community when no matter how bored you are there's nowhere else to go? And what if it rains? Villages whose only attraction is a beach are no fun in bad weather!

I'm left with just three of the Canary Islands yet to visit now that I've managed to tick the *'been there'* box with regard to La Graciosa. I shan't be back, but if I had a family of small children I well might.

Goodnight.

February 2012

P

PAPHOS

A tour de force?

I suppose one can say that reaching the age of three-quarters of a century is a significant milestone in life. That's how Margaret and I saw it when I reached that particular watershed, and an invitation to spend the occasion with my brother (Adrian) and sister-in-law (Myrtle) at their house in Cyprus was most welcome. They'd retired there a dozen years before, and built their own house outside Paphos on the west coast of the island to their own design and on the side of a hill, with a commanding view across twenty miles of countryside and no possibility of anyone ever obstructing it – short of building a skyscraper right in front of them (hardly likely). The other attraction was that as my birthday occurs in the middle of March the temperatures in Cyprus are most agreeable, as well as being a welcome alternative to those usual in England at that time of year.

The climate is one of the reasons so many other Brits have done what Adrian and Myrtle decided to do a decade ago: retire to Cyprus – though in their case not from their home in the UK but from Hong Kong. Another is that English is widely spoken or at least understood, the legacy of the island being a British protectorate between 1878 and 1960 and the language of administration being, naturally, that of the colonial power. The problem with the expat community, so far as I could fathom it in a short stay, was that few of them had bothered to learn the local language – the same problem as occurs in those parts of France and Spain which have seen English retirees descend in droves and then set about creating England-over-the-Water rather than integrating with the indigenous population and adopting or adapting to the indigenous language. Granted, Greek may be harder for an English person to learn than French or Spanish – particularly as they almost certainly won't have learnt a bit in school (if they can remember that far back). But surely if you *choose* to go and live somewhere where the local language is Greek, then . . .

There's lot of history in Cyprus! We tend to think of it simply as part of Ancient Greece, but in fact it was settled two millennia BC by people from Asia Minor and remains of those settlements and civilisations are much in evidence in the west of the island. Adrian set about with some enthusiasm showing me each and every mosaic within earshot, then every Mycenaean tomb, then Neolithic remains, Aphrodite's alleged birthplace and the spring named after her ('Aphrodite's Well') and finally the excavated site of Kourion. After a day of being shown archaeological sites followed by another day of another lot and then another, images become blurred and you forget which millenium you're in let alone which day of the week it is. 'Mosaiced out' probably describes my mental state after a week.

Tomb of the Kings, Paphos

To be perfectly honest, much as I enjoy watching archaeological digs on TV I'd never dream of going near one in person, and I have never felt enthused when looking at piles of stones and being told that they were once a round-house or the foundations of a temple or whatever. I'm extremely interested in history but pre-history leaves me cold. I want names, dates and events. Hadrian's Wall is interesting to me because I can see it and stand on it (and I have), and rather than have to use my imagination I prefer to visit a reconstruction or recreation to get an idea of what it was like to live then and in those conditions.

Getting Cyprus's history into focus is not easy, but if it's OK with you I'll try (if not, skip the next couple of paras). We all have ideas about Ancient Greece and Ancient Rome, even if only from blockbuster movies; most of us learned about them in history lessons in school, some of us even did Latin (me, for one). We then get a bit hazy. We've probably heard of the Byzantine Empire, but that's about it – we've heard of it. No idea where it was, still less when it was and nothing at all about who ruled it. Well, when the western half of the Roman Empire (capital: Rome) finally capitulated to the barbarians in 476 the eastern half (capital: Constantinople) carried on for another thousand years, though it was and remained Greek in character, culture and language and the form of Christianity differed – (Greek) Orthodox as opposed to (Roman) Catholic. Such trade as there was between Western Europe and the Eastern Mediterranean was conducted by intermediaries – Venetian and Genoese merchants – and direct contact not resumed until the coming of the Crusades seven hundred years later at the end of the eleventh century. The only exceptions were pilgrims, who throughout this time continued to travel to the Holy Land, risking their lives in the process and taking several years to make a round trip (if they ever came back at all, of course, as many perished along the way).

In 1191 Richard the Lion Heart was on his way to join the Third Crusade when his fiancée and sister were shipwrecked on Cyprus and the local king, Isaac Comnenus, was a bit flaky in his treatment of his royal visitors/hostages. He made a big mistake in falling out with King Richard, and paid for it by having his kingdom conquered – ending up imprisoned in silver chains (Richard had promised not to put him in irons – so he kept his word, sort of) and dying a couple of years later. Richard was now in possession of Cyprus but didn't know what to do with it, so sold it to the Knights Templar, who the following year sold it on to the titular King of Jerusalem, Guy de Lusignan, whose family remained in possession as kings of Cyprus for the next three hundred years until displaced by the Venetians, who held sway for the next hundred. Thus throughout the entire medieval period Cyprus was an outpost of Western Europe with Catholic kings and the feudal system exploiting the indigenous Greek Orthodox population while surrounded on three sides (look at the map) by lands ruled by Muslims – Palestine, Egypt and Asia Minor. Such an anomaly had a built-in sell-by date, which turned out to be 1571 when the Turks expelled the Venetians. This consolidated Ottoman total control of the Eastern Mediterranean and freed the Turks to embark on a long campaign of conquest in Europe which remained a very real threat right up to the Siege of Vienna in 1689. For the poor old Greek Cypriots and their Orthodox Church it just meant a change of master: feudal lords who were Roman Catholics replaced by Muslim pashas – and for the next three hundred years!

The Venetian castle guarding the harbour at Paphos

All of which helps to explain why Cyprus has so many medieval castles, of which one of the finest examples is at the harbour mouth in Paphos itself. It's open to the public, and the cells display the casual cruelty of the times when it was in use. But for a modern visitor it provides splendid views across the town and along the coast northwards, so it's well worth walking past the string of restaurants lining the harbour in order to reach it. With fierce competition, these restaurants provide excellent value and I very much enjoyed a fish *meze* at a table under a most welcome awning alongside tourist boats and touts seeking customers for mini-cruises.

Lunch beside the harbour with my brother and sister-in-law, Adrian and Myrtle (Jessop)

One of the first religious sites we visited was Ayios Neofytos, a hermitage not far from Paphos, whose principal attraction is a vividly decorated cave where the hermit lived in the twelfth century and which is now accessed by a rickety stairway up the side of the mountain (not recommended if you suffer from vertigo!). Even more sumptuously decorated is the monastery at Kykkos, once almost inaccessible high up in the Troodos Mountains but now easily reached by car thanks to a new road built with EU development funds. The preponderance of gold inside the church reminded me of the cathedral in Seville, with every surface glistening in the light of innumerable candles. But whereas Seville Cathedral has a high ceiling to its nave and so an airy space in which to stand to admire

Entrance to the monastery at Kykkos

6th century church at Ayios Georgios

Museum at Ayios Georgios of the Mycenean civilisation which flourished c1300BC

the ornamentation, here in Kykkos the effect is claustrophobic because there is so much of it in a confined space. Moreover, one must observe silence (or at the most, communicate in whispers and risk a sharp disapproving look from one of the ever-present monks). A short walk away is the usual cluster of souvenir stalls selling tourist tat, and also a rather attractive restaurant which at the height of the season must be absolutely packed but which we had almost to ourselves.

One of the finest sites for those interested in the Classical period are the remains of the major trading city of Kourion, just off the main road from Paphos to Limassol. This was founded in the second century BC but fine mosaics recently discovered date from the 5th century AD – and are protected by a huge over-arching roof structure supported on pillars allowing free movement of air. There are remains, too, of an early Christian basilica. The amphitheatre has been fully excavated and even brought back into use – as a venue for concerts. I didn't have an opportunity to experience one, but I can imagine an evening there must be a bit like attending the Minack Theatre near Land's End in Cornwall with the players performing against a backdrop of the open sea – only with the mercury a bit farther up the thermometer!

The north-west corner of Cyprus is a nature reserve, accessible only on foot. But the approach roads are interesting and lead to several favoured spots with beach-side or harbour-side restaurants. The most attractive spot in my opinion is Pomos farther along the north coast towards the Turkish Cypriot enclave of Kokkina. I was not overly impressed by the food on offer ('ordinary' would perhaps be a fitting description!) but from our table the relaxing view across the little harbour with its complement of small fishing boats and pleasure craft tied up alongside the jetty was adequate compensation.

Goodnight.

March 2008

Q

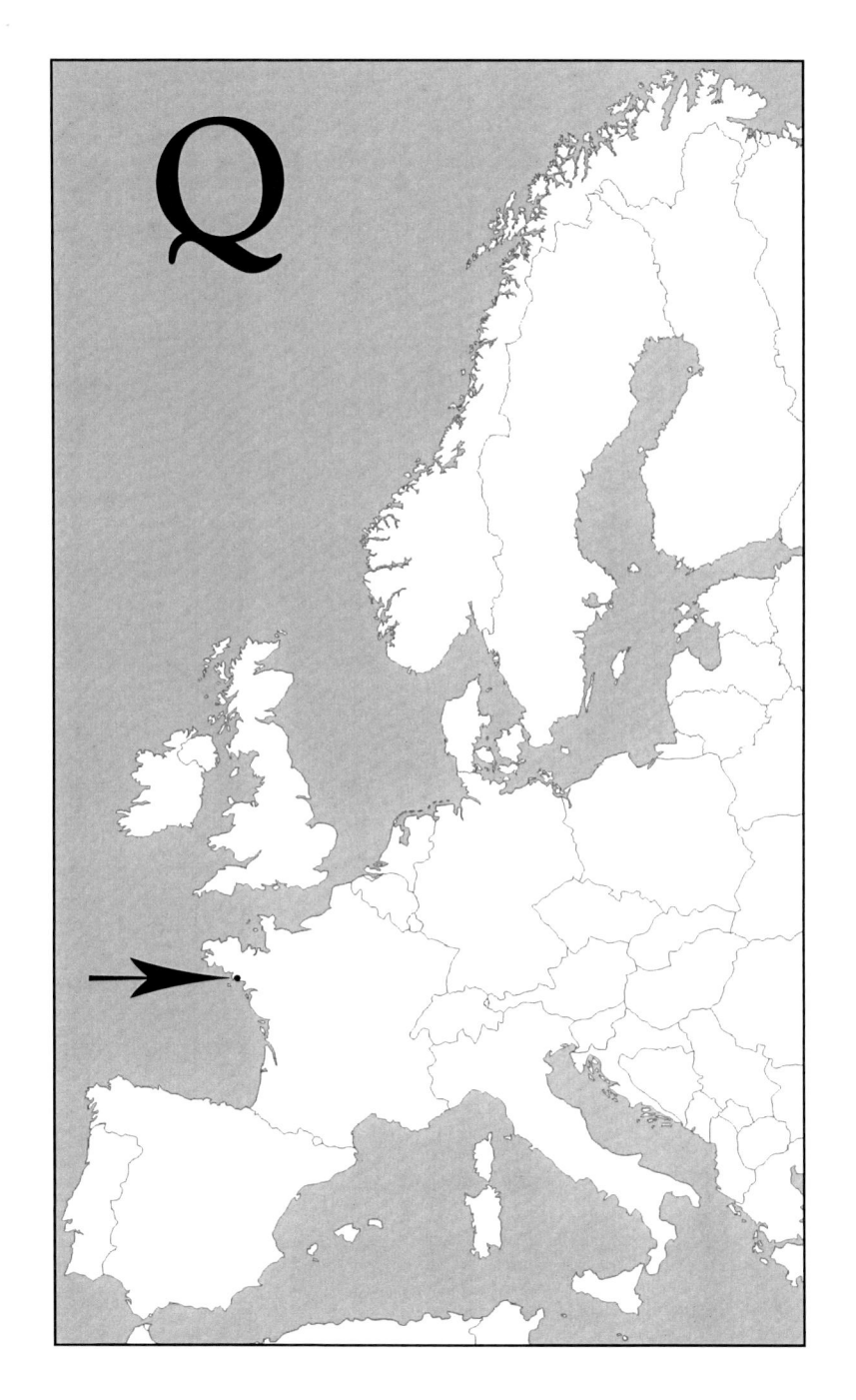

QUIBERON

Belle Île or bust!

I was over seventy before I finally made it to Quiberon, which I first heard of at school when we learned about the Seven Years' War with France which at least so far as naval warfare was concerned served as a dress rehearsal for the Napoleonic Wars forty years later. The Battle of Quiberon Bay in November 1759 was one of Britain's most decisive naval victories. It had the knock-on effect of making it impossible for the French fleet to send reinforcements to their colonists fighting in Canada, with the result that French Canada fell to the British and that country's future as a British possession was secured.

Quiberon is an attractive town, and I hope one day to stay for a proper visit. The journey there by car is fun, as it's at the end of a very long peninsula connected to the mainland by an isthmus only a couple of hundred metres wide, so of course there's only one way on or off – made even narrower because the road has to share the width with a railway line which carries tourists in the summer. But once on the *presqu'île* ('half-island' – interestingly, the Russians use a similar term to designate such geographical features), it's wide enough at some points to have side roads and smaller settlements with clusters of local shops and it's possible to drive along some of the coast away from the main spine road. Once you reach the far end and the waterfront, there are ferries to the three islands off the coast: Belle Ile, the largest of the French Atlantic islands, and also Houat and Hoedic, which mean 'duck' and 'duckling' in Breton and lie farther out. These two have tiny permanent populations, and although they cater for visitors in season there's not much to do. (*Sounds ideal!*)

Belle Île, on the other hand, is not so much 'popular' as 'overrun'. When we got there we were told by our guide that they have 5,000 permanent residents but 100,000 tourists a year. The result is that in high summer the cafés and restaurants can't cope, so unless you've booked a table you'll be lucky to find anywhere to eat.

The purpose of our visit was not to explore Quiberon but simply to use it as a jumping-off point for Belle Ile. Easier said than done. OK, there are frequent ferries. But there are also kiosks vying with each other to sell visitors a coach tour on arrival – which seemed to us a good idea and a lot cheaper than taking the car, especially as we were only going for the day. But although with the benefit of hindsight a ticket from a kiosk for a coach trip on Belle Ile doesn't as a matter of course also include the cost of the ferry to get there, they don't actually make a point of telling you that. It's not unreasonable to think that having bought your ticket, it's 'all inclusive'. But it wasn't, as we found out the minute we tried to proceed to board and were firmly directed to the queue at the ticket kiosk. With only fifteen minutes to departure, we had a fine old time worrying as the chap at the front of the queue seemed to be buying returns, season tickets and half price for children for his own extended family and several others besides, using up his OAP coupons and offering to pay by cheque drawn on the Royal Bank of Uzbekistan. Everyone was muttering and shifting from one foot to the other as he and the cashier argued and as fast as she showed him one set of papers he asked for another set and so it went on and on. We did manage to get a ticket in time, but only just.

That queue was my second major panic. The first was parking to go and see if I could get a ferry ticket anyway – i.e. it's July, the height of the season, was there room? – and having ascertained that there was I then discovered that there was no designated car park for ferry passengers. Where do you find an all-day car park in a major tourist town unaided and at short notice? Answer: you don't. I just went to the first one I could find with a vacant space, parked and left a hastily-scribbled note on my dashboard on the back of a till receipt, grovelling to the parking attendant that I couldn't find anywhere else and was going to Belle Ile for the day and would he be kind enough to overlook the fact that I was in a car park with a time limit. I just had to hope that he would take pity on a foreigner and not impose a fine, and while taking in the sights of Belle Ile I'd be able to worry about what would be pinned to my windscreen wipers when we got back or even whether the car would still be there, having been towed away and impounded.

> EXCUSEZ- MOI, S'IL
> VOUS PLAÎT.
> HORODATEUR NE MARCHE
> PAS ET JE VAIS SUR LE
> BATEAU À BELLE- ÎLE !!

From Quiberon on a clear day you can just about make out Houat, but Belle Ile is clearly visible as it's only 14km away. The crossing to the main town on the island, Le Palais, takes 45 minutes, and once there we found our way to the coach park and were taken for a twenty minute ride as far as Sauzon, the island's second town, for a coffee break and a chance to have a look round.

Waterfront at Sauzon

From April to September there is a direct ferry from Quiberon and in July and August also from Lorient (foot passengers only). Once back on the bus, our destination was the northern tip of the island to be shown the fort bought in 1894 by the famous French actress Sarah Bernhardt (1844-1923) and the private houses she built nearby for her family and friends. She's hardly a name to conjure with nowadays, but in her day she was probably the most famous actress in the world – and she also played in some early silent films. On an islet just off the north-west coast is the Pointe des Poulains lighthouse, accessible on foot at low tide.

Even on a fairly calm summer's day the Atlantic rollers were crashing onto the cliffs,and one can easily imagine how dramatic it must be in the winter during a gale. It's hardly surprising that the entire western side of Belle Ile, facing the open ocean, is a succession of wild indented cliffs and is known as 'le côte sauvage'. In complete contrast the eastern – sheltered – side of the island has gentle sandy beaches.

Back in Le Palais, we admired the fort built by the Louis XIV's military architect Vauban, famous for his defensive structures to be found all over France – principally on the coast to keep out the filthy British. Of these, the *Ville Close* at Concarneau is to my mind the most remarkable, as the fortifications enclose an urban village which although generally thronged with tourists is still a wonderful day out for a visitor because of all the shops and restaurants.

We didn't have time to visit the fort, as by now it was time to find some lunch. Not as easy as you might think. The influx of visitors means that during the summer the population rises to 25,000 and at the very peak in late July-early August to a staggering 35,000. It was hardly surprising that in high season none of the restaurants overlooking the fort or the harbour had an empty table and we only managed to find a place which could feed us by going up a side street to try our luck.

Back in Quiberon we found the car just as I'd left it. Either the attendant had humoured a visitor, or no one had come to check. I like to think it was an example of French *'sympathie'*, but I'll never know. Time now to find a seafood restaurant and enjoy *fruits de mer* – it's what you do in coastal towns in Brittany. No? Well, it's what *we* do, given half a chance. Quiberon's commercial fishing harbour lies on the eastern side of the peninsula protected from the open ocean, but the ferries operate on the south side, facing the Atlantic, and this is where the main tourist shops, cafés and restaurants lie. Unlike on Belle Ile, we were spoilt for choice!

Goodnight.

July 2007

R

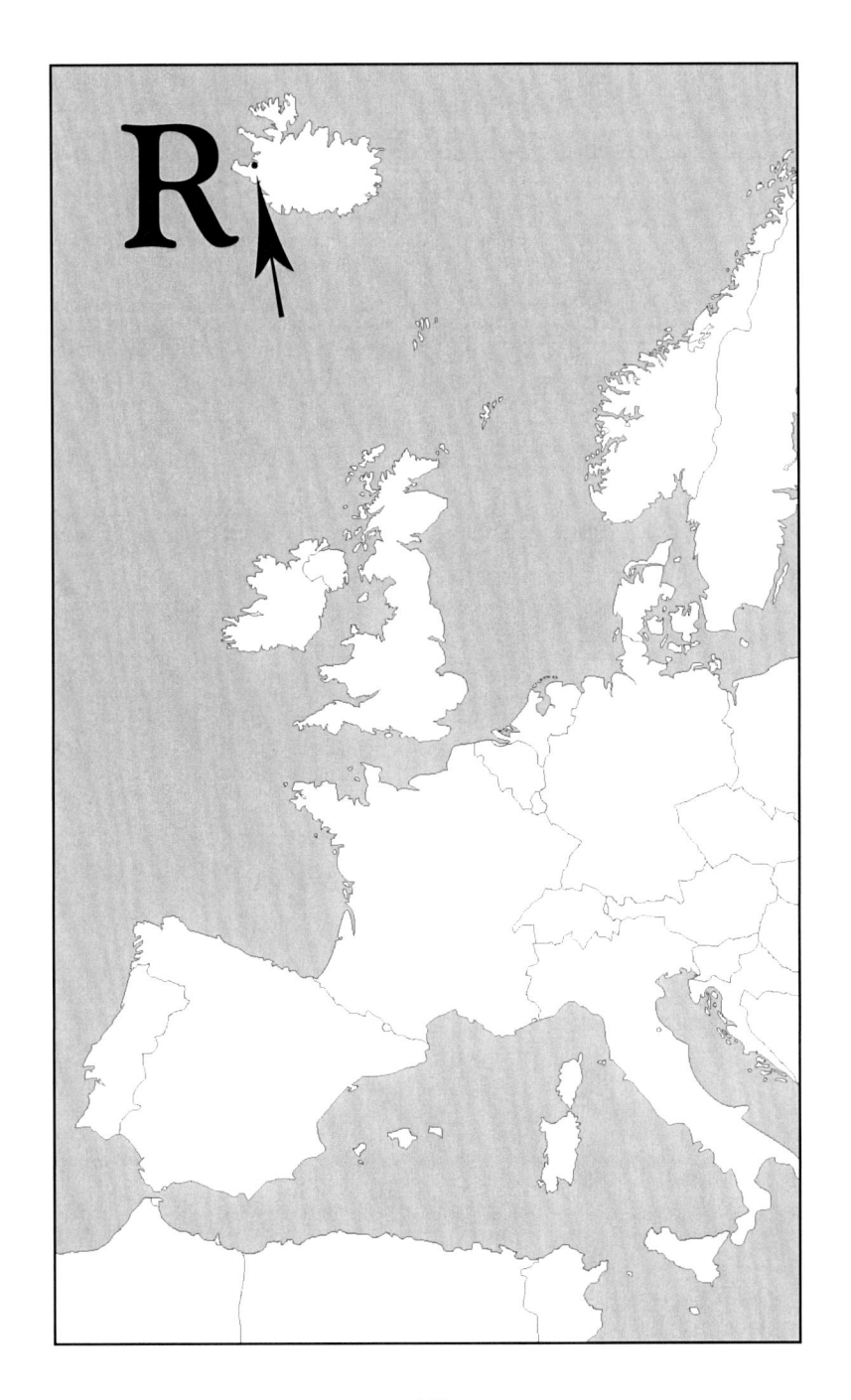

REYKJAVIK

Althing's for all men?

I'd always thought Iceland must be a fascinating place, and I'd love to go there. The chance came when it was announced that the Progressive Party – Iceland's Liberals – had invited the British Liberals to send an official delegation to meet them for an exchange of views and a general chewing of the fat. It would be led by our party leader in the Lords, Viscount Thurso, and ordinary party members interested in going – at their own expense, of course – were invited to apply. Two German FDP (Free Democrat) MPs, representing Bremen and Bremerhaven, joined us for the visit.

It was going to be more or less a long weekend, extending into the beginning of what was, luckily, half-term at my school. But I would have to have Friday afternoon off in order to join the rest of the delegation and catch the plane. I rang the Education Office in Winchester and explained what it was I wanted to do, and would they be prepared to give me half a day's leave of absence so that I could take the opportunity of a lifetime. No problem, they said, but you'll have to clear it with the Head.

Most headmasters, you might think, would be perfectly happy to indulge one of their senior staff who requested a half-day, on top of which the afternoon I wanted off was the end of the week preceding half-term and the school is winding down in preparation for the break. The actual cover I was asking for amounted, in fact, to just two lessons as I was free the other two. I canvassed my colleagues to arrange cover, and easily found two willing to help me out. But the Head refused me permission unless the LEA paid for a supply teacher to cover for me. When I relayed this to the Education Office they just laughed. Pay for supply cover for two lessons? No way. The Head dug his heels in, and kept me dangling until the middle of the week itself before accepting that the LEA was not going to give him a supply teacher and as they'd granted me formal permission he'd have to give way and let me go. Thanks, for nothing. I've been at the school for fifteen years, I'm in charge of pastoral care for 250 kids, but there's bugger-all pastoral care for me when I seek it. But that was the sort of man he was, as he showed many times in the way he treated his staff, though this is not the place to go into details.

I noticed two strange things about Reykjavik. One, there were no chimneys. Buildings are heated by hot water from deep underground, due to having geysers. Two, there were no dogs. I later asked a local why this was.

He asked in response, 'What do dogs eat?'

'Er, meat.'

'We have practically no meat in Iceland. We just have sheep, so apart from lamb it all has to be imported. Why should we spend our hard-earned foreign currency on importing meat just to feed it to dogs? You can have a cat – cats eat fish, and we have plenty of that!'

Apparently the only dogs allowed were working dogs on farms, and I presumed guide dogs for blind people – though I didn't see any.

As an official British delegation we were invited to a reception at the British Embassy, which turned into something of a memorable occasion. The ambassador was immensely tall and immensely thin, and had a passion for Gilbert & Sullivan. After a few drinks one of his staff sat down at the piano and we began a sing-song. In my student days I did four Gilbert & Sullivan productions in four years – my credits include Col Fairfax in '*The Yeomen of the Guard*' and Cox in '*Cox and Box*' – and I ended up singing duets with the ambassador while we all gradually got a skin-full out of his hospitality budget. Finally the evening ended, and as he'd had rather more to drink than intended he asked us to escort him back to his residence. That explained how two official delegates from the Liberal Party ended up staggering through the streets of Reykjavik in pitch darkness, trying desperately to hold the ambassador upright while all three of us singing chunks of '*The Mikado*' at the tops of our voices. It was just as well that his residence wasn't far and we didn't encounter any of the local constabulary.

A couple of other observations at that time may be of interest.

It was March, but still cold and dark much of the day. Yet I saw a bunch of boys in shorts and football shirts playing football on a cinder pitch in the near-freezing gloom, and marvelled at their hardiness. Perhaps being descended from Vikings? Then it was the hail – *horizontal!* I've never either before or since experienced hail which comes straight at you full in the moosh. No wonder the lads playing football were so tough. Wouldn't have survived otherwise.

The serious part of the visit was talking to Icelandic politicians, who took us to witness a session of their parliament, the *Althing*. But there was also time for some sight-seeing, so we were taken to see a geyser which although closed out of season was specially opened up for us. It spewed boiling water from a depth of, if I remember correctly, about 5000 feet, and could be timed exactly to one spout every twenty seconds – with a wet mark on the ground where the water came down, so watch out not to stand there as you'd get scalded. They also took us to see Gullfoss, perhaps the most famous waterfall in Iceland, and standing on a ledge immediately beneath the cascade I was able to stick my hand up into the torrent as it came over the ledge, but in perfect safety (unless you slipped and fell, in which case . . .).

REYKJAVÍK EXCURSIONS

GULLFOSS — GEYSIR
PASSENGER'S RECEIPT

Fare: I. Kr. 210

Nr. 05077

Icelanders are immensely proud of their claim that the *Althing* first met in the open air at Thingvellir in 930, nowadays the most sacred site in the country, and is the oldest democratic parliament in the world. 'But we English were first as a result of holding King John over a barrel in 1215!' you may cry. Well, maybe. The definition of 'Mother of Parliaments' depends on whether you base the claim on earliest foundation, in which case the Icelanders win by about three centuries, or continuity, in which case we do. The *Althing* was suppressed by the Norwegians at the start of their colonial occupation during the Middle Ages, and wasn't resurrected until 1843. Our parliament, although set up almost exactly at the time the *Althing* was suppressed, has had a continuous existence from that time.

The *Althing* is housed in a rather undistinguished detached building, with a door opening straight onto the street and no signs of security whatever. Visitors go up a broad, red-carpeted stair to the second floor, whence they can look down on the proceedings below. The feeling of being in the Upper Circle in a theatre is reinforced by the fact that the couple of dozen seats for the public

Thingvellir, the ancient meeting place of the Althing!

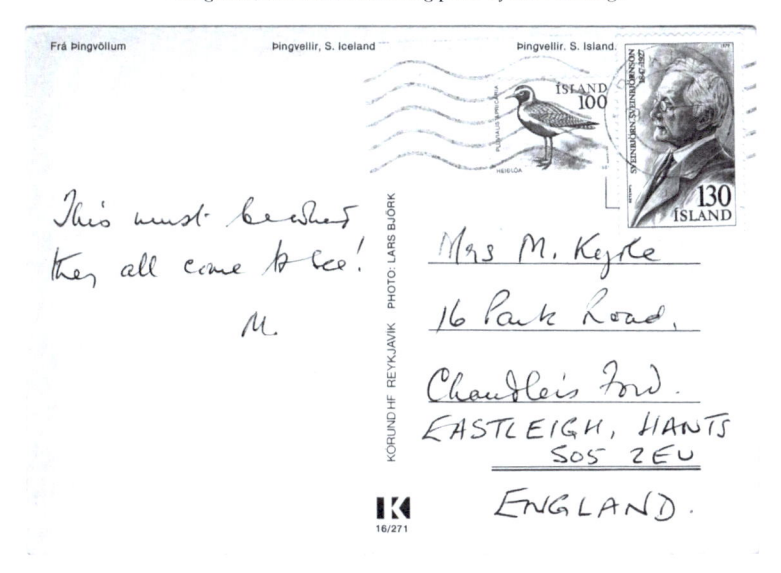

are arranged in three tiers, while on the left-hand side of the chamber below are a pair of double doors reaching from floor to ceiling which open into another room.

'What's that?' I asked.
'That's the Upper House', I was told.
The *Althing* comprises 60 members, all elected together. From these 60 they elect 20 to form the Upper House, and the remaining 40 make up the Lower House. While debate was continuing in the Lower House, officials bearing papers passed between the two chambers, the immense doors opening silently and closing equally silently behind them. The chairman (Speaker?) sat on a raised chair facing the members, but behind him were ordinary windows with plain glass through which one could clearly see pedestrians in the street outside, walking past without a second glance. There appeared to be no police on duty, no armed guards, nothing. And as the debate proceeded no one so much as raised his voice. A marked contrast with the yah-ing and boo-ing which passes for acceptable conduct in our House of Commons. One wonders if the original was conducted in such measured tones back in the tenth century – '*No battleaxes, and all helmets to be left in the sheep pen*' – perhaps?

We tend to think of Iceland as a European country, but in fact it's mid-Atlantic. OK, the people are of European stock, a mixture of Norsemen and Celts, but for centuries they were deliberately cut off from the rest of the world first by the kings of Norway who ruled Iceland from 1262 until 1380, and then when Norway lost its independence and became part of a joint realm ruled by the King of Denmark the Danes continued the embargo. Trade with Iceland was a royal monopoly from 1602, was slightly relaxed in 1787 to allow any subject of the Danish crown to trade but it wasn't until 1854 that commerce was opened up to all-comers. Denmark granted home rule in 1904, and independence under the crown in 1918. Only in 1944 did Iceland became a totally independent republic.

My brief visit taught me that for a country 80% of whose economy is dependent on a single product, fish, the so-called 'cod wars', after Iceland unilaterally extended its fishing limits to 200 miles in 1975 and British and Icelandic vessels squared up to each other and threatened violence in defence of fishing rights, may have been merely a sideshow to us but for them had been a matter of national survival. If countries aren't allowed to manage their local resources to sustain their population, how can we expect them to be peaceful neighbours and how do we expect to spread prosperity? Are Third World countries poor because they have no assets, or poor because what assets they have are exploited or plundered by First World countries which have bigger financial clout or more developed technology? But as examining that problem in depth will keep you awake all night, let's leave it for now. You can mull it over with your breakfast egg tomorrow.

Goodnight.

March 1982

S

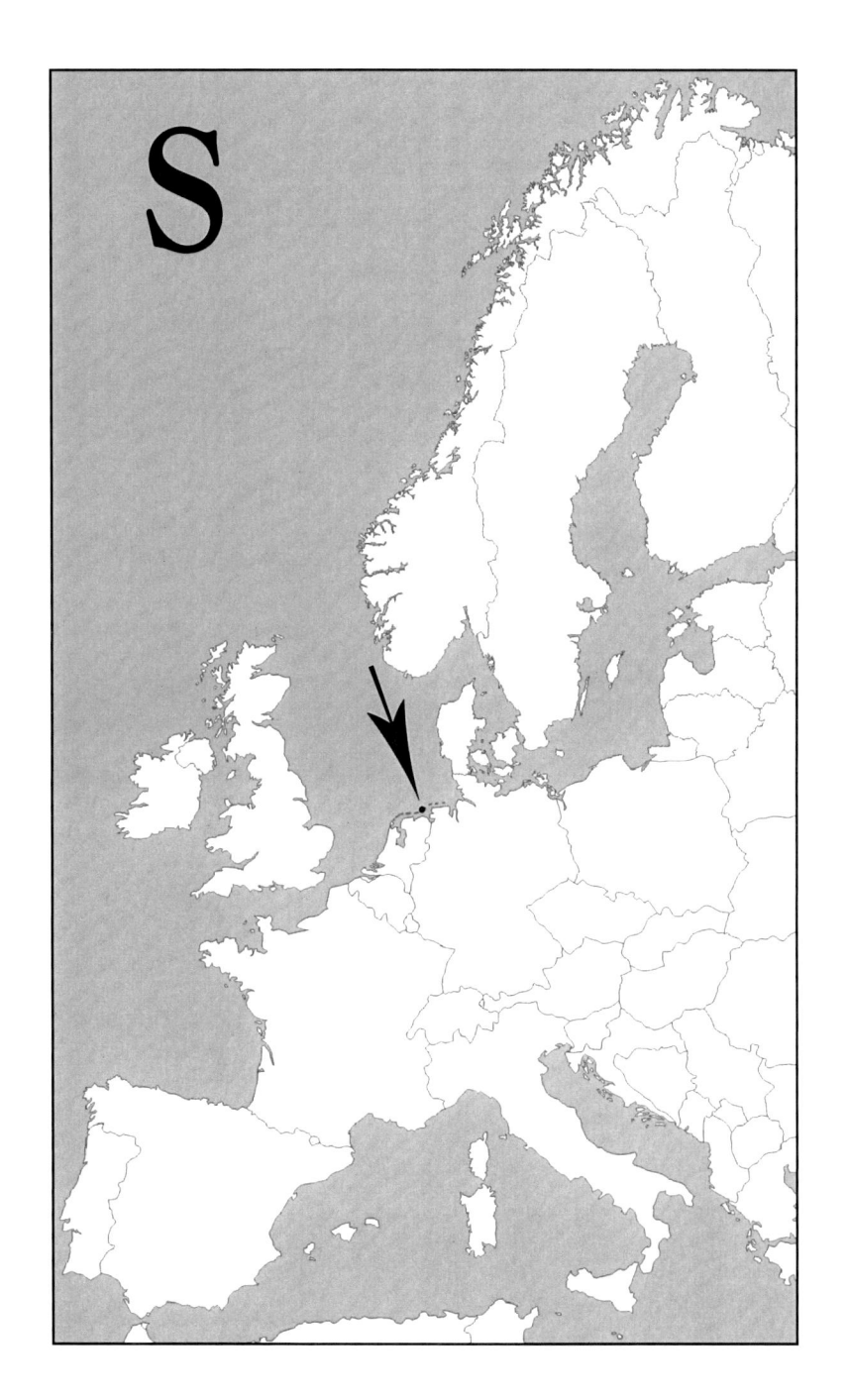

SCHIERMONNIKOOG

Schier delight!

One of the reasons few English people go to Schiermonnikoog is that they can't pronounce it – 'I want a ticket to... er, Seer, Skeer, Sheer' and by that point you've forgotten the rest of the name anyway. If you know not, it's usually described as the smallest inhabited of the Dutch Frisian Islands (it depends on the state of the tides when you measure it). Farther to the east lies even smaller Rottumeroog, a wildlife sanctuary, and then it's the border so other islands beyond and in some cases smaller belong to Germany.

Furthering my mildly sustained ambition of visiting them all, I asked Danny, my Dutch friend whom I've known since childhood (hers) and who lives in Amsterdam, to fix us a short break. We were coming over to attend her retirement party (*another story – you'll have to wait*), and being the right time of year it would be an opportunity to knock off another island. She fix.

Getting there is complicated. Danny doesn't drive, so it's public transport. Nothing wrong with the rail system in the Netherlands, although the locals complain all the time. But from Amsterdam you have to reach the far north of the country, which means finding a train to Groningen, and you come up against the first hurdle if you're not with a Dutch speaker because it looks like one thing in English but sounds quite different when the Dutch say it. It doesn't begin with a hard 'g' as you would expect – especially if you have a smattering of German – but with a guttural 'ch' as in the Scottish way of pronouncing 'loch'. Easy enough when you know, but an elephant trap when no one's warned you. Then there is the Dutch habit of not pronouncing the final 'n', so the town's name ends with an unstressed vowel, 'uh'. The result is something like 'Hroninga'. None of this mattered to me, as Danny was doing the talking. But it shows the obstacles facing an unaccompanied English speaker trying to get to such a destination. And if instead of via Groningen you opted for the alternative, slightly more direct, route, that means going via Leeuwarden – and try pronouncing *that*!

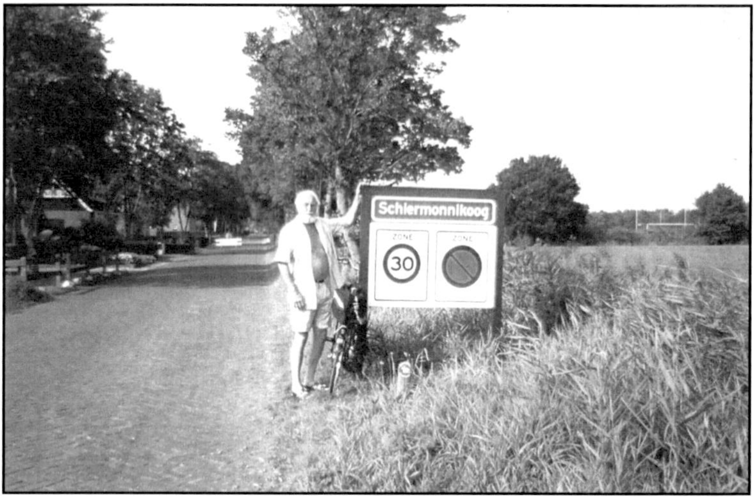
Schiermonnikoog
ZONE
30
ZONE

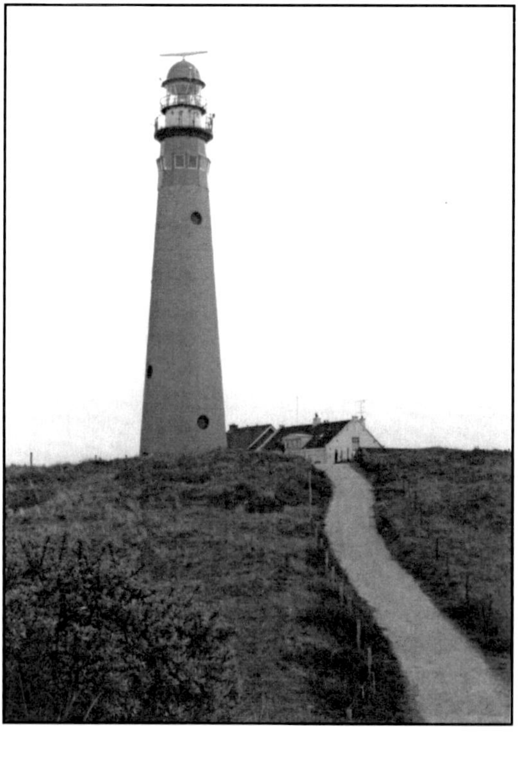

In fact, Danny had planned to go via the said Leeuwarden, but the train was delayed somewhere near Amersfoort for no obvious reason – it just stopped in the middle of nowhere, and there was no announcement – and when we got off at Leeuwarden we'd missed the connecting bus. Nothing for it but have some lunch in the station buffet, an enormous cavern whose walls were decorated with art from the great days of the railways at the end of the nineteenth century when they were all the rage and were opening up parts of the country which hitherto had been backwaters but were now able to join the mainstream and develop. We caught the next available train on to Groningen, where we'd pick up the bus to Lauwersoog, whence the ferry leaves for Schiermonnikoog. The bus leaves from right outside the railway station, but we found even the locals were having trouble making sense of the timetable and eventually Danny worked out that we'd missed it by ten minutes and the next one didn't leave for two hours.

But a temporary disaster can have an upside: we had two hours to kill and that gave us time to walk into the town centre and admire the architecture of the provincial capital. Well worth it, and I look forward to spending some time there at some future date and seeing the inside of some of the buildings I only had time to see the outside of. Back to the bus terminus, get on, relax and enjoy the countryside on the way to the coast and link up with the ferry. It's only a tiny island, so a rowing boat, perhaps? A flat-bottomed barge run on paraffin? No way – the ferry is absolutely enormous, as it has to take lorries to supply the islanders with every necessity.

The ferry terminal on Schiermonnikoog is right at the eastern tip, obviously built on reclaimed land for the sole purpose of providing a berth for the huge vessel. In former times, one supposes, people travelled in smaller boats which could tie up alongside a wall as they do in Vlieland, and before that you sailed as close inshore as you could get, avoiding the treacherous mudflats and sandbanks, and got off and waded ashore. The buses and taxis were waiting, and our bus had a scheduled stop right outside our hotel.

For so small an island, it is remarkably diverse. Next morning we walked down the road to the nearest cycle hire shop and within minutes were riding on the dedicated track through fields, then a small forest, then across water meadows where long-haired cattle grazed. The cattle, it appears, are the only means of keeping the land in good condition, as it floods in winter and because the ground is so soft no mechanical means exists to keep the grass down and the only possible alternative method is to leave cattle to roam free and graze it off. Walking off the tracks can be a bit risky, as there are muddy and boggy bits and in the wetter times of year you could find yourself in real trouble and all that's left of you on the surface is your hat and a few bubbles.

Een schierer monnik

We reached the edge of the beach, which stretched out of sight in either direction and it was perhaps a quarter of a mile from the water's edge to where we had to leave our bikes. The water was ridiculously shallow, so much so that the only way to get wet was to sit down or lie down and let the gentle breakers wash over you. But the currents in deeper water are lethal, and there were explanatory notices and flags flying warning visitors not to be tempted to go out of their depth to swim except at certain states of the tide. After all, this is not the beach in some sandy cove – it's the North Sea out there. Far out on the horizon were several beacons on platforms, and while we bathed or enjoyed a snack we could observe the periodic flashes of their beams and the passing ships which depended on them for safe navigation in what by any standards is a very dangerous stretch of water.

Danny thought the sea too cold to go right in, but I managed it if only to be able to tell Margaret when we got back that I had. 'We British', and all that. No, she wasn't with us. Why? A heat wave was forecast, and she's not good in heat (I said '*in*', not '*on*') and waived the trip. 'Go without me', she insisted. 'I'll cat-sit.' That was an extremely brave decision, not only because she actually didn't much like cats but also because Danny's cat, Pinguin, is worth a story in his own right, as, indeed, are several of her previous animals. Fierce, unpredictable, noisy and determined – some might say psychotic – how glad we all were that a previous owner had had his claws removed. We suspected he was a reincarnation, but were not sure what of. At five o'clock one morning we'd been woken by a thud on the door of our bedroom. Pinguin, determined to join us in bed, was shoulder-charging it.

The island's name is derived from Old Dutch 'schier' – 'grey', the word for a monk – 'monnik', and the Fris word 'oog' which means an island. In the fourteenth century the island came into the possession of the Cistercian monastery of Klaarkamp in Friesland, who sent some of their order – the Grey Friars – to see if their new acquisition had any economic value. Some farming people were brought in and gradually a small community grew up, supporting themselves and the monks who lived on the island by raising cattle for meat, milk and cheese and giving an income and some meagre profit to send back to the mother house. As in England after the Dissolution of the Monasteries in 1536 when Henry VIII sold off monastic land and the buildings themselves to anyone with the money to pay, similarly in 1580 staunchly Protestant Holland confiscated monastic property, and the island came into private ownership. Three centuries later in 1892 it was bought by a German aristocrat, but at the end of the Second World War in 1945 the Dutch government seized it as an 'enemy treasure' and it became once again the property of the Dutch state.

The original inhabitants have since been joined by a goodly number of retirees, attracted by the tranquillity of the place. There are buses and private cars, but no one's in a hurry. Some houses proudly display on their facades the fact that they date from the eighteenth century, others are of more recent construction. Plenty of shops, bars and restaurants, and although tourism is important – hence the abundance of cycle hire – out of season there is a sufficiently large resident population to sustain a retail economy. And there's always the ferry to the mainland and a bus to Groningen or Leeuwarden if you want a day out and a visit to the big stores but don't want to take your car.

Goodnight.

September 2005

T

TRONDHEIM

...the farther you go, the farther you still have to go!

This was the limit of the railway line from Oslo, and we were pretty knackered after the long train ride. 'We' on this occasion was Mike, who I still count as my best friend although we don't see much of each other. He had had a pretty roughshod childhood, his father having patented a battery-driven teaspoon and gone bankrupt trying the market it, and whose next invention – a half-size breadknife for when you only want to cut half a slice – was equally a failure. But I digress. From Trondheim north the only way is by road. As we soon discovered, after a time it wasn't road either, but track. Why spend public money putting a hard surface on a road which will break up in the winter and be impassable, and is hardly used in summer anyway? All serious transport of goods and people is by ship along the coast, and for hundreds of miles North Norway between the sea and the frontier with Sweden is so narrow that almost every settlement is either on the coast or within sight. Our aim was to get up to North Cape, so this was as far as we could get by public transport. We'd planned to hitchhike. Now we had no choice. We were barely one-third of the way. In fact, about 800 miles of not very much lay in front of us.

We were relaxing in the Common Room of the youth hostel with our pipes well lit and on the lookout for company to pass the evening. One lad, as black as your hat and in consequence standing out a mile because everyone else in the hostel was a North European (which is hardly surprising, as we were *in* northern Europe) turned out to be from the Belgian Congo and like us a student thumbing his way around Europe during the vac. I'd never met anyone before from his country, and we soon lapsed into conversing in French as he found that easier than English. He was studying in Belgium (the colonial power at that time, so no wonder), and taking the opportunity to see a bit of the rest of the continent before going back home to take up his career in the capital of his own country, Léopoldville. The chap next to him was a Swede, but from not far away right up against the border and amazingly he had never before seen the sea! Even more amazing was that he said he'd never heard of Belgium and had absolutely no idea where it was. We wouldn't have been so surprised if he'd said he'd never heard of the Belgian *Congo* – but Belgium itself? Maybe Swedish education wasn't as enlightened or enlightening as we thought. The third member of our group was Anders, a native, whose English was so good I asked him if he was studying it at university.

'No,' he said. 'I'm studying physics at what you call A level.'
'So how come your English is so good?'
'All our textbooks are in English.'
'Why's that?'
'Well, think how many Norwegians there are (about 3 million), then think how many of them want to study physics to A level. Maybe a hundred altogether? It just isn't economic to print physics textbooks in Norwegian for so few people, and anyway anyone going on to university and taking a science degree will end up working either abroad or for a Norwegian firm which is engaged in research or trade with international partners, mainly in the US, or in import/export, and for any of that you have to have English because no one speaks Norwegian except us.'

Seemed to make sense.

Amongst other travellers with whom we fell into conversation were a couple of canoeists who'd just returned from the Lofoten Islands, whose intriguing story about their journey and their experiences on the islands I related in the first book in this series, my *Little Green Nightbook*. Then there were a couple of Danes in their mid-twenties, one tall and thin and the other short and rotund – a sort of Laurel and Hardy in reverse. They were highly adventurous travellers who'd made it beyond the confines of Europe into North Africa, and had tales to tell about Morocco. On arrival in Casablanca they'd been warned of the ingeniousness and ruthless efficiency of the local thieves, evidenced by what befell a young German lad travelling alone who'd set up his tent on the beach with his rucksack, stove, sleeping bag and other necessaries arranged inside around him and who when he woke up next morning found himself lying on the sand in his pyjamas and that was all – everything else had been stolen.

Our two Danes explained that they had not been in the least put off by this story. 'We'll be fine', they'd said. 'We have a good Danish knife' (the speaker held his hands out about two feet apart, indicating just how big it had been). They proceeded to erect their tent out on the beach, stood their rucksacks side by side and when they got into their sleeping bags laid the knife on the ground between them – the slightest disturbance and either of them could reach out, grab it and confront the intruder. And it worked. Next morning they were still safely cocooned in their sleeping bags inside their tent and all their gear was just as they'd left it when they turned in.

Except for the knife, which had gone.

Moroccan Thieves 1, *Danes* nil.

The weather was very hot and sunny, and after looking round the city and its cathedral we found a deserted rocky beach where we could strip off, laze in the sun, read the copy of *The Observer* which we'd found at a newsstand and perhaps have a dip. Not expecting hot weather in North Norway we hadn't brought such luxury items as bathing trunks as it would be yet another thing to carry and hardly likely to get used. Mike, stark naked, jumped into the water, but after just a few seconds of delighted squeals leapt out again even more quickly – Trondheim Fjord is fed by melt water off glaciers inland and their low temperature doesn't encourage total immersion. Norwegian waters are serious matters, and not to be trifled with by 'occasional' bathers. It wasn't too bad in water up to the knees, and I myself was not in the least tempted to go in any farther, knowing that we were a lot farther north than either of us had ever been before and way beyond the northernmost parts of Great Britain. But as we lay starkers on the rocks enjoying the sun, suddenly we heard women's voices. A group of what looked from the distance like office typists out for their lunch break were coming along the beach towards us! We had no desire to end up in custody at the local cop shop for exposing ourselves, but the problem was that we were lying on the rocks and our clothes were twenty feet away on the beach and any attempted movement involving sliding off the rocks to reach them would mean we'd be spotted. So we tried to shrink ourselves down as flat as we could and just hope they wouldn't look up and spot us, holding our breath as the girls walked by oblivious of the fact that there were two naked young men only a few feet away. You have to picture us bollock naked, trying to lie as flat as possible on top of a rock, keeping absolutely silent while holding our breath and our stomachs in and crossing our fingers. That was us.

When someone asks me if I've ever had an embarrassing moment, I say 'Nearly'.

Goodnight.

August 1959

U

ULAN BATOR

Bator late than never?

Looking at landlocked Mongolia on a map, I always reckoned it amongst the least likely places I'd ever visit. However, planning a holiday partly around Lake Baikal put me near enough to consider popping over the border to tick another box. Then a second thought struck me: having got so far, what's the point of just 'popping over the border' and then getting back onto the Trans-Siberian Railway? Having reached Mongolia, it's daft not to spend at least a few days exploring it. The opportunity won't come again.

The country is about the size of Western Europe yet has only some three million people, and of these one million live in Ulaanbaatar (the double letters indicate where the stress goes). It's known by the locals simply as 'UB'. Mention Mongolia to most people and they have only one thought: Genghis Khan. They vaguely remember that in the Middle Ages he led the Mongols on a rampage across Central Asia and reached the frontiers of Europe, destroying everything in his way and on his way.

In real life, I'm not sure I'd have turned my back on him!

Modern Mongolians take a different view, and the huge statue of Chinggis Khaan (their spelling) in front of their Parliament Building says it all. He's seen as a national hero, the 'father of the nation' who united the nomadic Mongols for the first time at the end of the 12th century and created the largest land empire the world has ever seen. And he only destroyed those who opposed him. Those who submitted were allowed to keep their own customs and religion – a degree of toleration which was certainly not found in contemporary Christian Europe where Jews were persecuted and heretics routinely put to death and often in particularly nasty ways.

Arriving by train from Russia, we – Mike (remember Narvik?) and I – headed straight out to a country park 70kms north-east for a few days living in a traditional nomadic *ger* (*pron. 'grrrr'*) and experiencing a bit of rural life (*which I'll tell you about under another letter – but in another book*). Once outside the city limits tarmac ceased, and the road thereafter was of indeterminate and inconsistent width because it had no proper edge and drivers wishing to avoid a vast pothole or vertiginous rut just left the road, thus in the process increasing its width. As well as lacking any kind of kerb, the road across country was also devoid of a consistent surface, any lines indicating where the middle was supposed to be or any traffic directions, signage or lighting. Returning two days later, our driver seemed to be fleeing a wolf pack, so fiercely did he steer us around the world-class ruts and potholes. When we reached the city limits we had to go through a toll and pay 500 *tugriks* (the local currency, and worth about 20p in our money), which is apparently charged on all vehicles. With this additional income, you'd expect the city fathers to maintain the roads within the city to a higher standard than in the countryside. But no, hardly any difference until well into the city centre; not so many ruts, but still a plentiful supply of potholes. There were plenty of traffic police fighting a losing battle, with – a surprise – the word 'POLICE' across the back of their luminous jackets – just like that, i.e. in English. As well as being surprised that they use the English word and not whatever it is in their own language, on top of that Mongolian isn't written in Latin script but a slightly adapted version of Cyrillic.

Our tour of the city began with paying our respects to Chinggis Khaan and visiting the museum devoted to his times, which contained some interesting coins from the Early Middle Ages and banners carried by armies when approaching a town to show whether they came in peace (a white banner) or meant war (a black one). Then to the Gandan monastery, thronged with devotees buying bags of nuts from street vendors to feed to the hundreds of pigeons who knew which side their bread was buttered – so to speak. Coo! (*Sorry!*). There are plans to re-locate to a new site some 50km distant, and to erect a statue of the Buddha which will be taller than the Statue of Liberty. A model of his foot was displayed on a plinth, giving some idea of just how colossal the final statue will be.

After lunch in a Mongolian barbecue our guide took us to the memorial to Russian-Mongolian friendship and to those who died during the Second World War, erected at the top of Zaisan Hill requiring visitors to climb several hundred steep steps. It's very obvious that the architects and painters were strongly influenced by the concept of socialist realism, but in this instance it has worked incredibly well – even allowing for the element of propaganda contained in a succession of portraits depicting sturdy, good-looking men and women and every uniform smart and ready for a march past. We had an interesting encounter there with a young Chinese couple talking to each other in English. When questioned, they explained that they'd met on the train. The young man was from Hong Kong and didn't speak very good Mandarin, and the girl was from south-east China and couldn't understand his Cantonese – so they decided that as they'd both studied in Britain it was easier to talk to each other in English than struggle to communicate using two different versions of Chinese. An interesting example of the dominance of English as the world's *lingua franca* that two educated Chinese opt to use it.

Until the twentieth century the Mongols remained a largely nomadic people, even moving their capital – known at that time as Urga – with them. They were conquered by the Chinese in 1691, but when the Manchu dynasty fell in 1911 they declared their independence and turned to their religious leader, the lama Bogd Khan. His palace, built between 1893 and 1903, is open to tourists, and the interiors are well kept and full of examples of Buddhist art, calligraphy and especially *thangkas*; but while the skill and devotion of the artists are not to be doubted the fact is that the displays are largely meaningless to a viewer unfamiliar with the intricacies and symbolism of Buddhist belief. The open spaces between the buildings, on the other hand, are surprisingly unkempt. Bogd Khan agreed to become king, and even agreed to take a wife so that the people could have a queen. His throne is on display in the audience chamber, replete with 28 cushions representing the 28 provinces of Mongolia, and the seats where religious and lay officials sat. Ten years later he accepted constitutional limitations to his power, but when he died in 1924 the Communists took over and set up a dictatorship in imitation of what was happening at that time in their vast northern neighbour, Russia, and became to all intents and purposes a Soviet satellite. As we all know, the Soviet Union broke up in the 1990s and Belarus, Ukraine, the Baltic States and much of Central Asia became independent republics. It is less well known that at the same time the Mongolians threw off the Communist yoke and set about building a functioning democracy.

The cultural highlight of our visit was a performance of traditional Mongolian music and dance by a small, predominantly young, professional troupe who, dressed in elaborate costumes and quick-changing between acts amazed us with their dexterity on various traditional instruments and the obvious command of their repertoire – including the world-renowned local eccentricity, 'throat singing' (*hoomii* in Mongolian). Our guide said the show was staged between six and seven every night, and was essentially for tourists. But who can forget a contortionist who starts her act by standing on her right leg with her left leg at 180° with her knee against her ear – and as her finale sticks a peg in the floor, grips the top in her teeth and proceeds to perform a slow-motion head-stand!

On our final afternoon we popped along to the post office to get some stamps to post cards to friends and family, not having done so during our month in Russia prior to arriving in Mongolia. We'd been advised that they also stocked a wide range of souvenirs, and at keen prices. The problem in most cases was: the items didn't have any prices on them, so we had to keep asking one of the staff to show us each item and tell us how much it was. The next process was to tot up the total for multiple purchases and mentally convert the price in *tugriks* into sterling at 2200 to the £ – not the easiest of calculations to make in your head! While we're doing the mental arithmetic bit and debating the merits of this item or that, the assistant is standing holding the various items, eyes glazing over in boredom as she gazes into the middle distance. We then discovered – to our amazement – that in a shop geared up to accommodate foreign visitors and where all the serving staff spoke English they did not accept credit cards! So we had to go to the cashpoint, draw out the money, go and pay, take the goods (no wrapping paper or bags offered – the implication being 'You've bought it. Here it is. Take it away.') – and then if you decide you'd like something else go back and draw out more money and go through the whole rigmarole again. One of my additional purchases cost 2000 *tugriks*, which when I got my credit card statement back in England showed I'd been charged 92p for the currency and a £2 handling fee for withdrawing it!

This 5 tugrik note is worth approx. one-fifth of 1p!

Ulan Bator today is a thoroughly modern city, and its traffic jams bear comparison with the rush hour in any large conurbation – except that it has them all day long! From our hotel room on the 9th floor I could see a dozen cranes and as many half-built tower blocks, a clear indication of the influx of people into the city and the need to accommodate them. So it may not be beautiful – no 'old quarter' of the sort so keenly sought out by Western visitors to towns in foreign countries. But vibrant it sure is, and the smile on Chinggis Khaan's face doubtless indicates satisfaction with the modern Mongolia created by his descendants.

Goodnight.

September 2012

V

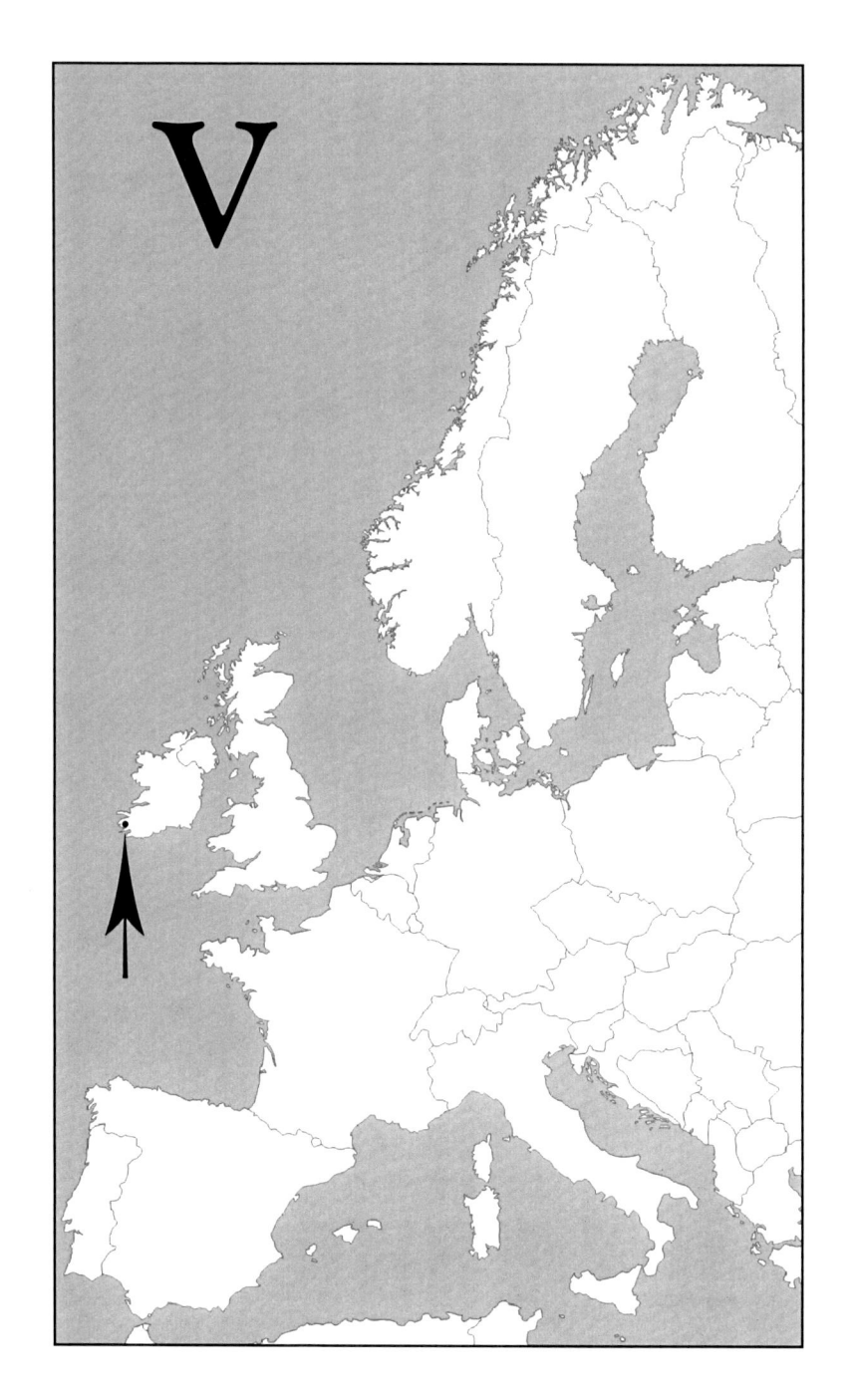

VALENTIA

Plan B to the end of the world

We arrived on schedule on the island, one of the departure points for boat trips out to The Skelligs. For those who don't know, these tiny islets lie off the coast of Kerry in the far south-west of Ireland.

Why go there?

For some four centuries up to about 1200 the larger islet, Skellig Michael, was the site of one of the most remote monastic communities in Christendom, where an abbot and twelve monks maintained their isolation from the temptations of the world by perching themselves on the top of a rocky outcrop which rises almost sheer some 700 feet above the sea, lashed by gales and most of the time inaccessible. They lie 8 miles out in the Atlantic – the farthest western point in the British Isles. There is a lighthouse. The next piece of land to the west is America.

We were booked into a B&B on Valentia where our host, who worked during the day at the Irish meteorological station on the island, informed us that due to adverse weather conditions no boats had ventured out to the Skelligs for a week and many visitors who had come intent on making the trip had run out of time and had had to go home disappointed. The boatmen stand with binoculars on various headlands and look at the landing stage on the island, and can tell through experience whether the height of the Atlantic swell is too great to permit landing. If it's too rough and no passengers could get ashore, there's no point in going.

We were, however, in luck. The very next day the weather moderated.

Down to the embarkation point, park the car and get aboard. The boat was tiny and completely open, and seemed quite inadequate for an eight mile voyage straight out into the Atlantic. But in the days of the monastery the monks used to make the trip in a coracle to fetch supplies or collect a novice or two. I guess they must have had supreme confidence in the power of prayer.

Eight miles out into the Atlantic in this!

The weather may have moderated, but it was still blowing quite hard and obviously we were in for a bumpy ride. Plan B, then: get on first, sit with your back against the wheelhouse and be out of the wind. The other passengers ranged themselves on the benches around the gunwales, backs to the sea and exposed to wind and spray. It was a case, I observed to Margaret, of the operation of Jackson's Principle. What's that, you ask? There was, so it's said, a shipwrecked sailor who, as he reached safety at the top of the rope ladder slung over the side of the other ship, said to his rescuers, 'Pull the ladder up, Jack, I'm alright' – while many of his shipmates were still in the water. 'Jackson's Principle' is how Margaret and I describe the phrase *'I'm alright, Jack'*, a reference to people who are indescribably self-centred and whose only concern in life is themselves and their own convenience. *(You may start now, if you like, compiling a personal list. But be warned: it may keep you awake, so obviating the point of this being a 'Nightbook'!).*

However, it soon became evident that operating 'Jackson's Principle' had been, as Margaret usually put it when I did something right, *'one of my better ideas'*. The boat bounced about like a cork in the ocean swell, with a German girl being discretely sick over the side most of the way. We passed Little Skellig, a small but steep rock with no possible place to land, the haunt of seabirds and covered in guano *(OK – have it your way: bird shit)* . Not far now to the landing stage on Skellig Michael. This, apparently, had only been built comparatively recently, for the benefit of tourists. The monks had simply launched their coracles straight off the rocks into the water. But then, not very often and only in the calmest of sea conditions.

The way to the monastic ruins is up a long, winding flight of slightly fan-shaped steps cut into the bare rock and without any handrails or safety features – and a real clincher if you want an answer to that nagging question you've always been wondering about: 'Do I suffer from vertigo?'. Make no mistake – or rather, on the other hand, *make* a mistake – and it's non-stop straight into the *oggin* and that could be a couple of hundred feet straight down. Even in a moderate wind it's pretty scary, as the steps are constantly wet from spray. What it must be like in a gale hardly bears thinking about.

Onward and upward – and no handrail

At the top of the landing-stage the resident tour guides were there to greet us. The Irish Tourist Board, it appeared, employed three or four students to stay out on shifts of three weeks or so at a time to take visitors round the ruins and explain them. The top of the island has just about enough level ground to allow for the construction of a reservoir to catch rainwater, individual cells for the monks, a tiny chapel and to lay out an equally tiny kitchen garden. Life must have been incredibly hard – but then, that's what the monks wanted. According to their beliefs, the greater the privation on earth, the greater the purity of the soul and the greater the reward in heaven at the end.

A monk's 'bee-hive' cell

The guides told the story of Viking raiders who carried off the abbot, who ultimately starved to death. The small patch of level ground which constituted the monks' vegetable garden seemed hardly big enough to have supplied them with enough to eat, but presumably they caught fish and in any case were the sort of zealots who had chosen this spot for the ultimate experience in self-denial and would have eaten the barest minimum to stay alive. The ruins have been partially repaired, and our intrepid band of visitors wandered around them freely, taking photos. In particular, of the altar cross silhouetted against the east window. It had no glass. But then, had it ever?

How long visitors could stay depended on sea conditions, as it was essential to get back to the mainland – there's absolutely nowhere to stay on the island and no proper shelter. The guides have a hut but often no visitors for days at a time because no boats can reach them. Once the summer tourist season is over, the island is abandoned except for maintaining the lighthouse on the far side. Being a lighthouseman there must have been about the loneliest posting in the service one could have experienced.

We had the wind behind us on the return trip, which seemed to fill the skipper, a lad of about 17 judging by appearances, with such confidence that he abandoned the wheel and sat on the stern with his feet on the seating, backside sticking out over our wash, chatting to the nearest passengers. One untoward wave and he'd have done a backward somersault into the sea – leaving us adrift without a pilot. I was glad when we made harbour and tied up safely.

A visit to The Skelligs is the ultimate in tourism to remote parts so far as south-west Ireland is concerned, because even though the Great Blasket is equally difficult to reach it's a proper island where ordinary people once lived by farming and fishing, and some of the cottages abandoned when the last residents moved out in the 1930s have been taken over by new owners and renovated as summer retreats. No one has ever lived on The Skelligs except for the tiny medieval community of monks – and even they gave up in the thirteenth century. I could only marvel at their devotion and hardiness – and feel thankful that I had a welcoming B&B to get back to in Valentia and the prospect of a good dinner in a restaurant.

Goodnight.

August 1990

W

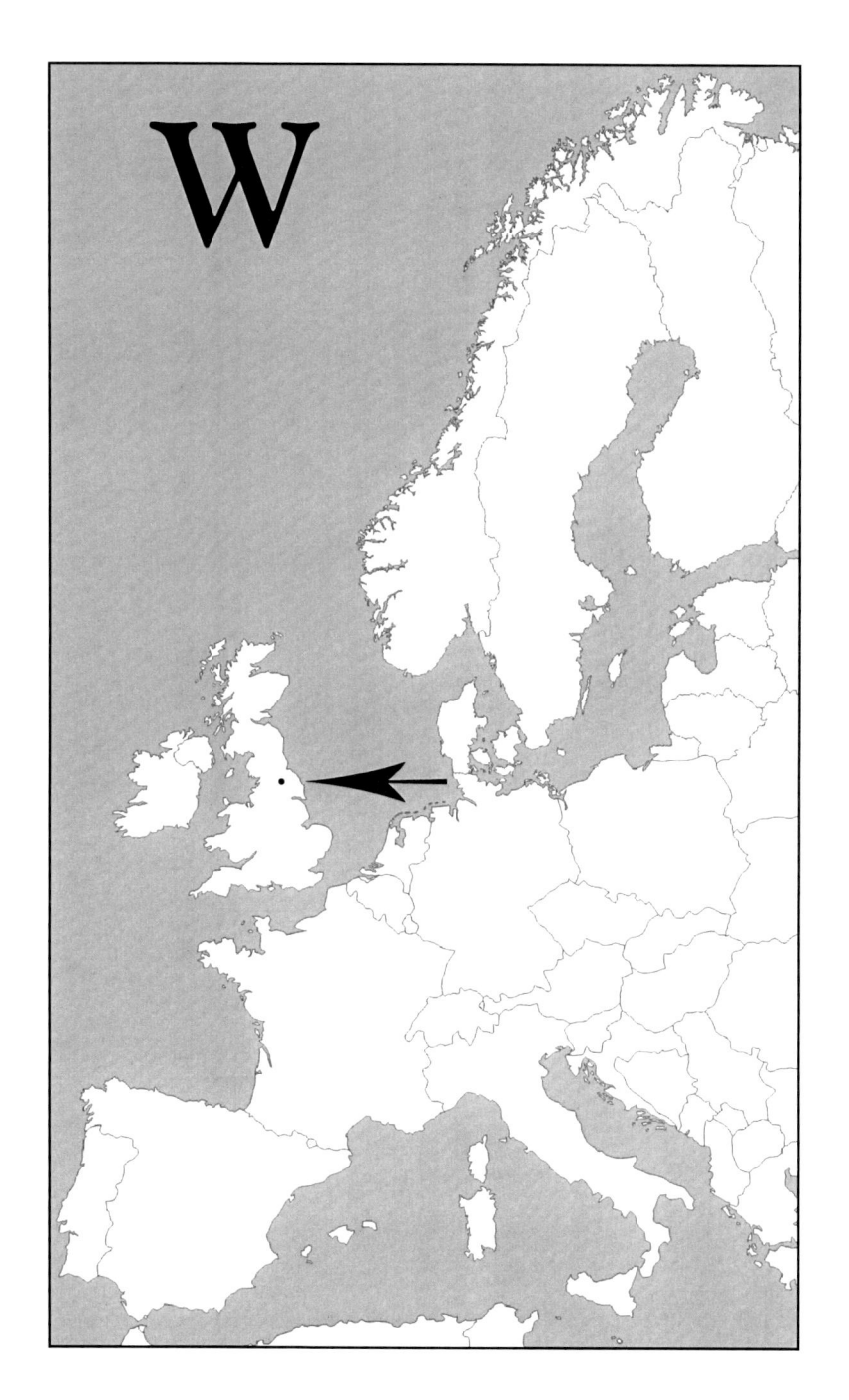

WETHERBY

As one life reaches its climax, two others begin

It was one hell of a dash. Mother's party was on Thursday, we had to get home and pack and be in Wetherby by late Friday ready for the wedding on Saturday – and it's a drive of 250 miles!

The run-up to Margaret's mother's hundredth birthday was long in the process and tough on the nerves – yes, it's pleasantly unusual to have your mother reach her century, but at the back of your mind is always the nagging fear that you'll have put in all this time and energy into making all the arrangements and then at the last minute she won't actually make it. It does happen. When I was mayor some twenty years ago I was all lined up to a present a bouquet of flowers to a lady whose 100th birthday was coming up, and she died the day before – leaving us with an expensive bouquet and no one to present it to. Very inconsiderate. Surely she could have just held on for another twenty-four hours, if only out of consideration for the council tax payers whose money she would be wasting by dying a day too soon?

The party itself went well, what with the local paper sending a photographer to the care home and all the residents joining in the celebratory drinks and nibbles. We all know that the Queen sends a card to people on their 100th birthday, but it's different when you actually see one. There are now so many people reaching three figures that it's hardly a phenomenon any longer, but in most families it's still a unique experience because whichever member of the family it is who's reached a hundred they are almost certainly the first one in *your* family to do so – however many others there are in other people's families up and down the country reaching the same milestone.

Ma enjoyed herself, and was more aware and alert than she'd been for months. She'd not been able to read for half-a-dozen years, and couldn't really even see the television. So what's the point of living if most of the time you're just sitting? You can't talk *all* the time, and frankly you run out of things to say. You can listen

I am so pleased to know that you are celebrating your one hundredth birthday on 19th May, 2011. I send my congratulations and best wishes to you on such a special occasion.

Elizabeth R

Mrs. Rita Round

to other people's conversation – but are you actually interested? Margaret spent a lot of time managing her affairs and visited every week, but it's a round trip of sixty miles across the New Forest and we had to be out by midday because that's when lunch is served and they wanted to get her downstairs into the dining room not only for the meal but also for a bit of company. Gave us the opportunity to investigate the menus of a whole host of country pubs all over the Forest (*arrangement: I pay for the petrol, you pay for the lunch*). But you're not back home till tea-time, so in effect visiting Mother took up a whole working day each week. Maybe not a problem if you have nothing else to do and no other responsibilities, but retired or not we both had busy lives and had to work round our other activities to find a day in the week when we could both be free to make the maternal visit. Can't go Saturday or Sunday – the A31 (the main road through the Forest to Bournemouth or the West Country) will be clogged with holiday traffic and likely as not we'll get stuck in a traffic tail-back. Monday's out – I've got a dentist appointment. Tuesday – no go, Margaret's got a meeting of the County Adoption Panel, and that takes all day. And she'll probably be so exhausted that she won't feel like visiting Mother on Wednesday. Etc., etc. Am I complaining? No. Just explaining.

Margaret was pretty knackered at the end of the party, what with reading out all the cards to Mother several times over, introducing all the family members, some of whom she hadn't seen for years, setting people up for group photos, liaising with the care home staff and regularly adjusting the transparent adhesive tape keeping her fixed smile in place. We got home, packed – posh clothes and lady's fancy titfer as well as usual holiday gear – and set the alarm for an early rise tomorrow.

The wedding was my younger nephew, Matthew, whose fiancée's family came from Yorkshire. We booked into a motel alongside the motorway, convenient for getting to the country house outside Wetherby where the ceremony would take place (no churches or religious element). It would also be convenient to get to anywhere else we fancied. Principally this would be York itself, which we both loved and wanted to re-visit and experience some of the major attractions again – possibly for the last time, as we're not likely to come this far north again. It would be interesting to see if the Jorvik Experience was still the same, and when we picked up a tourist brochure we read that there was a new medieval house to be explored, which had only been unearthed a couple of years previous when reconstruction work was undertaken and hidden walls were laid bare for the first time in five hundred years.

While in the North we also planned to take in some of the National Trust or English Heritage properties Margaret had always wanted to see but so far had not managed, in particular Bolsover Castle and the home of that extraordinary phenomenon Elizabeth, Countess of Shrewsbury, known as 'Bess of Hardwick': 'Hardwick Hall – more glass than wall', as it was dubbed at the time it was built during the reign of the first Elizabeth. Then there was Litchfield. We managed to find a space in a car park ideally placed for Margaret to take a photo of the famous twisted spire – only to find to her dismay that her camera battery was flat! Then to Knaresborough, where I sat for a moment on a bench in the main square next to an old boy dressed all in black and with a distinct frown on his face, but when I spoke to him he didn't answer so I didn't press him. There was a large wheel alongside him which he seemed to be guarding, so perhaps he was preoccupied with that.

The next day we made the journey to Bakewell, as I've been known to fancy a tart from time to time. The scenery is wonderful, and I made a mental note to come back another time and 'do' Derbyshire properly. The fly in the ointment with living on the south coast is that the attractions of the continent are just so close and the ferries so comfortable and so convenient if, like us, you have a penchant for French food and the pleasant scenery. It's less trouble for me to get to France than it is to get to the Midlands, and being as a result of many years of visiting pretty familiar with Normandy and Brittany and having a topped-up euro credit card in my pocket, it's naturally a first choice over driving a couple of hundred miles north to somewhere where I don't know the local geography when you've got a wife who's just as keen as you are to get stuck into an *assiette de fruits de mer*.

:he final drive home we managed to lose the road and
p making a detour through countryside where we had no
ere we were but ended up – using the map – taking a cross-
route back to the main A1. In a particularly deserted
ve found ourselves on a country road between the two main
)king for a lay-by to stop for a picnic. We parked facing a
)king over a wide field system with a tractor working away
r distance. On top of the fence posts local bird enthusiasts
ed small upturned tins into which, presumably, they left
encourage the local feathered wildlife to come, feed and
ved at close quarters – i.e. you parked close to the fence,
the car, kept quiet and waited for the floor show. Several
ls arrived, clearly familiar with the scheme, and proceeded
t one end of the fence, inspect the first tin and flutter on
ω ιπι πιεxt before finally flying off in disgust (the tins were as it
happened empty). But star of the show was a cock pheasant who
sauntered across the road behind us as though he owned it (no
hint of traffic sense whatever), flew nonchalantly up onto the top
of the fence and proceeded to promenade majestically tightrope-

style along the whole length investigating each tin in turn before finally dropping down on the other side of the fence and walking off in disgust – all the time apparently completely unaware that there were two humans watching his every move from barely ten feet away.

Goodnight.

May 2011

Y

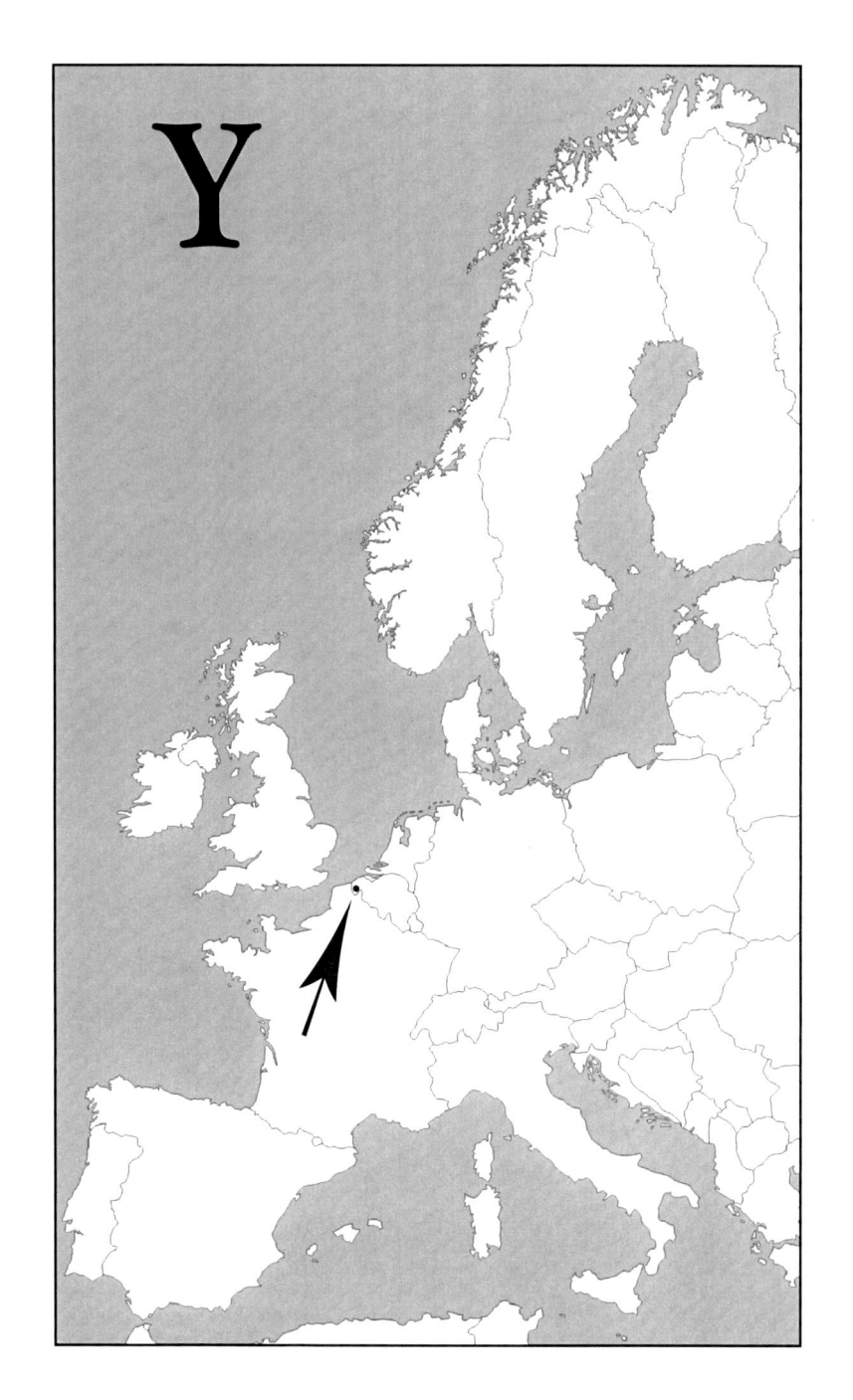

YPRES

Faith in the future

Ieper is much visited by the British, on account of the cemeteries and memorials to those who died in the First World War. Our visit was much more prosaic: a lunch stop on the way to the Channel Tunnel after a visit to the European Parliament in Brussels hosted by Chris Huhne, one of our MEPs.

Despite being a major centre of the wool trade in the Middle Ages, as were so many towns in Flanders, Ieper is not much visited, I think, by ordinary tourists interested in seeing something of Flemish history. They head for Bruges or Ghent. Maybe Antwerp. We've all learned in school that between 1914-18 Ypres was the site of not just one major battle but three, and we all know the Tommies called it 'Wipers' because seeing how it's spelled in French that was the way it looked as if it should be pronounced. We've all seen pictures of the devastation visited upon battlefield zones, how towns on the front line were reduced to rubble, and we just assume that postwar reconstruction was in 1920s architectural style, with modern public buildings, widened streets, art deco shopfronts if you're lucky and whatever the local equivalent was of council housing.

But the Flemings didn't do anything of the kind when rebuilding Ieper. They put it up again the way it was.

Parking our coach alongside the Cloth Hall, my first thought wasn't 'art deco' or 'concrete hangar' but my recollections of the Sukiennice in Kraków (built about the same time, too). I'm sure close inspection would reveal that the hall is a modern reconstruction, but from a casual glance just walking through it on the way to the main square and finding a restaurant it looks just like the original, begun in 1320, would have looked when completed. This is not deception big-time, it's recreating what was there, the way it was. It's about faith in the future. We lost a fine building in a war, but the war's over now, so let's have our history back.

The same attitude, I'm sure, inspired the Poles to rebuild the

Old Town in Warsaw after the Second World War even though millions of people were homeless, starving, unemployed and suffering all manner of extreme economic and social hardship. But money was found for rebuilding the city's historic heart, painting it up and re-creating the town centre just as it had looked in the seventeenth century – emphasis on 'looked'. The interiors were built to modern standards in terms of ceiling heights (we're generally taller than our ancestors) and modern plumbing, electric lighting and fire exits, but façade as near as possible a carbon copy of what was originally constructed four centuries earlier. If Poland were to recover, it needed also to recover its history – so, I'm sure, must have run the argument. The Russians re-gilded the domes of Orthodox churches, despite being officially an atheist state. We no longer believe in gods, but for centuries we did and isn't that part of our history? And they were rather fine buildings, weren't they? Christian Britain didn't demolish Stonehenge because it was constructed by bygone pagans. This is in marked contrast to the Taliban in Afghanistan who deliberately blew up the Buddhas at Bamyan simply because they were built by non-Muslims – even though in so doing they were destroying a part of their country's history.

The Cloth Hall

The object of our visit to Belgium was to visit the European Parliament, at the invitation of our MEP. Annie had made all the arrangements, as it was her idea in the first place. She knew MEPs could be approached to host visits by constituents, and wanted us to take advantage of this so as to be able to see the Parliament in session. What struck me was how unhurried and relaxed the atmosphere was in the debating chamber – very businesslike, speakers addressing the assembly in a variety of languages and no one waving papers in the air, shouting 'Hear! Hear!' or braying abuse as they do in our House of Commons or indeed showing much emotion at all.

We travelled by coach via Calais, stopped for lunch where Annie had booked us in and then on arrival at our hotel in Brussels found that two of our number had formerly lived and worked in the city so knew where to locate suitable restaurants for dinner. We negotiated a price for 28 of us, and were given wine 'on the house'. My most vivid memory of the city is of how the *Grand Place* more than lived up to its reputation when I saw it for real.

On the return journey we had planned to visit one of the many First World War cemeteries dotted all over Flanders. We had travelled to the European Parliament as an official delegation representing Romsey Liberal Democrats, and it had been agreed that as chairman I would formally lay a wreath on behalf of the Association. The day was a bright and sunny, but during the night it had been snowing. We were the first visitors to the cemetery that morning and it looked wonderfully serene and peaceful with its pristine covering of glistening white snow unblemished by footprints. The contrast now with what it must have been like in 1915 challenged the imagination.

I'm sure Ieper will repay a longer visit, if only to see if the restaurant we popped into on the street corner is still featuring a dish with includes sea urchin caviar. I'd been joined by my friend Carol, both looking for a snack in what looked like a bar. We thought it was merely a bar which also served food, but when we got inside and were conducted to a table by a waiter it was too late to turn back without embarrassment. It was, in fact, a top class establishment with excellent service and amazing food – including the afore-mentioned sea urchin caviar. I didn't know sea urchins *had* caviar – and I'm pretty sure sea urchins don't know it, either. But we ordered it just to see what it was. I'm none the wiser. It was there on the plate, somewhere. I just couldn't find it. The fish was beautifully cooked and served. The accompanying scallops white, fleshy and round. Maybe the 'caviar' was in the sauce. Preceded by an *amuse-bouche* of salmon mousse served up on a biscuit and garnished with what looked like horsehair and which was delivered to our table without being ordered – it was that sort of restaurant. I might go back to Ieper just to sit again at that same table and give myself the time to tackle their *gourmet* menu. Now there's a thought! Or I'll go back to see the rest of the town and do a bit of shopping, see the inside of the Cloth Hall, and then 'do' the Menin Gate just like all the other tourists.

Goodnight.

January 2004

Z

ZAGORSK*

If the opposite of 'uncouth' is 'couth', so the opposite of 'out of kilter' must be 'in'.

In the immediate postwar period a World Festival of Youth and Students was held in alternate years in Communist bloc capitals, and having spent half my national service studying Russian naturally I strained every sinew and knifed every piggy bank to come up with the money when it was Moscow's turn to play host. Like anyone who's studied a foreign language I wanted the chance to speak it with people for whom it was their mother tongue, and confirm that what I'd spent so much time and effort learning actually worked.

In those days it was nigh on impossible to get across the Iron Curtain into Eastern Europe or the Soviet Union unless you had a personal invitation from a local, were a member of some or other official delegation or were a member of your own country's Communist Party. But this was just a year after the Hungarian uprising and the Soviets were desperate to entice as many young people from the West as possible to take part in the festival, hoping for the propaganda benefits of drawing a veil over what they'd done in Budapest. By bragging about the numbers coming they could claim that our presence in Moscow showed our support for the Soviet Union and its policies.

Joining the special train in London, I fell in with a group of Scots. They seemed fascinated by my strange accent – mutual, I wasn't used to broad Glaswegian. But we stuck together throughout the long journey, turning our compartment into a fortress and keeping everyone else out. To improve personal comfort we put all our baggage on the floor, so as to provide a level space between the two banks of seats and support under the knees if you put your legs out straight. With the luggage rack therefore empty we could take it in turns to climb up and crash out full length and get some proper sleep. When the journey is going to take three days without getting off the train, such considerations are important. In Berlin food parcels were handed out. It was the first time I'd ever come across pumpernickel; I wasn't sure whether to eat it or mend the holes in my shoes. As we were crossing the interminable North European Plain through Poland – nothing to see but unchanging fields and woods, and you look through the window an hour later and it's as though you haven't moved – a farm worker in a field saw our train passing and made a dismissive gesture. So much for solidarity with the people. At each station we stopped at there was a welcoming party to wave flags and hand out refreshment. Even at Minsk, where we arrived at two in the morning. All volunteers, of course. Of *course* – and my other leg plays '*Rule Britannia*'.

Our hostel was on the outskirts of Moscow and we were fed communally, in cavernous marquees set out to seat hundreds. There were some fifty thousand young people attending the festival, with nationalities all mixed up. Meals were self-service. Our choice of breakfast food was laid out on long tables, and included both red and black caviar. This led to one chap queueing alongside me choosing some red, spreading it on a chunk of bread and then remarking to me 'This strawberry jam tastes fishy.' A bonus was that we were quite near the Vystavka, a permanent exhibition of life in each of the Soviet Union's constituent republics and autonomous areas. I went several times, and learned a lot. The staff in each republic's pavilion wore traditional costume and had products from their homeland laid out for inspection.

They all spoke Russian in addition to their regional language and were there to answer questions. It was the sort of 'live exhibit' that schoolchildren doing projects dream of. For us from the UK part of the attraction was that some of the regions were totally unknown to us – we'd never even heard of them and had absolutely no idea where they were. If you were given a map of Russia, could *you* indicate exactly where Tuva is or where to find the Evenki? Most British people wouldn't know whether Evenki is a place, a people, a small mammal, a wild flower or a sexually transmitted disease of reindeer ('*Sorry, Santa. Rudolph can't pull your sleigh tonight – he's got a touch of the evenks.*'). Let alone where it's spoken (*clue!*).

My new Scots friend Jock (yes – really!) had brought his kilt, and for some reason a spare one. I tried it on just for fun, but

The pavilion of the Turkmen republic

and Karelo-Finnish republic

discovering that in fact it was very comfortable I then wore it for the rest of our stay. Jock and I went round together as a lark to confuse the members of the other delegations who became totally bemused when on greeting me with the Russian word for a Scotsman – '*shotlandyets*' – I immediately riposted – '*Nyet, anglichanin.*' 'The

English wear kilts too?' 'No. Only me'. I dare say there exist family photograph albums in obscure parts of the world with pictures of two Scotsmen in national dress taken by granddad when he went to Moscow fifty years ago – only one of them said he was an Englishman. Huh? So was that an expression of cultural diversity? No. Just the English sense of humour.

In Gorki Park the city fathers had laid out paved areas for devotees of a wide range of activities: easels for artists, squares for chess players, tables for practitioners of table tennis, benches for string players and so on and so on. Whatever your hobby, if you wanted to spend time with others who shared your interest then in your free time you could go to Gorki Park to 'your' open-air space and meet other likeminded people. I was watching chess games when a group of amateur sculptors accosted me and insisted that I pose for them. I didn't kid myself that this was because of my personal pulchritude, universally admired though that has always been. It was because I had a beard. In those days that was so unusual that they'd probably never seen a real one and wanted the challenge of trying to model it in clay.

Within the walls of the Kremlin lie several cathedrals dating from the fifteenth century, and adjacent stands St Basil's. Elsewhere in the city, however, little remains of pre-nineteenth century Moscow. This is partly because the medieval town outside the fortified area (the 'kremlin') was built of wood and so unlikely to survive, especially considering the local climate. A second reason is that when Napoleon occupied the city in 1812 the inhabitants themselves set fire to it as winter approached in order to deny the invaders shelter and increase the pressure on them to abandon the occupation and go. To see more examples of medieval Russian ecclesiastical construction I would have to leave the city and travel to what tourist brochures nowadays heavily promote as 'The Golden Ring', north-east of Moscow.

My enquiries about making such a visit evoked a firmly negative response: participants in the Festival were not permitted to leave Moscow independently. I decided to see if this was really the case. The nearest town on the 'Ring' circuit, Zagorsk, was only some

50kms distant, so why not try just to get that far? If I turned up at the railway station and asked for a ticket, would I get one? Only one way to find out. It worked – no problem! Jock and I just got on the train, visited the Trinity Lavra monastery and got a train back. No one questioned us, and even though I was speaking Russian we weren't going to pass as natives when dressed in clothes obviously not 'Made in the Soviet Union' (and no – we ditched the kilts on this occasion. There is such a thing as pushing your luck!).

The Trinity Lavra monastery

There was a wide variety of organised visits and excursions on offer, and one I took was to the Valdai Hills some 350km north-west of Moscow. It was an opportunity – even rarer in those days than the chance to visit a Russian city – to see what rural Russia looked like. One of the local guides accompanying us made a lasting impression: by name Yefim ('Fima' in familiar Russian), he absolutely insisted on taking my rucksack off me and carrying it himself, even though it had only my jumper and a pocket dictionary in it and weighed practically nothing. I guess he was under instructions to make things as easy as possible for the visitors, but to take it to such an extreme was nonsensical. I protested, but he just refused to budge and I gave way to avoid embarrassing the rest of our party and maybe getting him into trouble with the authorities. But I didn't forget – as is demonstrated by the fact that although it's almost sixty years ago here I am telling you about it! (And I still remember his surname, too – but won't reveal it in case he's still alive and would be embarrassed to have the incident recalled).

In the Valdai Hills: Lake Seliger, near Ostashkov

Free tickets for performances at the Bolshoi Theatre were handed out at reception at our hostel, and I drew *Evgeny Onegin*. It was a wonderful surprise to see the inside of the theatre, knowing how much else of historic beauty and luxury the Russians had deliberately destroyed during the Revolution. We were taken on guided tours of the Kremlin, where for the first time I came face to face – literally – with Orthodox iconography (you can read more about that under 'N' – but in the Little Green Nightbook, not this one). The deepest impression was attending a service in the cathedral, because Orthodox ritual was so totally unlike what I was used to back home in my Anglican church choir. We were given places of honour at the side of what in an English church would be called the chancel, and we could hear the choir of three hundred singing behind the screen out of sight of us and the congregation. Except they weren't three hundred, just twelve. Then the archimandrite walked past us to the chancel steps, singing a rich bass *fortissimo*. As he passed me, and without any change in his facial expression, he doubled the volume! Reaching the steps, he raised his hand. The congregation, who had been standing in complete silence for nearly an hour, were awaiting this signal. He dropped his hand and they all started singing and continued for twenty minutes non-stop – all without hymn books, psalteries or anything whatever, all entirely from memory. Then the Patriarch came to the pulpit to preach his sermon, taking as his theme 'love'. He absolutely looked the part: long grey beard, very pale skin, piercing blue eyes and benign expression, and wearing a gold tiara topped by a cross and the sumptuous vestments that went with his rank. All familiar enough to most of us nowadays from television, but overwhelming to experience it for real in the Kremlin in the heart of Moscow when Russia was still the Soviet Union and officially an atheist state...

I said it left an abiding memory. After the service the Patriarch distributed tiny golden souvenir crosses to his Western guests.

I still treasure mine.

*Zagorsk, so named by the Communists in 1930 after the revolutionary activist Vladimir Zagorsky, reverted in 1991 to its original medieval name of Sergiyev Posad, which honoured its close connection with St Sergius of Radonezh, a Russian monk who in the fourteenth century founded some 40 monasteries.

Postscript
In September 2012 I visited again, in the company of my friend Mike whom you read about hitchhiking with me around Norway, and with me again (fifty-three years later!) in Ulan Bator taking photos.. Sergiev Posad is the official residence of the Patriarch of the Russian Orthodox Church, and the monastic compound was seething with tourists and all approaches lined with stalls selling souvenirs of every description. It was Sunday, and by chance also the beginning of 'term' for new seminarians, who were all gathered on the steps of the cathedral for a group photo under the gaze of proud parents and other family members (also taking photos).

Goodnight.

August 1957

EPILOGUE
TO MARGARET

And her eyes were of the sea, my lads,
And her eyes were of the sea.
And the blue of the far, far distant blue
Of horizons lost in the sun-dipped blue
Of the sea on a solent summer's day.
With a yacht sail thwart of a breeze o' the west
And a wafting gull and a wisp of my hair
And Beaulieu's creek and a tramper's smoke
And her eyes were of the sea, my lads,
And her eyes were of the sea.

On Lepe's mere strand and the distant isle
Which lead a-down to the needling crag
And the great full-riggers which once on a day
Proudly the name of England bore
To the lands which are far away.
And a tricorn hat and Elizabeth's men,
The walls of Southampton standing alert,
And Sally-port of Portsmouth old,
The Nab Tower's brood like chessmen placed
And the yachts of Cowes and Hamble a-port
Of this shade of a tree on the Solent shore
And her eyes were of the sea, my lads,
And her eyes were of the sea.

A shot in the arm and drug to my soul
Is the blue of the far, far distant blue
And the sun a-glinting the Solent's crests.
The toil of the world can pass me by
With its struggle of power and such worthless things
And its claim to dictate who is friend or foe
And where I may go and what believe
Be it mausoleum by Kremlin wall
Or he who died on Calvary.
For when these are forgotten and Man gone too
Who will remain with none to view
The blue of the far, far distant blue
Of horizons lost in the sun-dipped blue
Of the sea on a solent summer's day?
And the eyes that are of the sea, my lads,
And the eyes that are of the sea.

21 August 1957
Frankfurt a/Main

Between 1944 and 1968 the Students' Union at Southampton University published a literary magazine, *Second Wessex*. This poem appeared in the Spring 1958 edition.

ACKNOWLEDGMENTS

The author wishes to express his thanks to:

My one-time next door neighbour Derek Snowdon, now an established artist, for his creativity in many of the stories in providing amusing illustrations.

My long-standing friend Carol Boulton, proprietor of Russell Stables in West End, Southampton, and mastermind behind the Epona Trust, for reading initial drafts of these stories and suggesting adjustments.

My oldest friend, Mike Roberts, whose recollections of hitchhiking with me in Norway in 1959 helped shamfer the edges of those particular stories, and whose photos taken when we travelled to Mongolia in 2012 provided complementary visual material.

To Judith Blake, on behalf of Sarsen Press, for her forbearance in patiently accepting the frequent amendments over many months to which my original drafts were subjected in order to produce the final result.

THE SOME[

DAVID J. GATWARD

DG CREATIVE LTD

Ashes of Betrayal
by
David J. Gatward

Copyright © 2024 by David J. Gatward
All rights reserved.

Author photography by
@chrisbaileyheadshots, Facebook/chrisbaileyphotography

No part of this book may be reproduced in any form or by any electronic or mechanical means, including information storage and retrieval systems, without written permission from the author, except for the use of brief quotations in a book review.

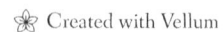

❀ Created with Vellum

This book is dedicated to all those I've been lucky enough to meet at Babington House; you have not only provided me with the most astonishing second home and place to write, but a level of support and friendship, during a really tough year, that still stuns me.

I would also like to give a very special mention to the following folk, for being particularly wonderful (and if I've missed anyone out, you can be in the next book!):

Fish, Haydn, Francesca, Hannah, Magda, Roman, Asta, Neil, Eleazar, Alex, Mannish, Rachel, Evan, Dom, Bryony, Olivia, Jack, Will, Aimee, Sophie, Ez, Mickey, Juan, Alex, Jon, and Donna.

> "The people who wound us get no say
> in how we clean up the blood."
> – Harriet Selina –

25 YEARS AGO, 1:45PM ...

Jennifer Clayton, Jenny to her friends, twenty-one and fresh out of university, and with the rest of her life ahead of her, was covered—no, she was drenched—in blood. With her t-shirt half ripped off and her jeans slashed, and her arms lacerated so badly that in places flaps of skin were hanging from her like swollen, blood-soaked bandages, she looked like a walking horror movie. And that, after all, was the point. Everything stuck to everything else, and her black fringe, thick with gore, hung down in front of her face like iron railings around a churchyard.

'You ready?'

The question was from Austin Clarke, a handsome young man with broad shoulders, scruffy brown hair, and an almost unhealthy interest in agriculture. This would generally surface whenever he spotted a random piece of farming equipment trundling along the lanes, or shuffling across the Somerset fields around the house Jenny had lived in her whole life.

Jennifer laughed to herself; calling where she lived a house was to undersell it a little, what with the dozen bedrooms, acreage, and walled garden. There was a woodland, too, not just the one by the lake, but another up a short footpath crossing a field, and she had spent many a day exploring there as a child.

As for Austin, they'd met during freshers' week, never once fancied each other, much to the bemusement of their circle of friends, and been like brother and sister ever since. Jennifer had often wondered why the spark of romance had never flared between them, had even tried to persuade herself to try and fancy him, but that essential flame had simply never been there. Friendship it was, and friendship it would always be; there were worse things. He had been the first person she'd asked to join her in making a movie that summer. And he'd said yes without a second's thought.

'How do I look?' she asked.

Austin took a moment to really take in the vision of violence before him.

'Like you've been chased around the house by a crazy person with a very big knife.'

Jennifer turned to look at herself again in the wall mirror at her side.

They were up in her bedroom, a place that had been her sanctuary her whole life, growing with her, yet still containing echoes of various versions of her past selves; her first teddy bear, some dolls she'd apparently pretended were the Prince and Princess of Wales and who would always come for tea at the weekend; various posters of boy bands, and her most precious item in the world, a handmade jewellery box sitting on her dressing table beside the mirror. It was a little rough around the edges now, but still beautiful, if not more so because of its well-loved, rustic charm. It had belonged to her mum. Jennifer had loved it as a kid, sitting on her mum's lap to lift the lid and hear the tune it played, and to watch the little ballerina rise and pirouette. Remembering her mum, she lifted the lid and watched the ballerina dance to the music. She thought about how the box still held so many treasures, both real and remembered, and a few secrets too, in the scratches and worn edges.

'Do you think we need more blood?'

'Not sure we've that much left,' Austin said.

'This is a horror movie though, isn't it? We need buckets of the stuff.'

'Which is what we've used,' laughed Austin.

Jennifer played with a flap of the skin on her arm.

'Special effects makeup was my favourite part of the course, you know?'

'I can tell,' Austin grinned, then poked one of the cuts on her arm.

Jennifer flinched.

'Ouch!'

'Excellent acting there,' said Austin with mock applause. 'Some of your best work.' Then he added, 'It's good of your dad to let us do this, you know? Film a movie in your house.'

Jennifer shrugged. There were eight of them in total, all staying in the house.

Though being asked first, Austin had made it clear he didn't want to appear on screen, so he had taken on the title of producer, and done a good job at keeping everything in check.

'He could hardly say no to a daughter who's just graduated with a degree in film, could he?'

ONE

Detective Inspector Gordanian Haig was sitting at a small table in a tiny room at the top of a short, narrow flight of stairs. Opposite her was another woman, bedecked in flowing garments of assorted colours and numerous scarves, her wrists adorned with so many bangles that they were part limb, part musical instrument.

The room's décor was really leaning into the idea that all surfaces must be covered in crushed velvet, and Gordy found herself wondering, if she fidgeted too much, would she get a shock from the build-up of static electricity? That thought reminded her of a scene from Superman III that had terrified her as a child, where a female villain had been pulled into a supercomputer and turned into a cyborg. There would be advantages to that, she thought; at the very least, she wouldn't have to keep thinking of the one thing that refused to leave her brain: Anna, and her dreadful absence.

To her left, a window stared out into a day that had promised sunshine but had delivered rain, the windowsill comprising a neat display of various crystals. No fairies and not a wand in sight, though, so that was something. Not even a tiny dragon guarding a glimmering egg.

The woman held out her hands and Gordy stared at the deck of oversized cards they were holding spread out in front of her.

'Point at the seven cards you would like to pick,' the woman said.

She had a very kind smile, thought Gordy, and counted out seven cards as instructed.

The woman removed the cards from the deck, then laid them out on the table in a cross, facedown, with five cards down the middle, and the two remaining cards on either side of the one in the centre.

'Now, is there anything in particular you would like to know or talk about?' the woman asked, as she rested the rest of the deck to one side.

Why the hell I'm here in the first place would be a start, Gordy thought, but kept that to herself; she'd never been to a card reading in her life, had always considered it to be abject nonsense, and yet here she was, sitting in a room in Glastonbury, doing exactly that. What the hell am I thinking? Am I really this desperate for direction, or just that lost? Both, she thought, and more besides.

Then Gordy saw Anna's face in her mind. But she always saw Anna's face, didn't she? Everywhere she went, every moment of every day, it was always there, smiling and laughing and filling her life with a joy now crushed and broken, a thing turned to ash.

'I'm not sure,' she said, hearing the huge lie in those words. 'I think I'm just intrigued.'

'About what?' the woman asked, an eyebrow raised enough to show she knew Gordy wasn't being entirely truthful.

Gordy gave a shrug. She didn't want to say too much. She knew enough from her decades in the police that reading people was a skill you learned and could use to your advantage. She was worried that if she started, she wouldn't stop, and she wasn't here to bare her shattered heart and broken soul to a total stranger dressed like an extra from The Voyages of Sinbad. Neither was she going to let the tears come, though they were there, as they always were, right on the edge of breaking through.

The woman smiled.

'Okay,' she said. 'Just relax, and we'll see what the cards tell us; how does that sound?'

'It sounds fine, I think?' Gordy said, her reply voiced as a question, because she really wasn't sure about any of this, and was half tempted to just get up and leave. But that would be rude. Also, she'd just forked out sixty quid for the pleasure, so she was going to get her money's worth, regardless.

After explaining how it worked, and having used the word *energy* just a little too often for Gordy's comfort, the woman reached out a hand. She turned over the card in the centre of the cross, the gems in the rings on her fingers catching the light like fallen stars.

'Ah,' she said, her voice bright. 'New beginnings.'

Gordy laughed, but heard and felt no humour in it.

'I bet you always say that, am I right?'

The woman cocked her head to one side.

'Only if the cards tell me to,' she said, then pointed to the card she had turned over. 'See? That's what this one actually says, and you picked it at random, remember?'

'Can't argue with that,' Gordy said, though knew just how easy it was for someone skilled enough to force a card to be chosen. 'What does it mean, then, this new beginnings?'

The woman clapped her hands together excitedly.

'Best way to look at it is like this ... you're standing on a bridge, behind you is everything you already know, yes? But you've decided, for whatever reason, to go and live on planet Mars ...'

Somerset isn't exactly Mars, thought Gordy, but she understood the point. Sort of. The reason she would keep to herself for now.

'You're not from round here, are you?' the woman stated, narrowing her eyes.

'The accent is a bit of a clue, I think,' said Gordy.

The woman shook her head.

'That's not what I mean. You're not on holiday though, are you? You're not dressed for it.'

'I didn't know there was a way I was supposed to dress.'

'There isn't, but my guess is that you're in your everyday wardrobe, rather than your away-from-it-all one.'

'I've just moved here,' Gordy said. 'Well, not here exactly, not to

Glastonbury, but to the area. Little place called Evercreech. Thought I'd go exploring.'

'New beginnings it is, then, see? Just like the cards said. And what's coming, well, it's really exciting, isn't it? But also, it's really petrifying.'

'Not so sure about the exciting part,' said Gordy. 'But the petrifying? That's about right.'

And it was, thought Gordy, because what she was facing every day, on her own, twisted her gut into knots made her feel sick.

'That's because this isn't a normal everyday new beginning,' the woman continued. 'This is going to challenge your very being, your very soul. And the reason for that is because there's a conflict between the part of you that really wants to do it, and this other part that wants to just run the hell away.'

Suddenly, Gordy was no longer in that room, but back in the flat she had just moved into. The furniture was built, not that there was much of it, but the boxes were still unpacked, huddled together in the corners of the rooms as though discussing among themselves how long it would be.

That was two weeks ago, and she was still living out of her suitcase. Living off microwave meals and meal replacement shakes, simply because she didn't have the energy to think, to plan, to care about food. She knew that she was trying to make what she was doing seem transient, but that was because anything else would make it all too real. Not just the move, but Anna's death.

Thanks to roadworks and awful traffic, the journey down from Wensleydale, where she had lived and worked for goodness knew how long, had taken her longer than she'd planned. She'd arrived late, and the removal truck not at all. Her first night had been spent in a sleeping bag on the floor of an empty flat, her only meal a collection of various things in packets she'd picked up at motorway service stations on her way down; nothing said *this didn't go according to plan* quite like a post-midnight feast of dry-roasted peanuts, a limp cheese and onion sandwich, a small packet of chocolate digestives, and a couple of cans of warm gin and tonic.

She'd told herself there hadn't been time to unpack, but that was a lie. All she seemed to have was time. Too much time. Too much time alone, in her head, in her memories, in her grief.

The woman's voice pulled Gordy back into the present.

'... writing letters to each other.'

'What? Who's writing letters?'

'The two parts of yourself are, that's who,' the woman said. 'You need to get them to communicate, that's all.'

'I do? By writing letters? Well, I'll no' going to be doing that.'

Gordy could see that the woman knew she hadn't been listening, but the deep frown that creased her face seemed to show that she wasn't so much irritated, as concerned.

'It's all about the pros and the cons; there's a part of you that doesn't want this change, wants to run away from it, and there's this other part that's telling you to embrace it, and get on with it.'

'But you just said something about writing letters.'

'You can do it like that if you want, or you can just write a list of pros and cons; either way, you'll have a better understanding of where you are right now and where it is that you're going.'

Good luck with that, Gordy thought.

'And just so you know,' the woman continued, 'that first voice, the negative one, it's just being protective, that's all. It's making sure you're okay, and that you're fully aware of the dangers that lie ahead. And that other voice, it can be a little bullish, can't it, if that makes sense? Likes to push you on, even when you really don't want to. You need to make all the parts of you work well together. Nice and simple, really.'

'I'll do the lists,' said Gordy, fairly sure that she would do no such thing. 'No letters though; writing to myself sounds like a step too close to losing the plot.'

The woman reached for the next card.

'Peace.'

'What about it?'

'Your soul needs a bit of a rest.'

Gordy shook her head, then rubbed her eyes to force the tears back inside. She wasn't going to allow them to fall, not today.

'You have no idea,' she said.

'The cards do though, don't they?'

Gordy said nothing, biting her tongue to stop her saying, 'Do they, though?'

'It seems to me that you've a lot going on,' the woman said, and Gordy was starting to see how good she was at what she did. Her voice was soft and calm and open, the kind of voice you could listen to for hours, that would send a room of children peacefully to sleep with a story. 'Personally, professionally, and every other *ly* you can think of; all of this change you're in the middle of, all the conflict, try and find some peace in it.'

'Easier said than done,' Gordy replied.

How the hell was she supposed to find peace when she was living with a broken heart so painful she could feel the hole inside her, the emptiness, a well of despair so deep that sometimes she wished it would just swallow her whole and be done with it.

'I know, but it doesn't take much,' said the woman. 'Go for a paddle in a stream, take a book and rest a while in a field, why not try a forest spa?'

Gordy frowned at that.

'A what now?'

She'd never heard of such a thing, but had a sneaking suspicion it involved getting naked and being hit by twigs, neither of which she was in the mood for, and certainly not as a joint activity.

'Go for a walk through the woods, breathe it in, that's all I'm saying,' the woman explained. 'The trees are wise, you know, and they'll help if you let them.'

Of course they are, Gordy thought, starting to lose her grip on the reality of the moment, panic creeping through her veins like an army of tiny spiders. She was getting fidgety. Coming here was a bad idea. It was making her think about things she didn't want to think about, and all of those things, every single damned one of them, centred around Anna. Yes, there was the move and the small issue of the new job she was starting in a couple of days, in which she had zero interest at all. But it was all so small when compared to the bottomless rift that had been carved so brutally into her by the loss of—

'...sex.'

'What?'

Gordy saw that the next card had the word *passion* on it.

'You need to have more sex.'

Ignoring how blunt and forward that statement was, Gordy waited for the woman to elaborate, if only because she had nothing she could offer herself.

'I don't just mean the physical,' the woman said, then tapped her temple with a bejewelled finger. 'It's about what's up here, in your head. And neither does it necessarily mean *doing it*.'

'Doing it?' Gordy repeated, laughing a little. 'Can't say as I remember the last time I heard someone call it that.'

'Well, you can do it in other ways, you know.'

'Sex? How do you mean? And please, for both our sakes, don't say tantric.'

'You need to think about how sex makes you feel, that euphoria, that release, that sense of abandonment, that's what this is about; finding something that gives you that, outside of everything else that's going on.'

'Easier said than done.'

'It can be sex, and who's going to ever say they don't need more of that? But it could be swimming or music or drumming, anything, really, that gives you that ... thing ...'

The woman did a sort of excited shiver, closed her eyes for a moment, then let out a faint moan.

Gordy very much hoped she hadn't just witnessed what she had a horrible feeling she very much had, or at least a very good impression of.

'You mean a hobby.'

'Can sex be a hobby? I suppose so. But yes, if that's how you want to look at it; see if you can find something outside of your everyday that'll give you—'

'You'll be moving on to the next card now, yes?' said Gordy, encouraging the woman to turn over the next card before she blessed her with another bit of hugely inappropriate acting.

For the next few minutes, Gordy watched the cards turn, listened to the woman's voice, and talked. She hadn't meant to. In fact, ignoring that she still had no real idea as to why she'd ended up there in the first place, she found herself talking so much that by the end of the session, she felt not just exhausted by it, but relieved.

They had talked about the move, yes, and the job, but in the end it was Anna who had pushed through to the front of everything, taking over the discussion as though it was her rightful place.

How could it not be? Gordy thought. Anna's absence was so raw, the echo of it so deafening, that Gordy found herself back in that hospital hearing the news, almost as though her life had, at that very moment, stopped, just like Anna's heart. Because, if she was truly honest with herself, it had. Yes, she'd moved forward, lived and breathed and spoken to people and gone for walks and gone to bed and got up again and moved house and ... and none of it meant or felt like she was living.

'You'll be okay, you know?'

The woman's voice cut into Gordy's thoughts.

'Pardon?'

'You don't feel it, love, I can see that and I hear it, too. And not now, either, because you can't. These things can't be rushed, not unless you want to damage yourself even more, but you will. Not today, not tomorrow, but little things will happen, small changes, and eventually the sun will break through the cloud.'

'Very poetic.'

'Hardly.'

The woman reached out and before Gordy could react, she took hold of her hands. Gordy hadn't realised that her own hands were even on the table.

Holding her gaze, she said, 'From what you've said, and from what I've heard, you're here because of someone else, not you.'

Well, that was perceptive, thought Gordy, and said, 'Pretty much.'

'There's a hurt in you,' the woman continued. 'I can see it as well as feel it. It's in your eyes, your body language, your skin.'

Gordy went to pull her hands away, but something kept them there. She wanted to keep everything private, to not let on, but there was something about the moment, the safety of it, the privacy, and the way the woman was staring at her, that made the walls she was built suddenly just crumble.

'Annd,' she said, her voice breaking with the hurt of it all. 'I moved here because of her. It was her job we were following, her "calling" as she would describe it, and there's very little you can do to argue your point with a vicar when God has told them to move house, trust me!'

Something splintered in Gordy, and she heard her own broken whimper, then felt the tears fall at last. She didn't care that the woman didn't exactly know what she was on about; she was saying things now as much to hear them herself as anything, as though voicing them made them even more real and forced her to face them head-on.

'I miss her,' she sobbed, her words thrown out into the room like driftwood on the crest of waves. 'Every moment of every day, I miss her. She was my heart, my soul, my every tomorrow! And now she's everywhere I go because she isn't there, you know? The absence of her fills my head with this god-awful silent scream and it's there all the time. Anna's right there, wherever I am, whatever I'm doing, because I can't call her, because I can't send her a text, because I won't see her when I get back after this, because everything that I'm doing now, from this moment 'til forever, will be without her! And that's why ... that's why I can't ...'

'Can't what?'

'Bloody well move on!' Gordy snapped back, her voice javelin-sharp and thrown hard.

The woman took a long slow breath, exhaled, looking again into Gordy's eyes, yet somehow deeper still.

'I'm going to break with protocol now,' she said, and gave Gordy's hands a squeeze. 'The cards, they had a few things to say, but now? Well, now I'm going to say something myself, so I hope you're listening ...'

'Not sure I've much choice in the matter, have I?' Gordy smiled.

'None at all.'

'Thought not.'

'I want you to be kind to yourself,' the woman said. 'Grief isn't something you just move on from, and the reason for that is that moving on means leaving things behind, and you can't really do that, can you? Don't answer—of course you can't! Why? Because grief is simply all of that love you have, but with nowhere for it to go. And this love you have—not *had*, okay, but *have*—for Anna, it's everything that you are, isn't it? She was your morning, your midnight, and she's never going to be anything else.'

'Not so sure that's healthy. I can't be like this forever. I just can't.'

'And you won't be, either, because Anna's love for you won't let you, and neither will your love for yourself.'

'This is stretching into the realms of counselling more than a card reading,' Gordy said. 'Though, from my own experience, counsellors don't usually give advice, do they? They usually just keep throwing questions at you to help you come up with your own answers.'

'Well, bollocks to that,' the woman said, the sudden change of tack in how she spoke making Gordy laugh. 'I see a broken heart before me, and a good soul, so I'm going to give advice. And I have; it's down to you whether you listen or not.'

'Be kind to myself, then ...'

'I've not finished.'

'Are you sure? Can you no' just bring it all to a close now?'

'No.'

'Oh ...'

For the next few minutes, Gordy just listened.

When the session came to an end, and she found herself outside, Gordy still had no answer as to why she had ended up in Glastonbury, sitting in a velvet room having her cards read. In a daze, she walked down the high street, wondered briefly about popping into the abbey, then decided against it, mainly because she needed cake.

Managing to avoid popping into any one of the numerous shops she passed, all of which were selling what looked to be the same collection of crystals, incense sticks, patchwork clothes, and candles, but from slightly different display units, Gordy navigated her way to a small, vegan café. She then ordered a huge slice of their chocolate cake and a pot of tea, and sat down in a corner, far enough away to give herself some space.

New beginnings, she thought, as she took her first mouthful, then noticed something; when she'd picked up her cutlery for the cake, she'd grabbed two forks, rather than just one.

The café shifted, melted, and for the briefest of moments, Gordy saw Anna sitting opposite her. She was smiling, and the few faint freckles she carried were shining brighter than usual. Then she was gone, the café was back to normal, and Gordy reached for her tea. She remembered something the woman had given her, having dashed off at the end of their session into another room. It was a sheet of paper. Gordy had thought nothing of it at the time, but now she removed it from her pocket, and unfolded it.

She saw the words, *Stages of Grief,* and beneath them, a simple diagram, like a valley, starting on the right with Loss and Hurt, dropping to the bottom of the valley then back up again to Loss Adjustment. Her eyes fell down the left side of the valley too easily, as she tumbled through shock and numbness and denial, banged into emotional outbursts and then anger, smashed herself to pieces on fear and searching and disorganisation, until finally she came to a stop, slowing down through panic and guilt, to lie in loneliness and isolation and depression.

Gordy stared at the sheet of paper for a long, long time. She felt all of those things all at once, and could see no way to ever crawl up the other side, out of the valley. Looking at it, reading what it comprised, almost terrified her more than where she was in her life right now. How could she have new strengths, new relationships, hope? Because if she did, then that meant she was leaving Anna behind, and she didn't want to, not yet ... not yet.

Later, with her day behind her, the memory of the chocolate cake as much as the card-reading still vivid in her mind, and the sheet on grief back in a pocket, Gordy let herself into her flat. She marched down the hallway into the lounge, and stood in front of a pile of boxes.

'Just the one,' she said to herself. 'That's all. Just the one ...' She grabbed the box sitting on top of all the others, placed it on the floor in front of her sofa, and ripped it open.

TWO

Monday arrived with all the clamour and symphony of a damp firework dying in a muddy puddle on a dank November evening. Gordy had spent the weekend trying to unpack. She'd managed three boxes, but given up on the rest. All of it had proved too exhausting. Instead, she'd spent her time walking some of the thin lanes that stretched out from the village of Evercreech as though tying the tiny, quiet outpost to the landscape like guide ropes on a tent.

When the unpacking had become too much, she'd tried to watch television. That had only served to put her on edge, making her feel like she was wasting the day. And perhaps she was, but she didn't need quiz shows and sitcom reruns to remind her.

The session with the card reader had been interesting. It had allowed her to talk through things a little, which she had never been all that good at, not really. Always better to put a brave face on it, and to help others, than to let others in and accept their help.

She had read the sheet on grief numerous times, even stuck it to the wall. It was a reminder that what she was going through was normal, that she shouldn't be afraid. But she was, because sometimes —even last night—she would feel out of control. It was the tears that confused her the most, because she had never been a crier. Now though? Now, she could cry at any moment. There would be no reason, no trigger, they would just come, and with them would be the memories and that god-awful emptiness inside, echoing the sound of a voice she would never hear again.

The village of Evercreech, her new home, was just away from the main road, which connected the small market towns of Shepton Mallet and Castle Cary. Had Anna been there, she would have been starting her new role as the vicar at the local church. On a stroll, Gordy had to force herself to walk past the ancient place of worship.

Gordy had ventured through Shepton Mallet only briefly, having driven into the car park for the supermarket before quickly driving out again, a strange sense of panic gripping her at the idea of going inside. All those people, busy with their lives, and her in limbo, just drifting from one simple task to the next, not living really at all, just getting by.

The lanes around Evercreech were narrow things, lined with a mix of wall and greenery. Though the deeper into the rolling countryside Gordy ventured, she discovered the wilder and taller the hedges grew, and the walls were less apparent. Along one lane she decided to venture into the fields, and hopped over a wooden stile to stroll through a pasture. Soon, she was by a tiny stream, and for a while she had simply stood there, listening to it, remembering what the woman over in Glastonbury had said about being kind to herself.

When Sunday afternoon slipped into the evening, Gordy had done her best to make it last as long as she could, dreading as she was the next day, her first on the job. She managed to unpack another box, had gone for a walk, only to find the evening had fallen dark quicker than she had expected, and she'd been left to depend on the torch on her phone to find her way back. Not that navigating was difficult, or that she had wandered far, but she'd found another little footpath across some fields. The ground was sunk deep with holes from cattle she'd seen roaming there earlier in the day, but were thankfully now shut in somewhere. What with cows supposedly killing more people a year in the country than any other animal, she was in no mood to deal with their criminal bovine ways.

The rest of that evening she'd spent reading up on the notes about the team she'd be looking after, the detective chief inspector she'd be working under, and anything else that had come to hand or seemed relevant to the sender. Gordy had no doubt that life here would be quite different to how things had been up in the Dales, but in exactly what ways, she couldn't rightly guess. Nor did she want to; she was trying to forget that life a little, to force herself to take on the challenge before her, but it was anything but easy. Caring about her new responsibilities, her team, the local community, seemed a big ask.

Forcing herself to go to bed, Gordy had pushed the window open to keep the room cool, then laid awake till past midnight, staring into the darkness, with half a mind to just get up, pack up, and sod off. Because in those moments, when the night crammed itself into her bedroom to suffocate her, she could think of nothing more than escaping, just running and running and running.

But to where? she thought. Because running would solve nothing, simply because she would always be there herself, wouldn't she, at the end of any journey? The memories would follow, the thoughts and the questions and the pain. Something had kept her where she was, prevented her from jumping into her car and heading for the horizon. Somewhere out in the garden, a pigeon had cooed softly, and yet more tears had come, these gentle, and with barely a sob, as they had slipped down her face to dampen her pillow.

GORDY'S new workplace was in the market town of Frome. She had pronounced that wrong immediately when she'd popped along to the small bakery in Evercreech to grab something for lunch, and ended up chatting to the woman at the checkout.

'No, it's not Frome as in Rome,' she'd said, 'it's Frome as in room.'

'Then why's it spelt like that?' Gordy had asked. 'Should it no' at the very least have two Os in it, instead of just the one?'

The woman had just shrugged.

'I guess.'

Driving to Frome from Evercreech, Gordy had had two choices: to take either the main road, which would be faster and, she suspected, probably more stressful, or the back roads, which would be anything but fast, but would at least give her time to process what she was doing. And she really needed that time, because the only way she was ever going to arrive at her new job was to physically force herself to get in her car and go, when all she really wanted to do was lock the door, close the curtains, and hide. So, the back roads it was, and with a carrier bag holding a generously filled coronation chicken bap, a slice of coffee and walnut cake, crisps, and a drink, she hopped into her vehicle and headed out of Evercreech towards the village of Batcombe.

Though Evercreech sat on relatively flat ground, the fields around it like a vast patchwork rug cast upon the Earth, soon the roads rose steeply. More so than Gordy had expected, and the hedges on either side quickly blocked the view. At points, she felt as though she were driving along a tunnel lined with hedge and hoary old trees, with nettles and long grass hanging out into the lane to brush her wheels as she rolled past.

Unsure of the road ahead, Gordy knew she was probably going slower than someone local to the area, but it hardly mattered. Even though Batcombe was only three miles from Evercreech, she ended up stuck behind three tractors on the way, one of which she'd had to do a double-take at, sure that it was being driven by a dog, only to see that the huge hound simply dwarfed its owner.

The sight of the dog actually made Gordy laugh, a sound that took her by surprise, and she found herself remembering the two dogs who had practically become members of the team in the Dales. One was a black Labrador called Smudge who belonged to Harry Grimm, the DCI who had moved to the Dales from this area a few years ago. The other was a Border Collie called Fly, who went everywhere with its owner Jim Metcalf, who was a PCSO and a farmer.

Gordy wouldn't be getting herself a dog, despite so many people advising her that it would be a really good idea. She begged to differ, and strongly; yes, she was on her own, and so suddenly that the wrench of it still pierced her mind, but putting that on an animal just didn't seem fair. Maybe one day, but for now, Gordy was set on getting used to being on her own, no matter how hard. If the thought of getting a dog seemed like a bad idea, then the thought of meeting someone else horrified her beyond all belief, because the Anna-shaped hole in her life bled freely still, and no one could stop it.

The road dipped sharply before rising steeply again. At a crossroads with zero visibility either way, Gordy eased forward, only to have the sound of a car horn blare at her, forcing her to slam on her brakes. A black Range Rover then flew past, at what speed she didn't dare to even guess, and was gone before she even had a chance to register its passing. Amazingly, she managed to clock the numberplate. Maybe she'd ask someone to look into finding the owner and then pop round to have a word about the importance of driving safely and appropriately, rather than like some creature breaking free from Hell's clutches.

Giving the crossroads another go, this time Gordy floored it, blasting out of the road she was on to dash across the one in front of her, and then up a small rise opposite onto another lane. This brought her to the top end of Batcombe. To her left she saw another ancient church, almost the twin of the one back in Evercreech, then a signpost to a pub, before she pushed on through the rest of the village.

Houses lined each side of the road as though facing each other off in some age-old staring competition. As she drove down the middle of the road, she was aware of expensive cars on either side, a good number of which were considerably outside her price bracket.

Though Gordy hadn't visited many of the villages and towns in the area yet, she had already seen a marked difference between the ones in Somerset and those in the Dales. Both were popular destinations for tourists. She had a sense that Somerset was home to a considerably more varied population, made up not just of those who had lived there for their whole lives, but people who had moved to the area either for work, or because they had plenty of money and fancied living the country life. And who could blame them? she thought. Though nothing like the Dales, the area had a beauty to it.

Coming to what was nearing the end of the village, Gordy spotted the same Range Rover that had nearly slammed her into a hedge. Well, perhaps that was an exaggeration, but there had been no need for the driver to blast along the lane like they had.

She checked the clock, knew she'd given herself plenty of leeway to get to the station without having to rush, and decided that there was no time like the present to throw herself into the new job. Yes, she was a detective inspector, and yes, there were probably other things to concern herself with right now, but if she just drove on and said nothing, it would bug her for the rest of the day. Even more so if the idiot at the wheel ended up having a prang, injuring someone, or worse.

Slowing down, Gordy pulled up in front of the Range Rover.

THREE

Before Gordy even had a chance to turn off the engine and unclip her seatbelt, her ears were witness to one of the loudest car horns she'd ever heard. It came again, twice more, but she ignored it, opened her door, and climbed out.

The driver wasn't entirely visible, the bright light of the morning reflecting harshly off the windscreen.

The horn came again, and Gordy wondered if the driver hadn't yet clocked her uniform; it was her first day, after all, and it was always sensible to make a good impression. Just because she had 'detective' in her job title didn't mean she got to race around the streets in jeans and a hoodie, lobbing criminals across the bonnet of her car and yelling, 'You're nicked, son!'

More was the pity, Gordy thought, because that was something she'd never done, and had always wondered what it felt like. Ridiculous was the only word that sprung immediately to mind, because she had never been able to see herself as that kind of detective.

Though, right then, with how she was feeling, that kind of activity might serve as good therapy. For a moment she dared to play out a scenario in her mind where the driver jumped out and attacked her, giving her no choice but to defend herself, and violently.

Gordy walked up to the Range Rover, then along to the driver's door. The window, darkly tinted and hiding the driver from view, was still up, so she rapped a knuckle against the glass.

The window didn't so much disappear into the door as get sucked down into it.

'Good morning,' Gordy said, her voice bright, and her smile not even forced. She'd been stressed beyond belief about this day, but now that she was all dressed up in her finery—she knew that was over-selling it, but she didn't really care—she found herself relaxing into the role she'd inhabited for decades. It was rather comfortable. She wasn't happy, not by a long shot, but this was a character she knew how to play, so that's exactly what she did.

The driver was a woman aged anything from thirty to fifty, and Gordy wouldn't have dared hazard a guess. She was confused as to whether it was due to the heavy makeup, a nip and tuck, a very healthy diet that no doubt comprised mainly kale and pine nuts, or a terrifying combination of all three.

The woman's hair, black enough to shine with the very faintest hint of blue, was pulled back into a ponytail, a pair of oversized and no doubt expensive sunglasses were perched on her tiny, perfect nose, and she was, from the little Gordy could see, wearing what would best be described as activewear.

Gordy, to put it bluntly, hated activewear. That it had become some kind of strange fashion statement baffled her. Yes, by all means, wear it *while active*, or when coming or going to some kind of fitness activity, but for the love of God, don't just go wearing it as a replacement for a T-shirt and jeans. But then, maybe the woman was doing exactly that, so Gordy did her best to not judge, not yet.

'I'm in a hurry,' the woman said, not turning to look at Gordy. Her accent was of no fixed abode, as though its edges had been eroded on purpose to allow it to fit in anywhere. 'I had to drop something off and—'

'So I gather,' said Gordy, her expression passive. 'You passed me a few minutes ago. Going at quite a pace, too, I must say.'

'Well, it's rather hard to hurry somewhere if you go slowly, don't you think? Kind of defeats the object.'

The woman then cocked her head forward and to one side just enough to allow her to look at Gordy over the top of her sunglasses, a gesture that in Gordy's current heightened state made her want to reach in, rip them from her face, and crush them underfoot.

'I think it's always best to make sure you give yourself plenty of time to get to where you're going, so that you don't have to rush in the first place. And even if you do have to rush, it's best not to, just in case. Because we all make mistakes, little errors, if we're no' thinking straight, don't we?'

Gordy watched her reply settle on the woman's face and turn from a look of mild condescension into an expression of wild irritation.

'Well, that's okay for you, I'm sure,' the woman snapped back. 'But some people—me, for example—rarely have plenty of time just sloshing about in the footwell of our car for us to dip into whenever we want, do we?'

Another voice, considerably younger and very tired, joined in the conversation from the darkness hiding in the back of the vehicle.

'Mummy, why are you talking to that woman?'

Gordy peered inside the Range Rover and saw, sitting behind the woman, a boy, maybe eight or nine years old.

'Don't worry,' the woman said. 'We'll be at school soon.'

'This is the school run, then?' Gordy asked, annoyance now turning to anger, because this woman had risked not just her own safety, but that of a child. 'And where would that be, if I wanted to find it?'

'Somewhere over there,' the woman said, waving a hand at nothing in particular. 'I don't know. I just follow the satnav.'

Gordy waved at the boy. He smiled and waved back.

'I don't want to go to school,' he said, looking at Gordy. 'We have to do hockey. The last time we played I got hit really hard on the ankle by Albie and he thought it was funny, but it wasn't, and he never said sorry, so I hit him back, and we got in dead big trouble, but it wasn't my fault, and that's not fair.'

'Well, you have to go to school,' the woman said, then turned to face Gordy. 'Will there be anything else?'

Gordy gave that question a fair amount of silence at first, to keep herself calm, but to also pile on the pressure a little.

'Just a wee word of advice,' she said eventually, leaning in close and lowering her voice. 'Ease up a bit, okay? You're carrying precious cargo back there, aren't you? And that's more valuable than any appointment, any deadline, any meeting you can think of, believe you me.'

'Well, of course he is,' the woman replied. 'And I don't like what you're suggesting at all.'

Gordy narrowed her eyes.

'And I don't like people driving like idiots and putting not only their own lives in danger, but the lives of others, too. That makes me angry, and when I get angry, I tend to keep an eye on those people a little more closely than others, you hear me?'

Shock lit up the other woman's eyes like fireworks.

'What? You can't spy on me! That's ... Well, it's an infringement of my rights!'

'Mummy, what's precious cargo?' the boy asked from the back of the vehicle.

'Nothing,' the woman said, her eyes still on Gordy. Then she said, 'I don't appreciate being told how to run my life.'

'And I don't appreciate turning up at vehicle collisions wondering what I'm going to find,' Gordy replied.

'But I didn't hit you! I didn't crash! What are you talking about?'

Gordy stepped back from the vehicle.

'Hopefully, I won't be seeing you again,' she said.

'You know, I didn't move all the way out here from London to be hassled by the police.'

'Then, what a relief it must be to know that you're no' being hassled at all, merely graciously advised on how to improve your driving.' Gordy tapped her cap badge. 'Here to serve, you see; to make sure people such as yourself arrive at their destination safe and sound. And it's been a pleasure to have helped.'

'A pleasure? But ... I mean ... What?'

Gordy went to head back to her own vehicle, but turned one last time to face the woman.

'One last thing,' she said, leaning in close enough that her head was now inside the vehicle. 'Try to stop thinking about everything as your right. It's a little bugbear of mine, you see, and it puts me on edge. Instead, why don't you focus on your responsibilities; you'll be surprised, not just by how differently you'll live, but how much happier you might be. Now, you get on and have yourself a good day, ma'am.'

Gordy gave the woman a tip of her hat, turned on her heels, and headed back to her own vehicle. She stood and watched as the woman started her engine and pulled out slowly into the road, almost resurfacing it with her caution, so thickly was it laid on.

Well, thought Gordy, climbing back into her own vehicle, that was certainly an interesting start to the day. In the Dales, she'd have more likely been stopped by an overheating campervan or a trailer with a snapped axle, rather than someone racing to the school run.

Quickly pushing the event to the back of her mind, Gordy continued on her way, leaving Batcombe by driving along a road once again lined with trees and hedgerow.

As the road rose in front of her, what struck her was just how green everything was. The Dales was green, of course it was, but there was a haunting bleakness to the place as well. It was a landscape of moorland and field, scarred with the bone-grey of drystone walls, and dotted here and there by clusters of trees, which huddled and bent together against the wind, as though whispering to each other their own ancient memories of when the place had been covered in woodland, and leaf and bower and dappled shadow had been the paintbrush of the sky.

But in Somerset, there seemed to be nothing but trees. Wherever she looked, the horizon was a broken by treeline after treeline, lanes were hung in deep shadow beneath branch and bough, and the borders and corners of field and pastureland seemed to be but the gathering places of ancient woody dwellers of copse and grove, their twisted, knotted trunks ever reaching for the sky.

At long last, the twisting lanes finally gave way to the main road, and swinging right at a roundabout, she joined a snake of urgent traffic. A few minutes later, the market town of Frome welcomed Gordy, and after navigating two more roundabouts, she was soon in a small industrial estate which housed a supermarket, a garden centre and a fast-food restaurant, as well as various other industrial units. They all stretched along a lane that rumbled to the drone of trucks and vans dodging parked vehicles and each other. What Frome itself looked like, what treasures it held, would have to wait. Gordy just hoped that it was a darn sight prettier and more inviting than the car park she was pulling into, and didn't smell so much of French fries.

Gordy parked up next to a handful of incident response vehicles, switched off the engine, then sucked in a deep breath, and exhaled slowly.

'Here we go, then,' she muttered, opened her door, and climbing out, took her first tentative steps into her first day. And each one felt like she was wading through wet tar.

FOUR

As buildings went, the station had about as much charm as a pizza chain restaurant, but without the birthday party balloons and all-you-can-eat lunchtime menu. Not that Gordy expected charm by any means, she knew she had been spoiled by where she had worked before, but it was hard to be anything other than a little disappointed.

Modern, industrial buildings made sense as far as costs were concerned, but there was no romance to them, no sense of being a part of the history of the area. Knowing it was too much to ask, Gordy forced an approachable, relaxed smile onto her face as she pushed through the main door and found herself in a reception area designed by someone who had been good with straight lines and very little else.

Walking past a handful of stackable chairs, the legs of some bent enough to give the disturbing impression they'd made a few attempts at escaping and failed in the task, she approached the front desk and rang the bell. It rattled with the buzz of a weary wasp trapped in a jar.

A door opened in a far wall and an Asian man with the most extraordinary white beard approached.

'Hello.' He smiled. 'And welcome to the Hut.'

Gordy looked around her, once again taking in the building.

'Hut? I mean, I know it's fairly functional, but to call it that seems a bit unfair.'

'It's not unfair at all,' said the man. 'Used to be a Pizza Hut before the old police station was knocked down to make way for housing and we moved in here instead. Detective Inspector Gordanian Haig, correct?'

'What gave it away?' Gordy asked, smiling to herself about her initial impressions of the building and just how accurate they had been.

'This,' the man said, and from beside him on the desk, he flipped over a sheet of paper.

On it, Gordy saw her own face staring back, beneath which was typed her name and rank and various other bits of official information.

'Ah.'

'That, and the uniform, obviously,' the man smiled. 'I'm Vivek Ramesh, the receptionist. Not the sexiest of job titles, I know, but I've never been one to attach someone's worth to the badge they wear.'

Vivek held out his hand, and Gordy shook it. The gesture was warm and welcoming, the grip firm, but not crushing. Gentle hands, but strong, Gordy thought, wondering if that was a summing up of the man's character as well. His voice and smile certainly gave that impression. A good start to the day, she thought, and welcome.

'I know it says Gordanian on that sheet of paper,' she said, 'but please, call me Gordy.'

Vivek raised an eyebrow.

'Why? Gordanian's your name, isn't it?'

'Just sounds so official. Four syllables ... It's a bit of a mouthful, isn't it?'

'Gordy it is, then,' said Vivek. 'Now, have you had breakfast?'

'Pardon?'

Gordy was immediately reminded of a certain Detective Sergeant from the Dales, Matt Dinsdale, a man whose enthusiasm for food had introduced so many on the team to the importance of pies and cakes no matter the time of day.

Vivek said, 'The smell of this place can play havoc with your mind, believe me; you get used to it, but every now and again, and especially if you turn up on an empty stomach, it's all you can do to not start the day by rushing out to buy half a dozen hash browns.'

Gordy laughed.

'And it always smells like this?'

'It does,' said Vivek. 'And you didn't answer the question.'

'Yes, I've had breakfast,' said Gordy, deciding against saying what, because she was fairly sure a double espresso that had made her eyes water, and a toasted slice of crust burned and covered in butter didn't really count. 'But I'm not sure it's going to be enough to fight off that smell. And who doesn't love a hash brown?'

'Then what about a good, strong coffee to take your mind off rushing out to buy one?' Vivek offered. 'Come on, I'll show you upstairs to your office. You're first in, you know. Very keen.'

'Good,' Gordy said. 'Gives me a chance to settle in.'

Vivek made his way out of reception by flipping up a hatch in the front desk, then led Gordy up some stairs to the first floor. He was smaller than she, and somewhat wider, but solid rather than soft and squishy. Or that was how he looked, anyway; it wasn't as though Gordy was about to pull out a pen and give the man a prod just to check.

'This way,' Vivek said, and guided Gordy through a plain door which swung open with about as much enthusiasm as a teenager told to tidy their bedroom. The squeak from the hinges made Gordy wince. 'Must oil that,' Vivek added.

On the other side, desks were set out, all of them sporting in and out trays, computers, phones, piles of papers, and items that the various users had brought in to try and personalise the workspace. Photos mainly, but on closer inspection, Gordy saw that one desk had a small display of medals, and another a collection of Lego models.

'Your office is just over there at the back,' Vivek said, and Gordy followed him over to a small room with a large window looking out onto the car park, and beyond that, the roundabout and supermarket.

Traffic was shunting its way along the roads, and horns were being beeped by tired drivers who were already edgy on the first day of the week. She watched a large minibus pull up at a bus stop, noting that the lettering on the side was for a school. Smartly uniformed children climbed on board before the minibus went on its way once again. It reminded her of the woman she'd met earlier, and she wondered if the minibus was heading the same way, though at a considerably more sensible speed.

The small office Vivek had directed Gordy to was everything it should be and nothing it shouldn't, with a desk and a computer, filing cabinets and shelves, and a small, circular table in the corner with a couple of chairs pushed under it. Every piece of furniture bore scars from being dragged around from room to room, perhaps even from building to building.

Gordy wondered if the scars she bore were as obvious, and made a mental note to keep her guard up. It wasn't that she didn't want to settle into things, and quickly. It was more that after everything she'd gone through recently, she wasn't sure enough of herself to reveal more than only the bare minimum. It was safer that way. She would maintain a distance between herself and the team, the job, the area, and that way, perhaps, she would survive.

'I'll go get you that coffee, then.' Vivek smiled. 'Let you get settled in. How do you take it?'

'Strong and black,' Gordy said. 'No sugar.'

'I'll be back in five.'

Left alone, Gordy stood for a moment breathing stale air. That she was there at all didn't seem entirely real, as though she was instead captaining a Gordy-shaped ship, hiding behind her own eyes, steering her body, controlling the voice.

She opened the window a little to allow a breeze to huff its way in, regretting it immediately, as car fumes and fast food jostled for attention.

Walking around to the other side of the desk, she sat down and decided that a few personal touches would definitely make a difference to the room. The walls seemed to have been attacked by someone with a little too much grey and blue paint to use up. What those personal touches would be, she really wasn't sure, because if it was photos, then of what, and of whom?

A collage of memories of Anna cascaded into Gordy's mind, sucking the oxygen from her lungs, and cramping her stomach to the point where she nearly doubled over.

The door opened.

Welcoming the distraction, Gordy looked up, expecting to see Vivek. Instead, what she was presented with was a slim woman about the same size as Vivek. She was wearing a deep blue trouser suit, a no-nonsense bob hairstyle, and an expression that told Gordy she had yet to decide on whether it was better to smile or look stern. The mix of both made it look like she was caught in a stuttering freeze frame, and Gordy felt for a moment as though she was in the presence of the living version of one of those live photographs she found so bloody annoying.

'Good morning,' the woman said, her voice clipped and professional, as she walked into the office.

Gordy rose to her feet as the woman came to stand in front of her desk and held out a hand. Gordy shook it, trying to ignore how tiny the hand was, like a child's almost, the fingers so thin and fragile that for a moment she was reminded of breadsticks and just how easy they were to snap.

'Detective Chief Inspector Ellen Allercott,' the woman said, and Gordy noticed then a faint note of an accent that she recognised from Harry, that soft, lilting tone of the west country. But it was distant and fleeting, as though DCI Allercott was trying to keep it hidden. 'I see you're wearing your uniform.'

The statement came out strange, Gordy thought, sounding a little like it was laced with suspicion, though of what, she couldn't guess.

'First day and all that,' Gordy said. 'Always best to make a good impression, I think, don't you? But tomorrow it'll be holey jeans and baggy sweaters all the way, I promise.'

'Well, I most certainly hope it won't be.' Allercott frowned.

Gordy said nothing for a moment, at first assuming that she was joking, then quickly realised she wasn't. Not good.

'So, tell me,' Allercott said, 'are you up to speed on everything for the month ahead at least?'

At least, Gordy thought, why would she add that? And she'd not heard anyone mutter the phrase *up to speed* in a very long time; it reeked of management speak from over a decade ago. Gordy had a pet hatred for such phrases and a memory made her smile; she had once informed a detective considerably younger than herself that if he said *blue sky thinking* one more time, she'd be happy to help him get as much as he could ever dream of by hoofing him one hard enough in the arse to send him into orbit.

'Something funny?'

The question caught Gordy off guard.

'Just thinking how friendly Vivek has already been,' Gordy said, then quickly added, 'I've a fair idea of what everyone is involved with, individually and as a team, and I'll be spending a good amount of time with them out and about, getting to know them, the local community, that kind of thing. I think that's the best way to be spending my first month here; help me get to know the place, the people, settle in.'

Allercott gave a serious nod. Gordy was already wondering if she had any other kind. She tried to place her age. She was definitely a good deal younger than herself, perhaps mid-thirties, but acted older.

'Excellent,' Allercott said. 'Now, I've looked at some of the cases you've been involved with over the past while, and had another glance at your personal statement; you're sure your experience up north will be of use here, correct?'

Gordy heard the inflection, ignored it.

'Aye, I'm sure it will,' she said.

Allercott turned on her heel, grabbed a chair from the small table in the corner, swung it around to face Gordy's desk, then sat down.

Vivek entered the room.

'Oh,' he said, seeing Allercott and placing Gordy's coffee in front of her. She was surprised to notice that it smelled very good, something she hadn't been expecting at all.

'Good morning, Ramesh,' Allercott said, and Gordy noticed immediately how the DCI referred to the man by his surname. 'I hope you're not giving DI Haig the impression that all you do is make coffee.'

Gordy took a sip.

'It's very good coffee,' she said, then smiled and added, 'Thank you, Vivek.'

She knew that using the man's first name was little more than her showing just the faintest glint of a blade drawn momentarily from its sheath, but it got Allercott's attention. It wasn't meant as a warning, just a demonstration of how Gordy liked to run things.

'I was a barista in a past life,' Vivek replied. 'I refuse to serve something I wouldn't drink myself.'

'Everyone chips in a little each week, to make sure we've always a good supply of freshly roasted beans,' said Allercott.

Gordy saw Vivek look at the DCI and widen his eyes briefly at her words. So, not exactly everyone then, she guessed.

'Can I get you one?' Vivek asked, stepping back towards the door, the question obviously aimed at Allercott.

Allercott shook her head.

'No, I'm fine, thank you,' she said. 'Only popped in to introduce myself to our new Detective Inspector.'

Vivek left the office, sending Gordy a quick, warm smile as he closed the door.

Allercott said, 'Now, I need to tell you that you won't see me all that often.'

'DCIs are busy people,' Gordy replied.

'They are, and I cover a large number of stations across the county, you see. Also, I generally work out of the central station in Bristol. Means I can really keep an eye on things, hear what's going on, keep up to date on all the latest working practices, that kind of thing.'

Hearing that reminded Gordy of something, and she said, 'Actually, I'm there tomorrow.'

'You are? Why?'

Gordy noticed that Allercott sounded not just surprised but a little put out, though why she would be either she had no idea.

'I'm meeting Detective Superintendent Firbank.'

Allercott's eyes went momentarily wide, and Gordy felt for a moment as though she was being stared at by a very annoyed cow.

'You are?'

'I am.'

'Oh.'

'A DCI that I know well worked with her before moving north,' Gordy explained.

'And you're off there tomorrow, then?'

'I'm never one for hanging about.'

'Clearly not.'

This whole conversation was both going nowhere and starting to get on Gordy's nerves, but she maintained her calm composure and waited to see where it would all lead, if anywhere.

Allercott leaned forward.

'Can I just say ...' Gordy watched the woman's eyes flit from side to side as though she was attempting to find what it was that she was trying to say floating in the air around her. '... I'm, well, you know, very sorry about what happened. To your partner, I mean.'

'Well, thank you,' said Gordy, in no mood at all to talk about it. It also seemed to her that the words weren't entirely genuine, said out of duty, rather than care.

'To be honest, I'm rather surprised you decided to come at all,' continued Allercott, shaking her head, almost as though she'd not heard Gordy's reply. 'Something like that is so difficult to deal with, isn't it? Really impacts on you and for such a long time, too.'

'If you're worried that it will affect my work, I can assure you—'

Allercott waved her comment away.

'Goodness, no, that's not what I'm suggesting at all. I'm speaking from experience.'

Gordy waited, sure Allercott was going to say something else, and also sure that was exactly what she was suggesting. Who had she lost? Gordy sensed she wasn't going to find out.

'This line of work, it doesn't mix well with external pressures, as I'm sure you know,' Allercott said. 'Well, of course you do.' She paused, and Gordy saw a change come over the woman's face, as she cocked her head to one side, and stared. 'I think you're going to do very well here, and I, for one, am very pleased that you made the brave decision to come, despite what you've been through. I can only respect that.'

That statement took Gordy back a little.

'Oh, well ... thank you?' Gordy replied

'I mean it,' Allercott continued, leaning forward now, like a doctor with a patient. 'And I would like to offer you something I do not do lightly or ever, actually.'

Gordy waited, waited some more, wondering what it was that her new DCI was going to offer.

'I'm here for you,' Allercott said. 'By which I mean that if you need anything, just call, yes? Life here can be quite mundane sometimes, but I'm sure something exciting will come along soon enough. But if you have any problems, any issues, or just want to chat? Please, call me.'

She handed Gordy a card with a number on it.

'I'm looking forward to working with you.'

'And you,' said Gordy, the card now in her hand.

Allercott stood up, giving Gordy a wide smile that her eyes seemed to be surprised at being asked to join, as though such a show of emotion was rare indeed.

'I'm glad we had this chat.'

Gordy rose to her feet, wondering what it was they had actually chatted about, if anything at all. The offer of help, though, of support, and the phone number? That had caught her off guard and she wasn't quite sure how seriously to take it. Not yet, anyway. It was early days.

'Well, thank you for coming in,' she said. 'I'll be sure to keep you up to date with things as I settle in.'

'So long as you keep things running smoothly, keep me up to date, and call me as and when you need me, that's all I ask,' Allercott said. 'The devil's in the details, and all that, isn't it? And I think the detail is probably what you excel at. You're not one of those detectives who break down doors and chain-smokes their way through every investigation and interrogation.'

'I don't smoke.'

'Exactly,' said Allercott. 'See? We're going to get on wonderfully.'

Gordy replied with a non-committal 'Mmm ...'

Allercott moved to the door, then with one hand pulling it open, paused and said, 'Oh, and one word of advice before I go ...'

Gordy waited, expecting some gem of wisdom from someone who, though younger than her by enough years to wear fewer lines around her eyes, was still her senior officer.

Allercott leaned forward, lifted a finger, and when she spoke, her voice was softer, not far from a whisper, but loud enough to hear.

'Source your own stationery.'

Gordy narrowed her eyes, not quite sure she had heard correctly.

'Did you just say my own stationery?'

'Yes,' said Allercott, with such pointed finality that Gordy could tell that to her, this was vital information which she was imparting. 'There's never enough, you see, in the cupboard, and it's always a mess, and when you do find what you want, it's never any good, or it's broken, or dried up; just a few biros, a broken stapler, creased paper for your printer, you know what I mean. Very disappointing.'

'I can see how it would be.'

'There's a lovely little art shop in town, plenty of choice there,' Allercott said. 'My suggestion is that you pop in after work and stock up. Oh, and make sure you keep it all locked away; there are more thieves in the police than in prison, I'm sure!'

Allercott then laughed, as though what she'd just said was the funniest thing in the world.

Gordy, somewhat baffled, couldn't bring herself to join in with the jocularity, and watched, as without another word said, not even a goodbye, Allercott left her office, humming to herself as she went.

Gordy thought she recognised the tune, but then Vivek popped his head around the door, and she lost it.

'You probably won't see her again for a month or two.'

'She mentioned an art shop.'

'She does love a good pen. Not that she'll ever let you borrow it. Very protective about her pens, she is.'

'Not the pep-talk I was expecting, if I'm honest. It was an odd mix. Sort of like she was keeping me at arm's length, while also trying to reach out and give me a hug. I'm a little confused.'

'As well you should be.' Vivek frowned. 'Allercott doesn't hug. That's very out of character. Wonder if she's ill.'

'I didn't say she actually hugged me,' said Gordy, clarifying things, 'but she did try to be supportive, said I could ring her if I ever needed to, that kind of thing.'

'Are we talking about the same DCI?'

'I think so,' said Gordy.

Vivek didn't look so sure. He nodded out into the main area of the building.

'The rest of the team are here, by the way, if you're ready to meet them?'

Despite feeling even more on edge about what she was doing than she had been even that morning, thanks to Allercott's odd manner and strange approach to welcoming her to the new position, Gordy said, 'I am.'

'There might even be biscuits,' Vivek added, and with that temptation, Gordy followed him out of her office and into the main room.

FIVE

'What do you mean, you like cider, but you don't like scrumpy? They're the same thing!'

'Wensleydale's a place? I thought it was a cheese?'

'Cheddar's a cheese and a place.'

'So's Stilton.'

'Cider and scrumpy aren't the same thing at all. Well, they are, it's just that one's fizzy and everyone likes it, and the other has bits that float in it, and it makes you fall over really quickly. Oh, and it can smell a bit, well, farmy ...'

'Good point. Fizzy cider from a service station has nothing on the kind of stuff you can get at Wilkin's farm; that's nectar, that is.'

'Still farmy, though, just in a good way.'

'You said something about somewhere called Hawes; where's that to, then?'

Within minutes of meeting the team, Gordy was already reeling from the full-frontal assault of questions, none of which were about her police background, or coming at her in any semblance of order.

'It's not so much that I don't like scrumpy,' Gordy said, trying to bat away some of the queries by answering the one from the PCSO supervisor, Jack Hill. 'More that I just haven't really ever drank it.

I'm not even sure you can really get it up north. Pretty sure I've never seen it.'

Jack was late thirties, Gordy guessed, wore his hair razor short, and was carrying earphones around his neck. Not modern ones, though, Gordy noticed, and neither was what they were plugged into; a bona fide nineteen-eighties Sony Walkman.

'Well, I'm sure we can rectify that easily enough and get you some of the proper stuff as a welcome to Somerset present.'

That was from the detective sergeant, Patti Matondo, a black woman in her early thirties, with a soft Welsh accent.

'I wasn't really aware there was such a thing as proper stuff,' Gordy said.

At this, Patti's eyes went wide and her jaw fell open.

Gordy went to speak, but Peter Knight, the detective constable, got there first. He was in his mid-twenties and had fashionably spiky black hair that looked more like a dangerous weapon than a hairstyle.

'Anyway, this Hawes place,' he said. 'Where's that—'

Gordy held up a hand to quell the storm of questions throwing itself at her with wild abandon.

'First,' she said, 'I know you've all just told me your names, but I'll be honest, they've no' stuck in my head at all, sort of just gone in one ear and fallen out the other and onto the carpet. And looking at the state of the carpet, I don't fancy getting on my knees to try and pick them up. So, can we start again?'

For the next while, Gordy did her best to look and sound interested in what everyone was saying, allowing her professional side to take over, and wearing it as a shield almost. She knew she was supposed to care, to really be in the moment, what with it being the first day of a new job, and these being the people she would be working with for a long time to come, but she was finding it beyond difficult, and the conversation drifted on, with her taking part, yet simultaneously forgetting everything almost as soon as it was said.

She was again wearing the disguise of DI Haig, stepping into character just enough to keep people happy but at arm's length, but inside, she was, even then, sitting in a corner, crying.

'Well, that's agreed, then,' said Patti, with a clap of her hands so loud it was like the crack of a rifle shot.

'Certainly sounds like it,' said Gordy, realising she had no idea what was agreed on at all, so focusing on the sergeant she added, 'Over to you, then?'

'Actually, today you'll be with PCSO Hill,' Patti said, nodding at Jack. 'No one knows the area better. I mean, we're all local-ish, but Jack's born and bred, and I think it would be a good idea for you to just head out with him today, have a look around, meet some of the other PCSOs as well if you can. If that's okay? You're the boss, so if —'

'Sounds perfect,' said Gordy.

She was sure she'd had other things planned for the day, really important detective inspector things, a whole list in a notebook somewhere, but when she glanced away from the team to see the dark shadows of her new office, she shuddered. She wasn't quite ready for that yet, for sitting in a small, grey room at a tired desk and starting on goodness knew what. No, this was definitely a much better use of her time, she thought, and turned to Jack with a smile she hoped looked convincing, because on her side of it, she could feel the muscles resisting, her eyes not getting in on the act quick enough.

'Looks like I'm in your hands,' she said, then noticed that Jack was now holding a silvery, palm-sized box and was busy switching his headphones over from the Walkman.

'MiniDisc player,' Jack said. 'Such a great format.'

'Yes, wasn't it?' said Gordy, having absolutely nothing else to offer to the conversation.

'It was expensive, but it was brilliant,' Jack continued. 'Better than tape, better than CD. It should have never died. But that's often the way with things, isn't it? The good stuff just doesn't make it.'

Though Jack had no idea of the impact of what he had just said, Gordy felt it and stumbled a little, grabbing the edge of a desk quick enough to stop herself from falling.

'You okay, there?' Jack asked, reaching a hand out to rest it on Gordy's arm.

'What? Oh, aye, I'm fine,' Gordy said. 'You know how it is on your first day; not enough sleep, you don't eat enough for breakfast.'

'That I do,' said Jack. 'You okay to head off? We can wait?'

'No, I'm good,' Gordy lied, forcing her mind to bury deep the memories of Anna, which had resurfaced uninvited.

A few minutes later, Gordy was sitting beside Jack in a very clean and shiny incident response vehicle. A pair of furry dice hung from the mirror.

'We'll do Frome first,' Jack said. 'Give you a bit of a guided tour, wave to Paul, then head off somewhere else. You're over in Evercreech, right?'

Gordy gave a nod, and asked, 'Paul?'

'PCSO Edwards,' said Jack. 'The world's most unflappable man.'

Heading into Frome, Gordy tried to sound interested in everything Jack was saying. He pointed out various points of interest, from Gentle Street, which he seemed to regard as the most used film location in the world, 'Because of all those costume dramas we do,' to Cheap Street, a narrow lane where the flagstones were cut from top to bottom by a thin sliver of flowing water fed from a spring at the church it sat beneath.

Pubs featured fairly heavily, with particular emphasis on The Lamb and Fountain, which was historically important, sold proper cider, and hadn't been redecorated since the fifties; Gordy wasn't sure how all of those things together made the place sound good or worthy of a visit.

As for PCSO Edwards, Jack spotted him outside the Cheese and Grain, a venue used for everything from flea markets to stopover gigs for big names on their way to Glastonbury.

'Paul McCartney played here recently,' he said, as they climbed out of the car to meet Paul.

'Really?' Gordy said, finding that very hard to believe.

Jack took out his phone as the PCSO approached and a moment later was showing her photos.

'I was lucky enough to get a ticket,' he said, and there on the screen of Jack's phone was indeed none other than Sir McCartney himself.

Paul introduced himself, shaking Gordy's hand warmly.

'He's not talking about record fairs, is he?' he said.

'Not yet, no,' said Gordy, remembering that one of her team in the Dales, Constable Jadyn Okri, had a similar interest. Not that he talked about it much, wrapped up as he was now in his blossoming relationship with Detective Constable Jenny Blades. The thoughts of her old team made her smile, and she found herself wondering just why the hell she'd gone ahead with this move at all. She had kind of just let it happen, lacking the energy or the brain space to do anything to change the direction her life was taking. She wondered if it was a decision she would regret.

'Give it time.'

'It's the best format, and you know it,' said Jack.

Paul took out his phone.

'See this? I've got thousands of albums on it, and it just fits in my pocket. Why would I need to fill my house with plastic discs? Makes no sense at all.'

For the next few minutes, Gordy listened to Paul and Jack argue about the pros and cons of various music formats, and really didn't have the energy to interupt.

Once they were done, and Paul had given Gordy a quick runthrough of what things were like in the town, what the main issues they were dealing with were, and where the best coffee could be found, she was back in Jack's car and heading deeper into Somerset.

'We'll not take the main road,' Jack explained, taking them away from the centre and threading them instead through various streets lined with old houses and endless lines of parked cars. 'Can't see a place if you only take the fastest route, can you?'

Considering how young Jack was, that struck Gordy as incredibly wise, especially as, moments later, they burst out of Frome and down a steep hill into a world that seemed pulled out of history.

Gordy had driven around the area a little, but as she stared out of the window at the sea of green before her, she realised that most of her journeys had been by those faster routes. That morning had really been the only time she'd strayed from the more direct routes, and she'd been struck then by how green everything was, the trees, the lanes lined with hedgerows. And once again, it was the lushness of the area that grabbed her and refused to let go. She wasn't in the right mood to start liking the place, but as it drifted by her window, there was little she could do but stare in wonder.

Wherever she looked, trees danced along the edges of fields, holding onto each other with outstretched branches like hands. Woodlands tumbled down the sides of low rolling hills, as though only just managing to stop themselves from falling into the fields at their feet, like toddlers teetering on the edge of a giant puddle.

The road rose again, its high sides of bush and grass eventually dropping enough to afford Gordy a view of the way ahead.

'And this is Nunney,' Jack said as they rounded a corner and came to a village. 'Properly old place, this. We won't stop, as there's plenty of other places I've to take you to, but it's worth a look when you get a chance.'

Gordy was about to ask why, when the very obvious reason loomed ahead of them.

'That's a castle,' she said.

'It is, indeed,' said Jack. 'Nunney's a pretty little village, isn't it? But to have that huge thing standing over it really sets it apart. It even has a moat.'

Jack slowed down, and Gordy was able to take the place in. She was astonished. Though clearly a ruin, it was still very much a castle, and an imposing one, too. With towers at its corners, and high walls with windows that must have seen and witnessed so much, there was enough presence about the place, even from the comfort of a car, to be a little unnerved by it. It was as though, buried deep in its walls and foundations there were dark secrets long forgotten.

'That must bring in a fair bit of money,' she said, staring at the broken towers of the structure, which grinned down at her like the smashed teeth of a brawler.

'What? No,' said Jack. 'It's free. Worth popping over when you get a chance, maybe at the weekend or something. And the George is a decent pub, as well.'

He pointed ahead and Gordy saw where Jack was talking about, its sign hanging from a metal beam spanning the road.

'Nice way to hang that,' she said.

'Hanging being the key word there,' said Jack. 'Used to be a courthouse for travelling judges, and that beam was where they despatched the condemned.'

Gordy turned in disbelief, expecting to see a smirk on Jack's face. She was the new kid in town, so she fully expected to have her leg pulled a few times as she settled in.

She saw no sign of the expected smirk.

'You're serious, aren't you?'

'No reason not to be.'

Leaving Nunney, Gordy made a mental note to visit again, and soon. Though, she wasn't too sure about having a drink in view of a gibbet that had taken the last gasps of goodness knew how many. But the castle intrigued her. Not that she was some mad history buff or anything, but sometimes just soaking up the atmosphere of a place so very old could do your soul good. And if there was something her soul needed, it was that.

From Nunney, Jack took a twisting, turning route, through numerous villages, all hung along the lanes and roads like bunting on a line. Names of places whizzed past as Jack gave her a whistle-stop tour, pointing out woods to walk in, pubs to drink in, while also pulling over when necessary to meet another PCSO.

By the end of the day, when they rolled back into the car park at the station in Frome, Gordy's mind was full of people and places and the names they carried. She'd met four more PCSOs, and couldn't remember the names of any of them. For that reason, she'd sensibly jotted them all down in her little notebook, alongside something she'd noticed about them that would help her remember who they were when they next met. Whether it worked or not, she would just have to see.

'Thank you, Jack,' Gordy said, climbing out.

'You know, you're different to our last DI,' Jack said, as he climbed out as well, locking the vehicle behind them.

'Being Scottish,' said Gordy.

Jack shook his head.

'No, it's not that,' he said. 'You use first names. Spotted that right away. DI Matthews was always a rank- and surnames-only kind of man. DCI Allercott is the same. Though with her, I'm not sure she actually even knows our first names in the first place, like she's just not bothered to learn them, because to do so would be an inefficient use of her time, or something like that, anyway.'

'Didn't realise,' said Gordy, though she very much did, and was pleased it had been picked up on. 'Should I no' do it, then? Is that what you're saying?'

'Not in the slightest,' Jack replied.

'You're sure? I mean, if it's something Allercott doesn't like, then …'

'She's never around enough to notice,' Jack laughed. 'Today's probably the first and last time you'll see her for months. Well, unless something big comes up, then she'll swoop in with her vast array of pens to make lots of notes, before disappearing again, but somehow claiming responsibility for all the good stuff.'

Gordy laughed, even though she had a feeling she probably shouldn't have, out of respect for someone of a higher rank.

Heading into the building to grab what she'd left in the office, Gordy was soon back outside and in her own vehicle. The day had been good, enjoyable even, and it had helped her to forget for a moment the deep ache inside. Now, though, as she eased the key into the ignition, the ache began to throb once again. Starting the engine, she tried to ignore it, but it just came back worse, and by the time she had eased herself out onto the road, all she could feel was a creeping dread of heading home.

The drive back to Evercreech took forever, and yet seemed over in moments, as though time and distance had conspired to concertina and deposit Gordy outside her house, confused and disorientated.

The walk back to her flat echoed with the sound of her footsteps, and all Gordy could think about was how she missed Anna's, which had, not so long ago, walked beside her.

When the grey evening became night, and after a microwave bolognaise that tasted of ash, Gordy headed to bed and begged the darkness to swallow her.

SIX

Bill Halliday was cold and damp and had no doubt in his mind at all that he reeked worse than a nest of rats. None of this was on purpose, but simply an unavoidable side effect of his current way of life, and that wasn't something he'd chosen either. But life had a way of cutting the legs from under you, Bill thought, and for him, it had gone at them with gusto.

He felt sure that some nights the sound that woke him was of all the awful things that had happened to him happily gnawing on his bones, desperate to get to the marrow inside. And they were welcome to it. Not that he'd given up, not yet, but some days he wished he could fall asleep and never wake up, wondering sometimes if death was like being carried to your bedroom as a child, the bed warm, the darkness cosy, and the distant sound of family and friends below sending you to sleep.

Homelessness, Bill knew, was not a choice. To suggest otherwise was ignorance and arrogance all wrapped in a lovely, neat package he'd happily set fire to. It was not something he had decided to do on purpose. There had never been one marked day where he'd woken up and decided that a roof and a comfy bed to share with someone he loved, good food and being warm and maybe watching a bit of telly while drinking a beer from the fridge were just not for him.

At no point in his life had he determined to pack everything he needed into a rucksack and just head off into the wilds of England's rubbish-strewn streets to sleep in shop doorways and under bridges and in cheap tents, if you were lucky. And if you weren't? Well, he'd had plenty of kickings from drunk thugs, though a good number had soon realised they'd bitten off a little more than they had been expecting to chew. This was no romantic life, seeing the world by means of a knapsack and a wanderlust; it was a dark, damp, and unfriendly place, and he had, at times, done things to survive that he wasn't proud of.

No. His way of life was definitely not a choice. It was something that had happened gradually over time, an odd sort of slumping through various small events, from days that he could still remember where his life had been mostly good, to right now, where it was anything but, and could best be described as an absolute crock of shit.

How he'd ended up in Somerset, Bill wasn't entirely sure, but neither did he care. If he was going to be homeless, then the one thing he was going to do was use his lack of a fixed abode to see things a little. He'd seen enough of the world to know that wherever you went, you'd always end up meeting dickheads, so now his choice was to stay clear of the larger places, of cities and towns, and the absolute planks that seemed to live there, and stick to the countryside instead.

Bill had enough skills from his past life to enable him to survive in the wilds, so that was what he did. Generally, setting up a small shelter in a tiny woodland wouldn't lead to your gear being kicked around and stamped on or nicked, or someone trying to hoof you one in the head with their Friday night specials.

The Army had been good, Bill thought, as he scurried through a small gate in a wall, and onto a gravel footpath that bowed to his left. It was a life he'd loved, not just for the friendships he had made, but for the things he'd got to do, what he'd learned. He was no John Rambo or Andy McNab, and had never wanted to be, but he'd been a decent squaddie, a good infantryman, and a damned fine shot, which had helped in a few situations, that was for sure.

The memory of just such a situation had Bill laughing as he continued his way along the path, before taking a right across a small bridge. Ahead of him a huge shadow loomed, cut through with occasional blades of moonlight, their razor edges glistening with a thin mist catching the air like the gossamer sails of a ghost ship dancing through the waves.

Why he was laughing, he wasn't entirely sure, especially considering the brutality and awfulness of the memory which had floated to the surface, though that had always been the way, as far as he could remember; the worse the situation, the more uncomfortable and unpleasant and dangerous, the more important it was to try and see the funny side.

A vast shadow swallowed Bill as he stepped into the place where he would spend the night, out of the wind and hopefully out of the rain if he picked his spot right. He stood for a moment, enjoying the stillness. Something flitted by his head, and he recognised it as a bat, the soft flutter of its leathery wings barely noticeable in the air.

He heard the solemn, sorrowful hoot of an owl, chased by the high-pitched yap of a skulk of foxes racing each other somewhere far off. Bill hoped he wouldn't be bothered by them tonight. Generally, foxes in the countryside were more wary of humans and would stay away, though he'd had plenty come up for a sniff. In the city, though, they were confident, brave, brazen. He'd lost precious provisions he'd taken from large bins at the backs of restaurants to the hungry bellies of too many foxes. Not that he begrudged them the forage; they, like he was himself, were simply trying to survive, and he had to respect that.

Finding a sheltered corner against a wall, Bill kneeled on the ground before laying out his bedroll. It provided little comfort, but insulated him just enough to make sure he didn't freeze to death. Next was the sleeping bag, which was protected from the elements by a waterproof, breathable bivi bag.

Bill sometimes wondered if passersby looked at him as though he was too well prepared, almost as though, because he was homeless, he wasn't allowed to have good kit. But it wasn't just the memories he had from the Army, he'd also kept his gear, and it had saved his life too many times to mention. He'd not just heard tales, but known people who had been frozen in the night and never woken up. He wasn't about to let that happen, which was why he also stayed away from drink.

There were other reasons. Alcohol had caused him enough problems in the past to make him decide one day that he wasn't going to use it as a crutch anymore. He had grown tired of how easy it was to pop the cork, sink the drink, feel the buzz, then wake up worse than ever. Not with a hangover, because he'd drunk so much over the years that they were a thing of the past. It was the way the booze hit his mood, turned a magnifying glass on the worst bits of his life, turning into a spiral. A helter-skelter to hell he'd chosen to ride so often and for what, just so he could drown out the noise it had caused in the first place? So, that had gone, and he didn't miss it.

His only vice now was a cheap, wooden pipe he carried close to his chest, and the small amount of tobacco he dipped into now and again, if only to help still his mind, and to take away the stale stink of his own life.

With his bed set up, Bill set to with a little camp stove and soon had some water boiling. Into it, he poured some pasta. The sauce would be margarine and some extra salt, with a few chunks of cheese and some cut-up sticks of spicy meat, all things he'd bought with the takings of the worst part of how he now lived; sitting in a doorway with a cup and a piece of cardboard, on which he had written, ever so politely, just enough to tell people who he was, what he was, and to thank them for their time and their spare change, however small.

Once the pasta was done, and the other ingredients were mixed in, he took his most treasured item from a jacket pocket: a bottle of Tabasco sauce. He dotted the food with a few precious drops of the red spice. That was another echo of his soldiering days; Tabasco went on everything. You went into the badlands carrying that as preciously as you did the rounds for your rifle.

Leaning against a wall, Bill tucked into his food, his mind drifting back and back and back, and for a while it seemed to him as though he was walking through a jungle, his memories hanging from branches like vines, and with each one he brushed into, another moment in time would present itself. Soon he had to force himself to stop remembering, and he raced out of that tangle of thoughts, though they tried their hardest to snag at him and trip him and trap him, to remind him of the things that had gone wrong.

Tears stung Bill's cheeks, and he just allowed them to fall, because he knew there was little point in stopping them. He tasted them in the last few mouthfuls of the pasta, an additional seasoning of pain.

Diligently, he cleaned away his gear, wiping the single pan with a stale piece of bread, before giving it a rinse with water. Then it was time to get his head down and to let the night take him. First, though, he unwrapped a small cellophane package he kept in a tin with some rolling tobacco and cigarette papers. A few minutes later he was having a much-needed pull on a spliff. Nothing too strong, mainly because he had to make what he had last and last, but enough to take the edge off the day, and help him relax.

Sleep took a while, not because the ground was rough, or that he was cold, because he had become hardened to both things. It was his mind that kept him alert, refusing to switch off, despite the cannabis in his system, but eventually it and the fatigue won over, and he slept.

The nightmare that woke Bill some hours later left him short of breath and sweating. His heart was pounding and for a moment he had no idea where he was, just that the darkness around him had teeth.

Shivering, he sat up. He shook his head to dislodge whatever awful thing had entered his mind to wake him with the whining scream of missiles slamming around him in some dark, hellscape of war. When nothing came loose, he considered lying back down again, but he was so awake that instead he just fell comfortably into a habit from his soldiering days, which he depended on even now. If in doubt, have a brew.

Scrabbling through his pack, Bill soon had his stove out and lit, and on it rested a small pot of water. The bright orange and purple glow of the flame gave an illusion of warmth and comfort, and he held his hands over it to steal some of the heat.

Once boiling, he lobbed in a teabag and let it stew. Then he added some milk from a little sachet he'd snatched from a café, and let the golden-brown liquid do its work.

The deep, black pit of the dream that had ripped him from slumber came back to him, gut-punching him hard enough to make him grab his stomach. Then the whine of the missile twisted itself into a tune, and he realised then that it wasn't just the nightmare that had woken him, but the sound of someone whistling.

Grasping his steaming mug, Bill climbed out of his sleeping bag to go for a stroll in the moonlight. He knew all too well how the mind could take what it heard while he was asleep, and turn it into things which would then chase him into blood-soaked shadows, so he needed to calm his nerves by checking the area to make sure he was still alone, still safe.

It was then, as he wandered away from where he had slept, and out into the night itself, lifting the mug to his lips for a sip, that he saw it. A silhouette, standing still as a post, just outside of his camp.

The initial shock of seeing someone, not just so suddenly, but so close to where he had been asleep, made Bill almost spill his tea, but he calmed himself down by taking another sip.

The silhouette didn't move. Bill felt sure that they must be aware of him, whoever they were.

'Hello, there? Was that you I heard whistling?'

No movement, no reply.

'Everything okay? Anything I can do to help?'

Still nothing.

'I'm Bill. Just staying here for the night, that's all. If there's a problem, I can move on; don't want to cause any trouble. That's not what I'm about. Been long enough in this game to know to always take the path of least resistance, don't draw attention.'

Bill waited, stared, took another sip, the steam warming his nose.

'I'll be gone in the morning,' he said, now edging closer to whoever this was who had turned up in the middle of the night to freak him out, intentionally or not. 'That's only a few hours away, isn't it?'

Bill was used to being diplomatic to save his skin. To make sure he was in one piece to face another day of the life he wasn't exactly enjoying, but also didn't yet value so poorly that he was willing to let go of quite yet.

Still nothing from the silhouette.

Bill took a gulp of tea, felt the liquid burn as it raced down his throat, and his diplomacy turned to annoyance, his anger suddenly a grenade with the pin out.

'If you don't want anything, then can I ask you to just bugger off?' he said, noticing the grit in his voice now, remembering the trouble it had got him into before, so many times. 'I'm not doing anyone any harm, am I? Just having a kip, that's all. And I never leave a trace, always take my rubbish, because that's how I was trained. But if you've got a problem with me, then why don't you come over here and we can have a little chat? How does that sound?'

Bill took a couple of steps and saw that whoever they were, they were standing beside the small bridge he'd taken just a few hours ago. He wondered how long they had been there, just staring, but at what? It certainly hadn't been him, had it, because he'd been hidden away, out of sight?

Bill's annoyance mixed with his anger, a chemical reaction that had exploded too many times before, and caused damage he had never been able to repair.

'The least you could do is bloody well say something!' he said, his voice the vicious growl of a starved wolf cornering its prey. He stepped forward, closed the distance between himself and this absolute git trying to mess with his head. 'How long have you been standing there? What the hell do you want? And just who the hell are—'

Bill's voice caught in his throat, hooked as it was on the barbs of the vision now before him, one so bizarre, so horrifying, that at first, he couldn't see how it was real.

The silhouette was that of a man, or so Bill assumed, though it was hard to be sure, all things considered. As for the individual's age, Bill had no idea and certainly couldn't guess, and not because of what the figure was wearing, the colour of their hair, or their wrinkles.

What it had more to do with, and what certainly drew Bill's eye, was the huge metal spike which jutted out of the ground and thrust upwards through the figure's body, its end bursting from their mouth to point at the sky. Even in the dark, Bill could see that what the figure was wearing glistened with a wetness he didn't need to guess at. Teeth hung by strands of flesh against the body's lips.

His tea forgotten, Bill ran across the bridge, down the path, through the little gate. He hammered on the door of the first house he came to, loud enough to wake the whole village. The living, as well as the dead.

SEVEN

Gordy was already awake when her phone rang, and had been for over an hour, thanks to a restless few hours in bed, courtesy of her mind refusing to give her the break she so desperately needed. The weeks since losing Anna had given her little rest, day or night, and she yearned to wake up feeling refreshed. But her mind seemed intent on continuing to harass her with a barrage of memories, and insisted most nights on firing them at her hard enough to scour her skin raw.

She had been about to get up and make a hot toddy, simply because there was little else more comforting in the early hours than a mug of hot water with whisky, honey, and lemon, and if she was feeling all fancy, a stick of cinnamon, as well. Tonight, she really wasn't, mainly because the reality of her new life had, after her first day in the office, hit her hard.

The team had welcomed her. Allercott had seemed a little cold perhaps, but maybe that was just the way she dealt with her own authority. All in all, it had been interesting and enjoyable. But the taste of it was still like ash in her mouth and Gordy had been careful to not allow too much of who she was to shine through the cracks, afraid that if she did, her vulnerability would be front and centre and that was just too much.

Perhaps it was a good thing that the phone had caught her before she got her hands on the whisky. Not that she would've drunk a lot, but then again, there was that temptation, wasn't there, to let the warmth of the liquid call her, and give her a moment of respite?

'Detective Inspector Haig,' Gordy said, announcing herself, her tiredness curling the edge of her words with a yawn.

'It's Detective Sergeant Matondo,' the voice on the end of the phone said.

'Matondo?' Gordy replied, pretty sure she didn't know anyone by that name. Then, as she was about to hang up on whoever the weirdo was calling her in the middle of the night, she remembered.

'Patti?'

'Yes, sorry to wake you.'

'Well, you didn't.'

A pause.

'But it's the middle of the night ...'

'Aye, tell me about it,' Gordy said, yawning again, adding, 'I don't sleep well, not at the moment, anyway. It's more a case of hello darkness, my old friend, I'm afraid.'

Patti was silent just long enough to make Gordy realise that she had guessed why. Though she'd only spoken about Anna's death with DCI Allercott, and even then hardly at all, she realised the rest of the team knew. It was right that they did, she thought, but it did make her feel momentarily exposed. That was an aspect of her life she was barely able to speak about with the people she knew best, never mind a new team she had only just met.

'I'm sorry to hear that,' Patti said, breaking the silence. 'Lack of sleep is a killer.'

'It really is.'

'I use audiobooks if I can't sleep. Not dramatised ones, but those where you have just a narrator doing the voices. Most times, I don't even care what the book's about. In fact, it's better if I don't.'

'I'll maybe give it a try,' said Gordy. 'Anyway, I'm assuming this isn't just a call to discuss insomnia.'

There was a pause, just long enough to worry Gordy, then ...

'Something's come up,' Patti said.

'Considering what time it is, my guess is that it's no' anything good, am I right?'

'Pretty much.'

'And this is my first week, too.'

Actually, it's not even my first week, thought Gordy. She'd managed one day in her new role, and most of that on a magical mystery tour of Somerset, and here she was already being called in the middle of the night to go and attend something or other. What, though, she almost didn't want to find out, because no one ever called in the middle of the night with good news and something fun and exciting to do.

Patti was still quiet, but Gordy waited. She had always preferred to give people time, instead of hurrying them along. Hurrying led to panic, which led to mistakes, and that just wasn't how she did things. But eventually, and with Patti's silence still holding, she decided that a gentle nudge was perhaps needed.

'Patti?'

'Yes?'

'You'll actually need to tell me what it is if I'm to do anything about it,' Gordy said, as lightly and relaxed as she could. 'So ...?'

'There's a body,' Patti said, blurting the words out like she just wanted rid of them and the bad taste they had. 'It's ... well, we don't ...'

Gordy heard a shiver of panic in Patti's voice. Or perhaps it wasn't panic, just a little dose of shock. Though she had no doubt that the sergeant had dealt with plenty of grisly things in her role; all part of the job.

'Where?'

'Nunney.'

'The village with the castle? Really?'

'Yes, why?'

Gordy couldn't believe it.

'Nothing, it's just it formed part of Jack's very detailed and entertaining tour, and I'd planned on making my way back there again soon. Just not this soon, or for such a reason. Where exactly in Nunney?'

'Actually, at the castle,' Patti explained. 'He—the body, I mean—it was found by someone sleeping rough inside the castle itself. Uniform have been sent to secure the scene, and we've an initial report of what's been found.'

'And what has been found, exactly?' Gordy asked, already dreading the answer.

She heard Patti take a breath.

'He's been impaled on a spike,' she said.

'I'm sorry, what?'

'A spike,' Patti repeated. 'That's all we know so far, really.'

'I'm on my way.'

Moments later, Gordy was dressed and in her vehicle, heading out of Evercreech, but instead of taking the route she had the previous morning, she turned left at the tiny hamlet of Stoney Stratton and pushed on up a steep hill. The road ran straight, with just a small number of corners once Gordy had reached the top of the rise, before cutting its way between dark, shadow-laden walls of hedge on either side. Soon, she was at the main road, now empty of vehicles, and taking a right, she accelerated hard.

With her headlights pulling her on, cutting a tunnel through the night, Gordy saw them catch the occasional glimmer of an eye from deer or fox or bird. Zipping past the entrance to a quarry, she eventually slowed to meet a roundabout, and followed the signs, taking her off left and on into the village of Nunney.

Along the side of the road, houses were dark as people slept on, as yet unaware of what was unfolding in the village's ancient heart. Right then, Gordy had little idea herself, but something in her gut told her that whatever it was she was about to walk into, it was nothing normal. But then, when would a body impaled on a spike ever be normal? she thought.

She could recall one similar event, a good few years ago now in the Dales, where a farmer had ended up skewered on a bale spike attached to his tractor. By some chance or miracle, or a mix of the two, the spike had managed to not only miss all of his main organs, but seal the wound shut. Unable to move, the farmer had had no choice but to wait until he was found by his eldest daughter, who worked the farm with him. She had driven into the yard where he was pinned, almost passed out at the sight of the spike rammed through her father's torso, but managed to call the rescue services. How he had been freed, Gordy wasn't sure, but the event had been the talk of the Dales for a good while after. Unsurprisingly, the farmer had been given the nickname Spike, and it had stuck with him ever since.

In the centre of the Nunney, Gordy took a left over the small bridge spanning a river, then an immediate right. There, directly in front of her, the vast stone structure of the castle sat silent and still. The broken walls, which a little bit of internet research the previous evening had told her had been smashed apart by Cromwell during the First English Civil War, were darker than the night that rested on the castle's shoulders like a thick, velvet cloak.

Climbing out of her vehicle, Gordy took a breath, exhaled slowly, then made her way past several police vehicles, until she came to a small gate in a wall surrounding the castle, at which a uniformed officer was standing guard.

Patti was there, waiting for her.

'That was quick,' she said, looking at Gordy.

'I sleep in my clothes,' Gordy replied, and watched Patti's eyes widen at her words. 'Joke.'

Patti's face wrestled with the idea of smiling, then gave up.

'It's through here,' she said, then pointed over to the castle. 'Just over there, on the other side of the bridge that crosses the moat. We've put cordon tape both here and round the other side as well, to cut off that half of the path, and stationed an officer on both sides. The path goes all the way around, you see, and the moat is a pretty good deterrent to anyone wanting to sneak in and see what's going on.'

'More fool anyone trying,' Gordy said, as she came to stand next to Patti and saw, just a ways below where she was standing, the inky black water of the moat. It sat around the feet of the castle, still and foreboding, and though Gordy doubted it was all that deep, it was still an eerie thing to stare down into, and for a moment she felt sure that it was calling to her to just slip beneath its depths. She added, 'Swimming that is asking for goodness knows how many revolting things to enter your system.'

Patti headed off, but Gordy held her back.

'We need a scene guard,' she said. 'Or was that officer at the gate supposed to take my details?'

'Scene Guard is a bit closer to the crime scene,' Patti said, pointing into the darkness ahead, which swirled around the base of the castle, thick and silent.

'Forensics?'

'Scene of Crime team are aware of the incident and await your call. An ambulance is on its way.'

Falling into step behind Patti, Gordy followed the sergeant through the dark, her footsteps crunching on the gravel path like shingle on a beach.

Ahead, she saw another figure in the darkness, smartly dressed in uniform, and recognised Detective Constable Knight immediately.

'Morning, Pete,' she said, coming to a stop in front of him, barely holding back a yawn. 'It is morning, isn't it? Something like that, anyway.'

Behind the constable, another strip of cordon tape was across the path.

'You're the Scene Guard, then?' Gordy asked.

Pete revealed a small clipboard.

'Have you made a reservation, ma'am?' he asked, glancing at the clipboard. 'Booking for two, was it? I can check to see if we have space or not, though there might be a wait.'

Gordy was genuinely impressed. She had been in plenty of situations where, to anyone else, humour would seem out of place, but she knew the value of it, and apparently, so did Pete, which was impressive for one so new to the force.

'Has anyone other than the officer first on the scene been to have a look?'

'That was me, and no,' Pete said.

Gordy saw a dark look flitter across the young man's eyes, the horror of what he had seen obviously still vivid in his mind.

'You were first on-scene?'

'I was the closest, and I was on duty, so yes.'

'What about the witness?' Gordy asked, then looked at Patti. 'Someone sleeping rough, I think you said.'

'He's back there,' Patti said, pointing back up the path to the small gate and the collection of police vehicles. 'PCSO Edwards is with him, making sure he's calm, keeping him warm with some hot, sweet tea and a few biscuits, that kind of thing.'

'And there's no one better to do it, either,' added Pete. 'That man could calm down Leatherface.'

Gordy frowned at that, confused by a reference she didn't understand.

'Leatherface?' Pete repeated, clearly picking up Gordy's confusion. 'Wears someone else's face, wields a chainsaw, and runs around chopping people up with it?'

Gordy had a vague recollection of the title of a film she'd never watched and never would, either, for that matter.

'I'll want to have a chat with him once we're done here,' she said.

'Of course,' said Patti. 'The witness's name is Bill Halliday. Ex-soldier. Homeless. Nice and chatty, actually, especially considering what he stumbled on. My guess is he's seen a few things himself, if you know what I mean.'

'He's been in theatre, then?'

That got a quizzical look from both Patti and Pete.

'Sorry,' Gordy apologised. 'Used to work with an ex-Para; picked up some of his jargon. What I meant was, he's been on tour, you know, active service?'

'Judging by his stories, very much so,' said Patti. 'And I think dealing with them, or not, is why he's ended up living as he does.'

Gordy asked, 'You said he found the body while he was sleeping rough in the castle?'

'Yes,' Patti answered.

'And that the body is on the other side of the bridge?'

Patti gave a nod.

'Then I'm confused as to how those turn of events took place,' Gordy said. 'If the body was there before he entered the castle, how did he not see it? And if it wasn't, how did it being put there not wake him up?'

Neither Patti nor Pete could provide an answer, and both remained silent.

Gordy gestured towards the castle.

'Come on, then,' she said, pulling a torch from her jacket pocket. 'Let's go and have a look for ourselves, shall we?'

EIGHT

Dipping under the cordon tape, Gordy led Patti along the path a little further to where she saw the small, wooden bridge crossing the moat. To the side stood an illustrated information board, and even just a glance at it showed her just how much history was in these broken walls. She put on some disposable covers for her shoes and Patti did the same.

Stepping onto the bridge, she was aware again of the moat, but wondered at how effective it would've been as a defensive measure. Perhaps it had served as more of a decorative design feature than anything else. No doubt the information board would tell her, but there were more important things to examine, and even from where she was now standing, it was utterly impossible to avoid exactly what. Still, it was unnerving to shuffle over the stagnant water.

Above her, the castle walls loomed and staring up at them made her a little dizzy. It was as though she was acutely aware of their vastness, their weight, and she felt suddenly very small and insignificant. She could see the night through the empty windows and cracks in the walls, the eye of the moon glaring through one high in the wall opposite, as though it was trying to see what she was doing. Wind whistled faintly through the structure, calling out with a tune both sorrowful and haunting.

To say that the body drew the eye would've been a huge understatement, Gordy thought, because it was utterly impossible to look at anything else. Though the finer details were not yet visible, the hideous shape of it was enough to cause Gordy to pause.

'Everything okay?' Patti asked, coming up alongside her.

'Just taking my time,' Gordy said, pulling her eyes away from what she was walking towards. 'I'm assuming you've informed DCI Allercott?'

Patti fell quiet.

'Something the matter?' Gordy asked.

'No, it's just that ...' Patti paused.

'It's just that what?'

'Well, you see, I haven't actually informed her,' Patti said, then held up her hands in defence and added, 'Not on purpose ... I mean, I didn't do it on purpose, you know, not tell her, and I will, it's just that with you here, and then with how our last DI worked, and she's not on duty tonight either, so ...'

Gordy turned her back on the castle and its horrifying visitor for a moment.

'And how exactly did your last DI work?' she asked. 'Matthews, wasn't it?'

'It was,' Patti said. 'And he ... well ... he kind of didn't tell her things.'

'Any chance of you being a wee bit more specific there, Sergeant? What kind of things, exactly? What he had for breakfast, his twelve favourite shapes?'

'Favourite shapes?'

'It's both late and early,' Gordy said, failing to hide a yawn. 'Even I don't know where that came from. But answer the question.'

'I guess they just didn't really get on,' Patti explained. 'She—'

'You mean Detective Chief Inspector Allercott,' Gordy corrected, albeit gently.

'Yes,' said Patti. 'DI Matthews always thought that she just ... got in the way.'

Gordy's eyes went wide.

'She's our DCI!' she said. 'It's kind of her job to get in the way, I think, don't you? Comes with the rank. And you'll have noticed, I'm sure, that I'm not Matthews. Call her. Now. And while you're at it, the SOC team as well; I think we've seen enough already to know that this is not simply a case of someone tripping over and oh, whoops, a spike has impaled me from backside to bonce.'

Gordy heard the edge in her voice, and backed it up by folding her arms across her chest. Considering how she had felt yesterday, almost as though she was piloting herself from inside her own skull, protected from the outside world, right now, on the site of a truly horrific crime scene, she felt oddly alive, something she hadn't felt since ...

'Done,' said Patti, cutting through Gordy's thoughts, much to her own relief.

'And?'

'She's on her way. At least I think she is.'

That answer confused Gordy.

'How do you mean?'

'She hung up before I had a chance to give her the location. Think I got caught up in the finer, more gruesome details, and she just said she'd be here ASAP, and that was that.'

'You called her back, though, yes?'

'I did, but her phone went to voicemail.'

'Then how will she get here if she doesn't even know where here is?'

'I sent a text. Hopefully she'll get that.'

'Well, that's the best we can do, I suppose,' Gordy shrugged. 'But you agree that calling her was the right thing to do, yes?'

'I do,' said Patti.

'Good,' said Gordy.

'Called the SOC team as well,' Patti added. 'And you'll know when they arrive, that's for sure.'

Gordy looked at Patti through narrowed eyes.

'And what exactly do you mean by that?'

'I think it's best you discover that for yourself.'

'Not even a clue? A hint of some kind? I'm not one for mystery if it's not needed, which, I'll be honest with you, it isn't right now, is it, seeing as we already have plenty to be getting on with?'

Patti shook her head.

'No clue, no hint, no mystery, just something you have to experience firsthand.'

Gordy gave a shrug.

'Well, if that's how it's going to be, how's about we crack on and see if we can work out how our friend over there ended up being skewered like a kebab?'

Gordy caught the cold scent of the wind whipping around the castle as it explored every nook and cranny it could. Then the air brought with it another taste, something metallic, and she allowed her eyes to fall again on the reason for her middle-of-the-night trip.

Using the beam of her torch to trace the figure, the light stroking its contours like the gentle bristles of an artist's brush, Gordy gave herself a moment to take it all in.

The body was on its knees, which gave it the look of someone deep in prayer. They were wearing a boiler suit, though Gordy couldn't make out if it was blue or black, so dirty was it, and so dark the night.

Gordy guessed by the figure's build that it was a man, but really, at this point, everything was a guess, not least because their head was hidden beneath a rotting, threadbare sack, the kind she had seen potatoes in at market stalls and farm shops, to give them that rustic, artisan feel. Though how a potato could be artisan, she hadn't the faintest idea.

The figure had the build of someone who had, she guessed, once upon a time been rather sporty, muscular even, but had let it all sag a little over the years, with the weight of life taking over from weights at the gym. He certainly wasn't skinny, but the fact that he was on his knees made Gordy think that getting him into position hadn't been too difficult. If he had been standing, that would have been an entirely different matter. Regardless of the practicalities of how he was displayed, she could see that at some point in his life, he must have been quite imposing to behold. And in death, no less so. Perhaps more so, considering how he was dressed.

Gordy dropped the beam of her torch to the ground, the sallow light catching the end of the spike the figure was impaled on, pleased to have taken her eyes from the awfulness for a moment. Keeping the beam steady, she circled the body until she was able to see where the spike had entered, and also where it was thrust into the ground.

Crouching, Gordy went in for a closer look.

'What do you think about this?' she asked, calling Patti over.

Patti joined Gordy, easing herself down beside her.

'How do you mean?' she asked.

'The ground,' Gordy said. 'Where the spike goes in, just there, you see? There's something off about it, isn't there?'

Gordy pulled on a pair of disposable rubber gloves, then reached out a finger, brushing gently at the earth.

'Looks just like soil to me,' said Patti.

Gordy edged her finger towards the spike, poked down a little, and came to a stop.

'There's something hard just beneath the surface,' she said.

'You mean like a rock or something?'

'Not a clue,' Gordy replied. 'And between you and me, I've plenty of experience with SOC teams to know it's generally best to leave well enough alone and let them find out first. Otherwise, they get a bit antsy about it all and think you're stealing their thunder. And believe you me, I've enough of a storm going on in my own life and have zero interest in adding to it.'

That last comment got a quizzical look from Patti, so Gordy quickly moved on.

'Bit odd though, isn't it?'

'A marked understatement, that,' muttered Patti.

Gordy traced the beam of her torch back up the spike, dreading what else she might see, though was fully aware that it was unavoidable, no matter how awful. She had already detached herself as best she could from what was in front of her, but that didn't make it any easier. Instead, it simply enabled her to view things objectively, clearly, and not get wound up in the horror of it all, and the numerous possible reasons as to how and why it had happened in the first place.

'Dear God in Heaven,' she said, staring at the entry wound.

The boilersuit the figure was wearing had been roughly pulled or hacked apart at the seam, and the iron spike entered his body through the most obvious route.

Staring at it, Gordy wondered briefly if there was something a little wrong with her own head that she wasn't at all surprised, and had almost been expecting it. She noticed then, that the man's lower back and his buttocks were a smashed up, bleeding mess. It looked as though numerous attempts had been made to insert the spike into his anus, the surrounding area dotted with seeping stab wounds.

'I'm surprised it was that difficult to hit the target,' said Patti.

'How do you mean?' Gordy asked.

'Well, and I know this is going to sound a bit weird, but a bit of lube and it would've slipped in easily, wouldn't it?'

Patti then, for reasons Gordy couldn't immediately fathom, proceeded to push a finger from her left hand into the closed fist of her right, and made sort of a squelchy sound effect with her mouth.

'Well, I can't say I was expecting any of that at all,' Gordy said.

'I warned you it would sound weird,' said Patti. 'So, why do you think they, whoever did this, took so many attempts?'

Gordy realised that Patti had a point. Why had they made such a mess of trying to take the obvious route, and instead gone somewhat off-piste?

Standing up, Gordy stepped back and allowed her eyes to drift upwards once again to where the spike exited the figure's mouth. Though the face was mostly hidden behind the scant threads of the sack pulled over their head, the white of their teeth caught the glare of her torch and shone brightly. A number of them had been rammed out of the way, and hung loosely on threads of bleeding gum, the lips ripped and torn with the violence of what had taken place.

'In answer to your question, I haven't the faintest idea,' Gordy said. 'Fury, rage, alcohol, drugs, confusion, who knows? All we know is what we have in front of us.'

'And that it's horrific.'

'Aye, that pretty much sums it up.'

'Do you think he was alive when it happened?'

Gordy felt her eyes go wide.

'I bloody well hope not,' she said, but even as she did so, she noticed something else, and to confirm it, reached out to pinch the material of the boilersuit between her fingers.

'He's sopping wet,' she said.

'All that blood I should think,' said Patti.

Gordy shook her head.

'No, it's not,' she said, then checked elsewhere, up and down the figure and what they were wearing. 'It's water. Yes, there's blood, but it's like he's been …'

She stopped talking and swung her beam to the moat. The dark, oily water beckoned to her silently, promising things she didn't want to hear.

'But if whoever this is, was in there,' she said, staring into the dark, reed-strangled depths, before placing her torch beam once again on the figure, 'then how the hell did they end up like this? And why?'

Patti was given no time to answer as a voice called across the bridge.

Gordy glanced over and saw the petite figure of DCI Allercott.

NINE

Gordy waved at Allercott, a little too cheerfully, she thought, and immediately regretted it. The smile she could feel herself wearing like an ill-fitting shirt, didn't help any either. What the hell was wrong with her? Well, she knew exactly what, didn't she? The person inside was not the person she was allowing everyone else to see, not by a long shot, so she was having trouble maintaining some sense of continuity in how she was coming across.

She didn't want to let people in, she just wasn't ready, didn't know if she ever would be. Frankly, right then, it was all about surviving, so she'd deal with any fallout from it at a later date. A much later date. Maybe never.

Pulling on a pair of disposable rubber gloves as she approached, Allercott crossed the bridge, trip-trapping across it like one of the three Billy Goats Gruff. Gordy wasn't too sure which one.

The DCI was small, yes, but something told Gordy that she was disguising a strength, both physical and mental. Perhaps it was the way she carried herself, walking with a sense of awareness of her own body that, to Gordy, suggested she looked after herself. And perhaps it was also in the haircut, and her focused stare as she came to stand with her and Patti. Whatever it was, and whatever she'd learned about Allercott from the people she'd met so far, she was going to reserve judgement.

Perhaps Detective Superintendent Firbank would be able to shed a little more light on this somewhat enigmatic DCI later on, assuming she was able to get there, and didn't get held up by this. Which, she probably would, because that was police work; you made your plans, then someone decided to inconvenience you with a gruesome murder. It was the way of things.

For a few moments, Allercott said nothing, just stood and stared at the scene before them, only moving her head to take it all in. Gordy was fairly sure she didn't blink either, and she felt as though she was in the presence of a wax doll from Madame Tussauds. She saw no emotion, bar a final narrowing of the eyes, and a clenching of her jaw.

'SOC team's on their way as well,' Gordy said, mainly because the silence was unnerving her, as was Allercott's body language. 'Patti gave them a call after she spoke with you.'

This got a reaction from Allercott, but not one she expected. The woman startled, snapping around to stare at her, her oddly sombre mood popping like a balloon.

'What? When? I mean, of course they are, but what time? Do we know how long? Before they get here, I mean?'

Gordy, taken aback by the sudden barrage of questions, glanced over at Patti, who gave a noncommittal shrug and suggested, 'Half an hour maybe? Ish? But that was when I called so, I'm not really sure.'

Allercott removed her gloves and turned sharply to face Gordy, handing her the gloves.

'I believe you have this all in hand,' she said. 'Keep me updated.'

'Of course, aye,' Gordy said. 'I just thought you might want to be Officer in Charge.'

Allercott shook her head.

'I'm putting you on as OIC,' she said. 'You're new to the area, so this will be a great way for you to stamp your authority on the team.'

'I'm not one for stamping anything on anywhere,' Gordy replied, but Allercott was already at the bridge.

As she watched her trip-trap across once more, Gordy was sure that she could hear music. It jarred with the peace of the village and the castle, almost more so than the body.

Allercott was on the other side of the bridge when she turned around and called over, 'I hope this isn't a sign of things to come, Detective Inspector, and that you've not gone and brought something with you from where you were before.'

'What?' Gordy replied, actually shocked. 'You can't be suggesting that my joining the team has somehow caused this?'

Then, bizarrely, Allercott's usually stern face broke into a grin.

'A joke,' she said. 'Humour helps with these kinds of things, don't you think?'

Gordy said nothing, because she had nothing to say, then watched as, instead of turning left to head back to where she must have parked, the DCI turned right, to take the long way around the castle.

The music was louder now.

'What is that?' she asked, looking at Patti.

'What is what?'

'That!' Gordy said, pointing into the air as though to do so would identify the sounds filling it. 'Who the hell is playing Country and Western music at this time of night, and here?'

Joining in with the music came the thrum of two large diesel engines and Gordy stepped onto the bridge to see a couple of tired-looking white vans pull up over where she had parked.

The driver opened his door, and the music grew louder, if that was at all possible.

'That's the SOC Team,' Patti said. Then she pointed at the driver, who was pulling open the side door. 'And that,' she then added, 'is Cowboy.'

TEN

Of the many things Gordy had seen in her life, a man skewered by a spike beside a castle and its moat, in the middle of the night, was certainly one of the most gruesome. However, what approached her then was, though not gruesome in any way, almost more bizarre.

Like a parade at a carnival, they came two by two in a line behind their leader, a tall man who was, against all sense and reason, wearing a large, white Stetson hat atop the usual garb of white, disposable PPE overalls.

Gordy actually did a double-take, shook her head, rubbed her eyes, but none of it worked; the hat was still on the man's head, a huge white thing more befitting a sheriff in a spaghetti Western than someone about to take apart a crime scene piece by detailed piece.

A figure with the fronds of a black fringe poking out from under the hood of their white paper suit, who followed closely behind the man she currently knew only as Cowboy, was carrying something Gordy had not seen in decades; an honest-to-God, 80s boombox, with a twin tape deck. The rest of the team were all lugging various other crates and aluminium boxes and everything else they needed to get to work on a crime scene. But a boombox?

Cowboy and his posse arrived at the other side of the bridge.

Gordy caught sight of movement over by the small gate and saw Allercott ducking through quickly, clearly not wishing to be seen.

Then Gordy noticed the tune and realised that she'd only been putting off recognising it because she absolutely despised it, every note putting her teeth on edge; it was Rhinestone Cowboy, by Glen Campbell.

As tunes went, it was one she would, if it came on the radio, turn the radio off, and if that meant using a hammer to do so, all the better, because no radio that had been allowed to send such awfulness into the world could ever be allowed to suffer again. It was surely the kind thing to do.

She had been known to walk out of pubs playing it, rip jukebox plugs out of the wall for daring to let the god-awful racket enter her listening space. She'd even threatened to arrest a busker for playing it, because back when she had been in uniform, and been out on patrol in a busy city centre, he'd played it six times in one hour. It had been all she could do to not smash his guitar over his head just to shut him the hell up.

She had issues with the song. Ones she had, until now, completely forgotten about, but once resurfaced, simply added a new flavour of poison to what was already swirling around inside her. So, as she headed across the bridge to meet Cowboy, she was already not in the best of moods, dark clouds swirling inside her as foreboding as a storm falling down the mountainsides of Glencoe.

'That, off, now,' she said, jabbing a hard finger at the boombox.

The man with the black fringe, who was holding the boombox, frowned at Gordy, did not do as she had ordered, and instead looked to Cowboy for direction.

The music still blared.

The storm in Gordy crackled with lightning, and thunder boomed inside her head as she waited.

'Whoa, take 'er easy, there, Pilgrim,' said Cowboy, in what Gordy could only assume was his attempt at a John Wayne impression.

To her, it sounded more like Foghorn Leghorn. Cowboy looked a little like him, too, she thought, though she wasn't entirely sure how that was possible. But he did have a huge mouth, which if she squinted, and really used her imagination, could perhaps look like a beak.

'I'm Detective Inspector Haig,' Gordy said. 'OIC for this crime scene.'

'And I'm Cowboy,' said Cowboy, then he scanned the area. 'No Allercott?'

'Already left,' said the figure with the black fringe, before Gordy could say the same herself, though how he knew, she had no idea. Must've spotted her as they were coming in, she thought.

'Now, ain't that a darn shame,' Cowboy lamented, the words falling from him lasciviously, Gordy thought, and immediately understood why Allercott had done a runner; intentionally or not, the man seemed very happy to make the worst of first impressions.

And still, the music was raking at the night. It was loud, it was misplaced in the extreme, and it was close to getting its hooks into Gordy to drag her somewhere she didn't want to go, and hadn't been to in decades.

Before anyone could react, she had the boombox in her hand. The shock in the eyes of not only the man who had carried it but Cowboy's was, she thought, quite delicious.

She switched it off, ejected the tape, and went to throw it in the moat, then pocketed it, much to her own surprise.

'Now,' she said, 'perhaps we can all have a sensible conversation?'

When Cowboy spoke next, his American drawl had faded and been replaced with something a little more at home around Birmingham. Not quite Ozzy Ozbourne, but not far off.

'Not a fan of Country, then?'

'My opinion on music is neither here nor there,' said Gordy. 'You're the pathologist?'

The abject disbelief in her question lit the words like petrol poured on a bonfire.

'Hell no,' Cowboy said. 'Pathologist is Charming.'

Gordy wanted to ask if that was a name or a description of the pathologist's character, but Cowboy was still talking.

'I'm head of the Scene of Crime team. Though I do pop by the mortuary on occasion to give a helping hand with things, should the need arise.'

'And I'm assuming you have another name, despite the one you've already given me.'

'It's what everyone calls me.'

'I'm not everyone.'

For a moment, no one said a word and Gordy used that time to hold Cowboy's gaze, her own face passive, but her stare strong enough to show she wasn't about to back down.

'Keith,' Cowboy said eventually. 'I'm Keith Brown.'

'But we call him Cowboy,' said a voice from someone in the team, though Gordy couldn't see who.

'Well then, Mr Brown,' Gordy said, 'your parade includes a photographer, yes?'

Cowboy called someone out from behind him, and a figure stepped forward wearing, like everyone else on the team, the disposable white paper suit that was the SOC team uniform. The suit was tight in all the wrong places and made him look like a really rubbish fancy dress version of the Stay Puffed Marshmallow Man from Ghostbusters.

That immediate comparison took Gordy by complete surprise. It was a film she had not seen in a very long time, but which had always been a bit of a guilty pleasure. But then she did have a thing for eighties movies. That had always made Anna laugh, especially the way she had been able to recite The Breakfast Club, word for word, when they'd watched it one evening, back in the early days of dating each other.

That quite unexpected, and very happy memory, took Gordy's breath away a little, and she stepped back to allow the photographer over the bridge, her mind elsewhere for a moment. Hearing Anna's laugh, as she shovelled in handfuls of popcorn and looked at her with the first sparks of love.

A few minutes later, a voice cut into her thoughts.

'DI Haig?'

Gordy shook herself free of the memory to see that Cowboy was talking to her.

'Yes?'

'I think we might have got off on the wrong foot.'

She saw that he was holding out his hand.

She reached out to shake it, and something buzzed in her palm.

Snatching her hand back, she stared at the man so hotly she wanted his face to melt.

'What in the name of—?'

Cowboy held up his hand to show, attached to a thin metal band around a finger, a metal device that had given her the deeply unpleasant buzz.

'Brilliant, right?' he said. 'Only cost me a couple of quid. Bargain.'

'Are you absolutely sure you're head of the Scene of Crime team?' Gordy asked, rubbing her palm, even though there was no pain, and narrowing her eyes at the man.

Cowboy wasn't given a chance to answer, as the photographer had returned from across the bridge.

'Well,' he said, 'that's something I'll never be able to unsee.'

'Didn't take you long,' said Patti.

'Not much to photograph,' the photographer replied.

'Over to you, then,' Gordy said, and gestured across the bridge for Cowboy to lead his team on.

As they passed, Patti leaned in close and whispered, 'The thing is, as annoying and clearly off-the-scale bonkers as he seems, he's actually brilliant.'

'Really ...' said Gordy, scepticism dripping from her lips.

'And he works really well with the pathologist. Mind you, the pathologist works really well with everyone. He's an acquired taste, though, I'll give him that.'

'And one I look forward to never acquiring.'

Over the other side of the moat, Cowboy and his team got to

work, and Gordy felt like she wanted to be anywhere but near them and their very strange leader.

'I think we should go and have a chat with our one witness, don't you?' she said, and without waiting for an answer, strode off along the path, with Patti following on behind.

25 YEARS AGO, 1:51PM ...

Austin gave a sigh.

'Mine would, but then he says no to most things. It's his favourite word, I'm sure.'

Jennifer saw a flicker of darkness in Austin's eyes.

'He's let you have these two weeks off though, hasn't he?'

'He's not happy about it, though. The estate needs me, apparently, what with shooting season round the corner, various properties needing looking at, the farm—'

A polite knock rapped against the open door, and a shadow cut across the floor. Jennifer turned to see a man standing there. He was around the same age as her father, perhaps a few years younger and slightly less well dressed, wearing as he was a worn waxed jacket and jeans, despite the sunshine of the day.

'Hi, Jack,' she said, smiling brightly. Then she gestured to herself, and asked, 'You like?'

Jack Harris cocked his head to one side.

'Not for me to say if I do or don't, Miss Clayton.'

'That's a no if ever I heard one, isn't it, Austin?' Jennifer said, raising a questioning eyebrow.

Austin shrugged and Jennifer waited for Jack to reveal the reason for his appearance. He'd turned up at her door numerous times over the years, a close friend of her father's, from his days in Sandhurst and then their respective careers in the army. Returning from a tour of duty, he hadn't fared so well as her father had, the experiences haunting him, and if it hadn't been for her parents stepping in to help, then ...

'Young Mr Cartwright asked me to tell you that you're needed on set in fifteen minutes.'

Jennifer rolled her eyes. Tristan had been the second person she'd asked to join in with the film, and he'd jumped at the chance, offering his services as director, and giving Jennifer no other option other than to say yes.

'You do know you don't work for him, don't you, Jack?' she asked. 'If he orders you about again, you just tell him to bugger off.'

She saw a flicker of a smile in the corner of Jack's mouth.

'I was coming this way anyway,' he said. 'Your father asked me to fetch a jacket from his room, so it was no bother, really. Shall I tell him you're on your way?'

Jennifer shook her head.

'I'll be down in my own good time,' she said, then glanced at Austin. 'Honestly, you'd think we were working on something straight out of Hollywood!'

'Not sure Tristan understands what low-budget actually means,' Austin said, his voice quiet, conspiratorial. 'Seems to think he's Spielberg.'

Jennifer agreed.

'He's as mad as his dad.'

'Not quite.'

Jennifer sniggered.

'No, maybe not.'

She remembered hearing about Tristan's somewhat unstable father in the first year of her degree. It wasn't something he had ever told anyone himself, but then he hadn't needed to; the Tabloids had done it for him.

'He's not even that good,' she said, briefly wondering if Tristan really was taking after his dad. 'I'm amazed he even passed his degree.'

'Then why did you ask him to direct?'

'Well, first, I didn't; he offered, and second, everyone else was either busy or on holiday. He is a bit shouty, though, isn't he?'

'A little.'

'Also, and I know you'll laugh at this, but I kind of felt a bit sorry for him. It's not his fault, is it, what his dad is like? Can't be easy.'

'Even so ...'

'Miss Clayton?'

Jennifer hadn't realised that Jack was still standing expectantly in her bedroom doorway.

'Is there something else?' she asked. Then she saw a look in Jack's eyes, one she recognised all too well, and added, 'It's Dad, isn't it? I can tell. What does he want?'

Jack shuffled a little, clearly awkward.

'He's asked if you're free this evening, Miss Clayton, that's all.'

'Any reason why he's not come up here and asked me himself? No, don't answer; he's too busy.'

'He does the best he can,' said Jack. 'You're a lucky girl, I mean, young woman, living where you do, with what you have. He works hard, yes, but it's all for you, as well you know.'

Jennifer heard the gentle chastisement in Jack's voice.

'Mum would come and ask ...'

Jack said nothing, just stayed quiet.

Jennifer allowed the silence to grow just awkward enough before she said anymore, but Jack spoke first.

'I see you've your mother's jewellery box. Took me so long to make it. It's not very good, but with the kindness she showed me, I ...'

'It's beautiful,' Jennifer said, noticing the awkwardness in Jack's voice. 'I love it.'

'Your dad still uses the stick I made him as well,' Jack added.

'You're quite the craftsman,' Jennifer said. 'So, tell me, then, what does dear Daddy want to do this evening?'

ELEVEN

Gordy found PCSO Paul Edwards standing outside one of the team's vehicles, the rear door open. Sitting inside, his hands clasped around a metal mug of tea, was the dishevelled figure of Bill Halliday.

'I see the circus is in town,' Paul said, and Gordy knew exactly what he was referring to.

'Patti's attempted to convince me that Mr Keith "Cowboy" Brown knows what he's doing. I find it very hard to believe.'

Paul smiled.

'Please keep calling him Keith,' he said.

'Why?'

'He'll hate it.'

'A good enough reason, then,' Gordy said with a wink, then glanced over Paul's shoulder at Bill.

'Anything to report?'

'Well, he's certainly got plenty of stories,' said Paul. 'Put him on stage and he'd make a killing. Though some of it might be a bit too much for most people; he's had a rough time of it. Every now and again he'll just break off and sit there with this thousand-yard stare.'

Gordy took in Bill's attire, noting that he seemed to be wearing a good deal of kit usually found in a military surplus store.

'Why was he at the castle?'

'He likes to stay away from towns, areas where there are too many people,' Paul explained. 'He was in Frome earlier in the day, actually. When I saw him tonight, I remembered speaking to him. He was on the bridge, the one from the car park at the Cheese Grain, over to the shopping arcade. He was just trying to get a bit of spare change, if anyone was kind enough to give him some.'

'And were they?'

Paul gave a shrug.

'People like Bill, they're invisible, aren't they? I helped a bit, though, because that's what you do, isn't it?'

'Not sure everyone would agree with that sentiment,' said Gordy.

'I'm not everyone,' Paul replied, and Gordy couldn't help but warm to the genuineness of his response, and note how much milder his use of it was when compared to her own just a few minutes ago with Cowboy. 'I've already arranged for him to check in with some local support, see if we can't at least provide him with some new kit, some food, help him get cleaned up a bit.'

'What about a bed?' Gordy asked.

'You can't force someone off the street,' said Paul. 'That's not how it works. Build up trust first, provide a safe zone, I guess. So, I've also told him I'll check up on him over the next few days, which'll make sure he's still in the area while we're on with this investigation. He usually camps out in woodlands, leaves no trace either; ex-military, so he has the skills to survive.'

'That explains his gear and clothing, then,' said Gordy, adding, 'Well, I'd best have a word with him, then.'

'Oh, and there's something you need to ask him about as well; Allercott popped by to have a chat with him, probably to avoid being seen by Cowboy. They don't get on, you know.'

'I gathered,' said Gordy. 'Though my impression is that Cowboy would very much like to.'

'That's it right there,' Paul nodded. 'Anyway, Allercott, she had a chat with him, asked if he'd heard anything, and it turns out he did.'

'What?'

'A whistle.'

'You mean like a dog whistle?'

Paul shook his head.

'No, as in someone actually whistling, like a tune. She asked him about it, but said you should maybe push him a bit on it, just in case.'

Paul leaned into the car and said something to Bill. Gordy saw the man look up at her as she walked around to scooch in beside him.

'Hi,' she said, sitting down in the rear of the car. The smell wasn't enough to make her eyes water, but she was in no doubt that a good deal of time had passed since Bill had last had a decent wash or worn clean clothing. He didn't smell dirty, as such, more well lived in. There was an aroma about him of field and farm, of smoky fires and tobacco, and something sweeter behind it that she recognised well enough, too, but didn't begrudge him it, because who was she to judge how someone managed to survive living the life he had found himself in? There was no smell of booze, which struck her as a positive.

'Evening,' Bill replied. 'No, it's morning, isn't it? I think. God, I'm tired. I mean, I'm usually tired, anyway, but this is different; don't feel like I've been asleep at all.'

'I'm Detective Inspector Haig,' Gordy said. 'But you can call me Gordy.'

'Bill Halliday,' said Bill. 'Gordy ... that's a name I've not heard before.'

'It's short for Gordanian.'

'You a Highlander?'

Gordy smiled at that.

'Interesting statement.'

'Served with a couple of lads from that way, and the accent's softer than anything from Glasgow, isn't it? More musical.'

'I like to think so.'

'I know so.'

Gordy felt herself warming to Bill immediately. He had an honesty about him that spoke of someone who either had little to hide, or who had just decided that trying to hide things served no purpose.

'You've had quite the night,' she said.

'I've had better, that's for sure,' said Bill. 'I'm sorry if I'm not supposed to sleep in the castle. It's public access, and I promise I'll be away with no bother, no mess.'

'I don't think you've anything to worry about. And who could resist the chance to sleep somewhere so grand?'

Bill laughed.

'Must've been quite a place back in the day. And I'd have had little chance of sleeping in it then, I'm quite sure.'

Sipping his tea, Bill fell quiet for a moment, and Gordy allowed him that time to just get used to her being with him.

'Are you okay to take me through what happened?' she asked, once Bill had rested his mug on his lap once more.

'You won't take my stash, will you?' Bill asked suddenly, his voice hushed and nervous. 'I've not got much. I don't deal or anything. It's just something that, well, it helps, you know? With getting to sleep, helping me to relax.'

'I could not be less interested,' said Gordy, and she saw Bill's shoulders fall a little with relief. She took out her small black notebook and a pencil. 'I'm just here to listen, that's all. You okay if I take some notes?'

'I can't see what I've got to tell that'll be much help,' Bill said. 'And I've told your PCSO Edwards plenty enough. And that tiny woman with the dramatic hair. Can't remember her name ... Dovecote?'

'Allercott.'

'That's it.'

'Well, if you can tell me everything again, that would be really helpful,' said Gordy, making sure her voice was relaxed, calm, non-threatening. 'Then at least I'll have the information myself as well, and I can discuss it with PCSO Edwards and the rest of the team, make sure we've got all the facts. And you never know, you might remember something that you've not told them.'

Bill laughed, but with little humour.

'Trust me, I'll not be forgetting this night for years, if ever.'

Gordy said nothing more, waiting for Bill to allow the words to come.

'Can't remember what time I arrived,' Bill said. 'Been a long day, what with sitting on the bridge to try and get a bit of change from people passing by. I don't expect much, because that's not fair, is it? But enough people gave me a quid or two, and that PCSO of yours, he was quite generous. He's a good lad, you know, worth keeping a hold of. Anyway, after that, I took myself out of the town, because I always prefer to sleep away from anything too big, if you know what I mean? I've had enough run-ins with the post-pub closing time folk to know it's best to stay away. I hadn't planned on staying here, either, but the village seemed quiet, and like you said, it was hard to resist a spot like this.'

'Did you notice anything when you got here?' Gordy asked.

'No,' said Bill, shaking his head. 'I just made my way around the footpath, wondering if I could get inside, and when I saw that bridge, I just headed over. Couldn't quite believe my luck.'

'Did you see anyone?'

'Not a soul. Like I said, everything was quiet, so I didn't think I'd get much bother from anyone. And no one was in the castle when I arrived either, so I just settled in for the night; laid out my doss bag, got the stove going, had some scoff, then a bit of a smoke before I got my head down.'

'There was no one around the castle at all?'

'Well, I didn't walk all the way around,' said Bill, 'so I couldn't say for sure, but I didn't see anyone.'

Gordy thought for a moment, then said, 'If you were asleep, how was it that you then found the body?'

'I'm almost embarrassed to say, but it was nightmares,' said Bill. 'Me, a grown man, and that's what it was. Sometimes I'll go weeks without a single one, then they'll all come crashing in. Looks like I'll be having a few restless nights ahead of me.'

'Sleep is never easy,' said Gordy, 'not if you've had a tough time of it, have things on your mind.'

At that, Bill narrowed his eyes at her.

'You've said more with that than you realise, haven't you?'

'I have?' Gordy replied, a little taken aback.

Bill didn't expand on what he had said, just held Gordy's eyes for a moment, before turning back to his tea for another sip. He tapped his head.

'There's too much in here for it to stay inside,' he said. 'It leaks out. I woke up to the sound of missiles, bullets, you name it, it was all coming in at me. Couldn't recall it at the time, but I can now. It's not a specific memory, really, just fragments of lots of them all joining in together to give me this god-awful picture.'

'I'm sorry to hear that,' said Gordy, seeing pain in Bill's eyes.

'Not your fault, is it? Anyway, I woke up, and the missiles sounded like whistling, and I thought I'd best just check to see if there was anyone around playing silly buggers.'

Gordy remembered the sound of the wind through the cracks in the castle and could see how Bill's mind had turned the haunting song into something quite different and altogether more awful. But she also thought back to what Paul had passed on from Allercott.

'Do you think it was someone actually whistling? Or just your dream?'

Bill frowned, scratching his chin.

'Can't say I'm entirely sure, but maybe it was someone? It was more tuneful than what I usually get in my dreams, if that means anything?'

'It just may,' said Gordy. 'Can you remember what it sounded like?'

To Gordy's surprise, Bill pursed his lips and attempted to whistle a tune.

'Sorry, that's not very good, is it?' he said. 'It's like I can hear the tune, but at the same time, I can't.'

'Oh, I think it was a decent enough attempt, all things considered,' said Gordy. 'There's a tune in there somewhere, isn't there?'

'I think there is, so maybe it was someone? I wouldn't be able to swear on it, though.'

'But that was when you found the body?' she said.

'It was,' said Bill. 'Nearly shat myself!'

Gordy couldn't help herself and burst out laughing.

'Sorry about that,' said Bill. 'Squaddie talk. Old habits, right?'

Still smiling, Gordy asked, 'Can you describe what you saw then?'

'I'd rather not, but yes,' said Bill, and proceeded to detail everything Gordy herself had already seen. 'And then I just ran, found the nearest house, banged on their door 'til someone answered. They weren't happy, what with someone looking like me turning up at God knows what hour and screaming crazy stuff about a body in the castle. Pretty sure they thought I was pissed.'

Gordy looked again through her notes.

'Is there anything else, Bill?' she asked.

Bill scratched his chin, drained his mug.

'Not a thing,' he said. 'That's all of it, I promise. If there was more, I'd tell you, if only to get it out of my own head.'

Gordy sat for a moment longer with Bill, just chatting with him about anything and nothing. Then, having confirmed what PCSO Edwards had told her, and the arrangements he had made with Bill, she thanked him for his time, wished him well, and climbed back out of the car.

She walked over to Patti and Paul.

'What do you think, then?' Patti asked, as Paul headed back to deal with Bill.

Along the path and across the bridge, Gordy saw the ghostly figures of the SOC team doing the crime scene dance under the glare of spotlights, chasing each other through the shadows cast by the castle standing watchful under the moon.

'I think,' she said, 'that when we all get together in the morning, we're going to need an awful lot of Vivek's coffee.'

TWELVE

Gordy was in a hospital. Bright lights and stainless steel and white sheets and pale faces and dear God, what was the doctor saying, and the nurses, what was anyone saying, why wasn't anything making any sense? And Anna's hand. It was cold, so cold, and she was still, not moving at all, hadn't moved since she'd arrived.

The smell of the place, it was everywhere, in everything, on her clothes, her skin, and she needed to get out, but she couldn't. She didn't want to leave, couldn't leave, because if she did, if she left Anna now, then—

Gordy woke to the sound of her own scream. It ripped from her throat, pulling her heart out with it as she jolted upright in a desperate attempt to escape it, her duvet conspiring with the panic to wrap itself around her, trap her, force her to replay the very thing that she had just woken from.

Sunlight cut through a thin gap in the curtains, a blinding razor slicing across her legs as she tried to untangle herself, kicking the duvet off the bed and onto the floor.

Breathless, Gordy sat in the gloom of her room, heart pounding, gasping for breath, no idea of the time, bar the fact that morning had long ago broken and waited now to welcome her with its cold greeting.

Squeezing her eyes shut to force the images back down into the locked box where she kept them, she swung her legs out of bed and sat for a moment on the edge of the mattress. Leaning forward, she gripped its edge as though to do anything else would allow her to fall into an abyss, because that's what she was teetering on. How long she could hold on, she had no idea, nor what would happen to her if and when her grip on reality, on life, slipped, and she fell.

Anna ...

Another scream threatened to shatter her chest, but Gordy held it in, only to have it break free as a sob. Tears came, and she wept, long and hard and with no control over it, the sensation one that was both relief and terror; that she was crying was no surprise, and it only served to confirm the hurt that clung to her like a leech, but that it came so suddenly, and was beyond her control to do anything to stop it, was alarming.

Deep breaths, Gordy told herself, just take some deep, deep breaths, get a grip.

The crying eased just enough for her to finally take control. That was where she needed to be. She couldn't let it take over, couldn't give in to it, because where would she be then?

Gordy stood up, checked the time.

Today involved two tasks; a team meeting about the previous night's deeply unpleasant and disturbing events, and a trip to Bristol to meet Detective Superintendent Alice Firbank. There would be a trip to the mortuary as well, no doubt, but not today. And even if it was today, she would need time to build up the energy to deal with Cowboy again, and would delay it.

The next half hour was a series of simple actions into which Gordy put little thought, doing them on autopilot. She shut down her mind, closed it off completely, and as though on a conveyor belt, allowed her body to take itself from bedroom to bathroom to kitchen, washing, clothing, and feeding her, just enough to make her presentable and fuelled enough to get into her vehicle and take the back roads to Frome.

Why the hell would they pronounce it *Froom*, and not spell it like that? she thought, as high hedges guided her along thin lanes, a bramble luge track of thistle and thorn. It made no sense. All they had to do was get rid of the *E* and add in that extra *O*. Hell, they could even keep the *E*!

At the main road, she picked up speed. A roundabout came up a little too fast, but she held the steering wheel firmly and ignored the squeal of the tyres as they complained.

Arriving at the station, she lifted herself out into a thick concoction of smells, most of them delicious. Yet, right then, all they did was churn her stomach, and she couldn't get inside fast enough.

Vivek was at the front desk and, the same as yesterday, greeted her with a warm smile.

'Everyone's here,' he said. 'By all accounts, sounds like you had an interesting night.'

'Something like that,' Gordy replied, doing her best to hide the wobble in her voice.

Vivek stared at her.

'Do you need anything?'

'Coffee,' Gordy said, forcing a smile. 'Lots and lots of coffee, and I don't mean just for me, either. We're all going to need it, I think.'

'Not a problem.'

Upstairs, the room her small office was attached to was alive with the sound of late morning chatter.

'I'm last to arrive, then,' Gordy said, as Patti strode across from a desk to greet her.

'You're not late, if that's what you mean,' Patti replied, then nodded around the group. 'Jack's in because he's been sorting out various PCSO stuff across the region. As for Pete and Paul? I think they're just a little bit too keen after last night to find out what they'll be doing next.'

'And yourself?'

'Oh, I sleep under my desk, and live off stuff I find bin-diving behind McDonald's and Gregg's.'

Gordy laughed at that, but then she saw something resting behind Patti's eyes that choked it off.

'I hope you're not serious,' she said.

Before Patti could answer, Vivek entered, and to Gordy's amazement, he was pushing an honest-to-God trolley that wouldn't have looked out of place in a vicarage. That thought had all the potential to bring things crashing around her again, so she walked over to meet him, ignoring the hollow echo of Anna's memory knocking at the inside of her skull.

'That doesn't look exactly police issue,' she said, pointing at the trolley and smiling.

'This? Goodness, no; it's from a charity furniture shop just along from here. The last one we had gave up one day and took a load of crockery with it. So, I had to act quickly.'

Atop the trolley was a selection of mugs and plates, with no two the same.

'I've made a couple of pots of French press coffee,' Vivek said, nodding to the trolley's bottom shelf.

Gordy, however, wasn't listening. Instead, she was staring at something on a plate. It looked a little like a loaf of bread that had been run over by a bus, then covered in syrup, its squashed surface glistening under the glare of the harsh lights in the ceiling.

'I've a feeling I'm going to regret asking this,' she said, and pointed at the sad-looking thing. 'What is that, Vivek?'

Vivek's eyes flashed bright.

'That,' he said, 'is lardy cake.'

Gordy leaned in, fairly sure she hadn't heard him properly.

'A what cake?'

'Lardy.'

'As in—'

'Lard.'

'Of course.'

Patti came to stand beside her.

'Vivek's a bit of a baker,' she said. 'This is somewhat of a speciality, though.'

'I don't do it often,' Vivek said, 'but thought you might appreciate it on your first week.'

'Dare I ask what's in it?' said Gordy. 'Apart from the obvious clue in the name.'

'Think of it like a sweet, spiced, fruit bread,' Vivek explained. 'You roll the dough out, then cover it with blobs of lard, sugar, dried fruit, spices, fold it over, and repeat a few times, bake it, then cover it in a sugar syrup.'

Pete, Jack, and Paul gathered around the trolley.

'Thought I smelled something delicious,' said Jack.

Vivek proceeded to cut up the lardy cake, while Jack poured the coffee.

Gordy took a plate handed to her, and a mug of coffee, then turned to find herself a chair to slump into. The coffee, like yesterday's, was sublime.

A prickling sensation at the back of her neck caused Gordy to look up, and she saw that the rest of the team were all staring at her.

'Well?' Jack asked, his own plate already empty. 'What do you think?'

Gordy picked up the slice of lardy cake.

'It's still warm,' she said.

'Fresh this morning,' said Vivek.

'What time did you get up, then?'

'Early enough to bake it.'

Gordy took a bite.

'Bloody hell ...'

'Good, isn't it?' said Pete.

Gordy wasn't quite sure how to answer the question. She knew that what she was eating was clearly the most appalling thing to put into her body, just animal fat and sugar and dried fruit, but at the same time, she immediately wanted more, and soon polished her own plate clean. The coffee chased it superbly, its earthy, smooth bitterness working to cut through the sweetness.

A moment or two later, the caffeine and sugar hit home, and

Gordy, at last, felt as close to being awake as she had done in weeks, which wasn't saying much, but it would have to do for now.

She stood up.

'Good?' she said. 'It's fantastic! So, how about another slice before we decide what to do about last night and the body in the castle?'

THIRTEEN

At first, the conversation had bounced around the room like a loose rubber ball, but Gordy had soon called things to order and asked for something to jot down her notes on.

'What do you mean, what is it?' Paul asked, as he stood beside Gordy. Behind them, attached to the wall, was what looked to be a huge computer screen. 'It's an interactive whiteboard.'

'Then, I refer you again to my original question,' Gordy replied. 'What is it?'

Paul showed Gordy how to use a special pen to write on the board, click on various icons to turn the writing a different colour or to make it bold, how to select text and move it around, and lots of other things which, after a few minutes of Paul talking, she'd already forgotten. Why did things have to get so complicated? Usually, it was in the name of efficiency, but in Gordy's experience, that was rarely the case.

'That all make sense, then?' Paul finished.

Gordy leaned over and said, 'I don't suppose you have anything as old-fashioned as a normal whiteboard and some pens, do you? Even a flip chart would do.'

'A flip chart?' said Paul, looking back at Gordy as though she'd just asked him to put his hand in a blender. 'But what about the interactive one?'

'I don't think now's the time for me to be learning how to use new technology,' replied Gordy.

'It's not new. It's been around for years. Every primary school has one, and has done for at least a decade.'

Gordy said nothing more, just stared, one eyebrow raised slightly to force her point home.

'I'll go have a look,' Paul said, a note of disbelief in his voice.

'Aye, you will,' Gordy said. 'Thank you, Paul.'

Paul wandered off, shaking his head as he went. Gordy heard him muttering the words *flip chart* to himself, and she did her best to not smile.

Paul returned a few minutes later, pushing a rickety board on squeaky wheels. Steering it was clearly an issue, as from the moment he came through the main door with it, the thing wanted to go anywhere but where he wanted it to be.

After crashing into three desks and knocking over a bin, Paul finally managed to navigate the board to where Gordy was standing. He presented her with a pack of pens. There were five in total, out of what Gordy guessed had at one time numbered eight. Three of the pens were without lids.

'First order of the day, then,' she said, 'is to jot the following down in the Action Book: buy new pens.'

Gordy saw that Patti was holding an iPad and tapping on it with one hand at an impossible speed.

'Patti?'

The sergeant glanced up.

'What are you doing?'

'The Action Book,' Patti replied, waggling the iPad in her hands.

'But that's an iPad.'

'I know.'

'So, where's the Action Book?'

The Action Book, a simple record of tasks to allow the team to plan and record what they were doing that day, was to Gordy a simple thing of paper and pen.

Patti flipped the iPad around so that Gordy could see the screen.

'Here,' she said. 'I just type in the notes on the screen, then we can all access it through a shared file in our—'

Gordy held up her hand to stop Patti right there.

'I'll take your word for it,' she said, and quickly turned to the board.

Ignoring the dried-up nibs of the lidless pens, she tried the two that remained. The one with the red lid turned out to be black, but also dry. The one with a black lid turned out to be red, but actually worked well.

'Right, then,' Gordy said, happy to at last be getting somewhere. 'Quick run-through of last night's events ...'

Once she had finished her recap, which included a description of the victim and various other relevant details from the crime scene, it was time to decide who was doing what next.

'First, as yet we've got no ID on the victim,' she said. 'So, we need to do a check of missing persons, see if we've had any reports locally of a man matching his description not coming home, that kind of thing. If we find nothing, move further afield. But my guess is, he's local.'

'I'll check up on the photos,' said Patti, 'and see if anything has come to light that might give us a lead in identifying who he is, even if we don't have anything like a credit card or driving licence.'

Pete suggested a bit of good, old-fashioned door-knocking would make sense.

'Not that I'm expecting anyone to have seen anything, considering the time, but you never know. Someone might have heard something, been woken up by vehicle lights; anything's useful, right?'

Thinking back to the crime scene, Gordy looked over at Jack and Paul.

'The spike,' she said. 'I've seen them before; it's a bale spike, I think, something you put on the front loader of a tractor to lift those huge bales you see all over the place.'

'Want us to see if anyone's reported one going missing?' Jack asked.

'Exactly that. Needle in a haystack, I know, or at least a giant one in a pile of straw, but sometimes that's the best we've got.'

'I'll check farms local to the village first, then move further afield,' said Jack.

Paul added, 'I could head out to that agricultural store we've got over in Standerwick; there's always a bit of chat going around that place about what's happening where, if any farms have had to deal with trespassers or poachers or whatever, that kind of thing.'

Gordy was genuinely impressed.

'I'll give our ludicrous friend Keith a call, just to chivvy him along,' she said. 'Then I'm away to Bristol for a meeting with Detective Superintendent Firbank.'

There was an audible gasp from the team.

'Something the matter?' Gordy asked.

Silence.

Gordy looked at them each in turn.

'You gasped,' she said. 'Now, that's either because of something I just said, or because something awful has just walked through the door behind me and shocked you all into silence. And, having witnessed the horror that is our friend Cowboy, it's worth mentioning that nothing will ever scare or shock me again. So, which is it?'

'It's neither,' said Patti.

Gordy was confused.

'How can it be neither and yet you all gasped in unison?'

'Does DCI Allercott know you're meeting with Firbank?' asked Pete.

'She does,' Gordy replied, 'though I'm not sure what that's got to do with anything.'

'They don't get on,' Patti said, clarifying things a little. 'That's all, really.'

'Not sure how that affects me,' Gordy said. 'You can't get on with everyone in the workplace, can you? I mean, the recently mentioned

Cowboy is a prime example, isn't he? Yet, I've been reassured that he's damned good at his job. So, whether I like him or not is irrelevant.'

The team was silent.

'Well, with that settled, then,' said Gordy, clapping her hands together loud enough to make everyone jump a little, 'shall we crack on?'

As the team dispersed, Gordy attempted to move the whiteboard that Paul had wheeled into the room. Neither pushing nor dragging improved its steering, but after a few minutes of barely disguised swearing, she had it in her office and against the wall, but not before being very close to reading it its rights and arresting it for assaulting a police officer.

Sitting behind her desk, Gordy viewed the notes she'd jotted down. There wasn't much at all, not yet, anyway, but there would be. There had to be. Someone didn't just end up impaled on a spike in a castle without anyone knowing anything, it just wasn't possible.

Reaching for her phone, Gordy realised that she didn't actually have Cowboy's number, so she called Patti into her office. Much to Gordy's dismay, she took her through the phone system, eventually bringing up the crime scene manager's number on the screen.

'There you go,' she said. 'Easy.'

Gordy gave a nod, but said not a word, knowing full well she had already forgotten every single instruction she had been given.

She dialled the number.

On the sixth ring, the line connected, and the voice of Birmingham slipped into Gordy's day.

'Keith Brown, speaking.'

'DI Haig,' said Gordy, and was fairly sure she heard the faint sound of a gulp. 'Just wondering how things are going, if there's anything to report yet? I know it's not long since you were on-scene, but I always like to check in, just in case there's something that might help, no matter how small.'

'Actually, there is something,' Cowboy replied, and Gordy heard the man's voice almost slip into his western persona, before stalling and sticking around Birmingham instead.

'Really? What?'

'It's a film frame. Just one. Like it's been snipped from a reel.'

'How do you mean?'

'Well, a film, a movie, it's just hundreds of thousands of still photographs, isn't it, all flying past at a hell of a rate to give the illusion of movement? Like that thing with the pictures of horses inside a spinner with slits in the side.'

'Hmm,' said Gordy, understanding enough and encouraging Cowboy to get to the point.

'So, there was one in the pocket of the overalls the victim was wearing. We've had a look at it, and it's fairly old now, but we can still see someone in the frame, and make out a few other details about their surroundings.'

'Any idea who the someone is?' Gordy asked, knowing the answer before it came.

'Not a clue,' Cowboy replied. 'A young woman. Looks like she's covered in blood.'

That detail made Gordy shudder. She'd heard of snuff films, movies made of people being tortured and killed, but had never really thought them to be anything more than an urban legend.

'Can you send a copy over?'

'Of course,' said Cowboy. 'Photos will be on their way later today as well, but I can get this sent over now if you want. It's been enlarged as well, so you can really see what's going on. I warn you, though, even though it's a fairly grainy image, it doesn't look pleasant.'

'I'll expect it shortly,' Gordy said, drew the conversation to a close, then hung up.

A few minutes later, when she opened the attachment Cowboy sent, she couldn't help but think that his description had undersold it more than a little.

FOURTEEN

The image on Gordy's screen, though grainy like Cowboy had described, was sharper than she had expected. Her reaction to it was visceral enough to make her flinch, and she found herself pushing her chair away from her desk just enough to make the wheels complain at her attempt to get away from it.

Blood. That was really all she could see for the first few moments, because there was just so damned much of it. So much, in fact, that she was sure she could smell it, the sight of all the blood, oddly frozen in time, stirring up memories she'd had more than her fair share of counselling sessions to learn to deal with. She leaned into a technique she'd learned through some of the tougher days of being in the police, focusing on her breathing to calm herself down and focus. Just simple breathing in through the nose, then out through the mouth, her lips tight enough to slow the breath down as she forced it out.

Once the initial shock had faded, Gordy edged closer to her screen, making herself examine what she was seeing and not be distracted by the horror of it or to let her imagination run wild with the hows or the whys.

The girl was drenched in crimson. Her clothes were sodden, her hair matted, her face running with thick beads of it like sweat. She looked to be in her late teens, maybe her early twenties. Beneath the blood, she could see a young woman with defined cheekbones and wide eyes, a thin smile cutting through all the blood with a flash of white teeth.

Elven, Gordy thought, thinking back to the stories of myth and legend her uncle told her when she was but a girl. Stories of dragons and wizards and elves and dwarves and men. The tales he'd read, and especially the ones he had spun himself from the darkness of an evening, had seemed so at home in the Highlands, as she had been herself.

Gordy's breath caught in her throat as memories of home, of mountains and lochs and the smell of bog myrtle, whirled around her head for a moment.

She closed her eyes, took another slow breath in and out, and focused again. Thoughts of her far away and long ago home filled her mind, and she found herself staring out across the dark waters of a loch, suddenly still after a passing storm.

Opening her eyes again, Gordy realised something: the girl, she was smiling ...

Now, that was odd, she thought. If she was covered in all of that blood and gore, why the hell would she look so happy?

Rubbing her eyes, Gordy gave herself a moment, then once again tried to take in what she was seeing, which wasn't proving easy. The fact that this was a film cell gave it a very surreal air. And that was a point that really struck a chord, though one that was out of tune and rang harshly in Gordy's mind.

Gordy ran through what this small and strange piece of evidence was trying to tell her, if anything.

It was a still frame from a film. It showed a young woman covered in blood. The young woman was smiling. Gordy also noticed that she was holding something in her right hand, though she couldn't quite make out what it was, the image too blurred in that area.

Moving away from the girl herself, Gordy turned her attention to examining where the girl was; perhaps that would help tell a little more of the story of this strangely selected moment from the past.

The girl was standing in a huge, open doorway which led out into bright light and faded hues of green and brown. Gordy had no idea if what she was looking at was real or a film set, the details insufficient to give her any further clues.

As to whoever was behind the camera, they were standing inside the building, though there was little detail visible of the room itself.

Gordy tried to see if she could make out any details beyond the open door. The green ... was that a lawn? And the browns beyond it... perhaps a field? That might give her some idea of the time of year, if the field was freshly ploughed, but it was hard to tell. The image at that point was fuzzy and out of focus, the girl being the centre of attention.

Something else caught Gordy's eye. Behind the girl, between where the lawn, if it was that, and the fields met, was something else, a building maybe? It was small, But what the hell was it? She leaned in closer, zooming in so that section of the still filled her screen.

Squinting, Gordy tried to make out the details, pushing away as best she could all thoughts about the blood, the odd smile on the girl's face, the thing she was holding in her hand.

There was an ornamental look to the building, the doorway somewhat ornate and arched. If it was a garden shed, it had certainly been over-designed. But why would a film set have such a thing?

Maybe it was part of another scene, Gordy thought, not that she had any idea at all about how films were made and sets constructed. Was it a cottage? No, that door looked too big. There was a temple-like quality to the place, though, and Gordy thought that she could make out carved stonework on the walls, and there were wide, shallow steps leading up to that large, ornate door. It reminded her of a mausoleum.

Perhaps this wasn't a film set and was actually a large house. If that were the case, having such a thing out on the front lawn seemed to be an oddly prominent place to have it, but perhaps this was the back of the house. It was impossible to tell, and Gordy's thoughts only swirled faster and faster as she tried to decipher whatever story lay behind the image.

Squinting at the screen again, Gordy tried to pick out any other details that would give her some clue as to what had been going on, and where, but she came up blank.

Leaning back in her chair, allowing her head to fall back, Gordy closed her eyes. Her mind drifted as she shuffled through a replay of what she had witnessed the night before at Nunney Castle, what she had learned and been told, the smell of the place, the atmosphere, and she tried to link all of that, and this. But the more she thought about it, the harder it seemed to be to do so.

What if there was no connection? Indeed, how could there be? The events of the night before had given her team a nameless man dead on a baler spike, and this film still frame was nothing more than a random picture. And maybe that's all it was. People kept odd things in their pockets.

Gordy was no different in that. Checking her own to prove her point, she found a parking ticket, a small penknife with a bone handle that she'd had since she was a child, a pebble she'd picked up from a stream months ago with Anna, an elastic band, and some loose change. Why she had transferred any of it from one pair of trousers to another, she had no answer for, except, perhaps, for the pebble. She held it for a moment, caressing its smooth, dark grey surface with the tip of her thumb, before stuffing it back into her pocket with the rest of the items.

Gordy checked her watch and saw it was time to head off to Bristol. Part of her didn't want to go. This case, as shocking as it was, had actually given her something to focus on beyond wishing she was anywhere else but here, a way to close the door briefly on the memories. But Firbank had been insistent, and maybe something useful would come from it, even if it was just a funny story or two about Harry.

With thoughts of her old DCI and the rest of the team up in Wensleydale dancing in her mind, she left the office, enjoyed a cheery farewell from Vivek, thanking him again for the lardy cake, and was soon in her vehicle and making her way out of Frome.

FIFTEEN

Detective Superintendent Alice Firbank's office was possibly the most organised room Gordy had ever sat in, and she immediately felt as though her presence alone was enough to make the place untidy and cluttered.

She had been met at reception by an officer, and then taken upstairs by another, neither of whom she had been given a chance to notice anything about other than their speed and efficiency in getting her from one place to another. The first had been a man, the second a woman, but that was really about as much as Gordy could recall.

Sitting in the D-Sup's office, waiting for her to arrive, she tried to imagine Harry sitting exactly where she was right then, and that thought was enough to turn her initial trepidation into a chuckling smile.

DCI Grimm, whose nature matched his name better than any person Gordy had ever known, must have filled the space with his own sense of awkwardness, she thought, the size of him enough on its own to make him seem out of place. Not that he was a giant, but there was certainly plenty of him to have her wondering if his entering the room had been a cause for concern, considering how easy he found it to knock into things as though they weren't even there.

He wasn't a bull in a china shop so much as a Pit Bull without a muzzle, and she could imagine him sitting there growling and grumbling to himself about how meetings were a waste of time, that he had other things to be getting on with, cases to follow up on. But like almost every huge, terrifying dog she'd ever met, underneath that gruff exterior was something considerably softer.

Not that he would flip over on the floor and ask for a tummy rub, a thought which made Gordy snort a laugh. Harry was a man with a big heart, and a sense of loyalty and kindness to those he cared about that just couldn't be matched, and though they had all been wary of him when he had arrived in the Dales a few years ago, they'd soon come to see just how lucky they were to have him there in the first place.

'Detective Inspector Haig,' said a voice from behind Gordy, and she stood up so suddenly that her legs caught her chair and knocked it over with a dull thud on the thin, hard-wearing office carpet.

'Ma'am,' Gordy said, unsure whether to salute or to hold out a hand to shake or to just stand there and wait for instructions. This confusion resulted in her doing an odd sort of wave at hip-height as Firbank went around to stand behind her desk.

'No need to stand,' Firbank said, and sat down. 'And no need to be calling me ma'am, either, though I do appreciate it, so thank you.'

Gordy retrieved her chair and lowered herself into it, careful to not cause any further mishaps.

'Sorry about that,' she said.

'You know, Harry once got stuck in that chair,' Firbank said, the thinnest of smiles cutting a line across her face, her black, pony-tailed hair bobbing a little with her laugh.

'Really?'

Gordy tried to imagine what that must have looked like.

'I still have no idea how he managed it,' said Firbank.

'He was actually stuck?' Gordy asked. 'This room must still echo with his swearing.'

'Not just this room, the whole damned building,' Firbank replied. 'And most of Somerset.'

'I can well imagine.'

'He's got quite the roar on him when he gets going, hasn't he? And he really does embrace guttural swearing with a passion matched by few.'

'He swears through gritted teeth better than anyone I've ever met.'

Firbank said, 'I've actually just been speaking with him. That's why I wasn't here to greet you when you arrived. Sorry about that.'

Gordy was surprised.

'You've been talking to Harry?'

'I know, he doesn't like phones much, and yet here we are.'

'Dare I ask what about?'

Firbank leaned back in her chair, folded her arms.

She was slight, Gordy noticed, but there was a presence to the woman that made up for it. She had a sense right then that Firbank was the kind of person who could silence a stadium just by holding up a single hand, perhaps even just a finger.

'You,' Firbank said.

'Ah.'

'You sound concerned.'

'Should I be?'

'Should I?'

'I don't think so, no,' said Gordy, a little unnerved by the rapid exchange, wondering if Firbank was playing games, trying to get the measure of her by being deliberately combative. 'What did Harry have to say?'

That got another chuckle from Firbank.

'You know Harry,' she said. 'Not much, but always just enough. I've long thought his approach to conversation was much like adding salt to a meal; he would put in enough to season it, but never too much to spoil it. Though I doubt that's anything like his thought process.'

'Doesn't quite answer my question though,' said Gordy.

Firbank sat forward again, and this time leaned her elbows on her desk, hands clasped together in front of her.

'How are you doing?'

'I'm fine?' Gordy replied, all too aware of the giveaway inflection at the end.

'In case you're wondering, Harry speaks very highly of you. And he really doesn't speak highly of anyone at all.'

Gordy wasn't quite sure how to respond, so said nothing.

'I don't generally call people in for a chat,' Firbank continued. 'If I did this with everyone, I'd never get my job done, would I? But Harry's a special case, and by default, so are you.'

'He's certainly that,' Gordy said, unable to hide her smile.

'Drove me up the bloody wall,' said Firbank, rolling her eyes. 'That's why you ended up with him, after all. But, by all accounts, it's done him a world of good.'

'And he us, actually,' replied Gordy. 'He's not as gruff as he'd like everyone to think he is, no' by a long way.'

'He's a bloody good detective, to boot,' added Firbank. 'Plus, he looks after his own, if you know what I mean.'

Gordy spotted something, not just in what Firbank had said, but in the way she had said it.

'He seems to lead from the front, but at the same time is always alongside you,' she said, looking at Firbank. 'Not sure that makes any sense, but I can't think of a clearer way to say it.'

For a moment, neither Gordy nor Firbank said anything.

Gordy broke the silence.

'I'm still not entirely sure why I'm here,' she said. 'If you have concerns, then—'

'I do,' said Firbank, cutting in, 'but they're not about your work. About you and how you are, though? Yes. Very serious concerns.'

Gordy's stomach twisted. This was what she had been dreading deep down, that the battering she had taken would have a knock-on effect that she couldn't do anything about. Was she about to be put on garden leave? Was that what this was? Had she been called in to be told to just stay at home, take some time off, only two days into her new job? How was that even fair?

'I know a little about what you've been through,' said Firbank, breaking Gordy's spiralling thoughts. 'Harry has, off his own back, kept me up to date, and given me a broader picture of things. His call earlier was little more than him asking me to tell you that you can always call on him, and the others, if you need to.'

'I know,' Gordy said, aware she had not reached out even once since moving South, preferring instead to keep her head down and push forward regardless.

'He's very much someone you can depend on,' Firbank continued. 'Believe me, I know.'

There it was again, Gordy noticed, the strange tone, as though something deeper was hiding behind Firbank's words.

'But it was you who sent him North,' she said.

'For his own good,' said Firbank. 'But that doesn't take anything away from the fact that he's had my back too many times to remember. He also saved my life, and in many ways that was the biggest reason of all for me to do what I did. He needed to rescue himself, and the only way for him to do that was to be sent somewhere else, somewhere completely different, where he'd be out of his comfort zone and forced to change.'

'He saved your life?'

'That's a story for another day,' Firbank smiled. 'Now, back to you.'

Gordy realised she was holding her breath in anticipation of what the D-Sup was going to say next, and forced herself to relax.

'I can't begin to imagine what it must've been like to lose Anna,' Firbank said, 'and even if I had lost someone so important to me, I wouldn't be so insensitive as to suggest what I had been through and experienced was in any way the same. Grief hits us all in different ways, doesn't it, and no two people suffer the same?'

Gordy felt pinned to her seat. She both wanted to burst out of the room and run like hell, and at the same time just listen to what Firbank was saying.

Firbank took a pad of blank sticky notes from the side of her desk and jotted something on the top note. She peeled it off from the rest of the pad and handed it to Gordy.

'That,' she said, 'is my personal number. I do not give this out lightly. And I do not expect it to be shared. Is that understood?'

Gordy felt her jaw drop open a little. She gave a short nod, staring at the number, not really sure what on earth was going on. First Allercott, and now Firbank. Nice, yes, but also a wee bit weird, she thought, but kept quiet about it.

'If you need someone to talk to, to shout at, whatever, just call. If I'm unavailable, leave a message, and I will call back. You have my word on that. Do not suffer alone and in silence.'

'I ... I won't,' Gordy said.

'I admire your courage in taking on this new role, considering the circumstances. But don't let that bravery cast too large a shadow, such that everything else gets blocked out and forgotten; that way madness lies. Harry knows that better than most, as I'm sure you're aware. Which is why I suggest you lean on him, too, when you need to.'

Gordy smiled, though there was no humour behind it.

'Sometimes, I think this is all madness,' she said, looking around Firbank's office, shaking her head sorrowfully. 'I don't know whether to run or to stay, but neither seems to be a good option, and that doesn't help, because then I feel like I'm just running on the spot, and that I'm only doing that to stop myself from falling flat on my face.'

'Running only takes you away,' said Firbank. 'Wherever you end up, you will still be you, and you will still have to deal with what you've been through. Staying might actually give you a bit of stability.'

'That's why I'm still here,' Gordy sighed. 'It's why I'm sitting here now, believe me.'

Firbank stood up.

'Well, I wish you well in your new role. I'm sure you'll fit in with the team; even Allercott.'

Gordy rose to her feet.

'Can't say I've quite got the measure of her yet,' she said.

'Let me know when you do.'

Firbank led Gordy to her office door and waved over another officer. She then held out her hand. Gordy shook it.

'I meant what I said, understood? Call. And if you don't, Harry won't be happy.'

'Oh, well, in that case,' Gordy said, then followed the other officer back down to reception.

When she was back outside and in her vehicle again, Gordy took a moment to let the meeting sink in.

She felt like crying, but she wouldn't, because she was strong, and tears weren't going to help.

Driving away, despite what she'd told herself, tears fell as softly as the evening, but for once, over a smile.

SIXTEEN

Come the morning, Gordy was back in the office, and this time earlier than the rest of the team. She had forced herself to head to bed at a sensible time, instead of allowing herself to drift off on the sofa, watching chewing gum for her brain on television. She had woken in the night only once, managed to push away whatever nightmare had sunk its claws into her, and to her own surprise, woken up again only when her alarm called her.

The conversation with Firbank had definitely stilled her mind a little, she realised, and knowing that Harry was out there, too, and the rest of her old team, rooting for her, wishing her well, and offering her their help should she need it, meant more than she'd ever given herself a chance to realise.

The only person in the office was Vivek, and Gordy's first words to him were a simple statement. 'This may only be my first week, Vivek, but I hope I'm not going to have to have words with you about working longer than you should.'

Vivek smiled, then opened his arms in a gesture at the reception area he manned.

'Oh, I know all about work-life balance. Why else do you think I'm here?'

He offered no further details, but Gordy left with the impression that Vivek had a backstory, and one she'd like to know more about, once she got the chance.

On her desk, she found a folder waiting for her. Opening it, she was presented with photographs from the crime scene. She knew that they would also be in her inbox, but the physical copies were so much more immediate and real.

Gordy flicked through the images, and the speed of them dashing past provided a short, silent movie of the horror they had all witnessed at the castle. It reminded her of the single film frame found in the victim's pocket, and again she wondered from where it had come, and whether it was relevant, or just a thread which, if pulled, would ultimately be found to be attached to nothing at all.

Leaving the photographs to one side, Gordy turned in her chair to stare at the board and the scant notes written on it. She'd not had a chance to get an update from the rest of the team, so as a focus for that, she tried to wheel the board back out into the main office. One of the wheels came off, and the jolt of the frame digging into the carpet caused her to stumble, and both she and the board tumbled forwards.

For a split second, Gordy felt as though she was frozen in time, neither standing nor falling, suspended in the moment. Then gravity claimed her, and she fell, the board not so much breaking her fall as making the sound of it so much more dramatic. The top edge caught a shelf and dislodged it, sending a cascade of books and folders over Gordy as she landed ungracefully on all fours, the board between her and the carpet.

A smell of stale coffee and dirt wafted up from the floor and Gordy pushed herself to her feet, swearing under her breath.

'Everything okay?'

Gordy turned to see Detective Sergeant Patti Matondo standing at her office doorway. Behind her, she spied the spiky hair of Detective Constable Peter Knight.

'Wheel came off,' said Gordy, brushing herself down, kicking at the board as it lay forlornly on the floor.

Patti and Pete came into the office. Pete lifted the board back up onto its three remaining wheels.

'Any idea where the other one went?' he asked.

'Not a clue,' said Gordy, her palms stinging a little from her landing.

'Well, you can have a look for it while we're out, can't you, Pete?' said Patti, and Gordy realised the sergeant's eyes were now on her.

'Has something come up? Is it Cowboy?'

Patti shook her head.

'Not Cowboy, no. However, a car's been found in Nunney,' she said. 'Jack's there now.'

Gordy frowned.

'And he thinks it might have something to do with what happened at the castle?'

'One of the residents he spoke to yesterday called it in first thing. Said they'd remembered seeing someone parking it up, matching the description given of the victim. He's checked to see if it's locked. Turns out the keys have been left in the ignition.'

'That's odd.'

'Isn't it?'

Gordy looked at Pete.

'Find that wheel,' she said, 'and let me know if and when you hear from Cowboy and the pathologist.'

'Prince? Sure.'

Gordy narrowed her eyes at Pete.

'Prince?'

'As in Charming,' said Pete. 'Suits him, too.'

'In what way?' Gordy asked, still trying to get over meeting Keith 'Cowboy' Brown, and now with the image of meeting Adam Ant at the mortuary...

'Dunno really,' Pete replied. 'He's just properly nice, I guess. One of those people you just find yourself talking to. Really good at remembering things, like the names of your family, dates you've been on, that kind of thing.'

Intrigued, Gordy then remembered the film frame she'd printed out, and took it from a drawer in her desk, handing it to the constable.

'What's this?' Pete asked.

Patti leaned over for a look as well.

'Bloody hell,' she said. 'That's horrific ...'

'Aye, it is that,' Gordy agreed. 'What it actually is, is the enlarged image of a single film cell found in the victim's pocket. I don't know what to make of it, but there's a lot off about it, for sure.'

'Like all the blood and the fact that she's smiling,' said Patti.

'Exactly,' said Gordy. 'She's holding something, but I can't make it out, and I've no idea if what we're looking at is real or fake, a film set, or an actual place ... Anyway, it's worth having a few pairs of eyes looking at it for sure.'

Pete took the picture.

'Come on then,' Gordy said, with a nod at Patti. 'You can drive.' She marched out of her office, the sound of Patti racing to keep up following her.

TO GET TO NUNNEY, Patti left Frome behind to head out on the main road towards Shepton Mallet, taking a right across oncoming traffic to drop them onto a narrow lane. Just a few minutes later, they were in Nunney, taking another right to thread their way through the village, where a sharp left took them over the small bridge spanning the river.

On the outskirts of the village, Patti pulled them into a small parking area and Gordy spotted Paul leaning against his vehicle, patiently waiting. The only other vehicle parked up was a black car, its glimmering paint dancing with the sunlight dropping through the high cover of bowed trees now well on their way with fresh buds of spring.

Patti pulled her vehicle to a stop and Gordy was first out.

'What've we got, then?' she asked, walking over to Paul.

'BMW,' Paul replied. 'M3 model, so not exactly cheap. The person who called in was out with their dog when they saw the driver park it up. They'd not made the connection until they'd been out again this morning and spotted the car, which is why they called.'

'And who is this they?'

Paul checked his notebook.

'A Mrs Clough,' said Paul. 'I've her address and contact details so we can follow up if necessary.'

'What time did she see the driver?' Gordy asked.

'The same evening,' said Paul. 'She walks her dog twice a day. Eight-ish she thinks, which is later than she usually goes out, but she had been busy with work and hadn't been able to get out until night was falling.'

'What does she do?'

'Dog groomer. Though hard to tell, considering how scruffy her own dog is. Looks like a hair explosion on legs.'

Gordy headed over to the black BMW, and Paul and Patti followed.

'If this was parked here,' she said, 'at the time Mrs Clough has said, then what was the driver doing between then and ending up at the castle? The car's open, yes?'

'It is,' said Paul. 'I've not checked inside, though; figured it would be best to wait for you, what with me being just a PCSO.'

Gordy narrowed her eyes at Paul.

'You mind saying that again for me, just to make sure I heard you right?'

'Say what again?'

'About being a PCSO.'

Gordy saw confusion in Paul's eyes.

'But I am, aren't I?' he said again. 'I'm just a PCSO, I can't—'

'There's no such thing as "just a PCSO,"' Gordy said, her tone edged with flint sharp enough to cut his sentence in two. 'So, you'll no' be saying that again, you hear?'

She gave Paul no time to reply and, with disposable gloves pulled on, grabbed the handle of the car door and gave it a yank.

The smell from inside the car was a mix of leather and aftershave, one expensive, the other eye-wateringly cheap. The carpets were spotless, the dashboard shiny to the point of being a little off-putting.

'Nice car,' she said, then started searching through the various pockets and cubby holes, instructing both Paul and Patti to do the same, Patti handing Paul a pair of disposable gloves.

As Gordy and Patti scrabbled around in the main cockpit, Paul headed to the back of the car.

Gordy heard the boot open, the sound of the PCSO rummaging around whatever was in there, then a hissed *yes*, followed by, 'Er, ma'am?'

Pushing herself out of the car, Gordy went around to the rear of the car.

'Please,' she said, 'don't call me ma'am.'

'But Allercott prefers—' Paul began, but Gordy cut him off.

'I'm not Allercott,' she said.

'Then what should I, or any of us, call you?'

'You'll think of something, but keep it polite when it's to my face. What have you found?'

In the boot was a small, brown leather suitcase, the flap hanging open.

'This,' said Paul, and he handed Gordy a leather wallet that was well worn, but had a feel to it of a quality only big money could buy.

Opening it, Gordy found a neat selection of notes, ranging from fivers to a couple of fifties, and a collection of receipts, all folded. There were no photos, no hint of the life of the man who owned it. A number of bank and credit cards were stacked together, behind which Gordy found three more; one for collecting supermarket points, one for somewhere called Holcombe Hall Club, and another for a roadside rescue organisation. Then, she struck gold, and removed another card, this one pink.

'Driving licence,' said Patti.

Staring back at Gordy from the card in her hand, was the small, black-and-white picture of the victim from the castle. Brian Shepherd, and he lived in Frome.

SEVENTEEN

She instructed Paul to catch up with the rest of the team and get back to her with any updates, especially with regards to the baler spike.

With lunch on the horizon, she was with Patti outside an iron-gated entrance on a narrow street in Frome. Cars lined one side of the road, leaving only just enough room to drive past, and there were no parking places available.

'This would drive me crazy,' Gordy said, as Patti took them back around the block to have another pass, in the hope that someone might have moved on. But no one had, so she was forced to navigate to another street to find a space.

'Yeah, parking can be an issue,' Patti said, as they both climbed out of her vehicle to head back down to the address the driving licence belonged to. 'Popular place though, so people are happy to put up with it if they get to live in a beautiful, if not a rather overpriced, pile of stone.'

As they approached the house, Gordy was struck not just by the size of the houses, each of them being at least three storeys, but by just how old they were, and how different, with no two having their doors or windows in the same place. She wondered if the terrace had been built ad hoc rather than all at once, with various new builders over the years adding their own slant to the next house to join the line.

Coming to a stop outside the gate, which sat at the end of an arched throughway leading to a rear yard, Gordy saw that the gate itself was locked.

With no idea yet if the victim lived alone or not, the best and also simplest and most sensitive way to find out was to speak to someone in person.

'I think this is the front door,' said Patti, pointing at a simple wooden door to the left of the gate, and she gave it a firm knock.

Gordy waited long enough for someone to come to the door, then leaned past Patti to thump the heel of her hand against the door, the dull thud echoing through the house beyond.

'Well, if they didn't hear that—' she said, when a voice from above called out.

Gordy stepped back and looked up to see a woman with striking silver hair leaning out of an upstairs window from the house next door.

'Brian's not in.'

Gordy introduced herself and Patti.

'The police? What's he done? He's not had any problems for years!'

That statement was enough to make Gordy want to take the conversation off the rather public road.

'Could we have a chat inside?'

'But I'm going out.'

'I promise this won't take long,' Gordy said. 'We just need to follow up on a few things, and any help would be greatly appreciated.'

The woman stared down at them for a moment before ducking back inside the house and pulling the window closed.

Gordy readied herself to knock at the door once again, not entirely convinced the woman was coming down to let them in, but then there was the rattle of keys and various locks from the other side, and the door opened. The woman's silvery hair shone in the light from inside the house and Gordy realised the colour was natural. Whoever she was, she was growing old disgracefully well, she thought, putting her in her early sixties, but with a look that she not only carried off effortlessly but seemed to knock at least a decade off her, if not more.

'Ten minutes,' the woman said, and stepped back, gesturing to Gordy and Patti to enter.

Inside, Gordy was presented with an open-plan space, a lounge leading to a dining room and, beyond that, a kitchen. It all looked very high-end, not a penny spared. The walls of the lounge and dining room were painted in dark hues of green and blue, which somehow managed to make the space seem both cosy and huge all at once.

The kitchen drew the eye with a brightness Gordy knew instinctively that she couldn't afford. Even from where they were standing, she could tell that it was all hand built, the craftsmanship as apparent as the cost in each and every line, the granite worktop sparkling in the sunlight cutting its way through the windows.

Gordy decided to not wait to be shown a chair, and sat down, Patti following suit, taking out her notebook as she did so.

'Can we take your name and a contact number, please?' Patti asked.

Gordy took in what the woman was wearing, and found that the only word that sprung to mind was linen. Swathed in the oat-coloured material from neck to ankle, she seemed not so much to stand as float.

'But you're here for Brian, not me, aren't you?' the woman replied.

'We're just trying to find out a little bit more about Mr Shepherd, yes,' said Gordy. 'And it's in your interest, as well as our own, if we record your details as well. Simply means we can maintain a good line of communication if we need to.'

The woman sucked in a long, slow breath through her nose, then sat down opposite as she exhaled.

'Lovely house,' Gordy said, trying to crack the ice enough to allow conversation to flow.

The woman's somewhat chilly front thawed immediately at the compliment.

'I'm an interior designer,' she said. 'So, this isn't just a home, it's a shop front, really.'

'And a very effective one, I'm sure, Ms ...?'

'Williams,' the woman replied. 'Christina Williams. Would you like tea? Coffee? I've some filtered water as well. And some biscuits. They're vegan.'

'No, we're fine, thank you; we won't take up much of your time,' Gordy said, wondering why mentioning that the biscuits were vegan was important, 'but thank you.'

'When was the last time you saw Mr Shepherd?' Patti asked.

'Brian? A couple of days ago, perhaps. We don't talk much really. We're very different. I've offered to help him with his house, but he won't of hear it. Seems to think that minimalism to the point of achingly empty is the best way to live. Never been in a house that feels so cold, even with the heating on, if you know what I mean.'

'How long have you lived here?' Gordy asked.

'Ten years,' Christina replied. 'This place was a shell when I bought it. I swear the previous owners kept horses in what's now the kitchen. The smell! Sometimes, I'm sure I still get a waft of it, like the stink of them is in the brickwork.'

'Was Brian here when you moved in?'

Christina shook her head.

'Moved in a couple of years after me. He's from here though, you know? Proper local. I think he was in London for years, for work, but then decided to move back and set up his own company. Fair enough though, it's a lovely place to live. So many artisan producers, lots of independent shops, and there's a huge market every month as well.'

Gordy was beginning to realise that Christina liked to ramble and embellish.

'He has a business here?' Patti asked.

'Shepherd's Solicitors,' said Christina with a nod. 'On Stony Street. Are you sure you don't want some tea?'

'Very sure,' said Gordy. 'Have you noticed anything out of the ordinary recently, with regards to Mr Shepherd? A strange question, I know, especially as you've told us that you don't really talk much. But anything at all, anything he's said, perhaps a visitor ...'

Gordy watched as the faintest of frowns appeared on Christina's forehead.

'I'll be honest,' Christina eventually said, 'everything about Brian is out of the ordinary.'

'Really? How do you mean?'

'I've never seen him receive a visitor other than the postie or a delivery van from the supermarket. Not one. Doesn't seem to have any friends. I don't think he's dating anyone. He's either at work, grabbing some shopping, at Holcombe Hall, or in the house. He's often still awake in the early hours of the morning; I hear him walking about, like he's pacing. He shouts sometimes, too. The walls of these houses are thick in places, thinner in others, and he's managed to wake me up sometimes. Then there's the crying.'

Gordy noticed Patti glance at her, and she gave the sergeant enough of a nod to indicate that she should ask the next question and probe a little deeper.

'Do you know why?' Patti asked.

'It's hard to make out words,' said Christina. 'Whatever it was or is, it was an accident. That's all I've ever been able to make out.'

'He cries about an accident?' Gordy said. 'Do you know what kind or what he means?'

'I've never asked,' said Christina. 'I mean, when he first moved in, I tried to get to know him, introduced myself, turned up with a bottle of wine and a card, that kind of thing, but it was clear from the off he wanted to keep his distance. He looks haunted, you know? Like there's something behind his eyes. That sounds a bit dramatic, but it's the only way I can describe it, really.'

'No, that's a very accurate description, I think,' said Gordy. 'If someone is carrying a trauma with them, it's often very hard to disguise completely.'

Christina leaned forward.

'Can I ask what's actually happened with him?'

Gordy ignored the question.

'When we first arrived and told you we were with the police, you said something quite interesting; you said, *"What's he done?"* then something about him not being in trouble for years; can you tell me what you meant by that?'

At this, Christina rolled her eyes.

'Well, he may not have any friends that I know of, but he certainly has a reputation locally. I half wonder if that's why he goes to Holcombe Hall; it's a safe place really, isn't it?'

Gordy glanced at Patti, not having a clue what Holcombe Hall was.

'It's just a private club really,' said Patti. 'Like a spa-hotel kind of thing. Quite posh, by all accounts. Not that I've ever been.'

Gordy had an idea of just the kind of place they were talking about, and also of the people who frequented it.

Patti asked, 'What do you mean by Brian having a reputation locally?'

Christina mimed taking a drink from an invisible glass.

'How he manages to keep his business going, I don't know,' she said, 'what with the trouble he's found himself in over the years. Though it's been a good while now since one of you knocked at his door to have a word.'

'He drinks, then,' said Gordy.

'Honestly, it's been a fair few years since he was in trouble, and I think he just drinks alone now in his house, which is probably why he's up most nights pacing about and shouting and crying. But the first few years? It was either the police, an angry pub owner, or someone he'd had an argument with at the bar. He would always be very remorseful, and I think because people sort of know him, being as he's local, they've let him off. And anyway, it's been a good while, like I said, since he's been out and about and caused a problem.'

Gordy allowed the conversation to fall quiet for a moment, then she stood up and Patti did the same.

'Thank you, Christina,' she said, using the woman's first name to add a more personal tone to their chat, 'this has been very useful.'

'You didn't tell me what's happened,' Christina said, pushing herself to her feet. 'Is Brian okay? Is something wrong? Is it serious?'

Gordy moved to the door, opened it.

'If we need to ask you anything else, we have your details and we will be in touch. Again, thank you for your time.'

Then she was outside and with a swift farewell, heading back up the street, Patti right beside her.

'We need Brian's house looked over,' she said, as Patti led her back to their vehicle.

'I can get Paul on with sorting the search warrant,' said Patti. 'Shouldn't take too long; two, maybe three hours?'

Gordy stopped mid-stride.

'Which means you're leaving me with the unique pleasure of calling a certain Mr Charming, the pathologist; does he have a first name other than Prince?'

That got a laugh from Patti.

'James,' she said. 'You'll love him, everybody does.'

'I'm not everybody,' Gordy replied.

Patti smiled, took out her phone. 'Once we've both finished our respective calls, I'm assuming we'll be heading to Stony Street? Unless you fancy a visit to a spa, that is?'

Gordy lifted her phone to her ear.

'Jacuzzis and wall-to-wall aromatherapy aren't quite my thing,' she said, then punched in a call to the pathologist.

EIGHTEEN

Patti drove them into town and parked up outside the Cheese and Grain, which Gordy recognised from her first trip out with Jack at the start of the week. A market was taking up half the car park, and Gordy followed Patti through the stalls, tempted by the smell of sausages cooking on a huge skillet.

They had briefly discussed on the way that a check of the records back at the station with regards to Brian Shepherd's supposed various run-ins with the police would be a task for later in the day. But to hurry things along, Gordy had called James Charming, explained what they needed, and asked him to look into it as soon as he got the chance.

A quick phone call was hardly enough to make a judgement call on just how nice someone was or wasn't, but she'd been struck by the warmth of the man's voice. For all she knew, though, the honeyed voice was simply a disguise, so she would delay judgement until they met face-to-face.

'Hungry?' she asked, stopping by the stall.

The look in Patti's eyes was enough of an answer for Gordy to buy them both a sausage in a bun with plenty of onions, and they both munched in silence as they walked on over River Frome and into the town itself.

The name Stony Street suited it, thought Gordy, the road ahead was cobbled, and it rose steeply, each side lined with shops.

Following Patti, she saw everything from a shop selling stationery —clearly the one Allercott had referred to—a wine bar, and a tattoo parlour, to a café, a charity shop, and a small boutique kind of place selling the type of underwear she would love to wear, but wasn't sure she had the confidence to pull off. That thought made her a little cross, and she kept it to herself, annoyed that her self-confidence had taken such a hit that she would even think such a thing. That surely needed to change. She just wasn't sure how to make it happen.

'Here we are,' said Patti, and opened a door to allow Gordy to enter first.

Inside, Gordy walked up to the receptionist, who greeted her with a smile that had not informed her eyes it was taking place.

'Can I help?'

Gordy presented her ID.

'Detective Inspector Haig,' she said. 'And this is Detective Sergeant Matondo.'

'Do you have an appointment?'

'Is it possible to speak to one of the partners?'

'Mr Shepherd is unavailable, I'm afraid.'

'It's because of Mr Shepherd that we are here.'

At last, the receptionist's eyes joined in with the rest of her face as they went wide with shock.

'Oh! Has something happened? Is he okay? It's not his ex, is it? Oh God …'

'How many staff work for Shepherd Solicitors?' Gordy asked, wondering if the whole conversation was going to be nothing more than questions batted back and forth across the room. As for the statement about Shepherd's ex, she logged that for later.

'Five. Mr Shepherd, his partner, Ms Jones, their PAs, and myself.'

'Can I take your name, please?' Patti asked with a smile.

'Yes, of course,' the receptionist answered immediately. 'I'm Louise Abbott.'

'And the other two members of staff are?'

'James Barker, and Hazel Thackery.'

'Are they all in the office today?' Gordy asked.

Louise gave a sharp nod.

'Would it be possible to speak to them?'

'Ms Jones and James are with a client.'

'And Hazel?'

'Snowed under with paperwork, as always,' Louise replied.

'Well, why don't we start with Hazel?' Gordy suggested. 'Then, while we're having a little chat with her, you can inform Ms Jones that we're here and would like a chat when she's done. How does that sound?'

'I think I should speak to her first, really,' said Louise.

'Whatever you think is best,' Gordy replied, then pointed at the handful of chairs in the reception area. 'We'll grab ourselves a seat while we wait.'

Sitting down, Gordy watched as Louise sprang up from behind her desk, then raced off through a door in the far wall. Not even a minute had passed before she returned, hot on the heels of a woman in a deep green trouser suit, her hair short and smart and, Gordy had to admit, rather bloody nice. She'd never had short hair herself, certainly not short enough that clippers had been involved, and for the briefest moment, she wondered if it would suit her.

'Amanda Jones,' the woman said, coming to stand in front of Gordy, hand extended. 'Can I help?'

Gordy stood up and shook her hand.

'We could do with a minute or two of your time, if that's okay,' Gordy said. 'I understand you're busy, but this is, as I'm sure you will understand, a wee bit important.'

'If you're here to speak with Brian, I'm afraid he's on leave this week.'

'Just a minute or two, that's all,' Gordy said, repeating herself.

Amanda turned to Louise.

'Can you nip up and tell James and my client I'll be a few minutes? Maybe see if coffee or tea are required, biscuits, that kind of thing? We've some chocolate ones, haven't we? That usually works to keep people relaxed.'

She looked back at Gordy.

'This way, please.'

Amanda didn't wait for an answer and marched to the door Louise had disappeared through just a few minutes ago.

Gordy followed, with Patti behind, and they were soon in a small, private room, decorated with strikingly realistic plastic flowers, and three artistically taken and framed photographs pinned to the wall, all of which showed various locations in Frome.

Amanda gestured to the seats at the round table in the centre of the room and they all sat down.

'What's happened?' she asked, before Gordy had even managed to get herself comfortable. 'Louise said something about Brian's ex; what is she accusing him of this time? Not that she's in any position to accuse him of anything after what she's done.'

Once again, Gordy decided to leave the mention of Brian's ex for now, and said, 'We understand that Brian is currently on leave.'

'Which is a rare thing indeed,' said Amanda, reaching for a bottle of water in the middle of the table and pouring them each a glass. 'Never takes holiday. And there's nothing I can do to force him to, either. It's not healthy.'

'Do you know what he intended to do with his time off?' Patti asked. 'Did he have plans to go away, to stay at home ...?'

'He didn't say. It was all very short notice. Had to move a lot of things around, but I didn't mind; I was just pleased he was finally listening to me.'

'Do you have any idea about his movements these last few days, perhaps over the weekend?'

'Not at all. He's very private. Keeps himself to himself. He moved here from the city, but that didn't go quite according to plan, not for the first few years anyway, and that damaged him, I think. Or maybe it was something else. Hard to say.'

'How do you mean?' Gordy asked.

'I don't really know,' Amanda said. 'He's local, but I don't know of anyone he hangs around with, anyone he would call a friend. Seems to prefer his own company. Especially the first few years after he came back. But that's all down to Melonie, really. You'd think a restraining order would have some kind of impact, wouldn't you? But it took her a long time to get the message.'

'Melonie?' Patti prompted.

'The ex,' said Amanda. 'They met at university, got married soon after, and they kept it going long enough for it to fall apart somewhat dramatically.'

'What happened?' asked Gordy, and received a narrow stare from the solicitor.

'You've not told me why you're here, and I see no reason to divulge anything further. It's Brian's private life, and for him to share if and when he wants to.'

'Do you have any contact details for Brian's family? Does he have children, or siblings?'

'Single child, both parents are dead. As far as I know, no extended family either, certainly none that I've heard him talk about.' Amanda's jaw clenched. 'As I'm sure you know, my knowledge of how the police work, the questions they ask and why, is rather detailed, Detective Inspector. Can I suggest that you cut to the chase and tell me exactly what is going on and why you're here?'

Gordy allowed them all a moment of silence before she spoke again. She would have preferred to break the news first to a family member, but under the circumstances, she felt fairly sure she had little choice but to be open about what had happened. Amanda, after all, might well be the closest thing to a family member that Brian had.

'I'm very sorry to inform you that Brian has been killed.'

The words were harsh, but they were accurate, and Gordy had found over the years that there was no way to soften the message, because whatever words you used, they were still communicating something utterly horrendous and earth-shattering.

Amanda didn't move, staring at Gordy, who held the woman's gaze.

'What happened?'

'I'm afraid that at this point we are unable to go into much more detail, as I'm sure you understand,' Gordy explained. 'However, I can tell you that his body was found two nights ago at Nunney Castle.'

'Then it was Melonie!' Amanda said, her voice suddenly sharp and rippling with anger. 'Melonie sodding Cox! Do you have her? Surely you have her, you must!'

Gordy maintained her calm composure.

'Can I ask why you think that?'

'Because he bloody well proposed to her there, that's why!' Amanda said, then hurled her glass at the wall.

Gordy waited for the last of the shards to fall.

'I don't suppose you have her address?' she asked.

NINETEEN

Approximately forty-five minutes later, Gordy was once again slipping through somewhere she had never been to before, though she had recognised some of the roads Patti had driven them along, thanks to her own journey to and from work that week.

'Nice place, Castle Cary,' Patti said, as they pulled up at the side of the road.

Ahead of them was the address that Amanda had given them once her rage had eased a little and the smashed glass had been cleaned up by a very surprised Louise. She had also provided them with Brian's file on his ex-wife, which was kept under lock and key in his office. It contained an awful lot of detail and various photographs.

'It's one of those places,' Patti said, 'I've driven through dozens of times and always thought it would be nice to stop and have a mooch around, but I've still not done it. Always the way when something's on your doorstep, isn't it?'

They had approached the small market town from the direction of Shepton Mallet, first passing the train station, which, for whatever reason, sat far enough out of town for Gordy to wonder why it even held the same name.

Once in Castle Cary itself, Patti had driven them into the centre, then turned right, rolling them through a picturesque collection of stone buildings populated by pubs and various small businesses, and even an honest-to-God small museum of local history.

Though Gordy had never admitted it to anyone, not even Anna come to think of it, she rather liked museums, especially the smaller, quirky ones. They told stories of people and places, which was one of the reasons she had become a police officer in the first place. Yes, she enjoyed the pace of the work, the importance of it, but at its heart were people, their lives, the choices they'd made or that had been forced upon them, and helping them deal with the worst of times gave her a sense of worth.

The road they were on led out of the village. Both sides were lined with houses more than a little outside of Gordy's own price bracket. Not that she was even considering buying a house; she was having enough trouble as it was persuading herself to stay in the place she had rented, so putting down roots was something she couldn't imagine. Not yet anyway; perhaps never. She didn't know, didn't want to think about that. The future was still a huge, scary, and unknown place, and one she felt considerably more comfortable approaching one day at a time. She had dreamed of sharing it all with someone, and that someone was now gone. Forever. How the hell was she supposed to see beyond that?

Gordy quickly ran through what Amanda had told them about Melonie, omitting the quite exceptional display of bad language she had used.

'We need to remember the facts,' she said. 'Description first: Melonie is forty-six years old, medium height, and the last time Amanda saw her, she had long, brown, wavy hair. So, that could easily have changed. We do have photographs, though, so that's a huge help. Beyond that, she was married to Brian not long out of university. They moved to London together, he completed a law degree, passed the Solicitors Qualifying Exam, got a job, worked hard, earned well, while Melonie attempted to pursue a career as an actress.

'She had a few on-off jobs, various commercials, a few walk-on roles on some television shows, a bit of theatre, but it never took off.

The relationship became strained, and she blamed Brian and his career for taking over, or something along those lines. That strikes me more as opinion, really, so what I'm going to bear in mind is that as the relationship issues came to a head, she leaned on cocaine and drink a little too much. Not that there's any other amount of cocaine, other than a little too much, no matter how much you've had, but you know what I mean.'

'Then, once they separated,' Patti added, 'Brian ended up having to get a restraining order on her. And it sounds like she pushed that as far as she could, stalking him, calling him, turning up at his door, following his work colleagues, suddenly appearing at dates he had arranged.'

'But all of that was years ago,' said Gordy, rifling through the file Amanda had given them, to retrieve the most recent photographs of Melonie. 'Amanda said Brian hadn't seen or heard from his ex-wife in years. But if he was as private as his neighbour told us he was, there's always the chance that he just never let on.'

'She's a suspect, then?'

Gordy shook her head and reached for her door handle.

'Right now, she's a person of interest. She has a history with the victim, which is leaning towards a motive, but there's a world of difference between losing it when your career and marriage fall apart, and deciding to impale someone on a baler spike.'

'Fair point.'

Gordy opened her door.

'Ready?'

'Let's go meet Melonie,' said Patti.

Walking along to the small row of low terrace houses, Gordy tried to prepare herself mentally for who they were about to meet. Amanda's description had been less than flattering, and, at times, downright terrifying. She suspected, though Amanda never said so explicitly, that Melonie had invaded her life as well, so her professional concern for Brian, her business partner, would have become personal.

It was also something she had very much not signed up for,

having explained to them that she had been taken on by Brian only once the business had spent a year becoming established. It had grown quickly, and he had recruited accordingly. They'd never grown larger, however, happy to keep things small, and it sounded as though that was very much down to Brian's own experiences in a large law firm in London.

At the door to the house Amanda had directed them to, Gordy noticed that the building next door wasn't a house at all, but a pub. The sound of happy chatter oozed through a small gap in a window, and out of the front door, to mingle with the thrum of vehicles breaking the speed limit as they thundered past.

Gordy looked for a doorbell, found none, and gave the door a firm knock.

'Give it a minute,' she said.

When there was no answer, she tried again.

Still nothing.

Gordy gave her head a scratch, then held out a hand to lean against the door.

'Why is no one ever in?' she said, then the door jolted forwards, and she was falling. 'Bloody hell!'

With the door no longer taking her weight, Gordy's vision was filled only with the sight of the floor zooming up lightning-fast to crash into her face and smash her teeth out the back of her skull. She yelled out as much in shock as fear, her mind filled with images of a crushed nose, black eyes, a mouth of blood, then felt herself get yanked back with a sharp, painful snap.

Reaching out to grab hold of the door frame, Gordy managed to pull herself back up to standing, her heart racing enough for her to hear the blood pumping in her ears.

'What the hell happened?' asked Patti, as Gordy tried to get her breath back. 'I only just managed to catch you; hope I didn't hurt you.'

'I'm fine,' said Gordy. 'Door must've been on the latch. When I leaned on it, it just popped open.'

Patti leaned in through the now-open door.

'Hello? Melonie?'

The house replied with nothing more than the whisper of emptiness dancing on the tails of dust motes.

'Maybe she's just one of those people who pops out and never locks her house,' Patti suggested.

Gordy stepped inside.

'Melonie? This is Detective Inspector Haig. Just wondering if we can have a little chat?'

'Is it me, or is it a little too quiet?' Patti asked. 'Do you know what I mean, like the house has been empty for a little too long?'

'I know exactly what you mean,' Gordy replied, having sensed something off about the place as soon as she had stepped over the threshold. Her gut told her something was wrong, but what that was, or why she felt it, she had no idea as yet.

'Melonie, if you can hear me, but can't respond, I want you to know that we are in the house. If you can make any sound at all, even just a tap, please do so.'

'You think she's in, then?' asked Patti.

'I think it's always best to be clear about our intentions,' said Gordy. 'Last thing we want is to stumble in on Melonie when she's fast asleep in a chair or in the bath or something, and cause a scene.'

'Sensible.'

'My middle name.'

The room they were in was a small lounge with white walls, and it was lit mainly by the light from the window at the front of the house. Stairs led up directly in front of them, and moving around them, Gordy saw two doors in the far wall of the room, one opening to a kitchen, the other to a small room with glass doors leading into a courtyard garden. A wood-burning stove stood where an open fire would have once been, the floor was flagstone, and the furniture old-fashioned, but cosy, restful.

Gordy stepped further into the room, far enough to allow her to see into the kitchen and the room leading to the garden.

'Let's head upstairs,' she said.

The stairs rose steep and narrow, reminding her of the stairs in the house Harry had bought just over a year ago. He had since moved in with his partner, Grace, and though Gordy hadn't admitted it to them, seeing them so happy had only magnified her own sadness. She hadn't even sent them a housewarming card; that was something she needed to rectify very soon.

At the top of the stairs, the stillness of the house seemed to gather weight, the darkness thicker, with the landing cut off from the light by three closed doors. The first opened to a narrow bedroom overlooking the garden. It contained a double bed, a small wardrobe, and on a bedside table, she spotted a small collection of paperbacks. The next room was the bathroom, and it was surprisingly large considering the size of the house. Almost too large, really. Odd.

'One room to go,' said Patti.

Standing outside the final door, Gordy could hear something. It was a muffled voice, but she couldn't quite make out what it was saying. The tone was deep, putting her more in mind of a man than a woman.

Patti opened the door, then froze.

Standing right behind her, Gordy stared over Patti's shoulder into the gloom of the room on the other side of the door and saw the unmistakable shape of a body on the floor. Then the stink of it smashed into them like a runaway train, and Gordy knew for sure that Melonie was very much still at home.

TWENTY

Instinct mixed with training and Gordy stepped past Patti, taking from a pocket a small tub of vapour rub.

'Little trick I learned from an old friend,' she said, holding the tub out to Patti. 'Get some of that under your nose right now. This may look fresh, but the smells you get from a body aren't just down to decay, as I'm sure you know.'

The look Patti gave Gordy was enough of an answer, as was the liberal coating of the vapour rub she then dabbed under her nose.

'And breathe through your mouth.' She added.

Once they were both adequately daubed with the strong-smelling goo, she tucked the pot away, pulled on a pair of disposable gloves, and stepped into the room.

The room was lit by whatever was playing on a thin television attached to the wall and the tepid veil of light filtering in through the deep blue curtains drawn across the window.

Despite the body on the floor so desperately pulling at her attention, Gordy instead found herself drawn to the television.

'That's a bit odd,' said Patti.

'Never really been a fan,' Gordy replied. 'Sci-Fi just isn't my thing. I know it was visionary when it came out, but how they've managed to spin it into numerous films, other shows, cartoons, and goodness knows what else, I'll never understand.'

'My dad's a fan. He thinks the original series is the best, though he does have a soft spot for Jean Luc.'

Gordy gave a shrug, no idea what Patti was talking about.

'Next Generation?' said Patti. 'Patrick Stewart? Anyway, he thinks that's okay, but it's Kirk he goes to, almost like it's some kind of comfort blanket.'

'It's a bit silly, though, isn't it?' said Gordy, as on the screen Captain Kirk said something in his inimitable style to Spock. Then she realised how she was in no position to talk, what with her love of reading fantasy, to the point where she'd even toyed, very briefly, with the idea of penning her own fan fiction. It had come to nothing in the end, but she still had a little notebook somewhere full of ideas; something else Anna had never known about.

'It must be set to replay,' said Patti, then glanced down at the body on the floor. 'Maybe she used it to help her get to sleep?'

'I can see how it would be a little hypnotic,' Gordy agreed. She realised that the sound of Kirk's voice was starting to grate somewhat and scanned the room to see if she could spot the remote control.

'Looking for this?' Patti asked.

Gordy took the remote and hit the power button. The TV shut off and the room fell quiet, deathly so.

'I think it's one of those TVs with an integrated DVD player,' Patti said. 'Can't see any other devices, can you?'

Gordy shook her head.

'I know I'm stating the obvious,' she said, turning her attention from the television to the body, 'but let's try to leave things as we see them, so that when we call the SOC team in, nothing else is disturbed.'

'Shall I call Allercott?'

'After we're done, aye,' Gordy said. 'Right now, let's just see if we can get an idea of what we've got. And if at any point you need to step outside, just go ahead.'

'No, I'll be fine,' said Patti. 'After finding Brian at the castle, I'm not sure there's much left my stomach and mind can't handle.'

'You'd be surprised.'

'I'd rather not be.'

For the next few minutes, Gordy and Patti were silent, as they both took a moment to simply look.

The room was small, neat, and plain, but in a fresh, clean way, with crisp white bed linen and pale walls, dotted here and there with exposed brickwork. Gordy felt that it had been put together to be a place of peace and rest, but if that truly was the case, then such an aim had been violently ripped apart.

She remembered that the rest of the house had been similarly decorated, with white walls, a comfortable sofa, and an armchair. This was a house where someone had come to recover, or that was the impression it gave her, though she knew she was undoubtedly reading too much into too little. But the plainness of it all seemed so at odds, not only with what had taken place in it, but with what they had been told about Melonie. Gordy just couldn't square the circle between the two. They just didn't match.

Though the body on the floor was truly horrible to see, it was made all the worse by the sprays of blood that painted the room, as though an artist had made them with a brush. It was hard to make out if any surface hadn't been touched by it, and Gordy had a sense that probably nothing had escaped, because the attack had clearly been frenzied enough to mist the blood, and there would be microscopic droplets of it everywhere.

The white of the bed linen seemed to be brighter still because of the red it now sported, and that struck a chord with Gordy.

'Point of note,' she said, impressed with Patti's composure, 'the blood; it's still a fairly lurid red, isn't it?'

'It's almost impossible to look at anything else,' said Patti. 'Even with the body at our feet.'

'Blood, when exposed to the air, begins to lose oxygen.'

'And changes colour.'

'Exactly. So, if this had happened a few days ago, it would be dry, and more of a deep brown than the red we're seeing here and now.'

'Could've happened the same night as Brian's murder,' said Patti.

'Possibly.'

Pulling her attention away from the blood spatter, Gordy took the photographs from the file out of her pocket and knelt gently beside the body on the floor. Like the room, the clothes were sodden with blood, and she could make out small cuts in the pink, short-sleeved top and denim trousers, which were clearly stab wounds.

With a slow breath in and out, she closed her eyes, then opened them on the face of the victim, holding up the photos to compare.

There was no doubt about it. The body was that of Melonie Cox.

Patti came to kneel beside Gordy.

'It's her, then.'

'It is,' said Gordy, holding out the photos for Patti.

'Well, she obviously didn't kill her husband, did she?'

'That, we don't know.'

'But ...'

Gordy stood up.

'Right now, all we have are two bodies, yes? As yet, we don't know whether Brian or Melonie was killed first; that's down to the SOC team to find out. We may think there's a chance that their deaths are fairly close together, but really, we don't know much else. For all we know, Melonie killed her ex, and was then murdered by someone else, perhaps a boyfriend or a house invader, or someone who just followed her home and decided to get busy with a kitchen knife.'

'That's a bit far-fetched.'

'Maybe Brian killed Melonie, and then he was killed by someone else in revenge for what he did here, or perhaps one of his cases didn't go quite so well and an ex-client paid him a visit with payback on his mind.'

'You should write this down. It's good stuff; I'd read it.'

'All I'm saying,' said Gordy, 'is that right now we don't know anything. And it's better to start with that than to jump to any conclusions because more often than not, they're the wrong ones.'

'So, what now?'

Gordy stepped away from the body and exited the room, then took out her phone.

'Cowboy?' said Patti.

'Yee-haw,' said Gordy, and she rolled her eyes as she pulled up the SOC team leader's number.

25 YEARS AGO, 2:04PM ...

'I don't rightly know,' Jack answered. 'He's asked me to drive, though. And Ellen and I, we had no plans for tonight, so she's happy for me to head out. I'll have to make it up to her, but she'll probably spend a bit of the evening with Lucy anyway; girl's night in, that's what you call it, isn't it?'

Jennifer brightened up at this.

'Dad wants to go out? Really? Like, for real?'

'That would be my guess, yes,' said Jack.

'Did he say where?'

'No, I'm afraid he didn't say any more, just asked me to come and ask if you were free, that was all.'

Jennifer scratched her chin, picking at a flake of dried, fake blood that had been irritating her.

She couldn't remember the last time she'd been out with her dad. More often than not, their time was stolen from his very full diary, squeezed between appointments and meetings. But a whole evening, and one that involved being driven somewhere by Jack?

'Well, in that case ...'

A shout from somewhere far off in the house rolled up the stairs to barge into the conversation. Though the words were impossible to make out, the meaning was there all the same.

'Tristan's getting antsy,' Austin said. 'Maybe, if we stay up here long enough, and he keeps shouting, he'll not be able to get his breath back and pass out.'

Jennifer ignored Austin.

'And how's my lovely little Smelly Helly doing?'

'She asks after you a lot,' Jack replied, smiling at Jennifer's use of one of the nicknames she had given his daughter.

'Of course she does,' Jennifer smiled. 'She's my adopted sister!'

'Well, she does miss you when you're away, as you know. And she's not seen much of you since you've been back, but that's to be expected. I've explained you can't be popping round to see her all the time, not now.'

Jennifer rested a gentle hand on Jack's shoulder.

'Well, tell her I'll come over tomorrow, and we can do whatever she wants. How's that?'

'That would make her very happy, I'm sure, but only if you're not too busy.'

'And tell Dad I'll be ready for seven,' Jennifer added.

'What shall I say to Mr Cartwright?' Jack asked.

'Nothing,' Jennifer said. 'I'm ready.'

With a last look at her ghastly reflection, she followed Jack and Austin out of her room.

Downstairs, Jennifer found the rest of the crew and cast waiting, though those were grand terms indeed for a handful of friends she'd managed to pull together to see if they could turn a little script she had written into a real movie.

The story was nothing special. It was horror, a genre she had, much to the bemusement of her parents, fallen in love with as a child, always wanting to read creepy tales and ghost stories, watch old movies about monsters and vampires. But it was a script she had written, and she wanted to prove to her dad that, even if the film came to nothing, it was still a film, something she had created, and that her degree hadn't been a total waste.

'About bloody time!'

Jennifer didn't respond, just waited, as Tristan marched over to *meet her halfway across the hallway, pushing past Carol, who was checking the camera, and nearly dropped it as he bumped into her.*

Behind Tristan, the huge front door of the house was open, and sunshine bled in across the tiled floor.

'Hey,' Jennifer said, spreading her arms out, 'the lead actress was just making herself look beautiful.'

'You're the final girl,' Tristan said. 'It's not about being beautiful, it's about being a survivor. It's a cliché, yes, but it's one everyone loves. You know that!'

'It's about both, actually,' said Jennifer. 'Name me one final girl who isn't hot?'

Tristan's mouth bobbed open for a moment, then slammed shut.

'Exactly.'

'Do you know your lines?'

'It's mainly screaming and running away before I manage to stab him with his own knife ... and anyway, I wrote them, remember?'

Tristan scratched his chin.

'About that; I've rewritten them.'

Jennifer wasn't the only one who gasped.

'You've what?'

'I'm the director,' Tristan said. 'It's my prerogative.'

'Then why did you ask if I knew them?'

'I was testing you,' Tristan said. 'I knew you wouldn't have looked at the script. And I was right.'

Jennifer caught the stares from her friends, and fed on them a little, as she wondered why the hell she'd felt sorry for him if this was how he was going to repay her.

When she spoke next, she punctuated every word with a sharp, blood-covered jab into Tristan's chest.

'My script. My film. My house. Oh, and my dad's paying for it all, in case you've forgotten.'

TWENTY-ONE

'Funny you should call,' said Cowboy, after Gordy had explained where she and Patti were, and what they had found.

'It is? Why?'

'Because I was going to call you, see if you fancied popping over if you had a moment spare.'

'Give me a second, won't you,' Gordy replied, 'while I have a good old rummage around in my little bag of spare moments to see if I ... Nope, it's empty.'

Cowboy laughed, and to Gordy's surprise, it sounded genuine.

'You know, you're growing on me already, Detective.'

'I'm sure there's an ointment you can get from the chemist to sort that out.'

Another laugh, this one louder.

'Anyway,' Gordy continued, 'as your team has the first victim's house to be looking at, and now this second crime scene, I'm not sure you could spare the time, even if you wanted to.'

'Which I do.'

'Which you do what?'

'Want to spare the time, but you're right, especially now with what you've just told me. I've a small team of crime scene investigators gearing up to visit Shepherd's house once the warrant is through.

But this one you're at now? I'll be handling that myself. I should be over in about an hour and a half max.'

Gordy said, 'Detective Sergeant Matondo has just contacted emergency services, so an ambulance will be on its way once one is available. I'll have my team set up a perimeter, make sure everything is secure. See you soon.'

'Count on it.'

As she was about to hang up, Gordy went back with, 'Wait, why was it you wanted me to come over? Has the pathologist finished the postmortem?'

'He has,' said Cowboy. 'Asked me to call you as he was heading off to do something else. Doctors of pathology are busy people, contracted in when needed, so he isn't usually able to hang around too much. Anyway, much of it is as you would expect, if you can actually expect anything from a full butt-to-bonce impalement.'

Gordy laughed, recognising the phrase because she'd used it herself at the crime scene.

'I know you said the same,' he said, 'and I know I wasn't there when you did, but your detective sergeant mentioned it, and I couldn't help myself. Phrase like that, you can't really forget it, can you?'

Gordy ignored Cowboy's question. 'But if the postmortem is exactly what we'd expect, then why did the pathologist want me to come over?'

Cowboy was quiet just long enough for Gordy to know that what he was about to say next was going to be important.

'Well, the victim, Mr Brian Shepherd, he didn't die from the impalement.'

After a moment's pause to take that in, Gordy said, 'I don't know whether to feel relieved, confused, or both.'

'Oh, I'd go with both,' said Cowboy. 'Especially when I tell you the next bit.'

'And what's that?'

'He drowned.'

Gordy cast her mind back to the night at the castle, remembering what Brian had been wearing, and how wet his clothes were.

'You know, I was expecting more of a response than silence,' said Cowboy.

'His clothes were wet,' Gordy said. 'What you've just told me explains why.'

'Then you'll not be surprised that the samples of water we took from his lungs show that it happened in the castle moat.'

'It was either there or the river, and it would make sense for it to be there.'

Gordy remembered the size of Brian, and she'd thought at the time that to impale him, and to get him into the position they'd found him in, would have been seriously difficult, to say the least.

'He suffered from an impact to the back of the head,' Cowboy continued. 'Serious enough to crack the skull. The spike was sunk into what we think was a pre-made block of cement with a hole set into it for said spike to rest in. Must've been buried there and hidden prior to the events that then took place.'

'That takes an awful lot of planning.'

'It does, and it doesn't. That location, on a dark night, anyone could easily sneak over the bridge to dig a hole deep enough for the concrete block and no one would be any the wiser.'

'Even so,' said Gordy, 'that's not the kind of thing you just come up with on the spur of the moment, is it? But then, I guess none of it is. Someone doesn't just wake up one morning with an elaborate plan to off someone by drowning them and then follow that up with impalement.' Another question came to mind. 'If he was drowned, how did his killer get him out of the moat?'

'There's a set of steps near the bridge,' said Cowboy. 'They're not that old, probably put in to help clean the moat out. Judging by the drag marks we found in the mud on the bank, and the fact that the moat is so shallow anyway, we think they were able to get him to the steps, then winch him out.'

'Winch?'

'James found rope marks on the body. No idea what kind of

winch would've been used, but there's plenty of easily available gear out there, like for climbing and tree surgery, anything that needs rope access, so it's not much of a lead really, I'm afraid. But it would be easy to attach something like that to the bridge or some of the stones in the castle walls. Quiet, too.'

Gordy said, 'I've still had nothing back from anyone about where the spike itself might have come from.'

'Might be able to help you with that as well, actually.'

Gordy did a double-take at her phone.

'Really?'

'We found various grass and wildflower seeds stuck to the spike.'

'That narrows it down to a farm, and bearing in mind it's a baler spike, that's not much of a lead.'

'You'd be surprised.'

'Then surprise me.'

'Well, farming's changed considerably over the years,' Cowboy said. 'New strains of quicker growing grass, that kind of thing. Means you can cut it more times in a year than you used to, and provide more feed for your animals. Then there's the loss of wildflower meadows, the use of all kinds of chemicals to keep the weeds down, and what you end up with is what people now call a green desert; the countryside looks alive and beautiful, but it's pretty dead in a lot of places thanks to intensive farming. You'll have noticed there aren't as many songbirds now; that's a direct result of what I'm talking about.'

'You're painting a bleak picture.'

'I am,' Cowboy agreed, 'but there's also a move towards not just organic farming now, but general improvements in ecosystems, soils, plant varieties. There's grants available for all kinds of things to encourage getting a little bit of nature back into things, and that includes moving away from growing just a few types of grass. It's all about traceability as well. Butchers love to be able to tell their customers that they know the farm, even the farmer, where they get their meat from. If they can add to the story that the farmer has improved the grass fed to their animals, thus improving the flavour of the meat, it can only be good for business.'

'I'm beginning to feel like I'm in a university lecture,' said Gordy.

'In simple terms, that spike is from a farm that's not only organic, but is really pushing the whole biodiversity, rewilding, wildflower meadow agenda. There's some really rare stuff in what we found. And though there will probably be a few of them around the area, my guess is that will narrow down your search considerably. Especially if you throw in the fact that we found a few strands of goat hair.'

'Not a common farm animal,' said Gordy, realising Cowboy had a point. 'Thanks, I'll get my team on to that right away.'

'Happy to help,' said Cowboy. 'See you soon.'

Call over, Gordy shared with Patti what she had just learned, then instructed her to contact as many of the team as were available and have them head over.

'The more the merrier,' she said, 'but don't pull people away from leave, or get them doing a double shift. This is a small crime scene, so easy enough for us to secure. It'll just be good to have a few extra hands and faces, if only to reassure the public and to keep them far enough away from what's going on.'

'I'll go grab some cordon tape from the car as well,' said Patti, leaving Gordy alone with Melonie.

Gordy had been in the presence of numerous dead bodies, victims of everything from murder to fatal accidents. What always struck her the most wasn't so much the way the person had died, though that obviously caught her attention with the tenacity of a barbed fishhook, but instead, it was the emptiness of the flesh. She knew that sounded odd, even though the words were spoken silently in her own mind, but what haunted her most was the loss of a person, rather than how that loss had happened.

Staring now at the body, she remembered a phrase, though had no idea how she had first heard or come across it: When someone dies, a library burns.

Gordy was a reader. She loved books, bookshops, libraries, and the stories and knowledge contained inside them. She wondered about Melonie's library of life, what experiences and memories had been snuffed out when her heart had stopped, her loves and hates, her fears, her dreams ... all of them gone.

Heading back downstairs, Gordy was met by Patti returning from the car, a roll of cordon tape in her hand.

'I mentioned to Pete about what was found on the baler spike,' she said. 'He agrees that there can't be many goat farmers, hobby or otherwise, in the area. He's going to call in at the vets in Frome on the way, see if they can help; might be a quicker way of narrowing down the list.'

'Excellent,' said Gordy.

'What about next of kin?' Patti asked.

'Hopefully, the search of both Brian's and Melonie's properties will identify that.'

'So, what now?'

Gordy plucked the cordon tape from Patti's hand.

'We decorate,' she said, and stepped back out into the day.

TWENTY-TWO

By the time everything was finished at the house of Melonie Cox, the SOC team having carried out their full and detailed inspection, and her body taken away to the mortuary, late afternoon had drifted into late evening, and before anyone had a chance to notice, it was early morning.

The small team of CSIs Cowboy had sent to Brian's property had finished going over the place and would get back to Gordy with their findings as soon as possible.

Making sure she was the last to leave, and instructing the team that a late morning start was on the cards, Gordy had headed back to her flat in Evercreech. The drive had drifted by so quietly, the roads empty and the sky as dark as thick velvet, that when she arrived home, she could barely remember any of it, the whole thing like a fever dream.

Letting herself into her flat, the temptation to just fall into bed fully clothed was strong, but she forced herself to undress, visit the bathroom, then allowed her bed to reach out and embrace her.

She was tempted to get straight back out of it again and open a bottle of wine, but knew that way madness lay, so forced herself to stay where she was. The temptation though ... God, it was almost a physical thing, palpable, the bottle in the cupboard calling out to her.

But she didn't need a drink, and had lived with a general rule that if she ever found she did, then she wouldn't have one. Drink and her job just didn't mix. So the bottle remained out of reach for another time, and Gordy closed her eyes.

The room was cold, just how she liked it, the window open to allow a cool breeze in to stir the quiet with the sound of the curtains tussling gently together.

In the moments before sleep eventually took her, Gordy had felt herself sinking deeper into her mattress, as though something heavy was weighing down on her, pushing her into it. At first, the sensation had led to an odd feeling of panic, but then she'd leaned into it and just let herself drift.

When she woke, barely an hour later, in a cold sweat, heart racing, duvet wrapped around her like rope, her mind was a jumble of nightmares she couldn't recall but could still feel the claws of in her skin. Gordy screamed at the night, her voice ripping its way out, tearing at her throat.

'I just need to bloody well sleep! Please! That's all I'm asking for, okay? A break from it all. Please ...'

She had no idea who she was shouting at, but vocalising her anguish meant that it wasn't trapped like a wild animal inside her chest, trying to get out.

Sitting up, Gordy struggled to free herself from the constrictor-like grip of the duvet, eventually kicking it off the bed and onto the floor, swearing at it as it fell. Fully exposed to the cold of the room, a shiver rippled through her body. She became acutely aware of something squeezing her chest, twisting her stomach, as invisible fingers of panic reached deep inside to suffocate her.

Before she knew what she was doing, or could even begin to understand why, Gordy was up and out of her bed, scrabbling around in the dark for her clothes. She stubbed her toes, tripped, fell against the wall, cracked her head, but that only served to make the panic worse as, disorientated, she felt her way along until she found the door, then the light switch, and flooded the room with brightness.

Seconds later, fully dressed, Gordy was out in the hallway,

pulling on her shoes, wrapping herself in her coat, and out of the door, keys in her hand, no idea what she was doing, because something had caught hold of her now, and she needed to run.

Outside, the night greeted her with cold disdain, the moon hidden behind clouds, the sky starless and bleak, and she dashed over to her car, tumbling into it as she fumbled with her keys to stab them into the ignition. The engine burst into life. Gordy crunched the gear stick into reverse, spun around in the driveway, and was then out and on the main road before she'd even managed to clip in her seatbelt.

Staring ahead, Gordy's vision was blurred, and she realised she was crying. She wiped away the tears with the back of her hand, but more fell, and the tunnel cut by her headlights through the blackness ahead was quickly obscured, the road and the hedgerows bleeding into each other like water spilled on a painting.

She had no idea what speed she was doing, no thought as to where she was even going other than away, far away, and fast. Because back there, back in the flat, the emptiness was waiting for her still, sitting at the end of her bed, crouching on the worktop in the kitchen, burrowed deep in the cushions of her sofa, and she couldn't be around it anymore. It was too much, all of it, she had to get out get out get out just get the hell away from it and—

A T-junction swept up so fast that by the time Gordy realised and hammered her foot down on the brakes, she knew it was already too late. She pumped the pedal, tried to maintain control, but the car was gone, sliding now, the rear end taking its own path as it swung around to her right. Then she was sideways, had drifted past the junction, was now careering across the road at the end of the one she'd just shot out from, and all she could think of, all she could feel, was nothing at all, because right then, she didn't care, hoped whatever was about to happen would be painless, and that perhaps now she would get some rest.

The car came to a stop. Its momentum was brought to a halt by the far edge of the road, which caught the wheels, jarring Gordy hard enough to crash her head against the window.

The engine stalled.

Gordy snatched at the key, twisted it hard, forgot the car was still in gear, and the vehicle complained with a shudder and a thump. She yanked the gearstick into neutral, tried again, and the engine sparked into life. Then she slammed the stick into first and went to stamp on the accelerator, only to stall again. Ahead, she saw lights racing towards her.

Too late now to respond, to get her car out of the way, Gordy froze, the lights growing larger, blinding her, then the other vehicle shot past, horn screaming at her as it disappeared in her rearview mirror.

Gordy took a moment to calm down, to assess. Then, with shaking hands, she got the engine started, eased into first, and, checking there was no other danger of being crashed into by another late-night driver, swung around to head back home.

Pulling back into her space in the parking area, Gordy came to a stop, turned off the engine, heaved the handbrake on, and killed the lights. Then, sitting there in the darkness, cocooned by the utter idiocy of what she had just done, she leaned her head back into her seat and sobbed.

She couldn't do this, not anymore. Every moment was agony. She was lost in an unknown world, surrounded by strangers, broken-hearted and alone. The work had distracted her a little, but how healthy was that in the end, really, to be so shattered by life that the only way to keep her mind together was to focus instead on a murder investigation?

Leaning her head forward, and wiping her eyes once again, Gordy saw something on the floor of the passenger side of the car. It was the sticky note Firbank had given her, with her number on it. She reached over, picked it up, grabbed her phone, and tapped in the number. Her thumb hovered over the call, just a millimetre between her and waking up someone she didn't know, but who had offered to help.

Gordy deleted the number, felt her shoulders sag.

She couldn't do it. She couldn't call a stranger, no matter what she'd said. Because what could Firbank do anyway? She couldn't take away the pain, couldn't fill in the hole in her chest where Anna still lived despite being dead for months now, couldn't staunch the wounds of her broken heart.

No, Firbank couldn't help. No one could. She was alone. Would face it alone. Simple as that. Even if it meant that in the end, she would be broken beyond repair.

Gordy opened her car door, climbed out, and made her way back to her flat, each step leaden and slow. Inside, she went to her bedroom, collapsed on the bed, didn't bother with undressing, just grabbed the duvet from the floor and gave it a heave, pulling it high enough to hide her head.

Her phone jabbed into her leg, and she struggled to pull it from her pocket, swearing as she tried to untangle it. She had to turn onto her side, which only served to wrap the duvet around her and make retrieving her mobile even more difficult. When she finally pulled it free, she saw from the screen that she'd somehow managed to open her contacts list, and there, in front of her, one name stood out. She punched it in, let it ring once, twice, thought better of it, and killed the call, before switching her phone off completely and hurling it into the dark to thud against the wall.

When sleep eventually came, it was a dead thing, but Gordy welcomed it anyway. Its embrace was little more than a cold mockery of the comfort she so desperately yearned for, and wondered if she would ever feel again.

TWENTY-THREE

Gordy knew that no amount of Vivek's exceptional coffee was going to help. As first weeks went, it had been the longest. The broken night, punctuated hauntingly by her extraordinary behaviour, had only added to the pain of waking up to a Thursday she wasn't sure she could face. She was now so tired that she had somehow come out the other side of it, beyond the reach of sense and caffeine. As the team gathered around the board, she felt both tired and wired, like she could at any minute both fall fast asleep and run a mile in four minutes flat.

She had arrived before everyone else, and had run through the postmortem report on Brian Shepherd. It was too early to expect anything yet on Melonie, but Cowboy had already been in touch to see if she could head over later to chat it through before he wrote it up.

The whole team was in, including the other four PCSOs Gordy had met during her guided tour on Monday, though their names eluded her. If they needed any more uniformed officers, she'd call for them, but right now, she was happy to keep things small. Large teams led to things getting unwieldy and overly complicated, and days quickly became months became years.

Gordy had a sense that the cases they were investigating were about to offer something up that would help them better understand what was going on, maybe find the person or persons responsible.

The reason she felt that was because there was a theatre to what had been done, as though those responsible were showing off. And if they were, there was every chance they would also unwittingly give themselves away; no plan, no matter how detailed or well thought out, was infallible. In fact, Gordy had often found that the more elaborate the crime, the faster it unravelled, because there were just too many plates to keep spinning.

Standing by the board, Gordy saw that the wayward wheel had been found, but was now utterly useless, stuck to the frame as it was by being wrapped with sticky tape.

'Sorry, best I could do,' said Paul.

'Well, maybe we can get another ordered, then?' Gordy suggested. 'But for now, I'll just have to make sure I don't lean on it, or sneeze.'

Everyone was hugging a mug of coffee, provided by Vivek, though today the biscuits were just from a packet. Gordy was a little thankful for that, because as delicious as the lardy cake was, she wasn't sure having it as a daily snack was all that sensible.

Gordy glanced over at Patti.

'Anything important in the Action Book, or are we good to crack on?'

'Nothing urgent,' Patti replied.

'Bill Halliday, then,' said Gordy, and looked over at Paul.

'I met up with him yesterday,' said Paul. 'We actually managed to persuade him to take a bed at a local hostel for the next couple of weeks. Means he's more secure, and we can keep an eye on him while we work on all of this.'

'I'm happier with that,' Gordy agreed. 'Has he mentioned anything else?'

Paul shook his head.

'He mentioned that whistle again, the one that woke him up because it sounded like a missile in his dream.'

'So, he does actually think it was someone whistling, then?' asked Gordy.

'He does. Though equally, it could've been the wind whipping through the ruins.'

'Exactly what I was thinking,' Gordy agreed, 'but worth remembering anyway. Now, victim one, Brian Shepherd ...' She pointed to a display of photos from the crime scene on the wall beside the board. It made for grim viewing indeed. 'What he's dressed in has to be significant. I doubt very much he arrived in Nunney wearing a boilersuit and with a sack over his head.'

'Could the killer have dressed him?' asked Pete.

'According to the postmortem report, he suffered an impact on the head,' Gordy said. 'Considerably more blood from this was found on the clothes he was wearing underneath the boilersuit than on it, suggesting he was dressed in it after being knocked unconscious. Once that was done, he was drowned in the moat, winched out, and only then was he impaled on the spike.'

She pointed to a number of other photographs. 'These are the various items found in the moat by a diving team sent over the day after. As you can see, it's mainly just beer cans and animal bones, along with some random stuff that's been in there for years; shoes, a couple of rusting penknives, a bike wheel, an ice hockey mask, even an old air pistol. Nothing fits the shape of the wound.'

'How did they display him like that, though?' asked one of the other PCSOs, a woman called Helen Kendrick, who had the most ginger hair Gordy had ever seen. 'And who the hell takes a hockey mask to a castle, then throws it in the moat?'

'By planning ahead,' said Gordy. 'The spike was sunk into a pre-made concrete block. According to the SOC team, it was buried there sometime before the events took place.'

There was an audible gasp from the team on hearing that little fact.

'That's some serious forward planning,' said Jack.

'Which is why,' continued Gordy, 'I think it's all significant; what he's wearing, the fact he was drowned before being impaled.'

'And the film still frame,' added Patti.

Gordy drew everyone's attention to that next.

'Right now, we've no idea who the girl is, what's happening, or even where this was filmed. You can see something behind her, a building of some sort, but it's hard to make out. For all we know, this was a film set.'

'Odd that she's smiling despite all the blood,' said another of the PCSOs, a man called Travis Waring, who had the build of a pub-going rugby player, and sported a huge, black, bushy beard.

'When the pathologist sent it through, it was the blood I saw first,' said Gordy. 'I found myself wondering if it was a snuff film. But that smile, it looks too natural, doesn't it, like she's happy, enjoying herself?'

'So, it could be from an actual movie, then, couldn't it?' said Pete. 'Some kind of slasher or horror flick or something. Don't recognise it, though.'

'And what's that she's holding?' asked Travis, coming up for a closer look.

'Haven't the faintest,' said Gordy.

Travis sat back down.

'A few other points of note about Brian,' said Gordy, keen now to get the team moving. They had plenty to be thinking about, and being active would help them think harder and faster. Sitting in a meeting for too long would have the opposite effect. 'One, no next of kin. Two, there's hours missing from when he was seen parking his car, to when he was eventually killed. I need another walk around, check the pub, knock on doors, see if we can find what he was up to, or if he met with anyone. Three, according to his neighbour, he would shout out about an accident, though we have no idea what that could be, whether he was in one or not. Worth checking up on his medical records, see if there's anything there. And, as for the location, his business partner informed us that he proposed to his ex-wife, Melonie Cox, who is also our second victim, at the castle. Once we're done here, I'm heading over to meet with the pathologist to go through the post-mortem.'

'Melonie's parents will meet you there to identify her body,' said Patti. 'Family liaison from Bristol has already visited them.'

'What about the info on the spike?' Gordy asked.

'Very helpful,' said Pete. 'Narrowed it down to two farms. I've rung both, found the one that's missing a spike, and will head out to Holcombe after this.'

'Why've I heard that name before?' Gordy asked.

'Probably because I drove you through it on Monday,' said Jack.

Gordy checked her watch.

'Right, post-mortem and body identification for me,' she said, the tone of her voice a clear indication of how little she was looking forward to it. 'Patti, can I leave you to divvy up tasks? And everyone, just keep me up to date, and if you need to call me, do.'

Handing it over to Patti, Gordy left the office and was soon driving to the city of Bath. She'd not had a chance to venture there yet, and didn't really know what to expect. She knew it had Roman-built baths, after which it was named, and that it was a desirable, and therefore very expensive, place to live.

She also knew it had a couple of really excellent, independent bookshops. She wouldn't get a chance to visit them this time, but that was enough of a draw for her to consider maybe a trip out on a day off. Today was anything but that, so she put on the radio and allowed the roads to guide her.

TWENTY-FOUR

When Gordy arrived at the mortuary, Cowboy, instead of James Charming, was there to meet her.

'Can't say I was expecting to see you here,' she said. 'And it's hard to recognise you without the hat.'

'Can't help who I am,' Cowboy replied, that western drawl to his voice thick and syrupy.

'I'm sure you can,' Gordy replied, but with enough warmth in her voice to bring a slight smile to the pathologist's face. 'Where's James?'

'Getting ready for you,' said Cowboy.

Gordy asked, 'Have you always been into, well, whatever all that is or was, with the hat and the music?'

Gordy wasn't sure how to describe it, whether it was Country, or Country and Western, or something else entirely, such as a love of reenacting historic scenes from the days of the Wild West, maybe even an odd obsession with a TV series she remembered from the 80s, The Dukes of Hazzard. Perhaps it was best to not even attempt to describe it.

'I do love me some country music,' Cowboy said, and his accent was again of dust and whisky and riding a horse across a sun-drenched ranch. 'Always have, always will. My dad, he was a singer, you see, toured clubs and pubs, dressed in all the gear. Did covers mainly; Hank Williams Jr, Waylon Jennings, Kris Kristofferson, Willie Nelson, Don Williams. So, it's what I grew up on. The hat? It was his. Left it, his gear, his guitars, all of it, to me in his will.'

'Do you play as well, then?'

'I do. Not as well as Dad did, but I do my best. Do gigs now and again as well; you'll have to come see me sometime.'

'I'd like that,' Gordy lied, unable to think of anything worse than sitting in a pub listening to live country and whatever music.

Once in the mortuary, Cowboy directed Gordy to a rack of white overalls and a row of white rubber boots. 'Face masks, gloves,' he added, pointing to some boxes on a shelf. 'When you're ready, just come join me and James through those doors over there.'

Cowboy left Gordy to change. As she did so, she noticed the smell of the air. There was a tang to it, faint in this little side office, but she knew that as soon as she entered the examination room it would be considerably stronger. For that reason, she applied a liberal dabbing of the vapour rub she'd pulled from her pocket, before following on behind.

The first thing Gordy noticed when she entered the exam room wasn't the white walls, the stainless steel, the bright lights, or the body under a white sheet on a metal trolley, but the music.

'You have got to be kidding me,' she muttered, wincing as John Denver sang something dreadful about the wind being the whisper of Mother Earth.

Doing her best to ignore it, and failing terribly, she strode over to stand opposite Cowboy and the pathologist, James Charming, the body under a white sheet on the trolley directly between them.

Gordy stared at the pathologist, or at his eyes, seeing as that was really the only part of his face that was visible. They were brown, and stared back at her, before the right one winked.

'I'm James,' the pathologist said, and Gordy saw the corners of the man's eyes crinkle a little with a smile she couldn't see behind the face mask.

'Gordy,' Gordy replied.

'I've heard plenty about you from Keith, all of it good.'

That statement took Gordy a little by surprise.

James was still speaking.

'You're having a busy first week, aren't you? How are you finding it? Oh, and I know about Anna, too; really sorry to hear you've been through something so tough. I've worked with your team a few times, and I've no doubt at all that they'll give you all the support you need.'

'They've been great,' Gordy said. 'And yes, it's been tough, the worst, actually.'

'Remember to give yourself time,' James said. 'It doesn't heal, not at all, but it does allow you to gradually come to terms with your loss, to sift through things, remember the good times. Worst thing you can do? Run away from it, ignore it, let it fester.'

'Easier said than done.'

'Just because it's difficult, doesn't mean it's not the right thing to do.'

Cowboy interrupted, 'As you're aware, the parents will be arriving soon. So, once we're done here, James will move Melonie over to the viewing window.'

Despite the nauseatingly cheery voice of Denver echoing through the room, Gordy heard a reassuring depth of sincerity in Cowboy's voice.

'One of the worst parts of the job,' she said. 'The damage something like this causes to those closest to the deceased.'

'It's a cruel world,' James agreed. 'Ready?'

'No, but I never am for this, no matter how much I try and mentally prepare myself.'

James reached up to the top of the white sheet and slowly, gently pulled it down to reveal Melonie's face, torso, and finally her legs, until she was fully exposed under the harsh hospital lighting.

Gordy closed her eyes for a moment, paused to calm herself with a slow breath in and out, then opened them again.

Melonie's body bore the scars of the pathologist's careful, yet no less brutal for being so, dissection work, with lines sewn across her chest and down her torso. The wounds to her body, inflicted by whoever had attacked her in her own home, dotted her flesh like a scattering of small, thin twigs, each no longer than maybe a centimetre or two.

'This was brutal,' she said.

'She was stabbed a total of nine times,' said James.

Gordy was now looking at the rest of Melonie's body, especially her arms.

'But there are no defensive wounds,' she said. 'Something like this ... I'd expect to see cuts, lacerations, up and down the arms, the hands to be damaged, but there's nothing.'

'Not a thing,' said James, then he pointed to Melonie's throat.

Gordy looked to where his finger was resting and saw a thin line of purple bruising reaching right around Melonie's neck.

'Strangled?'

'With this,' Cowboy said, and from a trolley at his side he lifted an evidence bag, handing it over to Gordy for a closer look.

Inside, Gordy saw a tangle of wire flex.

'And that is?'

'Telephone cord.'

'Do people even have landlines anymore?'

'Well, Melonie didn't,' said Cowboy.

Gordy stared at the wire.

'Which immediately makes me think that the killer took this with them and left it there on purpose.'

'Looks that way,' said James. 'She was strangled with that first, then stabbed. The flex killed her, not the knife.'

'Where was the knife found?'

'It wasn't.'

'What?'

Cowboy shook his head.

'No sign of it anywhere.'

'Might be worth having another look?' Gordy suggested.

'We looked everywhere.'

Gordy was quiet for a moment, then said, 'Anything else?'

Cowboy handed her another evidence bag.

'First, this,' he said. 'And you might recognise it. Well, not it, as such, but what it's from.'

Gordy took the bag. Inside was another film still. It was similar to the first one Cowboy had sent her, showed the same girl, only this time she wasn't covered in so much blood. To Gordy's surprise, a much younger Melonie was standing beside her. It looked to her like they were talking. They were outside, and she could see fields around them, but there was no sign of either the doorway from the other still, or the building she had spotted beyond the girl in the garden or whatever it was that lay beyond.

'They knew each other? So, there's obviously a connection, then.'

'Looks that way,' Cowboy agreed. 'There's also this ...'

Cowboy handed over yet another evidence bag.

'We didn't find a handbag or anything like that, but we did find a coin purse. Wasn't much in it, just some loose change, a few notes, and those cards.'

Gordy examined the cards. One was the business card of someone going by the name of Lily Twelvetrees, a counsellor specialising in neurolinguistic programming, relationships, and life coaching. Gordy had to wonder if the name was made up.

'This could be useful,' she said. 'Might be able to learn a little more about Melonie.'

The other was a membership card for Holcombe Hall.

'I knew I'd heard that name before,' Gordy exclaimed, holding the card up for a closer look. It was a simple design, containing the outline of a large house etched in gold, and set on a plain black background.

'What name?' asked Cowboy.

'Holcombe,' said Gordy. 'The spike that Brian Shepherd was impaled with? It's from a farm over that way. Brian Shepherd was also a member.'

'Coincidence, surely.'

'I don't believe in them,' said Gordy, and heard the voice of Harry, her last DCI, saying those exact same words in her mind, as he had done so many, many times. 'One other thing,' she added, 'there was a DVD playing when we arrived. Was there anything on it? Prints, that kind of thing?'

'Star Trek: The Original Series,' said Cowboy. 'One of my favourites. Have you ever seen the episode Space Seed? It's the one with Khan.'

Gordy didn't answer, just stared.

'No? Well, you should. It's amazing how they then brought back the character for what is clearly one of, if not the best, movies of the whole series, Star Trek II: The Wrath of Khan.'

'You've lost me.'

'He's got a point,' said James. 'Wrath of Khan is excellent.'

'See?' said Cowboy. 'But no, there was nothing on it at all. Not a thing.'

Gordy was a little surprised.

'What? How's that even possible? Surely it had Melonie's fingerprints on it.'

'Wiped clean. Thoroughly, too. Done with the kind of spray people use to clean vinyl records.'

'That's a bit odd, isn't it?'

'You're the detective, not me.'

Gordy thought for a moment about this tiny piece of information.

'Why would Melonie wipe down a DVD before putting it on? We wondered if she had it playing to help her get to sleep or something, but what you've just said doesn't add up.'

'Then what does?' Cowboy asked.

'Someone else could have done it,' Gordy suggested. 'The killer, maybe? But why? What's the point in putting it on at all? And where the hell is the knife?'

'Good questions. Can't say I've the answers.'

Gordy shook her head, baffled now.

'What the hell's the point of putting an old sci-fi series on a DVD? Why do that? What's it telling us?'

'Maybe it's what they like to kill to,' Cowboy suggested.

'That's a very strange tack to take.'

'All of this strikes me as strange,' said James. 'And believe you me, in this line of work, I've seen some very, very strange things indeed.'

'Fair point.' Said Gordy.

James reached for the white sheet and covered Melonie's body once more.

Gordy realised that from the moment he had pulled it down, she hadn't noticed the music. It was still on, and it was still John Denver, but she'd not heard a note of it.

Unfortunately, it was now back with a vengeance, and Mr Denver was now talking about poems, prayers, and promises, none of which would help Melonie, though Gordy felt that she could do with a few prayers herself.

'Her parents will be here in ten,' James said.

'Then I'll go and get myself ready to meet them,' said Gordy.

James went to move the trolley Melonie was lying on, but paused, and looked again at Gordy.

'I don't know how you do it, and I've the utmost respect for you,' he said, his voice quiet. 'Breaking the news to family, I mean, to friends. I know people look at what I do, wonder how I'm able to do it. It's not that I don't feel, or anything like that. I treat each person with respect and professionalism and care. But there's no interaction, is there? They're gone, and it's my job to see if what's left can help you or whoever find out what happened to them, who did it, even the why. But meeting kith and kin? Being in that moment with them? Like I just said, I've got nothing but respect for that.'

Gordy stood for a moment, a little stunned by the pathologist's words.

'Someone's got to do it,' she said. 'And sometimes, I'd just rather it was me than anyone else. Death, it's never a simple thing to deal with, to understand, and sometimes, actually a lot of the time, all people want, all they really require, is that you stand with them in that moment of grief and just let them be. Sometimes, just your presence is enough.'

'But how do you know what to say?'

'I never know what to say,' Gordy replied. 'I just go in there and let the moment lead me. There's no right way to do it, but I guess there are plenty of wrong ways, and I think, over the years, I've just got a feel for what's best.'

'Sounds to me like you draw a little on your own experience, your own pain.'

Gordy gave James a sad smile.

'More so now than you could ever believe,' she said, then turned away from him, and headed back out to the small room to remove the overalls, the boots, the mask, and the gloves, wipe the vapour rub from under her nose, and stand with Melonie's parents in their darkest of times.

TWENTY-FIVE

By the time Gordy was back in Frome, midafternoon had come around to greet her with open arms, and she welcomed them gladly. Seeing Melonie's body, experiencing its dreadful quiet, had affected her more than she had expected it to. Being there with her parents in that stark and brutal moment of appalling grief had only served to add to it.

It wasn't that she was a cold, unfeeling, hardened detective at all. In many ways, she wondered if the death of Anna, the love of her life, had shattered whatever protective shell she had developed over the years, exposing her to the raw grief she felt, even at the death of a stranger.

She did not know Melonie. She did not know Brian. They were the terrifyingly tragic players in a story she was now a part of, and one she knew she would have to see through to the end. Unlike a book, though, she couldn't skip a chapter when things got to be too much, or just jump to the final pages in the hope of a happy ending.

Seeing the wounds Melonie had suffered, imagining what her last awful moments of life had been like, had somehow given Gordy a deeper connection to both her and Brian. Someone was out there doing something awful, something so utterly against what the nature of humanity was surely about; to be kind, to care, to love, that she was going to do everything in her power to find them, and to stop them.

Worryingly, Gordy had a deep sense that whoever was responsible was not done yet. There was a message here, one she had not yet deciphered. Some killers murdered without reason, just for the thrill of it. Others were driven by a personal mission to prove something, to say something, to make the world shudder at the mention of their name. There were those who never wanted to be caught, and those who enjoyed being chased, staying one step ahead of the police. And then there were those who somehow managed to mix a little bit of each into one unholy, horrifying whole.

Gordy's gut told her that whatever the killer was doing, it had been long in the making, and something was driving them to do the unthinkable. There were clear links between Brian and his ex-wife Melonie's deaths; both murders were staged, but for what reason, she had not yet fathomed. There was also the obvious connection of the film stills, and the girl in both was clearly important.

Cowboy had given Gordy an enlarged copy of the second image found on Melonie's body, as she had left the mortuary. Who the girl in the film still frame was, and why she mattered, was still lost in the fog. The deaths themselves also seemed strangely elaborate; they had not just been killed, but despatched in a way that was neither spur of the moment nor quick.

Each kill had been unique. Each kill had been planned. Each kill was trying to say something.

Gordy wondered if the killer was hoping that someone would figure it all out and stop them. Not that it mattered; her job was to stop them, regardless.

On the way back from her meeting with Cowboy and James, Gordy had called the number on the card found in Melonie's purse. She had been immediately greeted by the warm voice of Melonie's counsellor, who was in the middle of her lunch break, and more than happy to meet up and chat.

After pulling into a parking space by the Cheese and Grain in Frome, Gordy made her way to the River House Café. Stepping inside, she was met by the delicious aromas of cakes and coffee, and the sound of happy, bubbling chatter, the tables filled with customers tucking into plates of deliciousness.

A middle-aged woman with short hair and lots of earrings waved to her, and Gordy headed over.

'Take a seat,' she said, gesturing at the chair opposite her. She was wearing an enormous, thick cardigan of deep red wool. 'Just finishing off my coffee. Do you want anything? The cinnamon twist is to die for. Actually, everything is. And you need to try the turmeric latte; sublime!'

Gordy declined.

'Thank you for agreeing to meet at such short notice, Ms Twelvetrees,' she said.

'Call me Lily. And I'm a Mrs, even though he buggered off a while ago now.'

'Oh, I'm sorry,' said Gordy, not sure whether Lily's husband had died or ran off.

Lily's accent was straight out of the heart of Yorkshire, and hearing it immediately warmed Gordy to her.

'Don't be,' Lily said, refusing to clarify what had happened to her husband. 'Also, Twelvetrees is rather a rare surname, so we try to make sure it's not used too much, otherwise it might wear out. That's why I went back to it.'

On saying that, Lily gave Gordy a wink, and she warmed to her even more.

Lily stood up.

'Right, shall we go to my office? A little more private than here, I think. But you must come back. Not just for the food, either; this is Black Swan Arts, and there's loads to see from local artists; it's one of my favourite places. Come on, then!'

Gordy scrambled to get out from under the table as Lily marched off at speed. Catching her up, she followed her out of the café, across the main road, and along a small lane beside the river, before leading her through the door of a house with large sash windows covered in numerous glass ornaments to catch the sunlight, and a handful of dreamcatchers.

'Here we are,' Lily said, showing Gordy through to a room on the left of a hallway decorated like the footpath of an ancient woodland, with numerous sticks lining the walls, the ceiling hung with bunches of dried flowers and herbs like the drooping leaves of trees. The smell, Gordy noticed immediately, was somewhat intoxicating.

The room Lily took Gordy into was small and cosy, with a floor-to-ceiling library on one wall, and the others bedecked in art, none of which she recognised. The furniture in the room comprised two deep, soft, olive-green sofas, a leather armchair, and a coffee table that looked to have been carved from one solid piece of wood.

Lily sat down, then was up again and out of the door, returning moments later with a glass jug of water and two tumblers.

Gordy took a seat as Lily poured the water and sat down opposite.

'Right then,' Lily said. 'Shall we get to it? You want to talk about Melonie Cox, yes?'

Gordy sipped her water.

'I must say that you're dealing with the news I gave you on the phone rather better than I expected,' she said, thinking back to their conversation when she had told Lily about both Melonie and Brian.

'I'll grieve in my own good time,' Lily replied. 'Right now, it sounds to me like you need all the help you can get to catch the bastard who did it.'

'Yes, quite,' said Gordy, taking another sip, if only to give her a chance to digest that reply.

As counsellors went, Lily was unlike any she had ever met. She was blunt, abrupt, open, and judging by her house, wildly creative.

'Warm, isn't it?' Lily said and removed her cardigan, revealing arms covered in a rainbow of tattoos.

'Wow,' Gordy said.

'You should see my legs,' Lily replied. 'So, how can I help?'

Working hard to push away imagined images of Lily's art-covered legs, Gordy said, 'Really, I'd just like some background on Melonie. I understand there will be patient confidentiality, but if there's anything you can tell me about her that you think might help ...'

'Do you have any specifics?' Lily asked. 'And as for patient confidentiality, I'm pretty bloody sure Melonie would want me to share something if she thought it might help to catch her killer.'

'Not every counsellor I've had to see would agree with you.'

'I'm not every counsellor.'

'So I gather.'

'Well, come on, then,' Lily said. 'What do you need to know?'

Gordy thought for a moment, then said, 'I've got two pictures of Melonie in my head.' 'One is of someone who went through a rough divorce and ended up having a restraining order. The other ... Well, her house doesn't match that description at all.'

'Explain.'

'It's peaceful,' said Gordy. 'There's a calm to it. Hard to put it into words, really, but it struck me as somewhere someone had gone to heal. I know that sounds a bit wishy-washy, but there we are.'

'No, that's accurate,' said Lily. 'Both points, actually. Melonie was very lost, very broken, but she was working very hard to heal, and she was doing so well.'

'How long had she been seeing you?'

'Years,' said Lily. 'She'd tried other counsellors, came to me as a last resort, I think.'

'Why a last resort?'

'I don't just sit and talk things through. I have my own way of doing things and it's not for everyone.'

'Not sure I understand.'

'I can get a bit shouty,' said Lily. 'I'm not insensitive, it's just that sometimes folk need a bit of a slap.'

Gordy was shocked, and it obviously showed on her face by Lily's reaction.

'Figuratively speaking,' she said. 'I don't actually slap people! But I won't hold with nonsense if that's what I'm hearing. I also encourage people to get out of their comfort zone, explore nature, join me for a cold dip in the river under a full moon, find a stick that speaks to them ...'

'A stick?'

'There's a lot of wisdom in a stick.'

That statement was said with such conviction that Gordy had no come back at all, so she said, 'How was Melonie the last time you saw her?'

'Happy. Genuinely, beautifully happy. At peace with herself, her past, everything. It was quite wonderful to see.'

'And what did she do, job wise?'

'Well, you know she was an actress, yes? I think she realised eventually that her strengths were not so much in being in front of the camera or an audience, but helping people to do it instead. She ran private one-to-one lessons, summer schools, children's clubs. She's going to be missed.'

Lily then provided Gordy with details about Melonie's business, her employees.

'Do you know if she had any contact with her ex-husband?'

'Brian? She was way beyond that, had left that life behind. It's why she came to me, really, to try and come to terms with what had happened, to heal and move on. And they did so together, you know? It was very brave of them, inspirational really.'

'How do you mean?'

'They did some joint sessions with me, decided to help each other, to forgive, instead of argue and fight.'

'That doesn't quite match what Brian's business partner had to say about Melonie,' said Gordy.

'They kept it all very private. I think they knew that they'd get flack from people if they said what they were doing. His business partner will have based whatever she said on what she knew of Melonie before the healing, rather than after.'

'So, what did actually happen?' Gordy asked. 'In their marriage, I mean?'

She knew she was prying, but she needed to find out everything she could about Melonie and Brian, because something in their joint past, something seemingly small and insignificant, could be vital.

'They were young, wanted different things, the usual kind of stuff. But there was something darker going on behind the scenes that I never got to the bottom of.'

That piqued Gordy's interest.

'How do you mean? What was darker behind the scenes?'

'Some kind of shared trauma, I think. I don't know what it was, but I felt like I was close to figuring it out.'

'No hints at all? Was it something that had happened to them both, do you think?'

'Absolutely. And whatever it was, it affected them both deeply enough to drive a wedge between them, but also into their own individual lives, too.'

Gordy wanted more information. This felt like something really important. But what if Lily really didn't know anything more than what she had already said?

'Can you think of anything, no matter how small, that might have given you some hint about what the trauma was?' Before Lily had a chance to answer, Gordy showed her the enlarged image of the film still. 'Do you think this has anything to do with it?'

Lily took the image from Gordy, and stared.

'What is this?'

'A film still. No idea when it's from, where it was taken. Do you recognise the other girl?'

Lily shook her head.

Gordy presented the other film still.

'And this one was found on Brian's body.'

Lily gasped.

'Good God ...'

'Whoever is responsible for Brian and Melonie's murders left those on them for a reason. I've just got no idea what it is.'

'The blood,' said Lily. 'That's surely not real. I mean, whoever this other girl is, she's smiling, isn't she?'

'' Melonie never mentioned anything that might make you think she was talking about this?'

Lily shook her head.

'She did acting at university, so my guess is that this is some student film she was involved with back then; she looks, what, early twenties? Looks quite horror-esque, doesn't it? Not my genre at all, I have to say.'

Gordy took the images back, but as she went to file them away, Lily held up a hand, and asked for them back again.

'What is it?' Gordy asked, as Lily stared.

'I ... I'm not sure,' Lily replied, swapping between the images, then resting mainly on the one found on Brian's body. 'But this one ... There's something familiar about it.'

'Really? What?'

Lily was quiet, then turned the image around so that Gordy could see it. She pointed at the strange building far off behind the mysterious girl covered in blood.

'That,' she said. 'I've seen it before. I know I have. But where?'

'Is it local?'

'Yes,' Lily nodded. 'I'm sure it is, actually. But where the hell is it?'

'Why do you think you recognise it?'

Lily held up a finger and Gordy fell quiet, a little stunned to have been shushed.

Lily narrowed her eyes, stared hard at the image, then stood up and started to pace around the room. Then, without warning, she dashed out, and Gordy heard her footsteps race down the hall and then up the stairs. The sound of Lily rummaging through something echoed through the house, then the footsteps sounded again, growing louder until she burst through the door.

'Got it!' she said, a wide smile on her bright face. 'It was a wedding!'

'What was?'

'This,' said Lily, and flipped the image found on Brian's body around. 'Well, not what's actually happening here, but the place, that building behind it. A wedding. I was at it because I was the celebrant.'

'You mean you officiated over a wedding in that building?'

'I did,' said Lily. 'I'm not just a counsellor. I also do weddings, funerals, naming ceremonies, that kind of thing.'

'So, what is it, then?' Gordy asked. 'The building, I mean.'

'It was built as a private church for the owners of the house,' Lily explained. 'When the house was sold on, it was deconsecrated, so that it could be more widely used. That way, you're not dependent on a vicar officiating a wedding; you can have someone like me do it if you want. It's such a pretty little place. Magical, really.'

Gordy's heart quickened. This was, at last, a potential lead.

'I need to know where it is.'

'What? Oh, sorry, of course,' said Lily. 'It's Holcombe Hall.'

Gordy sat up.

'The private members' club?' she asked. 'Brian and Melonie, they were both members.'

'That's a strange coincidence.'

'As someone I know once told me,' Gordy said, 'don't ever believe in them.'

She took out her phone and called Pete.

TWENTY-SIX

The late afternoon drive from Frome to Holcombe Hall was a collection of thin lanes knotted together by sharp bends and steep hills. A tangle of shadows was cast across them by high hedgerows, wayward brambles, and trees yawning with the breath of Spring. The sun was low, daylight dimming to a dull grey, and yet the countryside still seemed intent on blessing her with view upon view, as around every corner, and over every hill, some hidden corner of a woodland or vista of patchwork fields would reveal itself.

Despite everything that was going on, not just with the investigation, but with her own life, Gordy found herself so focused on the vast, unending palette of greens she was driving through, that when she arrived at Holcombe Hall, so lost was she to the pastoral splendour of the Somerset countryside, that she just swept on past it.

Pulling in at a gate into a field just ahead, she swung around and headed back, turning off the main road, and down a long, narrow driveway. A small cottage stood guard at its opening, and to its side, a saloon and an old, blue, short-wheelbase Land Rover were parked.

In the doorway, an old man was hugging a woman many years his junior, and Gordy smiled, warmed by the love so apparently on display. Glancing in her rearview mirror, the reflection of the hugging couple shrinking into the distance, something about what she was seeing caused an itch at the back of her mind. She looked up again, found that they were now hidden from view, having probably headed into the house, she guessed, and the itch faded.

Dropping her speed to match the five MPH limit requested by a small, polite sign at the side of the driveway, with all thoughts of what she had seen at the cottage gone from her head, Gordy glided along a tree-lined avenue. She noticed just how bright the sun was, having broken through the clouds to scatter them enough to give it a chance to bless the land below in liquid gold.

Not sure what to expect when she came to the end of the driveway, Gordy prepared herself for a country hotel, a large car park, and enough cheap chintz to attract twenty-something footballers and their wives from a thousand miles away. Then, like the opening credits to a costume drama, the house revealed itself. Before Gordy knew what she was doing, she'd slowed to a stop just to stare at the place, so awestruck was she by the sight.

Holcombe Hall was a large country house set in the most picturesque gardens she had ever seen. Flowers danced in a tumble of riotous colour in numerous flower beds, watched over by trees of all kinds. Towering boughs swayed gently as though conducting nature's orchestra of bird and beast. Lawns were laid all about; rich green carpets that Gordy felt the sudden urge to run across barefoot.

To one side of the house, she saw tables and chairs with parasols, occupied by people smiling and talking and drinking and eating. The front of the house comprised a huge, wooden door staring out onto an offshoot of the driveway she was on, a turning circle which, in its centre, held a pretty fountain that cast bright gems of water in shimmering arcs through the air.

Gordy realised that another car had eased to a stop behind her. She held up a hand in apology and pulled into a layby, and her pursuer's wheels crunched past on the gravel. It was a high-end sports car so low to the ground she was surprised it didn't just drive under her own car to continue on its way.

Gordy followed on behind, around to a car park hidden from view by tall hedges. Parking up, between a metallic-black Range

Rover and another expensive car she couldn't name, she grabbed the enlarged images of the film still frames, and stepped out of her vehicle. Following the signs, she headed to the main reception, where she would be meeting Detective Constable Peter Knight.

The path from the car park was lined with low box hedges, and forked at points to various buildings. Walking across cobbles, she made her way along the last bit of pathway before the main door. Gordy was struck by the peace and tranquillity of the place. It was clear to her that the only way to be a member of Holcombe Hall was to have a fair bit of money to your name, but right there and then, she would happily sell a kidney to get on the membership list, and she'd not even seen inside the main house yet.

Pushing through the main door, Gordy was hit by the sweet aroma of seasoned wood softly burning in an open fire in the front lobby. Pete was sitting in a soft armchair opposite and rose to greet her. At the same time, a man at the reception desk glanced up and smiled warmly.

'Nice, isn't it?' Pete said, coming over to meet Gordy in front of the reception desk. 'You know, I could see myself living in a place like this quite easily.'

Gordy noticed how the detective constable's spiky hair seemed even more violently opposed to being on his head than it had earlier. She wasn't sure if he had added more product to it, or if it was under some kind of dark occult curse, but from whatever angle she looked at it, every spike seemed to be loaded with the urge to launch itself from his skull and escape.

'Well, if it ever comes up for sale, I'm sure the owners will accept a sensible offer.'

Gordy returned the receptionist's smile and introduced herself.

'Is it possible to talk to either the manager or the owner?'

'Well, Holcombe Hall is actually owned by a small group of private shareholders,' said the receptionist. 'But we have a good number of managers around who might be able to help? There's the members' manager, the general manager, the floor manager, the bar manager ... sometimes, I think all we have working here are managers! Is there anything specific you need help with? Then I can see who would be best for you to speak to.'

Gordy thought about that for a moment, then said, 'The manager who's been here the longest and who probably has the best knowledge of the building, its history, that kind of thing.'

'That'll be the general manager, Felix Salmon.'

'That's quite a name.'

'We just call him Fish.'

'Behind his back or to his face?'

'Both.'

'Well, if we could have a chat with him, that would be great.'

The receptionist picked up the phone and made a call.

'He'll be five minutes at the most.'

Gordy walked over to the fire, Pete beside her.

'So, the spike, then,' she said.

'Well, it's not a recent theft,' said Pete. 'The farmer, Mr Combes, had actually forgotten all about it because it was so long ago.'

'How long?'

'He wasn't sure. A few years at least. Not a month or two or anything like that.'

'And he's sure it was stolen, not just mislaid or something?'

'Definitely stolen,' said Pete. 'Someone unbolted it one night and took it.'

'Did he report it?'

Pete shook his head.

'Didn't see the point. Just bought another.'

As Gordy was thinking about how this backed up her theory that the murderer had been planning it all for years, which in and of itself was terrifying in the extreme, a man approached. He was casually dressed in light trousers and a loose-fitting green linen shirt.

'Mr Salmon?'

'Felix.' The man smiled, holding out his hand, which Gordy shook firmly.

'Thank you for seeing us.'

'No problem at all. We can pop to my office, or if you would rather, I can give you a tour of the place as we talk?'

Gordy glanced out of one of the windows to the side of the main door. The late afternoon's greyness had been broken by the bright, farewell rays of the fading sun, and she rather fancied a bit of a stroll, instead of sitting in an office. She also thought that a look around the place might be helpful.

'A tour sounds good.'

'Then follow me,' said Felix, and led Gordy and Pete back out through the main door.

As she stepped over the threshold, Gordy realised where she was.

'Wait,' she said, and opened the file holding the film stills. She stared at the one found on Brian's body, then looked back at the door, the lobby, and across the lawn to a small building she'd not noticed when she had arrived. 'This one ... This is right here, isn't it?'

Pete and Felix leaned over to see what Gordy was talking about.

Gordy saw a frown plough a slow furrow across Felix's brow.

'What on earth? What is that? When was it taken?'

'Not sure and don't know are the only answers I can give you to those last two questions right now,' said Gordy. 'As to the first, we're still not sure, but I'm edging towards thinking that it's a still from a movie.'

Felix gestured for Gordy to give him the image, and she handed it to him for a closer look.

'This is at least twenty years ago,' he said, 'but I'd be inclined to think it's more than that.'

'Why do you say that?'

Felix lifted a hand in a wave at the space around them.

'Twenty years ago, after the owner sold it, the Hall was converted into the private members' club you see now. And that photo is from before that.'

Gordy stepped outside, standing back to really take in the front of the house.

'Do you know why they sold it?'

'The usual reason, probably,' said Felix, coming to stand beside her. 'Money. A place like this is a fortune to run. That's why so many places like it end up in the hands of the National Trust, because the upkeep is crippling, even if you are minted.'

Gordy took the image back from Felix and held it up.

'This happened when it was a private house, then?' she said.

'Undoubtedly,' Felix replied. 'Not just because you can see, even in that, how the place has changed, but because I doubt very much that the committee would greenlight something like that.'

'How do you mean?'

'Privacy is key,' said Felix. 'We've a lot of celebrity types here; actors, directors, even have a regular member who's a writer and often hides away in one of the snugs, tapping away at his next novel. Treats it like a second home, which is what we want all our members to do, though some do it more effectively than others. So, we have to ensure that this is somewhere they can come and not get hassled.

'You don't just get in by turning up with a credit card to pay the membership fee; you have to be proposed by a current member, then have your application put before the committee. So, it's kind of an ethos of the place; no photos, that kind of thing. We do allow weddings, but for that, you have to book the whole place and members aren't admitted when such an event is on.' He pointed then at the small building on the lawn in front of the house. 'Used to be a private place of worship for the family, but it was—'

'Deconsecrated,' said Gordy, remembering what Lily had told her earlier that afternoon. 'Can't be cheap getting married here.'

Felix laughed and shook his head.

'Eye-watering, if I'm honest. So, shall we do the tour? You can ask questions as we go.' Then he gave Gordy a wink. 'You never know, I might even be able to persuade you to become a member.'

This time, a laugh burst from Gordy.

'Me, with my celebrity lifestyle and movie star salary,' she said. 'Where do I sign?'

'It's not as expensive as you might think.'

'Aye, but I'll bet it's expensive enough.'

With that part of the conversation closed, Gordy followed Felix as he led them around the grounds of the Hall, taking in a lake, the spa, the pool, and telling them about the place as they strolled.

By the time they were back at the house, so effective had Felix's selling of the place been, that Gordy found herself half wondering if membership wouldn't be such a bad idea after all, and he'd still not mentioned the cost. She'd not actually asked any questions while they'd wandered around, the peace and tranquillity of the place seeping into her skin so much so that she was struck by a feeling she'd not experienced in a long time: a sense of calm.

'Ready to see the house?' Felix said.

'Too right I am,' said Paul. 'This place is amazing!'

Walking back through the main door, they were guided around various snug, cosy rooms where members could relax, and others where they could work, then to a bar that made Gordy want to take a seat and order something strong. The walls were hung with art, the bar a walnut thing of beauty, and the bright display of bottles on the wall behind was hypnotic.

In one room, she spotted a man with a well-groomed beard, sitting on a sofa, earphones clamped to his head, typing away at a laptop, and remembered the writer Felix had mentioned. The man looked up, gave a nod to Felix.

'A boulevardier later, then?' Felix said.

'I'll need one after these chapters are done, that's for sure,' the man replied, a weary smile on his face. He glanced at Gordy for a moment, gave a nod, then got back to his work.

Felix guided them down a long hall decorated with more art.

'Wait 'til you see the restaurant,' he said, and led them into a large, high-ceilinged dining room decorated with plants and yet more stunning pieces of art. Two walls were given over to large glass windows, which looked out over the gardens, and on one side, they opened out to tables on a veranda.

Picking up a menu, Gordy asked, 'What do you know about the original owners?'

'The Claytons? Not much,' Felix replied. Dropping a finger onto the menu, he added, 'The scallops are to die for, trust me.'

'You must know something, though.'

'All I know is that there was some tragedy and that, combined with the upkeep of the place, had the owner or owners sell up. You'd be better off talking to Gamekeeper John.'

'I would? Why?'

Felix ignored the question for a moment, leading Gordy and Paul up a flight of stairs and into a room with the largest, most comfortable-looking bed Gordy had ever seen in her life. The sight of it, and the room it was resting in, was enough to stop Gordy from pushing Felix to answer her question. Then she saw the bathroom, the huge cast iron bath, and the rain shower.

'Just out of interest, how much is a membership?'

Felix's answer was enough for Gordy to shut down any further enquiry, so she said, 'The gamekeeper, then ...'

'What? Oh, right, yes,' said Felix. 'He lives in the cottage at the end of the drive; you'd have spotted the place as you drove in.'

Gordy remembered the old man, and the tight hug he had been receiving from the younger woman.

'He knew the family?'

'Worked for them,' said Felix. 'The cottage was left to him by the original owner. I don't know much about it. Keeps himself to himself. House doesn't need a gamekeeper now, obviously, as most of the land was sold off, though a few fields around the perimeter were kept, and a bit of woodland, to help with keeping the place private.'

'Do you know his full name?'

'Gamekeeper John, like I said,' said Felix. 'That's what we've always known him as, so that's what we call him. He doesn't work for the hall or anything like that, but he does have permission to do a bit of vermin control, that kind of thing.'

Gordy realised that while Felix had been talking, she'd ended up sitting on the bed.

'God in heaven, this is comfortable,' she said, patting the mattress with a hand.

Felix smiled.

'And just so you know, this is one of the smaller beds ...'

TWENTY-SEVEN

Having parked up in front of the cottage at the end of the drive, with Paul pulling in behind her, Gordy headed over to the front door and gave it a sharp knock.

'Gamekeeper John, then,' Paul said, coming to stand beside her. 'Sounds like a character from an old-fashioned children's book, doesn't he?'

The front door opened, and it was all Gordy could do not to say, 'Looks like one, too.'

Gamekeeper John was tall and weathered like an ancient tree, standing on a lonely hill, and hardened by the storms it had faced over the centuries of its life. He was wearing a checked shirt of browns and greens, a waxed gilet, brown corduroy trousers with worn knees, held up by a belt from which hung an old leather knife sheath, and, in startling juxtaposition to the rest of the outfit, Homer Simpson slippers.

His face was lined like an outcrop of limestone on a Dales' fellside, the craggy overhang of his bushy eyebrows casting shadows over eyes narrowed against the daylight, but no less bright or keen for doing so. His hands were scarred, and his fingers sported a number of plasters.

Gordy waited for Gamekeeper John to speak, but when nothing

was forthcoming, she introduced herself and Paul and showed her ID.

'You'll be after coming in, then,' John said.

'We won't take up too much of your time,' Gordy said. 'Just need to ask you a few questions.'

'About what?'

'The house, its history. Would that be okay? It's to do with an ongoing investigation. I can't really give you the details of that, but any information you can provide may prove useful.'

'And what if I say that it isn't okay, seeing as I'm just about to skin a few rabbits, if you know what I mean?'

That phrase immediately struck Gordy as one of the most sinister-sounding euphemisms she had ever heard, though about what she didn't dare imagine. It was then that she spotted the knife in Gamekeeper John's left hand, and the blood. The knife was small, the kind she would expect to find in a kitchen, so clearly not the one that belonged in the sheath on his belt.

'We won't take up too much of your time,' she said.

Gordy waited as John glanced at Paul, then back at her, before stepping to one side.

'Best get yourself inside, then.'

Once inside the house, Gordy was greeted by numerous glass eyes staring out of various fur-covered faces, all of them following her with suspicious stares.

'Bloody hell,' said Paul, a little too loudly, Gordy thought.

'Don't mind them,' John said, leading them on through. 'They'll just be wondering who you are, that's all.'

'Where did you get them?' Paul asked.

'I didn't,' said John. 'I made them. Keeps my old hands busy and my mind focused. Easy to let the first become lazy and weak, and the second blurry and confused. And that's no good at my age, son, no good at all.'

A few steps later they were in a small, cosy lounge, the room heated by a fire roaring behind the glass-fronted door of a wood-burning stove.

'Lovely place you have,' Gordy said, hoping she sounded convincing. She wasn't lying as such, not really, because the house was cosy and well-kept. Those eyes, though, she thought, were just a bit too much, and could easily turn cosy into ghoulish.

'Coffee?' John asked, then said, 'Actually, I've only got tea.'

'That would be lovely,' Gordy replied, taking a seat, and John left the room, humming tunefully to himself as he went.

The humming continued, muffled by the walls and doors of the house, only to then grow louder as he returned with a tray holding a teapot, mugs, milk, and a packet of Rich Tea biscuits. Gordy noticed the blood on his hand was gone, and the small knife was nowhere to be seen.

Once the drinks were poured, he settled himself down into an armchair by the stove.

'So, how can I help?'

'Well, I was wondering if you could tell us anything about the original owners of the Hall,' Gordy said. 'You used to work for the family, I believe?'

'I did,' said John. 'That's why I'm still here, on account of them leaving me this cottage. Very kind, that was. Lived here for years now.'

'What did they do? Must've been something that made a lot of money to afford somewhere this grand.'

John gave a shrug.

'The owner was an old friend of mine and a successful businessman,' he said. 'That was never my thing, so I never really showed much interest in it. Happy to keep myself to myself. Not sure I could've offered much at a board meeting of shareholders, if you know what I mean. And I can't see them being that impressed by my bringing along a brace of pheasant or two. Though a good number of them did attend the shoots I ran. Good times.'

John took a sip from his mug.

'What about his family?' Gordy asked.

'Sad, really,' said John. 'Cancer took his wife early, left him with a daughter. Never remarried.'

'Do you know why he sold the property?'

'I do,' said John.

Gordy waited, saw Paul was staring at her, and gave him a nod, inviting him into the conversation.

'And what was the reason?' Paul asked. 'Was it a business thing?'

'Yes and no,' said John. 'He lost interest in it, the business, I mean, and the house. Can't say as I blame him.'

Another sip of tea, then a munch on a biscuit.

'How do you mean?'

'By what?'

'You said you couldn't blame him for selling up,' Paul clarified. 'Why?'

John fell quiet, and to Gordy it seemed as though the shadows from the corners of the room gathered around him like the wings of a crow.

He shook his head.

'Lost his daughter,' he said. 'Broke his heart so violently, I swear I heard it happen; like a gunshot it was, but that's no surprise, really, considering how she died, if you know what I mean? He was never the same. First his wife, then his daughter gone as well. That's too much grief, isn't it?'

'That's awful,' said Paul. 'How did she die?'

Gordy had noticed John's mention of a gunshot, and the mysterious way he'd suggested a connection between saying it and what had happened to the daughter. For now, though, she let Paul take the lead.

'It was just an accident, that's all I know for sure,' said John. 'Something to do with some film or other up at the house. I wasn't there when it happened, and even if I had been, there's not much I could've done. At that range? She didn't stand a chance.'

That statement caught Gordy's interest, more so than John's confirmation that there had been a film made at the property, or his comment about the gunshot.

'Range?' she said. 'That's a strange choice of words.'

'Is it?'

Her own tea finished, Gordy set her mug back on the tray. She was thinking about the images she was carrying with her, and decided to show them to John.

The old gamekeeper took them from her in silence, held them, stared at them, rubbed his chin, gave it a scratch, and Gordy saw the shadows gather darker still, though now behind his eyes.

'That's her,' he said. 'Jennifer.'

'The owner's daughter?'

John gave a nod, albeit one where his head barely moved.

'Just her and a few friends, that's all it was. They'd finished university. Were here making a film she'd written, I think, before they headed off into that big, scary world of work. It's a long time ago now, isn't it? Twenty-five years, give or take. She'd have been forty-six now. Hard to believe that time's gone so fast. She was the spitting image of her mum, and her father loved her, I can tell you that for nothing.' He shook his head, clearly still unable to accept not just the tragedies he was recounting, but how so much time had passed, Gordy thought.

'What about the girl in the other picture?'

'That was one of her friends,' John said. 'Most of them were a bit spoiled if you ask me. They should've all checked though, shouldn't they? Made sure what happened hadn't, if that makes sense. Could've been prevented, that's all I'm saying.'

'What could've been prevented?' Paul asked.

John held out the image with the girl Gordy now knew as Jennifer Clayton, and pointed at the thing she was holding, the thing Gordy still couldn't make out.

'It was a horror film,' John said. 'No idea myself why anyone would want to watch that kind of rubbish, but kids, right? They like to be a bit more out there than us older folks, don't they? I was probably the same when I was young. Jenny was the lead character. Struck me as all a bit daft, but she was happy, and her father didn't mind supporting her.'

Gordy waited for John to continue, giving him time to put into words something from so long ago.

'Shotgun,' he said.

Gordy leaned in close to the image, but still couldn't make it out.

'I was told it belonged to the director's father, only it didn't, did it?' said John, his voice both hard as stone, and crushed, like it had been turned to gravel by the memory.

'Then whose was it?' Gordy asked.

'Know what he did?' John continued, as though he'd not heard Gordy's question. 'Dropped blanks into the barrels, but didn't actually check the damned things first. No gun sense at all. Doubt he'd ever even used one, though he certainly shouted enough about it like he had. Turned out there were two smaller cartridges jammed in the barrels, just below the breech. No one had any idea how they'd got in there, and that director, he was adamant he'd had nothing to do with it. Impossible to prove otherwise. They were for a sixteen-bore, and the one you see Jenny holding there, that's a twelve, so they just slipped in, then got stuck.

'My guess is that he did it himself, to make a bigger bang, make it all the more dramatic. It wasn't like Jenny was actually going to shoot the gun at anyone; he had sense enough not to let that happen. So, they were just going to film her firing it and then cut that bit of the film into the rest. Anyway, like I was saying, I think he did it himself. Probably thought, because what he'd put in there were blanks, there wouldn't be much danger, daft as that sounds, right? Yeah, he really didn't have a clue how guns work, or understand what happens if you fire one when the barrel's blocked.'

'And what's that?' Paul asked.

'Pressure like that is enough to split a barrel in two,' said John. 'In this case, it blew it apart. Shattered it. Killed Jenny instantly.' John shook his head, eyes closed as though to stop the horror of the memory being beamed out from behind them and onto the wall. 'She'd have not known a thing, or that's what I tell myself, anyway. I've seen some things in my time, but that? Nothing comes close. Nothing at all. Never will again either, and I thank God I've only a few years left in me, because that image, that memory, it still wakes me in the night.'

'But you said you weren't there,' said Gordy.

'Not when it happened, no, but I was on site, around the house, working in the garden, sorting a few trees out, that kind of thing. I heard the shot, the screams, ran to see what the fuss was about. I ... It was me who broke the news to Jenny's father.'

A stillness settled upon the room then, and Gordy wasn't sure any further questioning was necessary or right, but something had caught her attention, and she needed to know.

'You said you were told the shotgun belonged to the director's father, but it didn't; then whose was it?'

John clasped his hands together and Gordy saw the knuckles turn white.

'Mine,' he said.

'Yours?'

'Idiot broke into the gunroom, didn't he? Took Jenny's dad's set of keys—I always carried mine with me, you see—and sneaked in that morning, took one, and put the keys back before anyone noticed. Reckon he took the cartridges at the same time, but that was impossible to tell; not like we knew how many of the things we had in there, is it? I think he meant to bring a gun, just forgot. And because of that, Jenny was killed. Not that she'd have known anything about it, like I said. Out like a light, I would think.' He clicked his fingers in midair, the sound of it like the hard crack of a rifle being fired. 'Like that,' he said. 'Gone.'

Seeing how disturbed John was to be talking about something clearly so painful, Gordy drew the conversation to a close and rose from her chair. Paul did the same, and then John led them back through the house, opening the front door for them.

'Thank you for your time,' Gordy said, noticing again the empty knife sheath on John's belt, and wondering if what he'd said about gutting rabbits hadn't actually been too far from the truth. 'And my apologies for asking you to talk about something clearly so painful.'

'Not a problem at all,' said John. 'Hope it was useful.'

Gordy went to step out into the early evening, then paused.

'When we arrived earlier, I saw you with someone.'

'You did?'

'A woman, not sure how old, but clearly a lot younger than yourself.'

John smiled.

'My daughter,' he said. 'She loved Jenny, you know? Used to hang around together all the time.'

'Would she be happy to talk to me about it, do you think?' Gordy asked. 'Might be something else we can learn from her.'

'Don't see why not,' said John.

'Would you be able to give me her details?' Gordy then held out her card. 'If not, then she can contact me at this number.'

John took the card.

'Not sure as I need to,' he said.

'Why?' Gordy asked, confused by John's reply.

'My guess is you probably know her.'

'I do? How?'

'On account of her being in the same line of work,' John said. 'She's a DCI.'

Gordy remembered the itch she'd felt at the back of her mind when she had first driven past the cottage and seen John hugging the woman. She also realised that, distracted by John being introduced to them as Gamekeeper John, neither she nor Paul had taken his full name or contact details.

'Can I ask for your full name, please, John?' she said.

'Well, for a start, it's Jack, not John,' he replied. 'And as for my surname? That'll be Allercott.'

TWENTY-EIGHT

Gordy was on her hands-free all the way home to Evercreech, trying to get in touch with Ellen, her new DCI, but there was no answer. That didn't stop her from leaving numerous messages asking as politely as she could, which wasn't very, she had to admit, for a return call.

Paul had headed home, and a quick catch-up call with Patti had resulted in a team meeting arranged for first thing in the morning.

Having planned to grab something for dinner on the way home, Gordy completely forgot, and instead skidded to a stop in one of the parking spaces near her flat, carrying not a shopping bag of delicious things to munch on for the evening, but only bewilderment and frustration, as she sent grit skittering across the ground like jumping beans.

Just what the hell was going on? Two murders, both of them violent beyond measure, and now she discovers that her very own DCI was somehow connected. How was that even possible? And why had Ellen never said? Surely, she must've known from the off.

Gordy was angry, upset, and frustrated. A part of her was tempted to call in a team and swoop in on Allercott's home, but that seemed like it might be overkill. All that she knew for certain was that Ellen had known the girl in the film still, back when she had been a child. And that really wasn't enough to pin anything on anyone, and certainly not enough to be taking a mad leap into a pool of conclusions just to grab any that came close.

Climbing out of her vehicle, she tried to call once again, and to her surprise, it connected.

'DCI Alle—'

'This is DI Haig,' Gordy said. 'We need to talk.'

A pause, then ...

'We do? What about? Is everything okay? Do you want to meet for a coffee or something? Have a chat? I'm a bit busy, but I could do tomorrow morning?'

Allercott's questions sounded like the woman had a mouthful of sour gobstoppers and wasn't quite sure how to politely spit them out.

'It's about the investigation.'

'I'm afraid I'm rather busy at the moment, like I said. But I can come into the office tomorrow? I agree, it is probably sensible for us to have a catch-up, anyway.'

'It's important.'

'I'm sure it is. And I will be there, I can assure you.'

'Are you positive you can't meet up now? What about talking? Do you have a couple of minutes just to go over things?'

'I'm literally heading out of the door. I've an appointment, and I can't miss it.'

'For what?'

Silence, then, 'I'm not sure my private life is any of your business, Detective Inspector.'

'I saw you at your dad's house,' Gordy said, blurting the words out before she'd had time to think through where the hell she was going to go with what she was saying.

Another pause, longer this time.

'You did? What were you doing over there? Are you thinking of becoming a member at the hall? I can highly recommend it.'

'You're one yourself, then?'

'A perk of having Dad on site,' said Allercott. 'He provides a bit of free security, does odd jobs here and there, keeps the rat and pigeon and rabbit numbers in check, and as a thank you, we both get free membership. Not that Dad uses it. You've met him; can you imagine him in a steam room, or drinking champagne in a jacuzzi?'

'Champagne in a jacuzzi?' Gordy said, not quite believing what she was hearing. 'That's not something people do, is it?'

'It's something you can treat yourself to, and a loved one as well, if you so wish, at the spa. Don't knock it till you try it.'

Allercott laughed then, and the sound made Gordy wince. She also noticed that Allercott's voice wasn't giving away any sign that she had any inclination about there being a connection between the victims, Holcombe Hall, her father, and herself. But then why should it? Gordy thought.

'No, that's not what this is about,' she said, trying to work out what it actually was about and coming up blank, because she couldn't just say, could she? Mainly, because there wasn't much to say; she just needed to speak to Allercott, pull at a thread, see if anything was at the end of it, or if something still hidden would start to unravel somewhere in the dark. 'It's about something that happened at the hall some years ago now.'

A car horn echoed from Allercott's side of the conversation.

'Tomorrow morning it is, then,' Allercott said, not taking the bait. 'I'll be at the office first thing. See you then.'

Gordy was given no chance to say anything else as Allercott hung up. She stood there for a moment, not sure what to do, what to think, breathing the cool evening air deep into her lungs, sensing a build-up of frustration in her chest, breathing to stay calm. She heaved her arm back like a javelin thrower to hurl her phone hard across the car park when a shout caught her attention, and she paused mid-swing.

Glancing over to the steps that led up to her new home, Gordy saw a man strolling towards her. He was in his early sixties, stocky, with thinning hair, and a small, wry smile on his face.

'Looks like you have as much love for phones as someone else we both know,' he said, a laugh curling the corners of his mouth as well as his words.

Gordy recognised him, was trying desperately to flick through her mental filing cabinet of faces, when he closed the gap and held out his hand.

'Bloody hell,' said Gordy. 'Jameson.'

'One and the same,' the man replied.

'Last time I saw you was at Harry's housewarming.'

The memory brought a smile to Gordy's face, as she thought back to her old DCI, Harry Grimm, and his awkwardness at having so many people in his new house, yet at the same time clearly enjoying the fact that they were there in the first place.

'You're forgetting that little case I was involved just after,' said Jameson. 'At the house above Marsett, remember?'

Gordy frowned, then managed to grab the thread of another memory.

'The private investigator course?'

'That's the one,' said Jameson, shaking his head. 'Unsurprisingly, after that experience, I've not followed it up as a way to keep me busy in my older years.'

Gordy could understand why Jameson had attended the course in the Dales, hoping to use his many years of experience as a detective to become a PI. Unfortunately, the course had been put together by a chancer of the highest order, who had then ended up dead when his own past had caught up with him. Add in the worst snowstorm in years, and a gang of stranded and very violent gangsters, and the whole thing had gone pear-shaped very quickly. A few weeks later, Harry had described it all as 'exciting,' which had seemed to Gordy to be somewhat of an understatement.

'So, how can I help?' she asked, stepping past Jameson, the key to her front door in her hand.

'Oh, I don't need your help at all,' Jameson replied. 'But I think you might need mine.'

That stopped Gordy in her tracks. Then it was the night before once again, and she was racing out of her flat, driving into the night, screaming at the dark, making a phone call ...

'Harry?'

Jameson gave a nod.

'He called. Said there was a missed call from you in the early hours. No message. Struck him as odd. Called me to come round and see if everything is okay.'

'Well, everything is okay,' Gordy lied, not really in the mood for someone to swing by because they felt obliged to, or had been ordered to do so by someone else, no matter how well-intentioned the act might be. 'So, you can tell that battle-scarred bastard he doesn't need to go prying. I'm fine.'

She'd meant that to sound funny, light, amusing, but the rusty knife edge to her voice had been keen.

'Fine?'

'Yes, fine.'

'Interesting word choice that, isn't it, fine?'

'Is it?'

'No one really wants to be fine, do they?' Jameson said. 'Not really. It's one of those camouflage words, one that you use to disguise how you actually feel because you don't want to talk about it. And I get why you don't, but that doesn't mean you shouldn't.'

'But it's the truth. I am fine. And no, I don't want to talk about it.'

'Then why did I catch you nearly sending your phone into orbit?' Jameson asked. 'Never mind the way you broadsided into that parking space there.'

'I did not broadside!' Gordy replied, a little put out by the implication. 'It's a gravel drive.'

'And you came in hot. You're lucky there was no other car, bar mine, in the way. Pity you'd not bumped it; I could do with a reason to send it for scrap.'

'I had it under control.'

'Why did you call Harry last night?'

'What? Oh, that …' Gordy waved a hand dismissively. 'It was nothing.'

'And you left the door to your flat open,' Jameson continued. 'I called for you, had a look inside just to make sure you were okay. Obviously, you weren't in, and if I'm honest, with everything still in boxes, it doesn't really look like you are, even if you are, if you understand me.'

'I don't.'

'I think you do.'

Gordy's mouth fell open, but there was no response on her tongue, so she closed it again.

Jameson said, 'You tried The Bell yet?'

'The pub?'

'No, the one in the church tower,' said Jameson. 'Of course I mean the pub!'

Gordy shook her head.

'Hungry?'

Gordy remembered then how she'd forgotten to pick something up on the way home. She could easily take a stroll down to the little co-op in the village, but then she'd have to cook it, and sometimes cooking a meal on your own just wasn't that much fun, was it? And that meant she'd probably just get something to throw in the microwave, or maybe just a loaf of bread to toast, and a tin of baked beans.

'You buying?'

'I am.'

Jameson said nothing more, and with a smile, strolled past Gordy towards the main road. By the time she had caught up, the only thing louder than the confused thoughts in her mind about the case, was the rumbling of her stomach.

TWENTY-NINE

Gordy stared at what Jameson had brought over from the bar and presented her with as an appetiser.

'So, what is it, then?'

'That, Gordy, is a Mousetrap.'

Gordy was sure she hadn't heard right.

'A what now?'

'A Mousetrap,' Jameson repeated. 'I popped by here a while ago and saw it on the snacks menu. Been back a few times just to have it and a pint.'

'I'm no clearer.'

'Apparently, it was a traditional thing here years ago, so they've brought it back. No idea if it's local to the village or not, but I reckon it's a winner, regardless. Goes brilliantly with a pint of cider or beer.'

The pint in front of Gordy was Stan's Trad cider, by Thatchers, so that was something of a surprise. She wasn't so sure it was scrumpy as such, but it was the closest they had been able to provide. So, she'd thought, why not give it a go? It was cloudy, smelled dry, but thankfully there was no farmy aroma, not that she really knew what that was other than animal sweat and manure. And she wouldn't be drinking anything that smelled of that anytime soon, that was for sure.

She took a sip, then a gulp, immediately falling in love with the cool glass of golden liquid in her hand, and had to stop herself from just necking it. The Mousetrap, however, was holding her somewhat at bay.

'Go through the ingredients again,' she said, her glass back on the table.

Jameson leaned forward with a pointed finger raised.

'Constituent parts, I think, rather than ingredients,' he said, then pointed at what was sitting next to his pint of Cheddar Ales Potholer. 'Packet of salt and vinegar crisps, inside which the lass at the bar has lobbed in a giant pickled onion, and a huge lump of strong cheddar cheese.'

Gordy picked up the packet of crisps in front of her and stared inside somewhat hesitantly.

'But why call it a Mousetrap?'

Jameson didn't answer; he was already eating.

Gordy took a deep swig of the cider, stared at the Mousetrap, then took another gulp for good measure. She reached in and grabbed the pickled onion. It was coated in crisp crumbs.

'What you have to do,' Jameson instructed, demonstrating as he spoke, 'is have a bit of each. So, take a bite of the onion, then the cheese, then the crisps. It's not fine dining, for sure, but it's bloody good!'

Gordy took another gulp of cider and realised she was already down half a pint ahead of Jameson. She crunched her teeth into the onion, followed that with some cheese, and finally a good pinch of crisps.

Confusion was the first thing she felt, laced with a noticeable amount of disgust at herself and how she was eating. Then all the flavours mingled, and her eyes went wide.

Swallowing, she went for the cider again.

'See?' smiled Jameson.

'But why does it work?' Gordy asked. 'It shouldn't. At least, I don't think it should. But it does. And it's absolutely amazing with the cider.'

'Which,' Jameson said with a nod at her glass, 'I'll be needing to top up by the looks of things.'

'No, I'll be getting the next in, you just stay sat where you are.'

But Jameson had already left the table. By the time he returned, the food had arrived; two steak and ale pies with chips and peas.

'The pies here are to die for,' Jameson said, placing another pint in front of Gordy, and a bottle of something beside his glass. 'You know, the non-alcoholic beers haven't half improved lately,' he added, gesturing at the bottle. 'Way better than filling up on fizzy stuff that tastes like a melted ice pop.'

Gordy finished her mousetrap and first pint, then took a sip of the golden cider from the fresh glass. The food in front of her looked so appetising it was all she could do not to just rip into it with her bare hands.

'Tuck in,' said Jameson, as he broke the pie crust with his fork, sending out a waft of delicious-smelling steam.

Gordy picked up her knife and fork and did the same.

A few minutes later, after they'd each made a start on their meals in reverential silence, Gordy said, 'So, Harry called you, then?'

'You called him. He called me.'

'But I didn't really call him,' Gordy clarified. 'I meant to, but I hung up.'

'Which I think he found more concerning than if you'd left a message. Plus the fact that it was the middle of the night? That got his sixth sense all tingly.'

Gordy ate a bit more of the pie, then sipped the cider, enjoying the crisp apple liquid as it chased the steak down her throat. She wasn't sure what to say next, or if she wanted to say anything at all. If she was honest, she was embarrassed about what she'd done, ashamed that she'd lost control, and that Harry had felt it necessary to send a friend over to check up on her. But at the same time, it showed her just what a friend he was.

'I'm finding it hard,' she said at last, hiding her words behind another sip of cider.

'Finding what hard?' Jameson asked.

Gordy went to speak, but her words caught in her throat, then started to scream in her head.

'Gordy?'

She wanted to tell him, wanted to yell and scream and shout the goddamn pub roof off, but the words just wouldn't bloody well come.

'You don't have to if you don't want to, or feel you can't,' Jameson said, sensing her struggle. 'It's okay. You don't know me that well, but just so as we're clear... With me? It's a safe space. Nothing goes further than me. Period. I can promise you th—'

'Life!' Gordy said, the word breaking out of her like a wolf from a cage at the zoo, ripping her throat raw. 'Everything! Every! Damned! Thing!' She saw someone on the other side of the pub glance over, but ignored the stare, because the dam had burst, and the words were coming now. 'It's that simple, and that complicated all at once! I don't know who I am, why any of this happened, why I'm here! It's like ... well, it's too much, and not just sometimes, either; it's too much all the damned time! And I don't really know where to start with explaining it because it all just comes at me in one huge wrecking ball!

'Anna's death, that I'm here now without her, that the only reason I'm here in the first place is because this was where she was moving to, rather than me, because I was following her!

'Then there's work, new people, getting to know a new area, missing the Dales, missing the old team, the flat, the fact I can't bloody well unpack because I don't know how to, or even if I want to. There's the tears, the relentless bloody tears, and this massive aching hole in my chest that just sits there day and sodding night! And I've got all these questions and memories and all kinds of crazy just rattling around in my head, trying to escape, and it feels like there's a swarm of bees trapped in here, trying to get out! No, not bees, wasps, just stinging me and causing me constant pain!' She tapped her temple with a finger in rapid succession, a rat-tat-tat of a machine gun against her skull. 'And on top of all that, if you can actually believe it, in my first week, we've a case with two bodies, and I think there's a link between it and my new DCI, and—'

Gordy stopped, exhausted by the waterfall of words and emotions that had tumbled out of her. She rested her eyes on Jameson, realised they were wet with tears, expected to see shock in his eyes, but instead, what she saw was something she could barely accept. The openness and kindness that stared back at her only served to disarm her even more. He put his cutlery down, took a sip of his beer, and reached out a hand to take hold of hers so gently that it was as though her fingers had been wrapped in the softest of mittens.

Neither of them said a word.

Gordy felt the ache in her chest shuffle down a little, one hand still in Jameson's, the other catching her head as she leaned forward.

'I don't know how to do this. I don't know if I can. I just know that I have to.'

'I'm afraid you're right,' Jameson said at last, and the bluntness of it was as much a shock as it was a relief. Usually, she expected people to pussyfoot around something so raw, but that obviously wasn't what Jameson was doing.

'I know.'

'You've a choice,' Jameson continued. 'You can be defined by the things that happen to you, or you can be defined by how you respond to them. Either way, it's your choice, and no one can make it for you.'

Gordy dropped her hand from her head, reached for her cider, and took a long, deep draught.

'God, that's good.'

'It's all about small changes,' said Jameson. 'Don't try and change or do everything all at once. Take life one day at a time. Because that's all you can do, isn't it? Sounds trite, but it isn't. It's freeing. As soon as you start living like that, you'll find that you can tackle things.'

Gordy smiled.

'So wise.'

'I've not even started.'

'What a terrifying thought.'

'But seeing as I want to finish this splendid pie, I'll finish with this for now: use the difficulty. Lean into it. Turn it to your advantage. Grow from it. Learn from it. Do not be defined by it. Accept the bad days, and begin afresh the next morning. Let the tears fall. Don't be afraid to feel sad, to feel broken. The difficulty of now, of what you've been through, has changed you and will continue to change you, so you need to ask yourself how. Make sense?'

'I think so.'

'Good,' Jameson said, removing his hand from Gordy's. 'Now, shall we get back to eating?'

Later, strolling back to the flat, Gordy noticed that Evercreech was actually a pretty little place. It wasn't necessarily a destination, somewhere you'd go to on your holiday, a place that you'd call a friend about and demand they visit. Instead, there was an honesty to it, like it had been there for centuries, happily looking after the people who were born and lived and died there. A mother hen of a village, she thought. Somewhere, she realised for the first time, that she didn't mind coming back to. She couldn't quite work out why she felt like that, but right then, she did.

Back in the small car park by the flat Gordy was doing her best to try and call home, she watched Jameson head over and stand by his vehicle.

'Thanks,' she said, as he opened the driver's door.

'You'll be okay,' Jameson replied. 'Might not feel like it right now, but I promise you, there'll come a time, something will happen, and you'll realise, all of this? Everything you're in right now? You've grown through it and become something more than you were before. It's terrifying to think about right now, but that's the truth, Gordy. And believe me, I know.'

Then he dropped into the car, closed the door, and started the engine. With a nod and smile, he headed off, leaving Gordy on her own.

That night, with pie and cider in her stomach, and a mind still busy with the hell of her life, Gordy started to unpack.

THIRTY

The next morning, Gordy had just gathered the team together to discuss the case when two things happened at once, and sent everything into a tailspin.

The first was the late arrival of Allercott.

And the second was the news she brought with her.

When Allercott arrived, the meeting had already started and Gordy could feel herself getting irritated with the fact that the DCI hadn't turned up first thing as promised. She was standing at the board, ready to go through everything, to discuss what she had learned the day before, and to go through her trip to Holcombe Hall.

The team was wired into the moment, keen to crack on, and Gordy herself was actually feeling oddly calm about things. Vivek's wonderful coffee and iced buns, all lovely and soft and fresh, certainly helped. Pete was especially keen to talk something through, but had agreed to share it with the rest of the team at the appropriate time. Ready to get things going, she quickly ran through a few things that were bothering her before opening it up for discussion and suggestions on what to do next.

They now knew there was some kind of connection, not just between the victims, but between them and Holcombe Hall, and the Claytons, the family who had originally owned it. John, or Jack or whatever he preferred to be called, had brought to light the tragic events of the film which Jenny, the owner's daughter, had been filming at the house with her university friends, and stills from that film had been found with both victims.

So, was this some kind of revenge thing for that event? And if so, who was responsible? Odds were it was someone involved in the film, thought Gordy, but there was every chance it was someone else entirely. As was the case with most investigations, it was rarely, if ever, the most obvious person who was guilty.

There were some odd things which didn't sit well. The violence of the killings, and the planning that had gone into them, stood out brutally amongst it all, but both of those had inexplicable things attached.

Ignoring how Brian had died, Gordy was drawn to wanting to uncover why he had been dressed in such a way. And with Melonie, there was the Star Trek DVD which had been playing; that it had been so clean, without even Melonie's fingerprints on it, strongly suggested it had been placed there by her killer.

Gordy also knew that she had to work out what to do about the clear connection between her new DCI, Ellen Allercott, and everything that had happened. Jack was Allercott's father, and she had certainly known Jenny Clayton when they'd been children.

There were definitely links being made, connections, and they all seemed to lead back to Jenny and her death.

With a clap of her hands, Gordy got everyone's attention. Heads turned, faces stared back, all of them keen-eyed, ready to get on with the job in hand. She quickly ran through everything from the previous day, her thoughts spilling out of her freely and at speed.

'So, with all of that in mind,' she said, a little out of breath from so much talking, 'my gut tells me that's where this all began, and where it is all leading. Someone is doing this for a very specific reason. I believe that reason to be what happened to Jenny Clayton while the film was being made.'

Pete put his hand up, and Gordy gave him a nod to speak.

'This is going to sound mad, but the murders ... I've been

wondering if they're linked to the film? I mean, I know they are, because of the film stills found on the bodies, but I'm wondering if there's more to it.'

'How do you mean?' Gordy asked.

'They're staged, aren't they?' Pete replied. 'And the film Jenny was making was a horror movie. I've watched a fair bit of horror myself, but then, who hasn't?'

Me, Gordy thought, but kept quiet, letting Pete continue.

'Anyway, they reminded me of stuff I'd seen, but I wasn't sure what. So, last night, I watched a few to see if it would jog my memory.'

'Memory of what?'

Gordy could see Pete was a little nervous about saying what was on his mind, perhaps concerned that voicing an idea would risk him getting shot down.

'This is a safe space,' she said. 'With something like this, there's rarely such a thing as a bad idea. In fact, sometimes, the most remote, out there ideas are what cracks a case.'

Pete did a very good impression of someone considering what they had just heard, before blurting out the words, 'Friday the 13th.'

'No, it isn't,' said Paul.

'Not today,' said Pete, 'the movie, Friday the 13th? The killer is Jason Voorhees. He wears an ice hockey mask. Not until the third film in the series, though.'

That piqued Gordy's interest.

'You mean like the one found in the moat at Nunney Castle?'

'I do,' said Pete. 'And the way the victim was killed, I think that's a nod to kills and killers in horror films as well.'

'Such as?' Gordy asked.

'Well, in Friday the 13th, the story is that he drowned when he was a kid at Camp Crystal Lake, which is where the film is set. His mother was the camp cook and takes revenge because she blames the camp counsellors for his death.'

'But the victim was impaled as well as drowned,' said Patti.

'That could be The Omen,' suggested Pete. 'A priest ends up

impaled on a spike that falls from a church tower. It's a lightning rod, I think.'

'What about Melonie, then?' Gordy asked.

'That could be from the first Halloween film. The first victim is stabbed nine times, and the final victim is strangled by a telephone cord.'

'Bloody hell, that's really specific,' said Jack. 'If this was a low-budget movie, what if Melonie played two victims?'

'The first and the last, like in Halloween,' grinned Pete. 'That's exactly what I was thinking!'

Gordy was hugely impressed and equally terrified at where this was potentially leading.

'If someone is killing off the cast in revenge for what happened to Jenny, then we really do need to find everyone else who was involved. And quickly.'

'This might help with that, then,' said Patti, and handed the iPad to Gordy.

Gordy frowned.

'Not sure this is the time to look at the Action Book, Patti.'

'It's not just the Action Book. The file that's open on there now is a list of names from the movie,' Patti said.

Gordy stared at the names, absolutely stunned.

'What? How the hell did you get this?'

'After you called me yesterday and told me what you'd found out, I went back over some of Brian's contacts, gave them a call, and one of them, Austin Clarke, he was really helpful. I think he had a bit of a thing for Jenny when they were younger.'

'Do we have addresses?'

'And telephone numbers,' said Patti. 'Then I did something else, which was just me with an itch to scratch.'

'What do you mean?' Gordy asked.

'Well, the first two victims were members at Holcombe Hall, right? So, I called that general manager you met, and he confirmed they were all members, too. And there's something else ...'

Gordy was reeling from the onslaught of information.

'Something else? What something else?'

'Not only are they all members, but they meet up once a year at the Hall and book out a private room for a meal and a few drinks.'

'What, like a memorial?' Gordy said. 'For Jenny?' A question rose to the surface. 'Do we know when they last met?'

'Better than that,' said Patti, 'I—'

The door to the room burst open and bounced off the wall.

Gordy turned around and saw Allercott marching towards them with keen purpose, a thin file under one arm, and a smile that looked like she'd just bought it from a shop on the way to the meeting and stuck it on her face to cover up what she was really feeling. She was wearing a long, winter coat that hung around her ankles.

A bit overkill, Gordy thought; the day was cool, not freezing, but then she'd never really felt the cold as much as most people, so who was she to judge?

When the DCI arrived beside her, Gordy was sure that she heard the woman humming a little to herself, and she recalled how Jack, her father, had hummed to himself while making the tea.

It made her wonder if Allercott suppressed things, if maybe this exterior of efficiency and distance and always being busy was something she buttoned on every morning to protect herself. Maybe now and again something would slip through, an echo of who she really was, or had been, once upon a time. She also wondered what it would be like to take the DCI up on her offer of support if she needed it; what exactly would a chat over coffee and a chocolate brownie be like, or maybe even a natter over a glass or two of something strong in a pub?

Allercott was standing front and centre as though she was about to take the meeting herself, except she was facing Gordy, rather than the rest of the team.

'Detective Inspector,' she said.

'Good morning,' Gordy replied, and was about to ask if the DCI would like to take a seat, because she wanted Patti to finish what she was saying.

'Do you have a minute?' Allercott asked, looking at Gordy with a firm stare. 'Something has come up.'

Gordy immediately suspected that this was Allercott's way of letting her know she was about to give her the reason as to why she couldn't stay for the meeting, tell her that there was something else more important for her to put her time to, and disappear. She wasn't about to let her do that, though, because they had arranged to meet for a chat, and she was going to make sure that happened.

'We're in the middle of going through a few really important things,' she said, 'and I think it would be best to get through that first before—'

'It wasn't a request,' Allercott clarified, then took herself out of the circle, walked over to Gordy's office, and let herself in.

Gordy looked at Patti.

'Can what you were about to tell us wait a few minutes?'

'I think it'll have to,' Patti said.

Gordy followed Allercott over to the office, a rare spike of anger at the way she had just been spoken to stirring the acid in her gut. She took a deep, calming breath as she shut the door behind her.

Allercott was standing at the desk, leaning on it with her hands, and facing away from the door.

Gordy was all set to have it out with her, as politely and calmly as possible, but something about the DCI's body language made her pause.

'You said something's come up?'

Allercott didn't move.

Gordy moved around to the other side of the desk.

'Ma'am?'

Nothing.

'Ellen?'

Allercott lifted her eyes to meet Gordy's, and Gordy saw that they were wide with shock and watery with tears.

'I need to show you something,' Allercott said.

'What?'

Allercott sat down, Gordy did the same.

'This …'

Allercott placed the thin file Gordy had seen her bring with her into the office on the table. She opened it, and slipped out the single sheet it contained, spinning it around so that Gordy could see it properly.

'I was looking through the evidence from the two crime scenes,' she said. 'This was found in Melonie's house.'

The image on the sheet was a photograph of a small hunting knife, its blade stained with blood.

Gordy was stunned.

'The murder weapon?'

'Yes.'

'Then why've I no' seen this before?' Gordy asked, her eyes flicking between Allercott and the image. 'Cowboy told me that no knife was found at the property by his team! So, where the hell has this turned up from? If I'm the OIC on this investigation, then—'

'After looking through the evidence, I decided to have another look at the crime scenes last night,' said Allercott, not so much interrupting as bulldozing Gordy's words out of the way. 'That's where I was going when you called.'

Gordy moved quickly from stunned to shocked.

'What? You went back to Melonie's?'

'Yes.'

'Why on Earth would you do that without contacting me first, or asking me to come with you?'

'I thought you had enough to deal with,' said Allercott. 'I called Cowboy. It's his area of expertise anyway, isn't it? And I thought it would look better if I went with the SOC team leader. It wasn't a personal slight, if that's what you're thinking.'

'I wasn't suggesting that it was.'

'Good.'

For a moment, Gordy and Allercott stared at each other in silence. Then Gordy rested her eyes on the image of the knife, and even though she didn't want it to, and couldn't believe it, she knew who the knife belonged to …

'Anyway,' Allercott eventually said, 'Cowboy found that knife at Melonie's. He had no idea how it was missed the first time. He was pretty pissed about it, if I'm honest. Not sure I've ever seen him that upset.'

'Where exactly did he find it at Melonie's?' Gordy asked.

'Under the bed.'

Gordy wanted to scream, not just because of what she'd been told, but because of what her gut was telling her about the knife.

It couldn't be, though, could it? The whole idea of what she was thinking seemed utterly ridiculous! But then again, when did killers ever look like the movies portrayed them? That would be never.

'How is that even possible? How did the whole SOC team miss it? I mean, under the bed? Bloody hell!'

'Cowboy thinks I dislodged it when I sat on the bed,' Allercott said. 'I had a bit of a funny turn, you see, needed to sit down, and there it was.'

'Dislodge it? From where?'

'Cowboy's not sure, but one thing he is sure about is that his team are going to get a royal kick up the arse for missing it.'

'I'm not bloody surprised!'

Gordy shook her head in abject disbelief, staring again at the knife in the image, knowing it, feeling it, understanding it, wishing to God—or whichever deity she believed in, and frankly, she just wasn't sure after everything she'd gone through if she believed in anything— that she didn't know in her gut to whom it belonged.

'Cowboy called me this morning, which is why I'm late,' said Allercott. 'He sent me that and I printed it off before coming over. The blade's been checked against the wounds to Melonie's body.'

'And it matches?'

'Perfectly.'

Gordy realised she was chewing her lip; something was telling her that Allercott was holding something back.

'You could've shared this with the rest of the team just now,' she said. 'Why did you bring me in here to talk about it? This is huge!'

'I know,' Allercott said. 'But ...'

'But what? What's wrong?'

Allercott didn't speak for a moment or two, and when she did, her voice was subdued.

'The knife is what's wrong,' she said, and rubbed her eyes, shook her head. 'You don't understand ... you can't ...'

But of course Gordy understood. How could she not?

She took another look at the image, saw the knife, the simple, leather-bound handle and brass pommel, the blade that looked like it had been used a lot over many years, its edge worn from numerous encounters with a whetstone to keep it razor sharp.

'You need to tell me,' she said, 'and you need to help me understand why we are talking about this in private.'

Deep down, though, she had the answer, the single point at the tip of the arrow all the evidence was pointing towards. But right there, in that moment, voicing it? Well, that didn't belong to her. That was someone else's responsibility; she needed to hear it from Allercott, because only then would it become real.

Allercott lifted her face to look at Gordy.

'The knife ... it's ... it's ...'

Gordy remembered something from the day before that had caught her eye at Jack's place. Something that had stuck with her and was now glaring at her, blinding her like headlights, and she was the startled rabbit unable to move out of the way of whatever was now racing towards her.

'It's your father's knife, isn't it?' she said.

'Yes,' Allercott replied, and burst into tears.

25 YEARS AGO, 2:15PM ...

Tristan narrowed his eyes, handed Jennifer a couple of sheets of fresh script, then spun on his heel.

'Right then, everyone,' he said, clapping his hands, 'now that our star is here, let's get this scene in the can, shall we?'

Jennifer tried to ignore the stinging barbs in Tristan's words as she read what he had just handed her.

'You've even changed the weapon!'

'Of course I have,' said Tristan. 'It's more dramatic than a knife, don't you think?'

'Where the hell did you get a shotgun?'

'I brought my own, if you must know. And, before you get all scared, I've got blank cartridges for it as well. They're from the crow scarers back home; you'll love it, I promise!'

'Are you mental?' The words were out before Jennifer could do anything about it, so instead, she just pushed on. 'I'm not using a shotgun, Tristan; it's far too dangerous.'

'Of course it isn't dangerous,' said Tristan. 'It won't be loaded, not until we do the final shot; I'm not a complete idiot! We'll have you fire it after we've filmed the fight, just so we can get a closeup.'

'I'm not doing it, Tristan; I'm not!'

An hour or so later, despite her protestations, Jennifer was short of breath from being chased all through the house, then around the grounds, by the Somerset Slayer, or as she knew him, Brian Shepherd. He'd taken the role because it was a non-speaking part. He was the largest of them all, and thus the most imposing, and all he had to do was chase after people while dressed in an oily, blue boilersuit, his face hidden beneath a grubby hessian sack.

The other reason was to be close to his girlfriend, Melonie Cox, who had been victims number two and five, out of a total of six, with Claire Green and Effie Hughes covering the rest between them. They'd done a great job, too, Jennifer thought, amazed at how effective a wig, a change of clothes, and some clever makeup could completely change how a person looked. She had noticed a few sharp looks from them while they'd been filming. Jealousy, perhaps, at her being the lead. But then, it was her film, so what did they expect?

With the final scene, the original plan had been to film the chase, and the death of the killer, at night, but they'd all agreed that doing it in the daytime was a nice and oddly sinister twist. Also, nighttime was much better spent partying, and they were all there for that as much as they were for the movie; the laughable promise of fame had nothing on booze and sex. Jennifer had had plenty of the first and none of the second, and she was more than fine with that.

'You ready?'

Tristan's question floated around inside Jennifer's head, but she didn't answer straight away; her mind was too preoccupied with what she was holding.

'I've never liked guns,' she said.

Tristan laughed, then glanced over at the house.

'You live in a place like that, a mansion, and you don't like guns?'

'What's that supposed to mean?'

'Your dad shoots, that weirdo bodyguard, butler, or whatever he is obviously does as well.'

'Well, I never have,' said Jennifer. 'Mum wasn't interested either. I suppose I just took after her instead.'

Tristan breathed through his nose, the sound harsh.

'All you have to do,' he said, 'is hold it like I've already shown you, and pull the trigger. You're not pointing it at anything, just an open field, okay? And the cartridges are blanks, like I've said. There'll be a big bang, you'll feel it kick back into your shoulder, so remember to hold it tight and not drop it, and that's all there is to it. Okay?'

Jennifer noticed a faint hint of warmth in Tristan's voice, and that was rare.

'I suppose,' she said.

'And try to remember not to close your eyes,' Tristan added. 'I want you wild and staring and full of vengeance; beautifully angry!'

Jennifer gave a shallow nod.

'Okay,' she said. 'I'm ready. I think ...'

'You'll be fine.'

There was the warmth again, she noticed. And had 'beautifully angry' been his attempt at a compliment? Was he coming on to her?

Tristan stepped away from Jennifer and headed over to where Carol Mitchell was holding their one and only camera. The quietest member of the group, she'd said little during filming, but everyone had agreed her work had been fantastic.

'Remember, Jennifer,' Tristan called over, 'all you have to do is hold it like I showed you; firmly in the shoulder, yes? Then pull the trigger; that's all there is to it. No lines, nothing else to worry about, just look angry as hell and imagine the killer's head exploding!'

Jennifer gave a nod.

'Not sure I can do beautifully angry though,' she said.

'Trust me,' Tristan said.

Jennifer took a deep breath, held it to the count of three, then exhaled.

'I'm good,' she said. 'Let's do this ...'

The next few seconds were silent and seemed to last an eternity. Jennifer became acutely aware of the weight of the shotgun in her hands, how deadly it was; but she told herself there was nothing to worry about; having watched Tristan load the gun, she knew the cartridges were blanks, and the only thing she was aiming at was thin air.

'Beautifully angry,' she muttered to herself. 'Beautifully angry ...'
'Action!'

At Tristan's shout, Jennifer heaved the shotgun upwards and planted it in her right shoulder, then, with a rage-filled scream, pulled the trigger ...

THIRTY-ONE

Gordy was up and out of her desk like a jack-in-the-box. She grabbed the handle of her office door, only to pause and turn back to Allercott.

'You know what we have to do, don't you?'

Allercott turned around in her chair.

'I do.'

'Can I count on your support?'

'I'm a police officer,' Allercott said, a shot of indignation in her voice.

'And he's your father,' Gordy fired back. 'So, I'll ask you again—'

'Yes, you can count on my support,' said Allercott, rising to her feet. 'In fact, so much so, that I'm going to come with you.'

Gordy stepped away from her door.

'Look, ma'am, I'm no' so sure that's a good idea.'

'And I'm not sure I give a damn,' said Allercott. 'I'm coming. If Dad did this, I need to be a part of it.'

'You're too close to it.'

'I'm not going to interrogate him. I just need to be there, when you … when you arrest him.'

Gordy still didn't like it and she was fairly sure that there was some protocol somewhere that wouldn't allow it. But Allercott was her DCI, and she really wasn't in the mood to argue.

With nothing else to say, she exited her office and marched over to the team, her mind focused on getting over to Jack's place with as little drama as possible. Except, right at the back of it, something was bothering her, though she wasn't exactly sure what. Possibly because everything about what was happening was bothering her, and the last thing she needed was to be distracted. This was sensitive, very out of the ordinary, and she needed to tread carefully. Then she remembered that Patti had been about to tell her something when Allercott's arrival had interrupted her.

'Patti, the meeting at the Hall you mentioned; you said you knew when it last happened?'

'Actually, I was about to tell you that I know when the next meeting is due to happen,' Patti said.

'You do?' said Gordy.

Patti gave a nod.

'Tonight. Ignoring Brian and Melonie, of the five left, two aren't local, so they stay over, and they've both booked in at the Hall for the night just gone and tonight. I think they like to get there early and enjoy the place. Fair enough, really.'

A chill raced down Gordy's spine.

'What, you mean they're there now?'

'Yes,' said Patti. 'Why?'

Gordy looked over at Allercott, who had only just followed her out of the small office.

'We're going,' she said, already moving towards the main doors. 'Now!'

Her walk became a run, and she heard Allercott racing up behind her.

'What's wrong? Why the rush?'

'I'll explain on the way,' Gordy said, then at the door, shot a look back over at Patti.

'Call the Hall,' she said. 'Speak with Felix. Get him to find the two who are staying there and have them secured in a room. The

Hall will have security staff, bound to have, so have them make sure no one other than myself and DCI Allercott, or you and Pete, are allowed to see them, is that understood? The rest of the team can contact the remaining three. My guess is that you'll be the first to arrive, as we've a stop to make on the way and we might not even get there at all.'

Gordy saw confusion blossoming in Patti's eyes.

'You mean you want me and Pete to go to the Hall?'

'Immediately!' said Gordy, allowing the door to close behind her.

Racing down the stairs, she gave no thought to Vivek's farewell, and was soon outside.

'My vehicle's over there,' Gordy said.

'We'll take mine,' Allercott replied, jogging past, her long coat pulled in at the waist by a belt flapping around her legs below her knees. 'Dad won't be so suspicious then.'

'Good point.'

Gordy followed Allercott and climbed into the passenger seat. Then Allercott had the engine alive, switched on the blue lights hidden behind the grill, and sent the wail of a siren into the air.

'I'll switch all this off before we get there,' she said, 'but it'll help us get there quicker, won't it?'

'And the quicker the better,' Gordy agreed. 'Shift it!'

Allercott shot her car out of the car park in front of the station, hammered around a roundabout, then two more roundabouts disappeared in the rearview mirror, and Gordy realised she was holding her breath.

'Can't say I expected you to drive like this,' she said.

'Oh, I'm full of surprises, believe me,' Allercott replied, overtaking a car ahead with such deft skill, Gordy was left feeling a little envious.

The road ahead melted as they sped along, the colours of the countryside blurring into a wash of swirling colour, like ink on wet paper.

Turning off the main road, thinner roads rose to greet them, but Allercott didn't slow down. If anything, she sped up, and Gordy found herself bracing her feet in the footwell and gripping the door a little more tightly.

'Ever thought of becoming a stunt driver or something?' she asked, as Allercott dropped a gear to deal with a dip and a corner ahead, before pushing the engine hard to come out of it.

'Too controlled an environment,' Allercott replied, eyes focused on the road ahead. 'This is a lot more fun.'

Gordy didn't know what to think. Allercott was a very confusing person to try and get to know, to even understand a little. One minute she was socially awkward, advising on the purchase of stationery, running away from a pathologist, and the next she was offering you her phone number and a chat, visiting a crime scene with said pathologist, and making a car speed along country lanes like a professional rally driver.

Forcing herself to relax, Gordy realised that something was troubling her. Well, a lot of things were, but a big one was motive. What the hell was Jack, Allercott's dad, doing killing folk? What was driving it? He was an old man living out his twilight years in a cute cottage, so why switch from that to elaborate murders of a group of people he'd known so long ago?

Glancing at Allercott, Gordy couldn't shift the disconnect in her head between what had happened and where they were going. But Allercott seemed determined, so set on it, so convinced, it was hard to not go along with it. But when had she ever just gone along with anything or anyone? That just wasn't in her blood.

As that thought settled itself comfortably in her mind, various things started to niggle at her, and together they turned into a jarring tune in her head, an unsettling soundtrack to what she was doing now, which, deep down, she knew wasn't right. The why, though, that was the problem.

Allercott killed the lights and sirens, then a few turns in the road later, and after a decent straight where she really picked up speed, the driveway to Holcombe Hall appeared. She slowed, clicked down through the gears, and pulled them up in front of her father's quaint little cottage.

As the engine turned off, Gordy heard the mechanics of it click and pop from the strain of being asked to do what the vehicle had just done.

'You don't have to do this,' Gordy said, unclipping her seat belt. 'Patti and Pete will be here soon. I can wait for them, and call ahead to the Hall.'

Allercott's answer was to unclip her own seatbelt, climb out of the car, then duck her head back in and say, 'I'm doing this.'

Gordy pulled herself out, easing her door shut as Allercott came around to join her.

'Something's bothering me,' she said, halting Ellen before they approached the house. 'Motive; why would your dad do any of this? Makes no sense. What's the reason for it, never mind the how?'

A flicker of something showed itself behind the other woman's eyes, but was gone as suddenly as it appeared, and Gordy took the smallest of steps back.

'It's revenge,' she said. 'He's bottled it up for so long. I thought he was over it, but he's old, and I think he just wants to get it done before he goes for good himself.'

'Revenge? For what? The accident that happened on set? That seems far-fetched.'

'He loved Jenny,' Allercott said, the words raw and rusted, like the blade of a hacksaw left in the rain. 'That's what this is about.'

Gordy saw a flicker of something like pain in Allercott's eyes, but it was soon gone, and she wondered if she'd seen it at all.

With nothing left to say for now, they walked over to the front door and Ellen rang the bell. As it sounded inside the house, another car pulled into the drive, and Gordy nodded at Patti as she and Pete drove on towards the Hall.

Footsteps sounded from inside.

Again, Gordy found herself turning to Allercott to give her another chance to back out, but as she did so, she heard the click of the door lock. The door swung inward, and there, for the second time in as many days, stood Jack Allercott.

'Hi, Dad,' Allercott said. 'Can we come in?'

Gordy watched as Jack stared at his daughter, then at her, and then back at his daughter.

'Ellie? I wasn't expecting to see you today. Is everything okay? What's up? What's happened? And why have you brought DI Haig with you?' He turned his stare on Gordy, and added, 'Why are you here? I told you everything I could remember about the Claytons.'

As he spoke, Gordy found herself looking for the empty knife sheath on his belt, and right enough, there it was.

'Please, Dad,' Ellen said. 'It would be best if we took this inside.'

Jack stepped back into the house.

'Come on in, then,' he said.

Gordy followed Ellen inside and a moment or two later was sitting in the same chair in Jack's cosy little lounge that she'd occupied the day before.

Ellen sat down as Jack joined them.

'Before you ask, Dad,' she said, 'no, we don't want any tea.'

'I was actually going to offer you coffee; popped out and got a few things last night.'

Gordy realised then that Ellen had the file she'd shown her in the office in her hand.

'I need to ask you something, Dad,' she said, then opened it, and showed Jack the image of the knife found at Melonie's house. 'Do you recognise this?'

THIRTY-TWO

Jack leaned forward, squinted to get a better look.

'Of course I do,' he said. 'That's my knife.'

As he said it, Gordy watched Jack drop his hand to the sheath on his belt.

'Lost it a few days ago, after one of your visits, I think. Not the last one, the one before that, maybe? Yes, last week, I think it was, when you were round to tell me about Detective Haig, here, starting in a few days' time, you remember? Where did you find it? Is that why you're here, because of that?' He looked over at Gordy. 'But why are you here, then? What's going on?'

'You really don't know?' Ellen asked.

Jack shook his head.

'I'm giving you a chance here, Dad,' she continued. 'Please ...'

Gordy could see confusion writing its way across Jack's face in the wrinkles and lines he wore, as they grew deeper, and twisted into one another like dancers. It looked genuine, but in a way that she found disconcerting. She'd seen plenty of criminals feign innocence, claim they had nothing to do with whatever crime they were being accused of. But Jack, he'd as yet not been accused of anything, and there, in his eyes, was something more, but what it was, Gordy didn't know, not yet.

'A chance? What for? I don't understand, Ellie. What are you talking about?'

Gordy noted that Jack called his daughter Ellie, not Ellen; a pet name, perhaps, something from her childhood that had stuck.

'The knife, Dad, what happened to Jenny ... It's been twenty-five years, hasn't it? Since the film, the accident?'

The lines on Jack's face grew deeper still.

'Jenny? What on earth are you talking about? What's that got to do with my knife?'

'Please, Dad!' Ellen said, and Gordy heard the strain in her voice.

Jack shot a look at Gordy.

'Can you explain to me what this is about, since my own daughter can't?'

Gordy decided it was best to play it straight.

'That knife was found at the scene of a crime.'

'What crime?'

And there it was again, thought Gordy, that confusion.

'The murder of Melonie Cox,' she said. 'She was strangled to death before being stabbed nine times in the chest with a knife.'

'Your knife, Dad,' said Allercott, voice quiet. 'Your knife.'

Jack's eyes grew wide.

'Ellie? You can't be thinking what I think you're thinking?' He turned his stare to Gordy, eyes blazing. 'Did you put her up to this? What the hell is wrong with you? What on earth are you thinking? That I'm a killer? Is that it? I'm eighty bloody years old! The hell would I be doing killing someone when I can barely get out of bed in the morning without my joints screaming at me in agony! Kill someone? Are you mad?'

Gordy asked Jack where he was during the two murders.

'How the hell should I know? I've trouble enough as it is remembering where I've left my teeth, and you expect me to give you a detailed account of my evenings?'

'It's important, Jack,' said Gordy. 'Your knife links you to the second crime scene. If you've an alibi, then we're good, aren't we?'

'Good? Is that the best you can do? Good? No, we are far from being anything at all like good.' Jack turned back to his daughter. 'Ellie? What's going on? What is this? Are you still blaming me, is that it? Is that what this is all about?'

'Something else crossed Gordy's mind, and she said, 'When we chatted yesterday, you mentioned something about sorting some trees, I think. Does that involve using ropes, that kind of thing?'

'What the hell has that got to do with anything?'

'Can you answer the question, please, Jack?'

'I use block and tackle, of course I do,' Jack replied. 'Heavier stuff I can't be lifting on my own, can I? Sometimes use my old Land Rover. I've a few bits of newer kit as well, which is a lot safer than the older stuff I'm more used to. But like I just said, what the hell has—'

'I never blamed you for Jenny's death,' said Allercott, cutting across her father's voice. Gordy watched her eyes widen, her jaw clench.

Jack's eyes swung back to his daughter.

'What are you talking about? Blame me? Why the hell would you?'

Gordy was confused now. The conversation seemed to have switched tracks and was heading off in a completely new direction.

'Mr Allercott,' she said, doing her best to lasso the reason they were there in the first place before it bolted from the room. 'The night of the murder …'

Jack said nothing, stood up, and before Gordy realised what he was doing, had left the room, heading through a door to some stairs, slamming the door behind him.

Gordy leapt out of her seat to chase after him.

'Jack?'

She grabbed the door handle and heaved it open, shouting the man's name once again, this time up the stairs.

'Jack? Jack!'

She ran up the stairs, wondering what Jack was doing, what he was going to do, what he had upstairs he so desperately and suddenly needed to get.

As she reached the top step, Jack appeared above her.

'You'll be needing to go back down again,' he said, and Gordy saw fire in his eyes. 'Unless you want me to stay up here, that is.'

Jack was carrying a carved wooden box.

'Jack? What's that?'

'Something for Ellie,' he said, and stood there, waiting for her to go back down the stairs.

Gordy turned on her heel and made her way back down into the lounge, Jack following on behind.

She sat down, and Jack did the same, the box in his hands.

'It would be best for everyone if you didn't make any sudden movements or exits from the room again,' she said. 'Please ...'

'I needed to get something,' Jack explained, his eyes on the box now on his lap. 'I needed to get this.' He looked up then and over at his daughter, who was staring at the box. 'And I sure as hell don't need yours or anyone else's permission to walk around my own damned house!'

Gordy saw that Allercott was staring at the box in Jack's hands.

'But ... but I thought it got lost when the house was sold,' she said. 'You've had it all this time?'

'Mr Clayton didn't want it,' Jack said. 'Couldn't bear to be around anything that reminded him of his daughter. You remember how he was when he lost his wife? Maybe you don't, you were young. But I do. And I understood that pain. We both did, didn't we, Ellie? Even if you couldn't and can't exactly remember it all. When your mum was killed, it was just you and me, then, wasn't it? I couldn't let him throw away a memory.'

'Especially not one you'd made yourself,' Ellen replied, and Gordy heard a sharp edge cutting through her voice.

Gordy held up her hands to bring the attention of both Allercotts back to her.

'I need someone to explain to me what's going on,' she said. 'And Jack, I still need you to answer the question about where you were when—'

Her phone buzzed. It was Jack, back at the office. Two Jack's, Gordy thought; as if things weren't confusing enough already.

She thought for a moment about killing the call, then decided to take it, stood up, and left the room, heading back towards the front door. As she closed the lounge door, the phone to her ear, she saw Jack turn the box towards Ellen and open it.

'Boss?'

'Yes, Jack,' Gordy replied. 'I'm assuming this is important. If it isn't, I'm hanging up.'

'Just had that Bill chap turn up at the Hut. You know, the bloke who was sleeping at Nunney Castle?'

Just behind Jack's voice, Gordy heard the sound of a music box playing from in the room she'd just left.

'Bill? What did he want?'

'He's remembered the tune he heard, the one he thought someone was whistling when he woke up, but wasn't sure if it was in his dream or not.'

'That's what this is about? Look, Jack, I'm about to arrest someone ...'

'He taught me it as well,' Jack said, and started to whistle.

'Jack, now's not the time for a solo performance ...'

For a moment, Jack's whistle wrestled with the music box she could still hear playing, then somehow the two melodies wove together, note for note, and Gordy realised that the song was the same.

'It's Swan Lake,' Jack said. 'Sorry if my version wasn't that good. Bill said it was important for you to hear it, so you'd believe him, because he thinks that whoever it was he heard at the castle, that's what they were whistling. He was pretty adamant about it, too.'

Gordy could hear Jack's voice, but she wasn't listening to it, not anymore. The sound of the music box was peeling away the top of her skull and forcing its way into her head.

'I'll call you back,' she said, and hung up on Jack, then opened the lounge door and walked back into the room.

Jack Allercott was staring at his daughter, who was holding the box he had brought down from upstairs. Gordy could see that it was open, and inside a tiny ballerina was turning as Swan Lake rang like a chorus of tiny bells in the air.

'I should've given that to you a long time ago,' Jack said. 'I'm sorry that I didn't. I wasn't sure how you would react to it, when you were young, I mean. Then I forgot about it for a while. Then I wasn't sure when the right time would be. Anyway, there it is. It's yours now, isn't it? You always loved the tune, and you'd whistle it to yourself, wouldn't you? And you still do, usually when you're nervous, though I don't think you notice.'

The music died.

Gordy's blood ran cold.

Allercott wiped a tear from her eye. Then, with a violence Gordy could hardly believe the DCI was able to tap into, she jumped to her feet and hurled the box at the wall, where it shattered against the brickwork, and fell to the floor like a broken bird.

THIRTY-THREE

The silence in the room was suffocating and Gordy could barely breathe, so shocked was she. She stared at the broken box as it lay in pieces on the floor, heard the music box tinkle again, then die.

'Ellie? I don't understand,' said Jack. 'Why?'

Allercott was staring at her dad.

'You're going to prison, Dad!' she said, the words spitting from her like poison from a cobra. 'You should've gone there years ago for what you did. I shouldn't have left it this long before doing something. I shouldn't. But that's on me.'

'What are you talking about?' Gordy said, still trying desperately to make some sense of not only what had just happened, but was clearly still happening, right in front of her eyes.

Allercott was holding handcuffs.

'Mr ... Jack Allercott...' she said, her father's name falling out of her mouth like it had shattered teeth on the way through, 'I am placing you under arrest for the murder of Melonie Cox and Brian Shepherd. You do not have to say anything, but it may harm your defence if you do not mention when questioned something which you later rely on in court. Anything you do say may be given in evidence.'

Her words seemed to swirl around awkwardly in the air, like they knew they didn't belong.

'Arrest me? I'm your dad, Ellie!'

'And she's dead because of you, can't you see that?' Allercott shouted back at him, her voice crackling with a pain so raw and deep that Gordy could feel as well as hear it.

'Ma'am,' she said, her eyes on the DCI, her voice as gentle as she could manage, 'I think we should take a moment. I need to check in with Patti and Paul anyway. Make sure that—'

'They're already dead!' Allercott snapped back. 'You know that, don't you, Dad?'

'Who's dead? What are you talking about?' Jack replied, voicing Gordy's own shocked, unspoken response to what his daughter had just said.

'They're all dead because of you, because of what you did. Can't you see that?'

'How do you know they're dead?' Gordy asked, still trying to get a grip on what was happening.

Her phone buzzed again. She answered it and Patti's voice came back at her, hard and serious.

'Boss? We ... we've ...'

Her voice died, and Gordy was left staring at the Allercotts, terrified at what Patti was going to say next.

'You've found them, haven't you?' she said.

'Yes,' said Patti.

'And?'

Silence.

'Patti?'

'They're ... the showers ... I ...'

'Patti,' she said, 'you know what to do, yes? Call Cowboy, get the SOC team over right away, get an ambulance, the rest of the team. Call in Uniform. With all the other guests there, you'll need to secure the site sharpish, avoid any panic, stay calm, get everyone's details, make sure no one leaves. Understood?'

'Yes, boss,' Patti replied.

'You'll be fine,' Gordy said, forcing her voice to sound firm and supportive and commanding. 'I know you will. You've absolutely got this.'

The call over, Gordy slipped her phone back into her pocket and tried not to think about what Patti and the rest of the team would be dealing with. She needed to gather her thoughts, because what was happening in front of her wasn't making any sense, but then again, what if it was? What if what she was witnessing made the most sense of anything she had seen all week?

'I need you both to calm down,' she said, focusing on gaining control of the situation.

'I've not killed anyone,' Jack said, still sitting in his chair, pinned there by the weight of what he had been accused of. 'Not out of theatre I haven't, and believe you me, after what I experienced? There's no way I'd ever go back to that again. It destroyed me.'

'It was your fault,' Allercott said again, untouched by her father's words. 'All of it. That's why you need to accept this, Dad. Please. You have to. Can't you see that?'

'I'm not accepting anything because I've not killed anyone! I haven't!'

Allercott held up the handcuffs.

'Please! Just put these on! You have to. Don't force me to do something I really don't want to do, something more than I already have.'

Gordy heard the pain in Allercott's voice.

'Ma'am, maybe you should let me do this,' she said, and went to take the cuffs from the DCI. But before Gordy could grab them, Allercott threw the cuffs at her father, then in a flurry of movement, pulled something from beneath her jacket.

'What the—?'

Gordy stared in horror as Allercott pointed the sawn-off barrels of a shotgun at her father.

'Just go to prison, Dad,' she said. 'Just accept it, please. You have to. That's the point of all of this. Can't you see that? You must see that! You should've gone there a long time ago for what you did, for the lies, for all of it. But I didn't know what to do, how to do it, couldn't do it, I guess. But I won't let you get away with it anymore. I can't.'

'That's my old gun!' Jack said, shocked. 'But the police ... They took it after the accident. The barrels were shattered because that idiot director had put two smaller cartridges in them, blowing them apart when Jenny pulled the trigger. I've not seen it since. How did you get hold of it? And what's happened to the barrels?'

'I'm police, remember?' Allercott said. 'Took me a while to track it down, and even longer to get my hands on it. But I managed, thanks to a little bit of flirting. The barrels were my own work, had to do that because they were so damaged, but also to conceal it for now, you see, because I knew you'd not come quietly.'

Flirting? thought Gordy. With whom? Cowboy? No, it couldn't be. That made no sense. But then Allercott had run at the mention of him arriving at Nunney, hadn't she? Then she remembered someone else, the one with the black fringe. What was it he had said? Something about Allercott not being there or that she'd already gone? How had he known? At the time, she'd wondered if he'd spotted her, but Allercott had disappeared around the back of the castle, so there was no chance of that, was there?

'You're pointing my own bloody gun at me and trying to arrest me for something I've not done? Why the hell would I come quietly?'

Gordy ignored all thoughts of Allercott having an accomplice for the moment, and stepped forward to try and get some control over things, only to have the barrels of the gun sweep around to hold her back.

'You'll no' be pointing a gun at me, Allercott!' she said, her voice cutting through gritted teeth. 'What the hell are you thinking? Speak to me! And while you're doing that, fill me in here, because I'm beginning to think you're the only one who knows what the hell's going on!'

'You need to ask my dad about that,' Allercott said. 'About Jenny Clayton.' She turned back to stare at Jack. 'You see, I know, Dad, I know everything. I always have. Jenny was your favourite, and you couldn't do anything about it, could you? Because she was your secret, yours and her mother's.'

'Wait, hold up, now,' Gordy said, trying to catch up once again. 'What are we talking about? What's Jenny's mother got to do with this? And please put that bloody gun down before you do something you regret!'

'I'm thinking she's already done something she regrets, haven't you, Ellie?' Jack said.

Gordy saw love in his eyes, but it was wrestling with confusion, hurt, and untold amounts of panic.

'Why did you never make me anything like that box, Dad?' Allercott asked, the barrel of the gun swaying a little. 'Why did you only ever make one for Jenny's mum?'

'It was a gift,' Jack said, 'a birthday present. You know that.'

Allercott barked out a cold, harsh laugh.

'You made the wife of your best friend a jewellery box for her birthday? And you didn't think someone would see that as a bit strange?'

'It was just a gift, Ellie, that's all.'

Gordy noticed a shift in the tone of Jack's voice, the shock and anger she'd heard there earlier, were now replaced with sadness.

'We need to all calm down,' she said. 'Allercott, I need you to put that gun down, please. I don't think any of us want anyone getting hurt or doing something they'll regret, do we?'

Another laugh burst from Allercott, the whoop of a hyena in the dark.

'I lived with this man's regret my whole life! Because I knew, you see? I knew! How could I not? The way you were with her, the way you treated her. I'd have to have been blind to not see!'

'See what?' Gordy asked, if only to get Allercott to focus on her instead of her dad, and to maybe give up with the gun.

'That Jenny was my half-sister, that's what. Right, Dad?' Allercott snapped back, shaking, and waving the shotgun around in her hands like a conductor's baton. 'That you had an affair with your best friend's wife, and she was the result. That mum found out after I'd arrived on the scene! That she took her own life, because she couldn't live with it anymore. That Jenny was always your favourite, not me, Dad, not me! Now put on the bloody handcuffs before, like DI Haig here just said, one of us does something we regret!'

Then, as Allercott's voice burned hot in the air, torching everything with a blistering wave of rage-filled hurt, the gun slipped out of her hand, landed hard on the floor, and fired.

THIRTY-FOUR

The sound of the shotgun blast blew apart the moment like a grenade going off, instinct took over, and Gordy realised too late that she was flying through the air towards a bookshelf, her body acting of its own accord to remove her from danger.

She crashed into the bookshelf face first. Unable to lift her arms in time to protect herself, the impact knocked her head back and sent the sound of a nasty crack reverberating from her neck through the rest of her body. Like a rag doll, the rest of her followed, legs and arms careering into the shelves, knocking books and sending ornaments flying, covering her as she fell to the floor, dazed and confused, thoughts buzzing around her head like mosquitos.

Rolling onto her knees, she shook her head to free it of the ringing filling her ears from the gun going off. The impact of hitting the bookshelf, then the floor, had stunned her momentarily, but she was already shutting the pain down, lifting her head to check on Ellen and Jack, pushing herself up onto her feet as dust and plaster and the acrid stink of the propellant from the cartridge filled the air.

She spotted Jack first. He was no longer in his chair, but on his feet, and he had the shotgun in his hands. He'd broken the barrel, and was removing the cartridges, one of which was responsible for the canon-like explosion that had happened when the gun had landed on the floor. He was staring down at his daughter, who was, to Gordy's stunned amazement, holding another weapon now, a small pistol this time, and it was pointing directly at Jack's chest.

'Where the hell are you getting all of these guns from?' Gordy yelled, unable to hear her own voice clearly, the question coming out like the annoyed enquiry of an irritated teacher dealing with a truculent child. 'Who were you flirting with? It's not Cowboy, I know that for sure. And by flirting, I assume you mean sleeping with, right? Was it someone on his team? His righthand man, the one carrying that god-awful boombox? Was it him?'

Forcing herself to her feet, Gordy could see Allercott's lips moving, pistol still raised at her father, but the sound of her voice was like listening to someone speaking underwater.

Gordy tried to read the woman's lips, but it was almost impossible to pull her eyes away from the pistol. If it wasn't someone on Cowboy's team, then had the DCI been pilfering weapons from old crime scenes? Was that even possible? Evidence, especially weapons, was locked down hard. But from what Jack had said about the shotgun being his and the police taking it after the accident on set with Jenny, she must've done. But a pistol as well? Who the hell was looking after it all to be so lax as to let such lethal items go on walkabout? Every SOC team she knew collected evidence and made sure it was secured safer than the crown jewels! And all of that just made her mind swing back to Cowboy's team, and the figure carrying the boombox.

Like a radio with bad reception, her hearing tuned itself back into the moment, and she heard the tinkling sound of the music box once again singing out its tune with a haunting sweetness.

'The whistling,' she said, staring now at Allercott, and remembering Bill at the castle.

Allercott, the pistol still trained on her father, turned her head just enough to stare at Gordy from the corner of her eye.

'I thought this would all go so much more easily than it has,' she said, sadness in her voice. 'That Dad would accept the punishment for what he did, and come along quietly. That's what was supposed to happen. You can see that, can't you? I didn't want any of this to go as far as it has.'

'But you brought a shotgun and a pistol!' said Gordy. 'How the hell else did you think this was going to go play out if you came so ready for violence?'

'You say that as though I like it,' Allercott replied. 'I don't. I hate it. All of it. But this was necessary. They were all responsible, you see? Each and every one of them. But Dad? It was because of him that it happened in the first place. That's why I had to do what I did.'

Ever so slowly, Gordy inched closer, her movements smooth, unthreatening. She was rattling through everything that had happened so far, what she had learned, not just from her own work, but that of the team, their ideas, their suggestions, even Cowboy... She stared at the pistol in Allercott's hand; surely he wasn't involved in this, too? But then who else would've given her access to the shotgun and the pistol?

'So, this all goes back to Jenny, then, right?' she asked, but in such a way as to suggest she didn't want Allercott to answer. 'That's why Brian and Melonie were killed, why we have more bodies up at the Hall to deal with, why we're here now, arresting your father for it all?'

'He's responsible, for all of it,' said Ellen, her eyes now back on her father. 'I just wanted you to love me like her, that's all! That's why I did it, that's why I put those cartridges in the shotgun when they were filming! I wanted to scare her, have her know it was me, and to leave and just let me have you as my dad! That's all I wanted! But I couldn't even have that, could I?'

Gordy saw Jack's shoulders sag.

'What are you saying, Ellie?' he asked.

'I was a kid, Dad, and I wanted everyone to be scared! I just wanted the bang to be extra loud so that Jenny would stop the film, everyone would go, and she would finally leave, just get out, get a job, and leave me alone with you! That's all I ever wanted!'

'I was never not your dad,' said Jack.

'But you were never all mine, were you? Part of you was always hers!'

Gordy saw tears on Jack's face.

'You've got it all wrong,' he said. 'I never knew that you thought this, about your mum, about Jenny ... I'm so sorry.'

'Sorry? Bit late for that, isn't it, Dad?' Allercott shot back. 'You could've prevented all of this happening, but you didn't.'

When Jack spoke again, Gordy saw that an odd calm had settled over him, though the tears continued to fall.

'Jenny was your sister, that's true,' he said. 'But your mum didn't take her own life because of that; she was ill, Ellie, that's all. Very ill. You wouldn't remember, you were too young, and I wanted to protect you from the truth.'

'This is the truth!' Allercott said, tears in her own eyes now, the pistol still aimed at her father. 'All of it!'

'No, Ellie, it's not,' Jack replied. 'Jenny's dad was away a lot. Too much. Work was all he could think about. Business. I was still a mess from everything I'd gone through as a soldier. Jenny's mum and I ... we ...' He closed his eyes, hung his head. 'It was wrong. We regretted it. We kept it a secret. She fell pregnant and Jenny was born and that was that.'

'You can't paper it all over with lies, not now, Dad! You can't!'

Gordy saw that Allercott's hands were shaking, and that made her even more worried about the pistol she was holding.

'Your mum, Jenny's dad, they never knew.'

'Mum killed herself!'

'She was depressed, Ellie. I tried to help, tried to love her as best as I could, but I was no use, no help, maybe I made it worse, you know? Sadness took over her life. To this day, I still don't know what it was, how the darkness inside her ate at her, eventually consumed her to the point where her only escape was to do what she did. She loved you. My God, she loved you. But something snapped inside her, she couldn't fix it. I didn't know how ...'

Allercott went to speak, but Gordy decided she needed to try and get control again.

'This was all you?' she asked, staring at Allercott. 'The murders? The way they were staged?'

Allercott's head twitched ever so slightly. 'A horror film destroyed my life. I've hated them ever since.'

Gordy had her eyes on the pistol, but her mind was racing, trying to take in what sounded like a confession.

'One of my team got the connection,' she said. 'Why so elaborate, though? Why any of it?'

She was asking questions, but the answers didn't interest her; they'd only be relevant if she could get them all out of this alive, and Allercott into an interview room. She just needed to keep her talking, and give herself a chance to shut this down quickly and safely, and without anyone else getting hurt.

'Because horror films are stupid, that's why,' said Allercott. 'Jenny's death, that was stupid, the film she was making, all of it. The whole thing was a circus of the ridiculous, making fun of death. Well, it's not fun, is it? I've lived with the guilt of what happened all these years, and it wasn't my fault, it was that film, those people, Jenny's mum, my dad, the secrets, all of it. Can you imagine it, being a kid who accidentally killed someone? They thought that director was responsible, but they had no proof, no confession. They certainly didn't think it was me. Why would they?'

'That's why you offered me all that support, isn't it?' Gordy asked, as everything started to slot into place. 'You wanted me to trust you, so that I wouldn't suspect, and I'd just go along with it.'

Allercott said nothing, so Gordy kept talking.

'I remember now, when Patti called you about the first crime scene, she said you hung up before she told her where it was. She sent a text, but you already knew anyway, didn't you?'

Allercott swung the pistol around and trained it on Gordy.

'Brian, he was the killer from Jenny's movie. I dressed him in what he wore on set. Thought it was appropriate. I had to bury the cement block the spike was slotted into a good few weeks ago. I knew you were starting soon, and I needed you to be the lead on it all, because your predecessor knew me too well. But you, you were new, and you were damaged by what you'd gone through, like me, you see?'

'No, I don't see,' Gordy replied.

'Jenny loved you, Ellie,' Jack said, butting in. 'Even had that nickname for you, remember? You used to laugh when she called you that; she'd hold her nose, then pick you up and hug you.'

'Smelly Ellie?' Allercott said. 'I hated that. I hated her.'

'No,' Jack replied. 'You didn't.'

'I did! You don't know. I loved her and I hated her. Because of your lies, your secrets. I just wanted you for myself!'

The pistol wavered between Gordy and Jack, and Gordy knew she'd have to act soon.

'The DVD playing at Melonie's,' she said. 'That was you as well, wasn't it?'

'Halloween,' Allercott explained. 'The mask worn by the killer, it's actually the face of William Shatner, who played Captain Kirk.'

'You've been planning this for years.'

Allercott's eyes were narrowed slits focused on Gordy with an intensity that nearly took her breath away. The pistol aimed at her chest was held firmly, steady, forefinger curled over the trigger.

'Planning it? No, not really. Thinking about it, yes, but when I knew you were moving down here, that's when I realised this was my chance. Figured I could use your state of mind to my advantage, thought you'd be distracted enough to go along with it all. Seems I was wrong about that, though, doesn't it?'

Gordy knew it was too late, that she should've acted sooner.

'Don't!' she cried, as she watched Allercott's arm stiffen, bracing for the shot that would likely end her life at such close range.

A blur of movement from her right drew her attention, and Gordy watched as Jack drove into his daughter's side, his arms wrapping around her, one hand going for the pistol, the weight of him sending them both to the floor.

The pistol fired. Gordy felt a sharp pain whip across her left cheek, but she ignored it as Jack wrestled with his daughter, struggling to subdue her. Jack got his daughter pinned, but the pistol was waving around.

Gordy lunged, focusing on the DCI's wrist, her hand, the pistol. Her hands wrapped around the weapon, then with a violent yank, she snapped it out of Ellen's hands, no thought given to the finger trapped inside the trigger guard, or what such a wrench might do to it.

Allercott screamed.

Gordy threw the pistol across the room, well out of reach, then pinned the woman's arm down under her knees, as she clipped one half of her cuffs around Allercott's wrist.

'No! This isn't how it's supposed to be!' Allercott raged, fighting against the weight of her father and Gordy on top of her, holding her where she was.

With Allercott's wrist now in the cuff, Gordy gave a nod to Jack. He slid himself down his daughter's back, and Gordy reached over for the other arm, clipping the other wrist into the cuffs before Allercott was able to respond and yank her arm away.

'Dad's responsible, can't you see that?' Allercott screamed, her face scraping against the floor, her breath short. 'It's because of him everything happened!'

'You were a kid!' said Gordy, pushing herself off Allercott, and helping Jack up onto his feet. 'Why the hell have you let this eat you up so much? It makes no sense!' She spotted the pistol, relieved that it was far enough away for it to not be a problem. 'If you tell me it's because of what happened that you ended up in the police to do this ...'

'Of course it's the reason!' Allercott said from the floor, turning herself over to lie on her side, kicking out with her legs. 'How the hell else was I going to find everyone, to get my hands on Dad's shotgun or do any of this? How?'

Gordy glanced over at Jack.

'I'm sorry,' she said.

Jack said nothing, just stared; not at her, not at Allercott, but through the walls and far away, and Gordy wondered what he was seeing.

'Can you walk?' she asked.

Jack gave a nod, but slumped down into his chair.

Gordy pulled her phone from her pocket, then walked over to where she had kicked the pistol, took an evidence bag from another pocket, and picked it up.

Her call connected.

'Detective Superintendent Firbank?' she said, her words a rasp as she sucked in breath after breath, adrenaline surging through her veins, muscles aching. 'Wondering if you have a moment ...'

THIRTY-FIVE

Gordy was crouched on the floor in the lounge of her flat in Evercreech, unpacking the last couple of boxes. Late morning sunlight was streaming through the large windows, both of which were open, and looked out onto a shared garden. Window boxes she hadn't even noticed when she had first moved in were now populated with flowers, grasses, and some young tomato plants. Sat amongst them was a fat pigeon cooing to itself, and the sound was soft, musical, and relaxing.

Reaching into the final box to pull out a small collection of framed photos, Gordy hesitated, as from one of them, Anna smiled up at her, eyes bright and alluring.

For a moment, Gordy couldn't move, the photo resting against her hand as she stared down at the love of her life. Memories swept through her like a flood, causing her to reel, fall back, and she snapped an arm around behind her to stop herself from tumbling backwards.

A harsh buzz chainsawed its way into the moment, ripping the memories to shreds, and Gordy pushed herself to her feet to go and see who was at the door. She wasn't expecting visitors, had plans anyway, but welcomed the distraction, if only to divert her attention from the shock of seeing Anna's beautiful face.

At the end of the short corridor, Gordy stepped into the small porch, and opened the door to find a man standing there holding a very large pot plant. The variegated leaves burst from the pot in all directions, two of which were poking the man in the face.

'Jameson,' Gordy said. 'It's you.'

'I'm surprised you can see me behind this ridiculous plant,' Jameson replied.

Gordy laughed.

'Oh, I can't, but I recognise your feet.'

At that, Jameson did a little jig, then popped his head around the plant to look at Gordy.

'Here,' he said, and held out the plant. 'You mind taking this from me? It's for you, anyway; a little housewarming gift. I always think a house doesn't feel like a home until something is growing in it. And I don't mean mould in the bathroom either.'

Gordy reached out for the plant, only to realise that she was still holding the photo of Anna.

'That's a lovely photo,' Jameson said. 'You'll be putting that up on the wall, then?'

Gordy placed the photo on a small shelf in the porch, then took the plant from Jameson.

'I don't know,' she said, gesturing for Jameson to step inside, and kicking the door shut behind him. 'Not sure how I'd deal with it, really.'

Gordy led Jameson down the hall and into the lounge.

'This is a lovely place you've got,' he said. 'Love those windows. And you've got window boxes as well, I see. Don't they do a great job of bringing a bit of nature closer to home?'

Gordy placed the plant she was carrying in the corner of the room on her small dining table.

'Might just leave it there,' she said, mainly because it was so big it was hard to think where else it would actually go.

Jameson sat down.

'Won't stay long,' he said.

'You can't anyway,' said Gordy. 'I'm heading out in a few minutes.'

'Going anywhere interesting?'

Gordy thought about where she was going and why, and decided she'd rather keep it to herself.

'Just out,' she said. 'Still getting to know the place.'

'A little adventure, then? That's good.'

Gordy watched as Jameson shuffled on the sofa, then leaned forward, resting his elbows on his knees, his hands together. She had a feeling he was there for more than just the delivery of an enormous plant.

'Tea?' she asked.

Jameson shook his head.

'No, I'll be fine for now,' he said. 'And I'll not keep you, not if you're heading out.'

There was hesitation in his voice and Gordy wondered if he had been chatting with Harry again.

Jameson looked up at Gordy and she saw concern in his eyes. Not as much as had been there when she had last seen him, but enough for her to know this was the reason for his impromptu visit.

'Out with it, then,' she said. 'Whatever it is that's brought you round here, tell me, because lovely though the plant is, I can tell—'

'I'm coming out of retirement,' Jameson said, the words blurting out of him like they'd been in his mouth for too long and needed to escape. 'Not completely. I mean, I don't want to go back to working full-time, do I? But part-time should suit, I think, and I've still got lots to offer, skills I've learned over the years, contacts. I could be a very useful resource, don't you think?'

Gordy said, 'You've just said all that as though I already have some idea about what it is you're going to be doing.'

'Oh, right, yes,' said Jameson. 'Sorry. Should've made myself more clear. I'm going to set myself up as a sort of advisor to the police.'

'You mean a private investigator?'

Jameson shook his head.

'I don't fancy that at all. Most of the work is spying on people's spouses; not me at all. No, this will let me use my police background to help out if needed, in an advisory capacity. I can be brought in for investigations, that kind of thing.'

'Makes sense,' Gordy agreed.

'And I'll be able to help you, too, won't I, what with this new job you'll be taking on?'

There was something in the way Jameson had worded that which made Gordy frown.

'How do you mean?' she asked. 'I'm already in my new role, aren't I?'

'Which is the other reason I'm here,' said Jameson. 'You've had a tough time of it, so I hear? A real birth of fire; more than, actually, what with Allercott and everything else.'

Gordy's frown eased into a knowing smile.

'Who've you been speaking to?'

'Oh, no one,' Jameson shrugged. 'But you know how it is. Word gets around, doesn't it?'

'Firbank?'

Jameson remained silent.

'You're right, it has been tough,' Gordy said. 'A case like this, it'll take months and months to sort out. I don't envy the team working on it now.'

'You'll still be involved, though.'

'I will be, but not leading it, not now, especially with Allercott's involvement. Conflict of interest and all that, not that I even know her, but it's a fair point. I'm relieved, if I'm honest; means I can focus on the job I moved down here to do in the first place.'

'That's not the job I'm talking about,' said Jameson.

'Then what are you talking about?'

'Allercott's replacement.'

'I'm not a DCI.'

'But you've put in an expression of interest, haven't you?'

Gordy shook her head.

'I've no' had the time.'

'Well, that's bollocks, isn't it?'

Jameson's language caught Gordy off guard. She went to reply, a little annoyed at what he was implying, regardless of how true or not it was, but Jameson didn't give her the chance.

'You're avoiding it,' he said. 'And don't tell me you're not, because I can see the lie in your eyes before it's even had the chance to get out into the open. Why, Gordy? What's the problem?'

'There isn't one.'

'You can't let the grief of your past shape your future,' said Jameson. 'Anna wouldn't be happy with that, would she?'

Gordy felt her stomach twist.

'Don't bring Anna into this.'

'I'm not,' Jameson replied. 'Because I don't need to. Because she's already here, isn't she? You're wondering if you can cope with her memory, trying to decide if you've got it in you to put up her pictures—because I'm going to assume there's more than just that one I saw earlier—overthinking everything to the point where you'll let this opportunity you've been presented pass you by if you don't reach out and grab it!'

'What if I don't want to grab it?' Gordy said, her voice rising. 'What if all I want is to get on with things, to do what I came here to do, and to deal with my grief in my own way? And I'll no' have you or Firbank or Harry or anyone else for that matter telling me what I should or shouldn't do!'

Jameson stood up.

'The job is yours and you know it,' he said. 'Firbank is waiting to hear from you as it is—'

'She's what? How do you know th—'

'The competency-based application will be a doddle,' Jameson continued, ignoring Gordy's shocked outburst. 'Then it's just an interview and an assessment or two, isn't it? It's an open door, Gordy, you've just to walk through it.'

'I don't want to walk through it!'

'Fear's stopping you, that's all, so don't let it. You know better than that.'

Gordy couldn't believe what she was hearing. Who the hell was Jameson to think he could just walk into her flat, hiding behind a plant, and start telling her how to live her life?

'I'm not afraid! Why would I be?' she said.

'You tell me,' replied Jameson.

'I just want to settle into the life I've already got, and get used to that. It's changed enough as it is, if you remember; why the hell would I want to go changing it even more?'

'That's the fear talking again,' Jameson said. 'Fear of change.'

Gordy laughed, then said, 'To reuse something you only just said yourself, that's bollocks!'

Jameson narrowed his eyes, gave a little nod, then smiled.

'I'll be off, then,' he said, as though what they'd just been speaking about hadn't even happened.

'Wait, what?'

'You're off out, remember?' Jameson said, walking over to the lounge door. 'Don't want to keep you.'

'You mean, you're just going to leave it like that, just walk away from what we're talking about?'

'Yes,' Jameson replied. 'Anyway, it sounds to me like you've already made your decision, doesn't it?'

'Does it?'

In the hallway, Gordy was following Jameson along to her front door. He gave the handle a twist, then stepped outside, before turning around to face Gordy again.

'Yes, it does,' he said. 'I just don't think you realise it.'

And with that, he gave a nod, and headed off, leaving Gordy standing alone in her own doorway.

For a moment or two, Gordy didn't move. When she did, instead of finishing off the last box, she grabbed her car keys and a jacket, and slipped on her shoes. Then she was outside, in her car, and heading back to somewhere, to someone, she had been to before.

Jameson was right; she hadn't realised she'd made her decision, not until he'd left her alone with what they'd talked about. Then it had flashed up bright in her mind and she'd known immediately that she needed to speak to someone about it. Not Firbank, and certainly not her old boss, Harry, but someone who had somehow managed to use a pack of strange cards to get her speaking about things she'd been keeping bottled up inside. And maybe that had been the reason she'd called up the day before to book another Tarot reading, she thought. Not that it mattered.

With the memory of the photo she had found in that last box in her mind, Gordy knew that she wasn't about to allow fear stand in her way. And neither was Anna. Glastonbury was calling her, and beyond that, so was her future.

WANT TO KNOW the hand Gordy is dealt as she faces another sinister killer in Somerset? Scan the QR code below to grab your copy of *Hatchet Hill*, the eagerly anticipated second book in the Detective Inspector Haig series.

You'll also be able to download an exclusive free short story, *When One Door Closes*, as an eBook or audiobook, and sign up for my VIP Club and newsletter.

ABOUT DAVID J. GATWARD

David had his first book published when he was 18 and still can't believe this is what he does for a living. Author of the long-running DCI Harry Grimm series, David was nominated for the Amazon Kindle Storyteller Award in 2023. He lives in Somerset with his two boys.

Visit www.davidjgatward.com to find out more about the author and his highly-acclaimed crime fiction.

f facebook.com/davidjgatwardauthor

Printed in Great Britain
by Amazon